For the Freedom *of* Her Race

For the Freedom *of* Her Race

Black Women and
Electoral Politics in Illinois,
1877–1932

LISA G. MATERSON

The University of North Carolina Press
Chapel Hill

Designed by Jacquline Johnson
Set in MT Baskerville by Keystone Typesetting, Inc.
Manufactured in the United States of America

The paper in this book meets the guidelines for
permanence and durability of the Committee on
Production Guidelines for Book Longevity of the
Council on Library Resources.

The University of North Carolina Press has been a member of
the Green Press Initiative since 2003.

Library of Congress Cataloging-in-Publication Data
Materson, Lisa G.
For the freedom of her race : Black women and electoral politics
in Illinois, 1877–1932 / Lisa G. Materson.
p. cm.
Includes bibliographical references and index.
ISBN 978-0-8078-3271-4 (alk. paper)
1. African American women—Illinois—Political activity—
History. 2. African Americans—Suffrage—Illinois—History.
3. African American churches—Political aspects—Illinois—
History. 4. African Americans—Migrations—History. 5. African
Americans—Civil rights—Illinois—History. 6. Sex role—Political
aspects—Illinois—History. 7. Elections—Illinois—History.
8. Political parties—United States—History. 9. Illinois—Politics
and government—1865–1950. 10. Chicago (Ill.)—Politics and
government—To 1950. I. Title.
E185.93.I2M38 2009
323.1196'0730773—dc22
2008035373

13 12 11 10 09   5 4 3 2 1

For Phil and Joshua
And for Rosa, Richard, and Larry

Contents

Illustrations

Acknowledgments

During the course of preparing this book, I have benefited from the generous support of many individuals and institutions to whom I wish to extend my sincerest thanks. Several grants and fellowships enabled me to travel to archives scattered across the United States and afforded me time to write up my findings. These included a Woodrow Wilson Dissertation Grant in Women's Studies, a Smithsonian Institution Predoctoral Research Fellowship, an Albert J. Beveridge Grant from the American Historical Association, a Horace Samuel and Marion Galbraith Merrill Travel Grant in Twentieth-Century Political History from the Organization of American Historians, an Ida B. Wells Grant from the Coordinating Council for Women in History, a King V. Hostick Award from the Illinois State Historical Society, a UCLA Roscrans Dissertation Year Fellowship, and grants from UCLA's History Department, Center for the Study of Women, Institute of American Cultures, and Center for African American Studies. Receiving the Lerner-Scott Dissertation Prize from the Organization of American Historians and the Mary Wollstonecraft Dissertation Award from the UCLA Center for the Study of Women gave me the confidence that this was a project worth transforming into a book. A University of California President's Research Fellowship in the Humanities and a UC Davis Faculty Development Award, as well as postdoctoral fellowships at Princeton University's Center for the Study of Religion and Harvard University's Charles Warren Center for Studies in American History, provided me the time and resources necessary for undertaking this task.

I relied upon numerous archivists for help identifying collections essential for recovering this history. For their guidance, I wish to thank the staffs of Howard University's Moorland-Spingarn Research Collection, the Library of Congress Manuscripts Division, the University of Chicago Library's Special Collections, the University Archives at the University of Illinois at Urbana-Champaign, the University of Illinois at Chicago's Special Collections, the Herbert Hoover Presidential Library, the Franklin D. Roosevelt Library, the University of Delaware's Special Collections, and the Presbyterian Historical Society. I would especially like to thank Archie Motley and Linda Evans at the Chicago Historical Society (now the Chicago History Museum), Michael Flug and Marc Chery at the Vivian G. Harsh Research Collection at the Carter G. Woodson Regional Public Library, Sheila Darrow at the Hallie Q. Brown Memorial Library, and Beth Shields at the Kentucky Historical Society.

During the years that I have been at work on this project, I have had the privilege of participating in several intellectual communities. I owe my greatest intellectual debt to Ellen DuBois. As my doctoral adviser and then my colleague, Ellen has taught me so many lessons and helped me in too many ways to mention here. Her scholarship and intellectual generosity have served as a constant inspiration to me as I have made my way through the many stages of preparing this book and becoming a professional historian. I am forever grateful for her steadfast support over the years. The other members of my doctoral committee, Brenda E. Stevenson, E. Victor Wolfenstein, and David N. Myers, were great mentors, as was Stephen Aron, who, though not on my committee, shared welcome advice. At UCLA, I had the good fortune of being part of an engaging cohort of graduate students that included Anastasia Christman, Sue Englander, Alexandra Garbarini, Daniel Hurewitz, Tony Iaccarino, Jennifer Koslow, Anne Lombard, Rebecca Mead, Adam Rubin, Eugene Sheppard, Allison Sneider, and Rumi Yasutake. In addition to their friendship, they provided invaluable feedback on draft chapters and practice talks. Jennifer Koslow repeatedly helped me get "unstuck" when I struggled with writing up my findings.

I am particularly indebted to Allison L. Sneider, who is the best kind of colleague, both a scholar of women's political history and a dear friend. I first met Allison in a graduate seminar at UCLA. In the years since, Allison's friendship has served as a portable community as I moved from California to Connecticut to New Jersey and back to California again. Allison read numerous drafts of this book with remarkable enthusiasm and always-incisive comments. I am so very thankful for her encouragement and willingness to read yet another chapter draft on a tight deadline.

After leaving UCLA, I was lucky enough to join the dynamic community at Princeton University's Center for the Study of Religion. There, Marc Dolinger, Penny Edgell, Marla Frederick, R. Marie Griffith, Tisa Wenger, and Robert Wuthnow furnished me with wonderful feedback. As my time at Princeton came to an end and I was facing unemployment, Jon Butler offered me a lectureship at Yale University. I am very grateful to him for this opportunity, as well as for the sage advice he gave me as I searched for a tenure-track position.

It was a great pleasure when this search ended at the University of California at Davis. UC Davis has been a supportive environment for completing this project. UC Davis released me from teaching several courses so that I could accept a University of California President's Research Fellowship in the Humanities and a UC Davis Faculty Development Award, as well as spend a semester at Harvard University. At UC Davis, I have enjoyed being a part of a vibrant community of scholars. My writing group, Richard Kim, Kimberly Nettles, and Bettina Ng'weno, has been a source of stimulating discussion and some great meals. In the history department I have enjoyed the collegiality of fellow Americanists Karen Halttunen, Ellen Hartigan-O'Connor, Ari Kelman, Kathy Olmsted, Eric Rauchway, John Smolenski, Cecelia Tsu, Lorena Oropeza, Alan Taylor, Clarence Walker, and Louis Warren. Clarence, in particular, has been a strong advocate of this project. Joan Cadden and Susan Mann have been great mentors. I cannot thank Lorena Oropeza enough for all the assistance she has given me on this manuscript. Lorena pulled me aside at a time when I was spinning my wheels and helped me to get back on track. She generously read the manuscript twice, sharing constructive criticism and a supportive ear. UC Davis graduate students Padraic Benson, Chris Doyle, Elisabeth Ritacca, Samantha Scott, Beth Slutsky, Alison Steiner, and Marie Basile were excellent research assistants. I am terribly sad that Chris Doyle did not live to see in print the research she helped me to uncover.

Harvard University's Charles Warren Center for Studies in American History served as a home away from home for my final months of work on the book. I am grateful to director Joyce Chapin and workshop conveners Lisa McGirr and Daniel Carpenter for this opportunity, as well as to Warren Center staff members Larissa Kennedy and Arthur Patton-Hock for all their assistance.

Commentators and co-panelists at the several conferences where I presented portions of this project spurred me to sharpen my arguments. I would especially like to thank Richard Blackett, Eileen Boris, Elsa Barkley Brown, William Chafe, Melanie Gustafson, Martha S. Jones, Michele Mitchell, Lori Schuyler, and Judith Weisenfeld for their helpful comments. I would like to express my gratitude to Eileen Boris and Kevin Gaines for their continued enthusiasm for this project over the years. Their support has been instrumental in my ability to obtain fellowships and has been a source of

Illustrations

encouragement during the revision process. I also want to acknowledge the helpful insights of the anonymous readers at the *Journal of Women's History* (Johns Hopkins University Press), where portions of chapter 4 appear.

I was thrilled to find a home for this book at the University of North Carolina Press. Chuck Grench showed an early interest in the manuscript and has been a patient guide as I made my way through the various stages of the review and publication process. Ron Maner has generously fielded my numerous questions. Katy O'Brien and Brian R. MacDonald have also been very helpful during this process. This book has benefited enormously from the extensive feedback of two wonderful readers. I sincerely thank Rebecca Edwards and Patricia Schechter for their meticulous and exacting readings of my manuscript. They pushed me to significantly deepen my analyses and expand my research. Their cogent criticisms and suggestions have helped to make this book far better than it would have been without their input.

I could not have completed this project without the hospitality and support of friends and family. Richard Fingard generously provided me with lodging during a freezing month I spent in Chicago. Allison Hertog, Seth Schachner, Susan Beren, and Jason McGill put me up during an equally extreme hot New York summer. Barbara and Peter Schwartz welcomed me into their home while I searched for an apartment back in Los Angeles. I am indebted to Jody and Gary Eglington, who took me into their home and lives while I read manuscript collections in Washington, D.C., for six months. Without the Eglinton family's warmth and generosity, I am not sure that I would have made it through the daily highs and lows of archival research. Without their company, I certainly would not have had as much fun as I did during my time in D.C. One of the greatest pleasures of finding employment at uc Davis has been the chance to live near my birth family. Ever since I met them in my twenties, Judy Loewe, Megan Mowery, John Swain, Regina Miesch, and Veda Dixon have embraced me and my interests, including my academic pursuits. They have patiently followed the progress of this book through its many incarnations, consistently expressing excitement over its eventual publication. I regret very much that Gladys Hicks, Norma and Jack Swain, and Mary Wood, who each offered critical financial and emotional support at key stages of the project, did not live to see the book's completion.

Finally, I am forever grateful to my dear family, my parents, Rosa and Richard Materson, my brother Larry Materson, and my husband Phil Kaminsky. Each of them has taught me the meaning of unconditional love. My parents and brother have been my unfailing champions through the years. Phil's incredible warmth, generosity, and great sense of humor have been a constant source of joy and comfort as I struggled through finishing this book. Their faith in my ability to do this project carried me through at times when mine wavered. For this and so much more, I dedicate this work to them.

Illustrations

Introduction

In 1913 Ella Elm rejected the life of limited and unsteady employment that was available to black women in Arkansas by relocating to Illinois, where she had heard "there was lots of work."[1] Work, or wage labor, had been a necessary component of Elm's life in Arkansas after she "went to school some."[2] Elm did not describe the nature of her employment in Arkansas to the interviewer who visited her home in downstate Illinois in the late 1930s. She would have been in the minority of black women in the state if she did not eke out a marginal income through agricultural and domestic labor. By the time Elm departed for Illinois in 1913, African American laborers were suffering from severe under- and unemployment in Arkansas's cotton- and corn-dominated economy.[3] Ella Elm's life in Arkansas was marred not only by tough economic times but also by political turmoil. As a child and then young woman, Elm watched Arkansas's white Democratic-controlled legislature disfranchise black men between 1891 and 1909.[4] These efforts reduced the black male vote in Arkansas from 71 percent in 1890 to 24 percent in 1892 and eliminated the presence of black men in public office throughout the state.[5] Along with limited employment opportunities, such disfranchisement schemes pushed many southern women like Elm northward.

Once in Illinois, Ella Elm set out to make a better life for herself than had been possible in Arkansas. Unlike the majority of migrant women, Elm did not have to rely long on her own wage labor. Shortly after her 1913 arrival in Illinois, Ella met and married fellow Arkansas native, "Texas" Elm. Ella and Texas were able to survive on his income, an aspiration of many black families who depended upon the wage labor of every member. Although raised in Arkansas, Texas had traveled across the South finding short-term jobs "to get by with" and, in fact, earned his nickname because of the considerable time he spent in the state of Texas seeking these odd jobs. He relocated to Illinois in 1912 because, as Texas told the interviewer, he "heard there was better opportunities for colored folks" up North. He quickly found employment with the Missouri Pacific Railroad on the "extra gang" and eventually channeled this physically demanding job into a degree of financial security for himself and Ella. By the late 1930s, the Missouri Pacific Railroad employed Texas as a foreman at one of its downstate railroad stations. One of the perks of the job was a small four-room house on a two-acre plot of land. Ella and Texas fixed up this house with great care. Ella created a flower garden in one corner of the property, and the couple devoted the rest of the land to raising vegetables and hogs. The two acres "ain't a whole lot," Texas acknowledged, but it supplemented the couple's diet with "fresh vegetables in the summer" and "meat for the winter."[6]

Even as Ella embarked upon her new life in Illinois, she did not turn away from the family and community that she had left behind in Arkansas. As surely as she carried her belongings on the long train ride to Illinois, Ella Elm also carried with her a commitment to use her newfound freedoms in Illinois to aid family and friends who remained in Arkansas. One of these freedoms was the right to vote. In 1913 women in Illinois acquired the right to vote in most municipal and federal elections, including presidential elections. A scarcity of archival records makes it difficult to discern whether Elm's politics were limited to voting, or if she was also active in the Jackson County Colored Republican Club. During the 1920s, the women of this club, mostly residents of Murphysboro and nearby Carbondale, canvassed voters on behalf of selected Republican candidates.[7]

Elm's father had certainly prepared her for participation in such canvassing work. As Elm told the government interviewer, "I can't remember much that happened in my childhood but one thing does stand out." Elm recalled, "When I was a little girl my daddy used to say to me. Ella you is a little girl now but when you grow up to twenty-one and can vote don't never vote a democrat ticket." Optimistic that one day his daughter would join the ranks of voters, Ella's father attempted to educate his daughter about the dangers of the Democratic Party and the virtues of voting the Republican ticket. Following her relocation to Illinois, Elm used her vote on behalf of her father and the thousands of disfranchised African Americans in Arkansas. Referring to her father's appeal not to vote for Democrats, Elm informed the interviewer, "And so to this very day I never have."[8]

This book is a history of African American women like Ella Elm who entered electoral politics to help their new northern communities and the ones they left behind in the South. It examines this history during what is often described as the "nadir" of black life in America. These were the incredibly oppressive decades between the demise of Reconstruction in 1877 and the beginnings of a major voting realignment in 1932. African American women who lived beyond the reach of southern white supremacists, this book argues, participated in the American party system during these years in a hard fought effort to put an end to the nadir. They served as "proxy" voters and canvassers for African Americans who remained under the tyranny of southern white supremacy. For the most part, this meant voting the Republican ticket. They sought to create an activist federal government that would use its power to protect African Americans' basic citizenship rights.

Twenty-first-century Americans often view party politics with cynicism. Since World War II, half or less than half of eligible voters cast their ballots in presidential elections. This figure drops further during "off-year" elections.[9] From a twenty-first-century perspective, it might be hard to comprehend the effort and hopes that earlier generations invested in the arena of electoral politics. Americans of diverse backgrounds have fought in the courts, on the streets, in the battlefields, and through the constitutional amendment process for the right to cast their ballot and participate in party politics. Since the rise of the two-party system in the United States during the 1820s, the mobilization on behalf of candidates from competing political parties has served as the principal vehicle by which American citizens have attempted to influence government. Historically, however, a privileged few have chosen representatives for the majority. This book explores how African American women mobilized to enter and reshape one of the most exclusive power institutions in America, the party system, so that it would protect the rights of all citizens rather than a privileged few.

African American women's turn to electoral politics to defeat white supremacy began during the crucible of Reconstruction before they even had the right to vote. In many ways, this book is an epilogue to or continuation of a story that began in the South during the 1860s and 1870s with a generation of women who attempted to influence electoral contests so that results would enhance black freedom. Subsequent generations of African American women kept this battle for basic citizenship rights within the party system alive by carrying it from the South to the North and from the nineteenth century into the twentieth.

Reconstruction, that is the years between 1865 and 1877 when rebel states regained admission to the Union, was a period of great promise for black Americans. With the end of the Civil War in 1865, southern roads were filled with newly emancipated people searching for children, husbands, siblings, and parents who had been sold away during slavery. Men, women, and children of all ages packed into schoolhouses seeking the education that the

[3]

slave regime had denied them. Black men held offices in southern state governments that had been newly reconstructed in order to rejoin the Union. Congress demonstrated a commitment to black Americans never witnessed before on the part of the federal government when it enacted the Thirteenth, Fourteenth, and Fifteenth Amendments to the Constitution between 1865 and 1870. The Thirteenth Amendment abolished American slavery. The Fourteenth Amendment defined American citizenship and who had the authority to confer it in such a way that newly freed slaves became American citizens. For the first time, the Constitution defined this fundamental concept as deriving from the federal government, not the states. Additionally, the Fourteenth Amendment established the concept of equal protection before the law, and it made unconstitutional any state laws that "abridge the privileges or immunities of citizens of the United States." In other words, southern states could no longer deny black residents the entitlements and protections that came with being an American citizen. For white American men, one of these key entitlements was the right to vote. The Reconstruction Act of 1867 recognized black male suffrage in the former Confederate states. The ratification of the Fifteenth Amendment in 1870 made black male suffrage part of the Constitution. Congress backed up these three Reconstruction Amendments with enforcement legislation and civil rights acts.

Although not entitled to vote themselves, African American women were heavily involved in politics during Reconstruction.[10] At the same moment that white suffragists were just beginning to establish national suffrage organizations, black women were attending Republican rallies and conventions. In Virginia, for example, both women and men poured into Richmond's First African Baptist Church in late August 1867 for a Republican state convention hours before the meeting was to begin. When white delegates arrived and discovered no available seats for themselves, they moved the meeting outdoors, much to the delight of the thousands of additional African Americans who had not been able to find space in the church. Similar scenes of women and men packing Republican meetings, large and small, took place across the South (see figure 1). At community rallies, women voted on issues and expressed their opinions, sometimes shouting them from the crowd. They made their politics known in other ways. In 1868, for instance, white employers in Mississippi were alarmed when cooks and maids showed up to work wearing campaign buttons with images of Republican presidential candidate Ulysses S. Grant. In Georgia and Virginia, women established political organizations that helped their neighbors

[4]

FIGURE 1. *Women appear on the balcony and the far left bench in this 1868* Harper's Weekly *rendition of a political gathering entitled "Electioneering at the South." The text that accompanies this drawing reads: "It shows the newly-enfranchised citizens of the United States engaged in the discussion of political questions upon which they are to vote."* Harper's Weekly, *July 25, 1868, 468. Provided courtesy HarpWeek, LLC.*

prepare to go to the polls and that financed Republican speakers. African American women also helped to register voters and marched with men to the polls. In fact, black women were so engaged in politics that white employers widely complained about their lack of domestic servants on convention and election days.[11]

At the polls, women did not stand by passively. One educated Savannah, Georgia, woman described her efforts to prevent white Democratic misconduct at the polls during the first election in which black men could vote in the state. Initially, as she told a *New York Times* reporter, she had merely intended to assist a few men: "I went out with four colored men from the country to help them vote. I suppose I was interested in the first place to see that my people had a chance to vote. Then these men could not read or write, and so I went with them." The widespread fraud that she encountered at the polls, however, led her to broaden her efforts. As she described, "The white people were giving the colored voters Democratic tickets, and the negro men did not know any better." There at the polls she remained after concluding that "I could be of use," helping illiterate men identify and reject the Democratic tickets that white poll workers were fraudulently giving them.[12]

Analyzing disfranchised women's Republican activism during Reconstruction, historian Elsa Barkley Brown argues that freed people in the South did not approach politics through the lens of nineteenth-century liberal ideology that characterized society as an aggregate of autonomous individuals each acting in his or her own self-interest. Rather, an "ethos of mutuality" and interreliance that enabled so many families and communities to survive the poverty African Americans confronted in the South following emancipation was also reflected within party politics. Freed people, Brown explains, viewed the ballot as owned by the community rather than individuals. Women's participation at these various political events was an expression of this view that men were voting on behalf of the entire community and not just for themselves.[13]

This expectation that men's votes would benefit the entire community helps to explain why women celebrated men's voting rights, even though they were denied the ballot. One white woman wrote derisively about the celebratory atmosphere that unfolded near her Virginia home on election day: "Negroes went to precincts overnight and camped out. Morning revealed reinforcements arriving. All sexes and ages came afoot, in carts, in wagons, as to a fair or circus. Old women set up tables and spread out ginger-cakes and set forth buckets of lemonade." To her surprise, "The all-day picnic ended only with closing of polls, and not always then, darkeys hanging around and carrying scrapping and jollification into the night."[14] The gathering of men, women, and children at the polls that this white woman tried to dismiss as typifying a carnival more than a civic duty was a demonstration of the hope that black communities invested in men's voting rights for creating a new political and racial order in the South.

Women also joined men at rallies and the polls to guard against violence.[15] When Ella Elm's father taught her about the dangers of the Democratic Party, he would have no doubt recalled the party's terror campaigns to reclaim power during Reconstruction. The 1868 elections in Arkansas were so violent that the state's Republican governor declared martial law in ten counties and called up a militia to restore order. Across the South, white paramilitary groups attempted to prevent Republican victories by murdering both black and white Republican leaders. Elm's father would have remembered the assassination of white Republican James Hinds in 1868, one of Arkansas's sitting representatives in the U.S. Congress. If her father had

[6]

attempted to cast a ballot, he may have encountered white marauders, including the Ku Klux Klan, who attacked black voters and shut down polling sites. In one horrible incident in Georgia, white Democrats shot at a black election parade, even chasing down and murdering terrified participants who fled for their lives. By accompanying men to the polls, women and children avoided the prospect of being confronted by white militias while the majority of men were absent from the home. Armed with a range of weapons from boards with protruding nails to hatchets, women also stood guard while men cast their ballots or Republican rallies were under way.[16]

Women may have expected men to vote on their behalf, but reality did not always match expectation. It is clear that not all men adhered to the notion that the ballot was collectively owned. Democratic violence and intimidation sometimes intervened. So too did economic desperation. White employers threatened to fire men who voted the Republican ticket and, in some instances, promised jobs for those who sided with the Democrats.[17] Moreover, not all men favored women having so much say in the political process. Because slavery had muted patriarchy within southern black communities, some African American men associated their freedom with the ability to establish a patriarchal system, a privilege that in the South had been the preserve of white men. During election season, establishing male authority sometimes translated into the exclusion of women from Republican rallies in various locations.[18]

In these circumstances, African American women who did not possess any formal political power relied on persuasion and threats to influence men's voting. Women chastised men who strayed from the Republican fold. Fiancées broke off engagements and wives refused to share beds with men who turned away from the Republican Party. Church congregations ostracized Democratic members. Women monitored men's voting at the polls, promising, as one woman told her husband, that "if he voted the Democratic ticket she 'would kill him dead in his sleep.' "[19] If women could not vote themselves, they could at least pressure men to represent them. By most accounts, this approach was often effective. As one black Democratic man described, "many more [men] desire to vote the Democratic ticket and on account of these women and the threats, they voted Republican."[20] In the end, however, black women of the Reconstruction South were dependent upon men's decisions at the polls.

Reconstruction had started with great hope that the federal government would recognize and protect former slaves as full American citizens. By 1877, however, after the Republicans lost the House in 1874 and nearly the

[7]

presidency in 1876, the federal government had abandoned black Americans in the South. W. E. B. Du Bois poignantly characterized both the promise and incredible disappointment of Reconstruction when he wrote in his 1935 study of the era that "the slave went free; stood a brief moment in the sun; then moved back again toward slavery."[21] In one state after another, former rebel leaders regained control of southern legislatures. In Arkansas, for example, Elm's father watched as white Democrats once again dominated the state legislature in 1874. A series of Supreme Court decisions gutted the Fourteenth and Fifteenth Amendments and "gave a green light to acts of terror where local officials either could not or would not enforce the law."[22] In 1877 the final remaining federal troops in the South withdrew as part of deal brokered between white Republicans and Democrats to resolve the contested presidential election of 1876.

The white South was free to trample over the rights guaranteed in the Reconstruction Amendments. Through a combination of state-sponsored violence and legislation, white southern Democrats were well on their way to nullifying the Reconstruction Amendments by the 1890s. The chain gang labor and sharecropping systems that had emerged throughout the South after the Civil War looked disturbingly like slavery at times. In 1883 the Supreme Court struck down the Civil Rights Act of 1875 that prohibited discrimination in public accommodations.[23] Between 1890 and 1910, all of the ex-Confederate states and Oklahoma legislated the disfranchisement of black male voters.[24] The Supreme Court's 1896 *Plessy v. Ferguson* decision that "separate but equal" accommodations were constitutional enabled legalized segregation to spread throughout the South. Widespread violence facilitated the "legalization" of disfranchisement and segregation. The federal government, of course, was complicit in this nullification process through decisions like *Plessy* and by refusing to enforce the amendments.

While the federal government abandoned American citizens of African descent in the South, aunts, mothers, sisters, and daughters residing outside the South did not. The pages that follow document how African American women in one state, Illinois, repeatedly entered electoral politics between the 1890s and 1930s in order to complete the unfinished goals of Reconstruction. They mobilized to elect representatives who would push for the enforcement of the Reconstruction Amendments in the South. In so doing, African American women kept alive a very distinct strain of Republican Party ideology that favored using federal power to protect black citizenship rights. This particular vein of Republican Party ideology had fallen out of favor with most white supporters by the close of the nineteenth century.

Beginning in the 1890s, black women in Illinois attempted to keep alive this strain of Republican Party ideology with one important difference from the generation of women who had preceded them: they participated in the party system as a new class of voters. Their ability to shape the party system was not dependent on men's willingness to extend an ethos of mutuality to politics. Persuasion and threats were no longer their only tools for ensuring Republican votes. Precisely during the years when black men in the South were being disfranchised, American women's access to the ballot box was gradually expanding. American women's enfranchisement did not occur in a single moment with the passage of the Nineteenth Amendment in 1920. Women in Illinois were among the millions of American women who acquired the right to vote selectively in various cities and states during the late nineteenth and early twentieth centuries. Women in Illinois acquired voting rights in three stages: suffrage for school officials in 1891, expanded suffrage for many municipal and federal offices in 1913, and the full franchise in 1920. The ability of states to enfranchise residents, even to vote for federal offices as was the case in Illinois in 1913, without federal authority was one of the peculiar qualities of the suffrage process and a sign of the continuing ambiguities of the demarcation between state and federal enfranchisement roles in the years after Reconstruction.

Black women in Illinois entered the electoral system not only as voters in the years after 1891 but also as canvassers and even candidates—primarily Republican voters, canvassers, and candidates. Because the Republican Party was the party of Abraham Lincoln and the Reconstruction Amendments, most blacks who retained the franchise favored the Republican Party. During the depths of the Depression, Franklin Roosevelt's New Deal programs helped to bring the majority of black voters into the Democratic fold for the first time in 1936, but before this major voting realignment, African American women in Illinois formed a plethora of Republican women's clubs devoted to canvassing on behalf of chosen Republican candidates.

Illinois is a very rich site for examining the history of black women's electoral activism. This is because African Americans acquired significant political influence in Illinois, and especially Chicago, during the first part of the twentieth century. The arrival of tens of thousands of southern blacks like Ella Elm was a key factor in the growth of black political power in the state. Illinois's black population expanded by more than 475 percent between 1890 and 1930, from 57,028 to 328,972. Elm eventually made her home in downstate Illinois, but the vast majority of southern migrants who arrived at one of Chicago's railroad depots remained in the city. This fact

[9]

was reflected in U.S. Census figures: the number of African Americans who made their home in Chicago skyrocketed by more than 1,500 percent between 1890 and 1930, from 14,271 to 233,903.[25] Black leaders in Chicago bartered this potential voting bloc for jobs, social services, and elected offices. Between 1915 and 1928, black voters in Chicago put more black men into office than in any other American city. The list of black elected officials included multiple city councilmen, a state senator, several state representatives, a municipal court judge, and a U.S. congressman. This congressman, Oscar DePriest—who in 1915 was also Chicago's first black city councilman—became in 1928 the first black American to serve in Congress since 1901. The first black Democrat to be elected to Congress also came from Chicago. This was Arthur Mitchell, who defeated DePriest in 1934. African American women in Chicago were heavily involved in these elections as voters and canvassers. They were also a driving force behind the campaigns of white candidates whom they identified as friendly toward black voters and, even more important, interested in promoting black freedom.[26]

Although organized around Illinois, and especially Chicago, this book is a history about national and southern politics as well. The narrative moves from the Midwest, to the South, to the national level because the women discussed here operated in, and linked, these multiple political arenas. By virtue of their location, Republican women in Illinois were at the crossroads of a great deal of national Republican traffic that passed through Chicago. Between the end of Reconstruction in 1877 and the 1936 voting realignment, nine of the fifteen Republican National Conventions took place in Chicago; and the Republican National Committee's main headquarters or its Western Division Headquarters was frequently located there.[27] Black Republican women in Illinois were not alone in their political organizing. Similar Republican clubs emerged in cities and states across the country during this period. By the mid-1920s, women in Illinois were part of a national network of black Republican women who worked together in both local and national campaigns in order to place desirable candidates in office. Politically active black women in Illinois also traveled the crossroads that connected southern and midwestern communities. Like Elm, many were originally southerners who had resettled in Illinois only a few years and sometimes months before throwing themselves into the fray of campaign work with longtime Illinois residents.

Glenda Gilmore argues that black men's disfranchisement in North Carolina at the turn of the century ironically created new public roles for black women. Black women in North Carolina became "diplomats to the white community" who negotiated for government services for black residents. Black women's ability to negotiate services from a government that excluded black men was possible precisely because women lacked voting rights. Unlike black men, women in North Carolina had never voted and this fact "camouflaged" the political content of their activities.[28] Once in Illinois, no longer needing to camouflage their politics, they joined the thousands of newly enfranchised African American women in the state who marched to the polls to cast their own ballots.

Migrant women, however, were more than just numbers. Their decision to cast ballots and engage in Republican canvassing work in Illinois needs to be understood within the larger continuum of their lives. While seeking to escape the oppressive regime of southern white supremacy, migrant women did not begin their lives "anew" upon relocating to Illinois, nor did they sever personal ties to the South. Rather, they carried with them a host of memories and experiences—political and otherwise—that shaped their future lives in the Midwest. Many newly arrived migrants had weathered disfranchisement battles against southern white Democrats. Others, like Ella Elm, learned about Democratic misconduct from relatives. Migrant women's infusion of southern political knowledge into the Midwest took place over several decades. The term "Great Migration" is most closely associated with the heaviest years of migration during World War I and the 1920s. Black migration out of the South, however, was a continuous process that stretched across the nineteenth and twentieth centuries. The pages that follow show that each new wave of migration reinvigorated the southern orientation of black Republican women's culture in the Midwest with fresh stories of southern Democratic abuses.

Together migrant and Illinois-born women created a hybrid political culture in Illinois that blended local political issues with a concern about black rights in the South. Both groups were acutely aware that they had access to the ballot box, whereas the majority of southern blacks did not. Each electoral battle in which they engaged had its own unique set of issues. Yet, a common goal emerged across the years and idiosyncrasies of diverse electoral contests. They repeatedly looked for moments in electoral races, even small local contests, to focus attention on the ongoing struggles against disfranchisement, segregation, and forced labor in the South—and to help elect officials who would do the same. For example, during the 1890s, black women in Chicago used a local school election that had nothing to do with federal power to generate a public discussion about the power and authority of the Reconstruction Amendments.[29]

It was never this simple, however. African American women faced a whole host of interlocking obstacles as they attempted to push forward the struggle for civil rights using the party system. One of the most challenging obstacles they faced was a lack of good choices. When African American women finally began to cast their own ballots, neither of the two main parties offered very much on the national level. The Democratic Party remained the party of southern white supremacy, and the Republican Party was in deep retreat from its antislavery origins. Increasingly, even white Republican candidates who talked about using federal power to protect black rights also sought southern white votes in order to break up the Democratic "solid south." At the local level in Illinois, however, black women voters and canvassers had more options. There, African American women found white and eventually black Republican candidates who, in return for black support, were willing to use their elected office to promote legislation beneficial to black communities. In 1928, for example, African American women across Illinois canvassed hard to help white Republican Ruth Hanna McCormick win a seat in the U.S. House of Representatives. Once in office, Congressman McCormick attempted to reduce southern representation in the House from states that disfranchised black voters.

One of the factors that distinguished African American women's electoral activism from men's during the nadir was black women reformers' belief that they had embarked on a new era in which women would help deliver the race from the injustices that it faced. African American women were so insistent that famed abolitionist and suffragist Frances Ellen Watkins Harper declared the late nineteenth century was the "woman's era." As historian Deborah Gray White explains, this "woman's era" philosophy was grounded in the "sad loss of confidence in the ability of most black men to deal effectively with the race problem."[30] Women reformers asserted that, as wives and mothers, women were better situated than men to instill in future generations the values of self-help and respectability that they believed to be so essential to race progress. Indeed, Michele Mitchell has demonstrated that many reformers, both women and men, held that properly educated mothers and homemakers were the key to the very survival of the race. Healthful and respectable homes would produce vigorous offspring who would lead morally upright lives.[31]

In addition to propagating a physically and morally robust race, personal displays of thrift and modesty, reformers believed, would go a long way toward undermining devastating racial stereotypes of African Americans as immoral and undeserving of citizenship. The expectation that the victims and not the perpetrators of racism should regulate their behavior was a problematic strategy for battling racism. Middle-class African Americans' reliance on such "racial uplift" and "racial destiny" ideology was indicative of the limited avenues available for challenging white supremacy during the late nineteenth and early twentieth centuries and also contributed to the construction of intraracial class divisions. Indeed, middle-class status, or what Mitchell characterizes as "aspiring class" status, was defined less by income and more by the determination to live a certain type of respectable life that entailed hard work and modest behavior. Black women reformers asserted that because they were unlike the mass of black Americans, they should not be lumped together with uneducated blacks in the white mind; yet, at the same time, they had an obligation to prevent the working poor from engaging in behavior that would injure the reputation of the entire race. Mostly middle-class black women established a plethora of self-help institutions that both provided social services that ensured healthful homes and instilled racial uplift values in the working poor. These included kindergartens, homes for the elderly and for wayward girls, health clinics, and classes that taught a range of homemaking and mothering skills.[32] African American women's social service was part of a more general turn inward among black communities that had been largely abandoned by elected representatives.[33]

This book unpacks the electoral manifestations of "woman's era" philosophy, what might be characterized as the "outward" electoral face of this drive among African American women to help guide the race out of the profound problems that it faced during the late nineteenth and early twentieth centuries. To be sure, women's efforts to save the race through social service was political, not only by the very definition of the project but also because women reformers regularly worked with government agencies to ensure healthful living conditions and the availability of public services for their communities.[34] Many of the very same women who established these self-help organizations, however, also carried on their work to save the race within the party system. Indeed, the notion that women had a responsibility to lead the race took on a life of its own within party politics.

From the 1870s through the 1920s, many black women reformers held that it was women's responsibility to keep men loyal to the Republican Party. From this vantage, party loyalty, and specifically Republican Party loyalty, was a virtue that would eventually reap rewards. Women's supposed moral superiority over men, women reformers asserted, enabled women to deflect vote-buying schemes. As women increasingly joined the ranks of voters, adherents of this view rhetorically lumped women of low social standing together with men when describing that group of African Americans most likely to succumb to Democratic malfeasance. In other words, class increasingly cut across gender in Republican women's partisan constructions of race disloyalty. Moreover, within local Republican circles, it was not always clear what example women should be setting for the masses. Republican women leaders, for example, disagreed about whether the race would benefit most by working with white-controlled political machines or by supporting black candidates over white ones.

This belief that women must guide the race toward Republican loyalty was not the only argument circulating about women's unique responsibilities within party politics. A minority of women tapped into this very same ideology of female moral superiority to make a very different claim: that if it was women's responsibility to lead the race, then they must lead the race *out* of the Republican Party. This explicitly gendered argument for abandoning the Republican Party helped to fuel what would eventually transform into a major voting realignment by the mid-1930s. To be sure, this assertion was not the primary factor motivating the mass of poor African Americans to switch to the Democratic Party. Among some middle-class black women reformers who had devoted their adult lives to trying to pull the race out of the nadir, however, the notion that women reformers had an obligation to guide the race into the Democratic Party carried weight.

African American women grounded their approach to party politics in their vast experience negotiating, bridging, and transforming contradiction, what contemporary theorists would describe as a womanist perspective to social change.[35] In addition to Republican duplicity, African American women regularly encountered blatant sexism and racism from groups who should have been their closest political allies, African American men and white Republicans (both women and men). Rather than throw up their hands in despair, politically active black women simultaneously criticized and supported these sometimes less than ideal partners. Far from illogical or contradictory, this strategy enabled them to work toward the multiple levels of social change that they demanded. They needed to build such alliances in order to gain a voice in powerful party circles. Even as they cultivated powerful allies, however, they also protested indifference, bigotry, and hypocrisy. African American women regularly criticized black men for what they perceived as failures of leadership while also expressing solidarity with them in a shared battle against white supremacy. The same could be said for black women's dealings with white women reformers: they denounced white women's racism while also expressing solidarity with them in the struggle to undermine sexism. And so it was in their approach to the Republican Party.

Black Republican women rebuked their party for its profound failings, but they also focused on the exceptions to Republican indifference when canvassing for candidates. These exceptions changed over the years and with different candidates. They included legislative efforts for black education, against mob violence, and for a reduction in U.S. representatives from southern states that disfranchised voters. African American women also supported positions that at first glance seemed to have nothing to do with the struggle for black citizenship rights. One of these seemingly unrelated issues was the enactment and then repeal of a federal amendment prohibiting the production and consumption of liquor. The Republican Party's support of prohibition gave women reformers a reason to work with the party as they increasingly struggled with Republican indifference toward the end of the 1920s. Ironically, however, African American women's stance in favor of prohibition also undercut their authority to represent the race during an era when many enjoyed the pleasures of commercialized leisure districts, from blues and jazz clubs to dance and gambling halls.

In their canvassing efforts, African American women relied on a range of institutions. These included churches, fraternal organizations, women's reform groups, and Republican and Democratic clubs. This study traces some of the key institutional changes that undergirded women's political activism between the 1890s and 1930s. The overall trajectory of these changes was from less organizational support to more: in 1891 when women in Illinois acquired their first voting rights, African American women in the state had few organizations at their disposal for campaign work, whereas by the 1930s they had a range from which to choose. This growth in organizational support, however, involved a complicated set of struggles for authority and resources that were refracted through gender and class hierarchies. Because historically they were among the only black institutions independent from white authority, black churches served as important sites for party politics. Churches were also patriarchal institutions in which key leadership positions were reserved for men. African American women regularly turned to the churches to conduct campaign work, but they also created their own set of clubs that theoretically enabled them to express their political views beyond the reach of clerical authority. In practice, however, the clubs did not

[15]

always achieve this intended goal, and this book documents tensions between women and male clergy that only increased as women's independent political organizing expanded in the twentieth century. The pages that follow also document how black women reformers missed several important opportunities to reach women voters who, because of a combination of poverty and regional differences, remained outside the fold of either middle-class women's clubs or mainline churches.

Chapters 1 through 3 explore African American women's Republican and eventually Democratic activism following each expansion of women's voting rights in Illinois: 1891, 1913, and 1920. These chapters identify the different ways that African American women in Illinois and across the nation used electoral contests to shine a light on the need for a stronger federal government, especially in relation to the South. Each new wave of migrant women who arrived in Illinois, these chapters show, reinvigorated this southern orientation of local women's politics. Chapters 1 through 3 also consider the diverse ways that African American women applied "woman's era" philosophy to party politics. This philosophy was articulated mostly with the Republican Party in mind. Chapter 3, however, also documents how some African American women, angered by the Republican Party's failure to push through federal antilynching legislation, argued by the mid-1920s that if women were going to lead the race, then they needed to lead it into the Democratic Party. This analysis of the gendered components of the voting realignment extends into chapter 4's discussion of prohibition politics and the 1928 presidential election. Chapter 4 continues to trace this gendered argument for switching to the Democratic Party. It also explores how the decline of women's racial uplift ideology intertwined with the decline of the Republican Party among black voters in ways that undercut the influence of Republican women's networks that were, after years of organizing, at the height of their organizing potential. Chapter 5 examines black women's use of these Republican networks to advance individual and group agendas in congressional elections in Illinois between 1927 and 1930. Despite or because of their embattled position, black Republican women remained fiercely loyal to the Republican Party not only to achieve long-sought policy goals but also to obtain paid campaign positions that would help them weather what was turning into the worst economic depression in American history. The book concludes with a brief discussion of women's turn to the Democratic Party with the election of Franklin Delano Roosevelt in 1932. Threaded across these chapters is an examination of the shifting institutional support—from churches, to women's clubs, to party organizations, to fraternal organizations—that black women relied upon, fought for access to, created, and sometimes overlooked in their campaign work.

ELLA ELM WAS NOT the only daughter who learned about the politics of Democratic white supremacy from her father. Several hundred miles to the east in North Carolina, another young girl by the name of Jennie Lawrence learned about the history of the Democratic Party during Reconstruction from her father, Abner Bernard Lawrence. Abner Lawrence had witnessed the establishment of the Republican Party in North Carolina in 1867 and its decline over the next eight years. In 1876 Lawrence was a seminary student at the Biddle Memorial Institute in Charlotte.[36] In addition to preparing for a life as a Presbyterian minister, Lawrence was engaged in a last-ditch fight to retain Republican influence in North Carolina.

On July 4, 1876, Abner Bernard Lawrence addressed a crowd of between 5,000 and 8,000 African Americans who had gathered in the grove near Biddle Memorial Institute to celebrate the nation's centennial. Some had traveled from as far as Statesville and Wilmington to participate in the festivities. Lawrence was one among several prominent black and white North Carolinians who, in between singing, prayer, and eating, delivered speeches to the crowd throughout the day. Several of the speakers, including Lawrence, had participated in the Republican Convention of Mecklenburg County ten days earlier where a heated dispute over patronage had nearly caused a breakdown in the convention and had divided black Republicans among themselves. Having survived the convention with the county's Republican Party battered but still intact, black Republicans sidestepped their disagreements and instead emphasized unity. As the *Charlotte Observer* reported, leading black Republican John Schenck told the crowd that "at present they had best disregard personal preferences and stand together for the Republican party." Days earlier Schenck had squared off with Lawrence over patronage practices and the nomination of candidates. Schenck, Lawrence, and others would have another chance to hammer out their disagreements over nominees in Raleigh the following week. They would travel there as delegates to the North Carolina Republican State Convention.[37] For the time being, they presented a unified front against a shared enemy, Democratic gubernatorial candidate Zebulon Vance. Vance, whose campaign rhetoric included a description of the Republican Party as "begotten by a scalawag out of a mulatto and born in an outhouse," had served as the

Introduction

governor of North Carolina during the Civil War.[38] Vance's victory would mean that the exact same man who had led North Carolina during the secession crisis would once again govern the state.

It was with good reason that Schenck emphasized unity among black Republicans in the upcoming election, even though he personally railed against the party's treatment of black members. The pages of the *Charlotte Observer* gleefully noted the presence of a black Tilden and Vance Club in the city.[39] Deeply frustrated with Republican Party scandals and general unwillingness to either support black candidates or reward black supporters with patronage, some black men turned toward the Democratic Party. Others succumbed to economic pressures and intimidation.[40] White employers coerced black workers to support Democratic candidates, in some instances accompanying them to the polls to make sure they voted the Democratic ticket. Black men of the Tilden and Vance Club were given badges that, as the *Charlotte Observer* reported, were "to serve as passports to the favor of those who wish to hir[e] labor."[41]

Black women in Charlotte openly challenged black men who for whatever reason considered voting a Democratic ticket. After a late October women's meeting, a local paper reported, "a bright colored damsel of probably 20 summers, was heard to say 'we'll make them forget Vance yet, d—n their black souls.' "[42] Days after the gathering, the *Charlotte Observer* made an unveiled threat against women who denounced black Democrats: "The colored women should not be so embittered against the whites, nor should they work so hard against the interests of those persons who give them their patronage and employment." Knowing full well that many black women in the city earned wages as washwomen—picking up dirty laundry from white households, scrubbing the linens clean on washboards at home, and then carrying them back to the white section of Charlotte freshly ironed and folded—the *Observer* predicted ominously: "If a steam la[u]ndry was erected, as is talked of, it would throw hundreds of colored women out of the means of making a support. Colored people think! who are your friends."[43] Defiantly, black women "held meetings and appointed committees on elections to look after the men and induce them to return to Radicalism."[44] On election day, they jeered at black Democrats and, by one account, lay "in ambush and stone[d] them as they return[ed] home."[45]

Despite black Republican efforts, Zebulon Vance won the election by about 13,000 votes. Democrats were also in control of the state legislature. North Carolina was officially "redeemed" from Republican influence asserted during Reconstruction.[46] Abner Lawrence must have been deeply disappointed about Vance's victory. Still, he continued to forge a life for himself as a minister, husband, and father. In early 1878, Abner married teacher Annie Henderson. Together they had seven children, three surviving.[47] Their eldest surviving daughter, Jennie, would carry her parents' passion for party politics northward. Jennie Lawrence emerged as a leading Republican organizer in Chicago's predominantly black wards between the 1910s and 1930s. During Reconstruction, disfranchised women expected men to use their vote on behalf of the entire community. Not all of them did, of course, but the expectation or pressure that men should act as proxy voters for women was there. By the time that Jennie Lawrence was ensconced in Republican politics in Chicago, African Americans' ability to cast a ballot was increasingly determined more by region and less by gender. The disfranchised, both men and women, resided in the South; the enfranchised, including women, lived outside that region. In Chicago, Jennie Lawrence would take on the role of proxy voter that her father had once performed.

Introduction

[I]

Tomorrow You Will Go to the Polls
Women's Voting in Chicago in 1894

The crisp clear autumn air of November 6, 1894, was punctuated with excitement and eagerness as thousands of women in Illinois traveled to the polls. Many dressed in their best attire, assembled at prearranged open houses or meeting places, and then took carriages or walked in groups to their precinct polling sites. The majority adhered to calls to submit their specially printed woman's ballot only between 10 A.M. and 2 P.M., so as not to interfere with men's voting before and after work and during lunch break. Working women, however, arrived early at the polls. Enthusiasm led others to enter polling booths before 9 A.M., in some precincts casting the day's first ballot.[1] Women were permitted to vote only for the University of Illinois's board of trustees, but their large turnout and the extensive news coverage made it seem as if women were voting for all the offices that were up for election in 1894. Those women who headed to the polls understood the historic significance of their errand. Not only were most casting their first ballot, but also four women—on the Republican, Democratic, and Prohibition tickets—were candidates for the board of trustees.

In 1891, following the narrow defeat of a state constitutional amendment that would have fully enfranchised the women of Illinois, the state legislature passed the less controversial Woman's Suffrage Bill, which legalized women's voting for school-related offices and matters in rural areas and unincorporated cities.[2] Three years later, women affiliated with the Republican, Democratic, and Prohibition parties ensured that four women were among the field of thirteen candidates who were running for the three open positions on the university's board of trustees. In the months leading up to November 6, women of the state's diverse ethnic population—immigrant and native-born Scandinavian, German, Jewish, Italian, Anglo-, and African American—participated, in varying degrees, in the university trustee campaign.

One group, however, was particularly well organized and committed to ensuring a large female Republican vote: those of Illinois's expanding African American community. Black women's widespread canvassing enabled white Republican candidate Lucy Flower to become Illinois's first woman elected to statewide office.[3] The success of these women's efforts on behalf of the Republican ticket was evident in the predominantly black precincts of Chicago's lower wards on election day. For instance, in the First Ward, the *Chicago Tribune* reported black women voting "in nearly every case," and Republican activist Fannie Brown counted 325 black women casting ballots for the Republican ticket.[4] African American women of the Fourth Ward made a showing equally as impressive as those of the First. The *Chicago Times* characterized black women voters as "[o]ne of the great features in the Fourth," having "far exceeded their white sisters in activity and eagerness."[5]

Examining this seemingly minor contest offers a window into the goals and canvassing strategies of black women who were active in Republican politics during the 1890s. One of the most striking features of these women's organizing was their rhetoric. Black Republican women sought to place individuals on the board who would address the educational needs of Illinois's growing black communities. Yet, in their speeches, leading black Republican women repeatedly embedded this contest within the Republican Party's historic connection with abolitionism, the Civil War, and Reconstruction. In other words, they nationalized a small local contest. They pointed to the power and authority of the Reconstruction Amendments. They urged women to vote Republican as an endorsement of the compromised emancipatory principles that the party had championed during Reconstruction and, on a much smaller scale, had briefly resuscitated during the early 1890s. By linking women's entrance into formal party politics to the ongoing struggle against white supremacy, these women maintained the historical and activist links between the struggle for black and women's rights. They also used the electoral leverage and public platforms available to them to reinsert into the party system a discourse about black rights and freedom that was deeply marginalized by the 1890s.

Migrant women drew upon their experiences in the South to shape politics in the Midwest. Though the heaviest years of migration were still more than two decades away, the arrival of southern blacks in Chicago and other parts of Illinois was already beginning to accelerate by the 1890s. At least two of the leading Republican women organizers of the 1894 campaign began their lives as slaves in the South.[6] It is no coincidence that a campaign drive with two former slaves at its helm focused on the Republican Party's historic commitment to black rights. These southern-born women and their families had personally witnessed the Republican Party's efforts to ensure black citizenship rights after the Civil War. They had also experienced the massive southern white backlash against such Republican efforts.[7] They carried these memories with them to the Midwest, where they continued to champion that strain of Republicanism that demanded black equality and the federal protection of citizenship rights.

WHEN SOUTHERN MIGRANTS ARRIVED in Chicago in the 1890s, they entered into a community that had gradually taken shape over the nineteenth century. A black Frenchman, Jean Baptiste Point de Saible, established Chicago as a permanent settlement in 1790. The first waves of African American migrants to Chicago, however, began a half century later. The small black community that emerged in Chicago during the 1840s and 1850s comprised for the most part fugitive slaves. The social life of these roughly 300 black Chicagoans revolved around two main churches established in the 1840s and 1850s, Quinn Chapel AME and Olivet Baptist. While nominally free, black Chicagoans lived under the restrictive Illinois "Black Laws," which from 1818 until 1865, required African Americans in the state to post bond and carry certificates of freedom. These laws also prohibited black voting, jury service, state military service, and interracial marriage.[8]

Black Chicago's growth, in terms of both numbers and institutions, was primarily a post–Civil War phenomenon. During the 1870s and 1880s, several thousand southerners who had the resources to quit the violence of the immediate postwar era entered into this community. The approximately 1,000 African Americans living in Chicago at the start of the Civil War expanded to 3,691 by 1870, to 6,480 by 1880, and to 14,271 by 1890. During the 1870s and 1880s, black Chicagoans added a range of community institutions to the handful that existed prior to the Civil War: about a dozen additional churches, three weekly newspapers, and several social clubs and lodges.[9]

Although black associational life had expanded since midcentury, it still remained relatively limited. With few independent institutions at their disposal, African Americans relied heavily on the churches as important sites for political gatherings during the 1870s and 1880s. Black men in Illinois finally acquired the right to vote in 1870 with the enactment of the Fifteenth Amendment. Like their counterparts in the South, African American women frequently attended such gatherings. As the *Inter Ocean* reported in the winter of 1876, "not a few of the gentler sex" were among the 300 African Americans who gathered at Quinn Chapel AME to arrange for the selection of delegates who would attend a national convention to discuss the "redemption" movement taking place across the South.[10] In 1876 organizers of a black Republican rally in the First Ward invited women's participation by promising "Good Seats reserved for the ladies."[11] While not entitled to vote themselves, African American women in Chicago also attended the yearly celebrations marking the enactment of the Fifteenth Amendment.[12] It is difficult to determine women's level of participation at these events. Unlike southern white newspaper coverage of African American politics in the 1870s, there are no reports of women shouting their opinions during debates or accompanying male relatives to the polls. For example, three companies of black men marched in a massive Republican torchlight parade that wound through the streets of Chicago in the fall of 1872. If women were more than spectators, even enthusiastic spectators, there is no mention of it in the press.[13] It is hard to believe that women did not voice their opinions at these various events or cheer on marchers, but little more than speculation is possible. What is certain, however, is that although women attended some political rallies, they were clearly not present at others, particularly those where white and black men gathered together.[14] Black men expressed racial solidarity with women, but they also distinguished themselves from the women of their race by enacting their manhood rights with white men at all-male Republican gatherings.

As black men began voting in the 1870s, machine politics was taking root in Chicago and the larger state of Illinois. What emerged over the next two decades was a decentralized array of competing political machines. As historian Thomas Pegram explains, "The two political parties were splintered into numerous factions that came together and split apart without ideological consistency."[15] The political parties and their various factions "functioned as the principal conduit for goods and favors between government and electorate."[16] With the exception of a few years, the Republican factions dominated Illinois state government between 1880 and 1932. The same could not be said for city hall in Chicago. The competition for control of city hall was fierce between the two main parties. During these same years, the Democrats won the mayor's office more than twice as often as the Republicans. Into this labyrinth of machinery stepped a handful of black men who began to craft themselves as professional politicians in the 1880s and who delivered black votes to white politicians in exchange for patronage and favors.[17]

Along with the maturation of machine politics, Chicago's political scene during the 1880s included some of the most radical and reactionary voices in the country. The various incarnations of radicalism that were quite literally exploding in Chicago in the late nineteenth century witnessed minimal black involvement. For the most part, the various groups that challenged the growing power of wealthy industrialists and capitalists did little to include black workers or address the racial components of class-based injustice. The struggle for the eight-hour workday, for instance, did not address the working conditions of the large number of African Americans who, because of limited job opportunities, found employment as domestic and personal servants. Lucy Parsons was one notable exception to the absence of black participation in Chicago's radical politics. Best known as the widow of Albert Parsons, who had been executed with three others for inciting the infamous 1886 Haymarket Riot, Lucy Parsons was an important voice in American radicalism in her own right.[18] A woman of color in a movement dominated by European immigrants, Parsons believed that trade unionism and, when necessary, armed conflict would emancipate the working class, including black workers, not the ballot box.[19] Another notable exception was the Knights of Labor (formed in 1869), which conducted the most concerted effort to attract black members that had ever taken place within the ranks of labor unionism.[20] For the most part, however, unions were hostile environments for black laborers. With the Knights' demise in the 1890s, black access to unions and the jobs they protected were eclipsed for at least three decades. Barred from the white-dominated railway brotherhoods and the American Federation of Labor, black men and women participated in the wave of strikes that swept late nineteenth-century America primarily as strikebreakers rather than strikers.[21]

Largely excluded from the labor movement, many African Americans attempted to overcome racialized class injustices through hard work and education. An education not only was a symbol of emancipation but also held the promise of individual and group advancement. Denied even the most rudimentary education under the slave regime, former slaves across the South crammed into Freedmen's Bureau schools and established their own makeshift schools where none were available.[22] Women from Chicago's growing black community were among the hundreds of northern women teachers who traveled south to fill these schools. For instance, before reset-

Women's Voting in Chicago in 1894

tling in Chicago from other parts of the North, Fannie Barrier Williams and Elizabeth Lindsay Davis made detours south to teach freed peoples during the 1870s and 1880s.[23] During the nineteenth century, because discriminatory practices also denied thousands of black students in Illinois access to a public education, black Chicagoans not only traveled south to help freed peoples but simultaneously fought and won several battles to open up educational opportunities for black students in Illinois. The new state constitution in 1870 promised free primary and secondary education for all children in the state regardless of race. In 1874 Chicago's municipal code was rewritten to prohibit segregation in public schools, and in 1889 the Illinois General Assembly passed legislation that held school boards across the state liable if they denied education to students on account of race.[24]

Despite these victories, black access to the state's only public university, the University of Illinois, was practically nonexistent. Located in Champaign, the University of Illinois opened its doors to black men in 1887. African American women were not admitted until 1901. Although technically black men's exclusion from the university ended in 1887, the enrollment of only one black man in 1894 suggested that very little had changed in the seven intervening years since desegregation had begun. This record can be compared to the enrollment figures of another group of relative newcomers, white women. The University of Illinois began admitting white women in 1870. By the 1893–94 academic year, fully one-fifth of the university's students were white women.[25] The black middle and elite classes perceived college education as an essential component for the creation of a black leadership that would offer guidance among their own communities, while also serving as a liaison between black and white America. Even before W. E. B. Du Bois articulated this particular vision of a black leadership class most forcefully in his 1903 publication *The Souls of Black Folk*, college training often served as a conduit toward leadership positions for black women and men.

In 1894 African American women saw their new voting rights as a tool that they could use to lead the race toward higher education opportunities. Although women had the power only to vote for members of the University of Illinois's board of trustees, these board members had significant influence setting university policy on admissions, campus expansion, tuition, salaries, hiring, curriculum, and scholarships for Illinois's only public university.[26] Republican candidate Lucy Flower pledged to secure scholarships for African American students if black women would help her win. No such pledge was forthcoming from Flower's competitors in the Democratic, Prohibitionist, and People's parties. While Flower's pledge did not necessarily convert these women into Republicans—most already supported the Republican Party—the pledge did have an "electrical" effect on their canvassing activities. As one journalist explained after Flower's announcement, "Women's social and charity clubs were temporarily converted into political organizations which threw their full strength into the campaign."[27]

Flower's black women supporters employed a strategy that they would use repeatedly in an era in which neither major political party expressed much interest in black voters: they focused on the exceptions to Republican indifference. Or, at least they worked with candidates with inconsistent records. If they did not, there would be very few candidates whom they could support. In deciding to help Flower, African American women either did not know about or had to make a deliberate choice to ignore Flower's troubling position on restrictive voting requirements. As an 1894 article in the leading woman's suffrage periodical the *Woman's Journal* noted, Flower favored property and educational requirements for voting.[28] These were of course key mechanisms that southern white supremacists increasingly used in the 1890s to disfranchise black men. In her support of voting restrictions, Flower was very much in line with the views of white leaders of the National American Woman Suffrage Association (NAWSA).

In 1890 a divided woman's suffrage movement reunited in the form of the NAWSA and embarked on a "southern strategy." Unable to get a federal suffrage amendment through Congress, the NAWSA turned its sights in the 1890s toward generating support for women's enfranchisement at the state level. White NAWSA leaders calculated that a groundswell of suffrage victories at the state level would pressure Congress to act. This new approach included building support among the traditionally antisuffrage southern states. In the 1890s, northern white NAWSA leaders joined forces with southern white suffragists to bring southern states into the cause of women's enfranchisement. In order to attract white southerners to the cause of woman's suffrage, NAWSA argued that extending the ballot to white women would ensure white supremacy by offsetting the black male vote: white women would outvote black men. Black women, the argument went, could be excluded from the electorate through educational and property restrictions.[29] Even if black readers of the *Woman's Journal* had encountered this article on Flower, they decided that they too could engage in political logrolling. At least temporarily, they focused on her promise to support black education as a university trustee and overlooked her conformity to the troubling strategies of the larger white women's suffrage movement.

[26]

Black women's extensive campaigning in Chicago in 1894 was not an anomaly. Where women were entitled to vote, even for small local offices, black women canvassed and marched to the polls in significant numbers. In the East that year, black women in Boston who would be voting in municipal school board elections warned black men to "not be indifferent to the women voters" when nominating candidates because women "hold a tremendous power over school matters."[30] In the West, women had already acquired full voting rights in Wyoming and Colorado. Preparing for the 1894 midterm elections, one black Republican women's club in central Colorado passed a resolution refusing to "support any candidate of any party that has ever been known at any time under whatever circumstances to oppose the right of the Negro to any and all privileges that any other race enjoy[s] as American citizens."[31] Black women in Denver organized Republican clubs, raised campaign funds, gave speeches, and, in one instance, served as a delegate to the Republican county convention.[32] One year later in the South, white Kentucky newspapers lamented the large turnout of black women voters in the school board elections that took place in the central and northern Kentucky cities of Lexington, Covington, and Newport.[33] In a front-page article entitled, "It Is a Bad Experiment," the *Lexington Press-Transcript*, complained that Lexington's "Negro women have shown a greater disposition to avail themselves of this newly acquired right" by out-registering white women.[34] On election day, the *Press-Transcript* similarly bemoaned: "The white women did not turn out in full force . . . but the colored vote nearly all went in."[35] While white Kentucky newspapers were taken aback by this strong turnout, black women in the Northeast celebrated it. The Boston-based *Woman's Era* enthused that "the colored women of Kentucky outregistered the white women two to one in their ambition to get a colored man on the school board," commending them for demonstrating their "earnestness and intelligence" at the polls.[36]

Black and white Republican women approached the 1894 elections in Illinois with both overlapping and separate concerns that revolved around educational reform, Republican victory, and placing a woman in office. The shared goal of Republican victory, particularly for Flower, was compelling enough to engender interracial mobilization. From its August 1894 inception, African American women were members of the predominantly white women's organization devoted to the success of Flower and other Republican candidates, the Illinois Women's Republican Educational Committee (IWREC). Of the August 16 inaugural meeting, one Chicago newspaper reported approvingly, "it is pleasing to know that color lines were ignored, and colored women were present by invitation."[37] Dozens of the white women's Republican clubs that organized by ward during the fall sought black participation. For instance, at their founding meeting, the white members of the Mary A. Logan Women's Republican Club of the Thirteenth Ward resolved "to try to bring the large number of colored women in the ward into the movement."[38] Conversely, black Republican women offered their time and skills to the campaign. In mid-September, members of the Ida B. Wells Club occupied "nearly a whole row of chairs" at the IWREC's third official gathering. This club, which had been formed just one year earlier and would go on to establish Chicago's first black kindergarten and orchestra, was already known in 1894 for its efforts to end lynching in America. According to the *Tribune*, the Ida B. Wells Club had "resolved themselves into a Republican club for work among their own race" and had come to the IWREC meeting "to report that they were ready for business."[39] By the fall, Ida Dempsey and Wells were members of the IWREC's state committee.[40]

Dempsey was born Ida McIntosh in May 1859 into the free black community located in Indiana, and she relocated to her father's home state of Illinois at some point before 1894 (her mother hailed from North Carolina). Around 1879, Ida McIntosh married another midwesterner, Ohio-native Dillard Dempsey, who was ten years her senior. Ida and Dillard Dempsey never had children. They were part of Chicago's small black middle class. By 1900 Dillard's job as a letter carrier for the U.S. Post Office enabled the couple to purchase a home. It also allowed Ida to avoid wage labor and devote her energy toward community work, that is, until Dillard's death at some point during the first decade of the twentieth century.[41] Along with her Republican activism in the 1890s, Dempsey was the first president of the Old Settlers Club upon its founding in 1904. She also served as a "board member and corresponding secretary of the Frederick Douglass Center," a settlement house providing social services to black Chicagoans during the 1910s, such as adult and child education, child care, and "mother's clubs."[42] After Dillard's death, however, Ida, like the majority of politically active black women, had to combine such activities with employment, in her case as a stenographer.[43]

Wells was a newcomer to Chicago in 1894. She had relocated to the city just months earlier. Easily the most recognized black woman journalist in the nation by the 1890s, Wells quickly emerged as a key figure in the political and social life of black Chicago. Wells's roots—like those of so many politically active black women of her generation—were southern. She was born a slave in Holly Springs, Mississippi, three years before the close of the Civil

War. While still a teenager, Wells and her family suffered a terrible tragedy. In 1878, a yellow fever epidemic in Mississippi took the lives of her parents and infant brother. Refusing to allow her family to be split up, Wells, just sixteen years old, assumed responsibility for her five younger siblings. Wells relocated the family to Memphis, Tennessee, where she lived with her aunt and acquired a job as a teacher on the outskirts of the city. There, in 1887, she began her career as a journalist when she was elected editor of the *Evening Star*, a newsletter put out by the teachers' lyceum that Wells had joined. Within a year, Wells's work was appearing in black newspapers throughout the country, and she had gained the distinction of being the first woman to address the Afro-American Press Association's national convention. Within two years, Wells had become part owner and editor of one of Memphis's three black newspapers, the *Free Speech and Headlight*. Her unapologetic *Free Speech* articles dissecting the harm and hypocrisies of southern racism caused her to lose her teaching job and eventually led to her exile from the South for thirty years.[44]

Wells's encounters with white supremacy in the South would shape the trajectory of her life for years to come, transforming her into one of the leading civil rights and women's rights advocates until her death in 1931. From a young age, she contested racial injustices not only with her pen but also through the courts. In this, she predated the NAACP's legal strategy by twenty-five years. In 1884 Wells brought suit against the Chesapeake, Ohio, and Southwestern Railroad after a conductor humiliatingly dragged her from the train's first-class car—what was commonly called the "ladies car"—when she refused to move to the segregated "smoker car." White passengers applauded as she was ejected. Wells won the suit at the circuit court level. The railroad, however, went on to successfully appeal the case at the state level. It was able to do so because just one year before Wells brought suit against the railroad, the Supreme Court had declared unconstitutional the 1875 Civil Rights Act prohibiting racial discrimination in public facilities and accommodations. Years later Wells reflected in her autobiography on the debilitating consequences of this 1883 Supreme Court decision: "The supreme court of the nation had told us to go to the state courts for redress of grievances; when I did so I was given the brand of justice Charles Sumner knew Negroes would get when he fathered the Civil Rights bill during the Reconstruction period."[45]

Wells's experiences in the South informed her interest in party politics. Growing up in Reconstruction Mississippi, Wells learned at a young age the risks that black women and men undertook so that men could vote and

Women's Voting in Chicago in 1894

participate in electoral politics. Wells's father, Jim Wells—as she recalled years later in her autobiography—was "interested in politics." Because of this interest, Wells explained, "I heard the words Ku Klux Klan long before I knew what they meant. I knew dimly that it meant something fearful, by the anxious way my mother walked the floor at night when my father was out to a political meeting."[46]

Wells's political training continued as a young woman in Memphis, where she witnessed the rise and decline of interracial politics in the state. Wells arrived in Memphis shortly before "Bourbon" Democrats (so called by opponents who likened their economic conservatism to that of the French ruling family of that name) began courting black male votes in order to gain a foothold in districts with large black populations. When black men continued to vote disproportionately for Republican candidates, however, the "Bourbons" changed strategy and joined forces with other white Democrats to eliminate the black vote. During 1889 and 1890, Wells watched the Tennessee legislature enact a patchwork of laws—poll taxes, complicated education and registration requirements, and gerrymandering—designed to disfranchise black men. As a result, regions of Tennessee that had been Republican strongholds since the Civil War produced Democratic victories in 1890. As the editor of one white Nashville newspaper enthused, the new legislation had "solve[d] the race problem in so far as the elections system is concerned."[47] In other words, black disfranchisement eliminated the two-party system in Tennessee. It removed the Republican presence in local government by removing one of the party's most significant voting constituencies. Wells and other black Tennesseans also saw how disfranchisement reshuffled the racial dynamics of local Republican politics. Without a political voice, black leverage within Tennessee's Republican Party rapidly declined, and in its place the "lily white" voices of white segregationist Republicans gained in strength.[48]

The events leading to Wells's move from Memphis to Chicago are well known. In 1892 the brutal lynching of three African American men who had opened a grocery store near an existing white-owned business in a black section of Memphis prompted Wells to write a series of antilynching editorials. In an 1893 *Free Speech* piece, Wells argued, "Nobody in this section of the country believes the old thread-bare lie that Negro men rape white women. If Southern white men are not careful, they will over-reach themselves and a conclusion will be reached which will be very damaging to the moral reputation of their women."[49] The implication that a white woman would willingly have sexual relations with a black man resulted in death

[30]

threats that prevented Wells, who had been out of town at the time of publication, from returning to the South. After stays in several East Coast cities and a trip to England and Scotland, Wells relocated to Chicago in 1894, where she continued her antilynching work.[50] Eight days before the first IWREC meeting, Wells returned from the second of her antilynching speaking tours through England.[51]

Wells and Dempsey were joined in their speech giving by another southerner, Fannie Brown. Like Wells, Brown was born a slave. She presumably experienced the hope and disappointment of Reconstruction. Indignities similar to those that had propelled Wells toward public life and Republican activism most likely shaped her, as one newspaper report put it, "ardent" support for the Republican Party following her relocation to Illinois. Once in Illinois, Brown's ties to the Republican Party were reinforced by her employment at the U.S. Post Office. The Republican Party controlled patronage in the city post office and rewarded black supporters with jobs.[52] For women like Brown who aspired to middle-class status, a postal job offered the possibility of class mobility that came with a steady income.

Brown, Wells, and Dempsey expounded upon the importance of women's educational franchise to audiences that varied in racial and gender composition.[53] In mid-October, for instance, Wells and Dempsey were among a field of six speakers that also included leading white Republican women. Dempsey began her address to this mixed-race and mixed-gender audience of 1,200 at the Central Music Hall by emphasizing women's shared interests: "It was her pleasant duty as a representative of the colored women of Illinois to say that she could not neglect anything that concerned all women." As Dempsey argued, "Education appealed to any truly womanly woman." She made her point by drawing a direct connection between child rearing and the nature of citizenry and government: "What the home was the children were, and what the children were the State was. So that it was their duty as women to be interested in the election." Wells similarly commented on the political implications of motherhood when she asserted that "mothers were throwing away all the time they had devoted to studying for the benefit of their children if they failed to vote for Trustees, and thus carry to the logical conclusion their efforts along the line of education."[54] Dempsey, however, also directed her comments to black women in the audience, who, she asserted, "in particular ought to be interested in education" because they "remembered the dark days of American slavery, when it was a crime to teach a black man to read." African American women understood that the "best legacy any man could leave his children was a good education." As

[31]

Dempsey concluded, "It was the particular duty of Illinois colored women to be interested in this election, as Illinois was the first state to allow mixed schools. The election would show how deeply interested they were."[55]

Even as a degree of interracial cooperation remained a hallmark of the campaign, black women carefully negotiated rather than assumed a working relationship with the dozens of predominantly white women's Republican clubs that emerged between mid-September and early November. This was because African American women entered the 1894 campaign season with fresh bruises from white women reformers' racism and betrayal. At the national level, black women reformers were reeling from the NAWSA's new "southern strategy." At the local level, black women reformers had recently completed a protracted and disappointing battle to gain black representation at the World's Columbian Exposition that took place in Chicago in 1893. The Board of Lady Managers that was in charge of the "Woman's Building" at the exposition denied black women's repeated requests to appoint just one black woman to the 115-person board. Eventually the Board of Lady Managers permitted "a small 'Afro-American' exhibit to be installed in a distant corner of the Woman's Building."[56] Chicago reformer Fannie Barrier Williams finally convinced the Lady Board of Managers to include a handful of African American women speakers, herself included, at the Congress of Representative Women taking place simultaneously with the fair. Significantly, Williams used her speaking opportunity to place black women squarely among the "best of American women" in a speech entitled, "The Intellectual Progress of the Colored Women of the United States since the Emancipation Proclamation." The concessions that black women reformers extracted from the Board of Lady Managers were a far cry from the type of participation they had sought in a spectacular event designed to "demonstrate American civilization's astonishing progress toward human perfection." Wells expressed her indignation over blacks' insignificant role by coauthoring a pamphlet with Frederick Douglass, Irvine Penn, and her future husband Ferdinand Barnett, *The Reason Why the Colored American Is Not in the World's Columbian Exposition*, which they distributed at the fair.[57]

African American women's cautious approach to mobilizing with white women during the Chicago campaign was evident in an exchange between two black women, one possibly Dempsey, and white members of the Women's Republican Club of the Fourth Ward. Representing the Fourth Ward's black female voting population, these two women informed those assembled for the late September meeting that "considerable interest was being taken in the women's movement by the women of the race." The Fourth Ward's black Republican female voters, however, were hesitant "about coming to meetings until they knew whether it would be better to organize a club of their own or join forces with the regular club." Club chairman Dr. Harriet Fox assured the representatives that "it was the unanimous sense of the meeting [that] no color line should be drawn and every woman of African race who came among them would be welcome."[58] About thirty black women attended the next meeting of the Women's Republican Club of the Fourth Ward in early October. Following a series of speeches, including an address by Dempsey on behalf of the group that was "received with enthusiasm," these approximately thirty women added their names to the list of members.[59]

Although in this instance party politics created a degree of interracial cooperation among black and white women, African American women continued their battle to tear down the "color wall" of a number of other institutions and professions across Illinois. While cautious about white women's intentions, they realized that this interracial campaign effort might serve as a wedge to open more opportunities for interracial cooperation and the antisegregation agenda that it could promote. Black women who canvassed with Flower and her white supporters were willing to see, but some wondered whether their hard work and votes would be remembered once the campaign was over.

Organizing Separately and through the Churches

African American women also participated heavily in intraracial political events within their own community. Black Republican women met primarily in two venues, homes and churches. Several of these events were all-female gatherings. In mid-October, for example, two black women's Republican meetings took place at the homes of Mrs. Ward and Mrs. Warner.[60] These gatherings were presumably limited in size because of their venue. A much larger women's rally took place on October 15 when 200 black Republican women from wards throughout Chicago met at Bethel AME Church. Although organized in Republican clubs by ward, these women came together for the purpose of discussing canvassing strategies and voting procedure for the upcoming election. Among those speaking before the large crowd were IWREC committeewoman Ida B. Wells and president of the Third Ward Colored Women's Republican Club Mrs. D. P. Moore.[61] A member of Bethel

AME since her settlement in Illinois until around 1904, Wells had made a riveting antilynching speech before a mixed-gender crowd of more than 1,500 at Bethel AME just weeks before.[62]

Alongside these women's meetings, mixed-gender church rallies also marked the political landscape of the 1894 campaign season. Women had attended political church rallies before. What was different this time, of course, was the fact that they were now participating as voters. Given the limited reporting during the 1870s and 1880s, it is hard to measure whether women were more enthusiastic participants at such rallies with the vote than without, although it is hard to believe that their partial enfranchisement did not heighten their level of involvement. Indeed, they did make their presence and opinions known. Following one mixed-gender meeting, for instance, the *Inter Ocean* reported that "the women were there in great throngs and just as enthusiastic as if they were to vote for the whole ticket from top to bottom."[63]

Between October 15 and November 3, women were in large attendance at the series of at least nine Republican church rallies that were called by Chicago's leading black Baptist, Methodist, and Presbyterian clergy. Eight of these rallies were held within the walls of five of the established AME and Baptist churches: Quinn Chapel AME, Olivet Baptist, Bethesda Baptist, Bethel AME, and St. Stephen's AME (see figure 2).[64] Of the October 15 rally at Quinn Chapel AME that initiated this series of church-based political rallies, the *Inter Ocean* described a scene of more than 600 men and women overflowing the sanctuary's capacity.[65] Former mayor George W. Swift, a speaker at the rally, commented that "[h]e was glad to see women present because they have the welfare of the city as much at heart as the fathers and sons."[66] Black women, of course, did not need to be told that they too had to take an interest in the city's welfare. They were embarking on what many believed would be the "woman's era." Swift's condescension hinted at a certain uneasiness with which men, both white and black (Swift was white), greeted women's formal entrance into party politics. They welcomed women, but they also wanted to maintain authority. The capstone event on November 3, which was organized by six of the city's leading black Methodist, Baptist, and Presbyterian ministers, was also notable for its large female presence. The Central Music Hall's massive ballroom could barely accommodate the crowd of more than 5,000 that "filled the vast ballroom from the front row of the parquette to the last tier of the seats in the galleries." Women and men were "seated and standing, crowding the aisles and foyer." At this "cheeringly enthusiastic" meeting, the *Inter Ocean* reported, "men and women

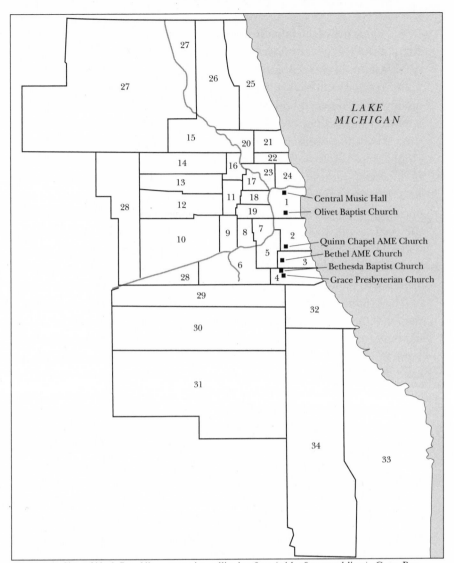

FIGURE 2. *Sites of black Republican campaign rallies in 1894 (with 1890 ward lines). Grace Pres-byterian was involved in rally planning, although the church itself did not host a rally in its sanctuary. Based on a map by C. Scott Walker, Harvard Map Collection, with information from the Center for Population Economics, University of Chicago, <http://www.cpe.uchicago.edu/publichealth/gis_analysis.html>; "Notes on Bethesda Baptist Church," folder 16, box 18, Illinois Writers Project; "Notes on Olivet Baptist Church," folder 21, box 18, Illinois Writers Project; "The History of Grace Presby-terian Church," folder 24, box 18, Illinois Writers Project;* Inter Ocean, *October 16, 1894;* Chicago Tribune, *October 23, 1894; and James Pierce,* Photographic History of the World's Fair and Sketch of the City of Chicago, Also a Guide to the World's Fair and Chicago *(Baltimore: R. H. Woodward and Co., 1893), 42.*

[were] vying with each other in applauding every sentiment that extolled the Republican Party and eulogized its sentiments."[67]

This flurry of rallies points to the centrality of churches and clergy in the politics of black Chicago at the close of the nineteenth century. Clergy were among the primary political brokers between black neighborhoods and white city bosses. The centrality of these churches to black party politics in the city affected women's electoral activism in several ways. First, these church-based rallies were directed at a very particular class of women, those of the middle and elite classes. In late nineteenth-century Chicago, Wallace Best explains, "[w]orship across class lines rarely took place, and it was not encouraged."[68] All of these rallies took place at or were organized under the auspices of Chicago's foundational congregations, whose memberships consisted of the middle and elite classes. These included Quinn Chapel AME and Olivet Baptist, both of which were pre–Civil War institutions, and Bethel AME, Bethesda Baptist, St. Stephen's AME, and Grace Presbyterian, all of which had been founded between 1862 and 1888.[69] By participating in these rallies, women claimed a certain class status that came with affiliating with these congregations and the political gatherings their clergy endorsed. Women who did not associate with these rigidly class-based institutions were presumably excluded from an important forum where the community came together to make decisions during election season.

These mainline churches were also patriarchal institutions that typically reserved key leadership positions for men. Since the antebellum period, women had been challenging men's leadership monopoly in the various black denominations by demanding the right to be ordained as ministers and to participate in church governing bodies. Methodist women met with some success at the end of the nineteenth century.[70] AME Zion women acquired voting privileges and the right to serve as lay delegates at the General Conference in 1876 and 1884 respectively. Also in 1884, AME women gained the right to be licensed, but not ordained, as preachers.[71] Efforts to expand women's voice and authority within the churches met with stiff opposition, however. Reports from the 1884 AME General Conference that approved the licensing of female preachers offers a small glimpse of this deep-seated opposition among male clergy to any significant power sharing with women. When the conference considered a resolution seeking to limit the church's formal recognition of women preachers, one minister who favored the resolution declared, "I vote in favor of their staying home and taking care of babies."[72] Another proclaimed that "[w]omen had no right to go into the pulpit to preach the Lord Jesus Christ." He denied any scriptural grounds for such public roles: "God has circumscribed her sphere, and whenever she goes out of it injury is done to society." Referring to Paul's frequently cited pronouncement in the book of Corinthians against women speaking in church, this minister concluded, "The Bible said she should keep silence in the church."[73] When in 1885 AME bishop Henry McNeal Turner ordained Sarah Hughes as a deacon, the protest among male ministers was so great that church leaders moved to disordain her. It would take another ten years for the smaller AME Zion Church to ordain two women as deacons, thus becoming the first black denomination to do so officially.[74]

The debates over expanded roles for women within the AME Church during the 1880s and 1890s demonstrated how both male clergy and women congregants perceived a connection between secular and religious politics. Both supporters and opponents of enlarged leadership opportunities for women in the AME Church pointed to women's drive for full participation in party politics in making their arguments. In 1887, for example, one opponent of women's voting complained in the AME *Church Review* that woman's suffrage agitation had caused women "to lift up their voices against God and the Bible, to demand that every word in Holy Writ restricting woman be eliminated."[75] Three years later an AME minister dismissed the calls for women's inclusion in church legislative bodies as "pressure from without." As he argued, "this is the spirit of the age . . . which demands that a place be found for woman in the Church, such as some aspire to fill in the state and in social life."[76] Women, however, also found powerful allies among clergy. In an 1886 AME *Church Review* article, for instance, Bishop John M. Brown endorsed both women's secular voting rights and their ordination within the church. Brown presented these arguments for woman's suffrage and ordination consecutively without directly linking the two, but the connection was certainly implied.[77] By contrast, Alice Felts, a minister's wife, was straightforward in linking secular and religious politics when she asserted that the church should lead in matters of women's political participation. In an 1891 *Christian Recorder* editorial, she explained that despite the separation of church and state, "as the church goes in a Christian Republic so will the State." Moreover, black women's involvement in secular politics, she insisted, was the antidote for race-based suffrage arguments that enfranchising women would enable white women to outvote black men. This, of course, was the heart of the NAWSA's "southern strategy." As Felts explained, "If the white voters want to over power the colored by the enfranchise [*sic*] for the women, where will the colored women be but by the side of their brothers to swell the colored vote in proportion?"[78] A breakdown of men's monopoly in party politics, these articles suggested, would undermine their monopoly of church leadership, and vice versa.

The church-based political rallies in Chicago upheld the existing patriarchy within both the churches and the party system. These institutions appeared to have been mutually constitutive in privileging male voices at the rallies—this despite, or perhaps because of, the slight loosening of male authority that had taken place in the party system and the churches as a result of women's partial enfranchisement in Illinois and the extension of some leadership roles to women in black Methodist denominations. At the all-women gatherings, such as the one held at Bethel AME in mid-October, women had an opportunity to address the meeting. In contrast, at the mixed-gender church meetings, men, a good number of whom were ministers, were clearly in control of the events. Men did all the speaking. Women remained in the audience and, in some cases, the choir seated on the podium. A notable exception to this format occurred at the Central Music Hall gathering that served as a capstone to the Republican church rally series. Eight women were among the several dozen Republican leaders who served as vice presidents of the massive event.[79] Even here, though, women did not have an opportunity to address the crowd as they did at all-female gatherings and the mixed-gender meetings organized by the secular IWREC.

Black Republican women took measures to expand the institutional base for their campaign activities beyond the purview of either black men or white women. In the late nineteenth century, the field of African Americans who claimed to speak for the race in party politics was diversifying. Alongside a handful of male clergy, journalists, lawyers, doctors, and professional politicians, the Ida B. Wells Club stepped into this increasingly crowded field when members "resolved themselves into a Republican club for work among their own race."[80] In so doing, the members of the Ida B. Wells Club created a new forum for black women's electoral work, one that served as an important alternative to both the male-centered political gatherings of the churches and the white-dominated meetings of the city's existing women's clubs. The black women's Republican clubs that cropped up in, for instance, the First, Third, and Twenty-third Wards also temporarily offered independent forums for black women's political organizing. In contrast to the Ida B. Wells Club, however, these ward-based organizations appear to have been campaign-specific and closed down after the election was over.[81] The Ida B. Wells Club was the first black women's club in Chicago to offer an independent organizational foundation for black women's political work, but it would not be the last. In the future, the independent black women's club would emerge as one of the primary vehicles through which African American women would express, debate, and carry forward their diverse political agendas.

Shifting Focus from the Local to the National

The women who attended these rallies and formed Republican clubs sought to accomplish goals that extended beyond any one local contest. Many looked to the South and to the nation in their campaign work. Wells, Dempsey, and Brown situated their strong Republican partisanship within broad contemporary struggles for political freedom. Their speeches are striking for their emphasis on party loyalty, and for their references to abolitionism, the Civil War, and the Reconstruction Amendments. Wells, Dempsey, and Brown nationalized a small local contest that was essentially about university education in one state—the availability of scholarships, the composition of incoming classes. In their public appearances, they drew attention to the Republican Party's historic commitment to racial equality and political freedom, and the unfinished business of Reconstruction.

Chicago was a city in ferment at the time that African American women first went to the polls. In 1893 a string of business failures plunged the nation into four years of depression, the worst the country had experienced to date. Widespread unemployment sparked urban and labor protests throughout the country. In 1894 alone, seventeen armies of unemployed industrial workers marched on Washington. That same year workers at the Pullman Palace Car Company, which manufactured railroad sleeper cars, went on strike over exploitative practices at the company town just south of Chicago. The strike brought railway commerce to a halt and was violently crushed when President Cleveland sent federal troops into Pullman to uphold a court injunction demanding the strike's cessation.[82] The black press noted the hypocrisy of a Democratic administration that, although unwilling to protect black citizens, sent federal troops to Chicago over the objections of Illinois's governor.[83] White Republican women in Chicago pointed to the high protective tariff that the Republican Party, with the backing of big business, promoted as a salve to the nation's economic woes.[84] Although there is some evidence of black women participating in these tariff and "sound money" debates two years later, in 1894 black women in Chicago strategically shifted the focus of the campaign away from the issue that captured the attention of white Republicans, the tariff, and toward the matter that was of central importance to black Americans, returning the

Republican Party to its emancipationist origins.[85] As Quinn Chapel's Reverend J. M. Townsend pointed out at one of the mixed-gender church rallies, protection in the Republican Party had once meant much more than a high tariff. The "Afro-American," he explained, "was by instinct and nature a Republican because he was for protection." As Townsend insisted, "He wanted labor protected . . . but above all he asked for the protection of life and limb—and that, too, he asked of the Republican party down South."[86]

African American women attempted to revitalize public discussion of Reconstruction-era goals. Renewed interest in these goals and successful midterm elections might help liberal Republicans recover from a crushing blow to the struggle for black citizenship rights that had occurred two years prior. The 1892 elections had been a smashing victory for the Democratic Party and for southern white supremacists. That year Democrat Grover Cleveland defeated incumbent Republican President Benjamin Harrison, and Democrats gained control of both chambers of Congress.[87] With their sweeping victory in 1892, white Democrats removed the Republican administration and Congress that had taken the most serious measures to end southern abuses of black citizenship rights since Reconstruction.

During 1890 and 1891, Republican congressmen had introduced two ultimately unsuccessful bills to protect voting rights and enhance black education. The Blair Education Bill promised federal moneys to states for their public school systems, but only to those states that raised and spent common school funds equitably among black and white communities, albeit segregation was permitted. Federal intervention in the southern educational system was much needed. Though African Americans made every effort to acquire an education, southern white officials allocated as little local tax revenues toward segregated black schools as possible, in some instances diverting funds that had been earmarked for black schools toward white schools. Even more threatening to southern white Democrats was the Lodge Federal Elections Bill that provided for the federal supervision of polling sites. The Lodge Bill—or, as its opponents called it, the "Force Bill"—was actually an extension of the federal elections laws that had been enacted between 1870 and 1872 and expanded in subsequent years. Lodge Bill supporters aimed to suppress voting fraud against mostly black Republicans with an eye toward revitalizing the Republican Party in the South and ending the Democratic Party's stranglehold on the region.[88]

Southern white Democrats' response was massive. As one historian has argued, Republican attempts "to reopen the 'Southern question' . . . provoked a counteroffensive from which the South emerged even more triumphant than it had in 1877."[89] Democrats took action at multiple levels to head off future federal interference in southern elections and to eliminate the black vote in the South once and for all. At the state level, Mississippi initiated a new phase in black disfranchisement in 1890. White Democrats revised the state constitution so that it included a complicated array of measures, including the infamous "understanding clause," designed to disfranchise black men without specifically mentioning race as a reason for disqualification. (To do so might result in Supreme Court intervention.) The new state constitution relieved white election officials from having to engage in the never-ending work of fraud and intimidation in order to water down the potential strength of black votes. African Americans would rarely have a chance to vote because the revised constitution greatly impeded their ability to register. White Democrats in South Carolina, under the leadership of Governor Ben Tillman, were preparing to do the same. At the federal level, once Democrats gained control of the presidency and Congress in 1892, they moved to eliminate the federal government's authority to enforce the Fifteenth Amendment. During the winter of 1893 and 1894, a Democratic-controlled Congress repealed the last remaining federal election laws. Politically, Democrats were well on their way to pushing the South as close to the pre-Reconstruction era as it had ever been.[90]

So it was in this context—the defeat of the Federal Elections Bill, the "legalized" disfranchisement of black men in Mississippi, similar pending legislation in South Carolina, Democratic domination of the federal government, and the Democrats' elimination of the last vestiges of Reconstruction legislation—that black women in Illinois were going to the polls for the first time. As Reverend J. M. Townsend told the 600 men and women attending the Republican rally held at Quinn Chapel AME in mid-October, "We have had harder times during the past year since we got the Democratic change than at any time since the armies of Sherman and Grant left the field. We expected a rough sail under Democratic rule and we are getting it . . . Under it we have had business depression, no work, little money, Southern lynching, chain-gang system, separate coach law, and southern disfranchisement of the negro." Townsend concluded with a challenge to black men that linked dignified manhood with Republican loyalty: "I hold that no negro can bring his conscience, his manhood or even his wife along with him to the polls to vote the Democratic ticket."[91]

Townsend equated Republican loyalty with respectable black manhood. Black women reformers would not have disagreed. But women's campaign rhetoric, by contrast, centered on women, not men, as the group that would

[41]

help redeem the race in party politics. In their view, women were not merely accessories at the polls against which men defined their manhood. Women were voters, and political actors in their own right who had a duty to use their vote differently from how men had so far. Only by acting differently could women help to restore value to black votes and help the race find its way out of a profoundly bleak political situation. African American women, however, disagreed significantly on exactly how men had misused their ballots and, consequently, on what corrective measures women should take at the polls. Had men carelessly sold their vote to white Democrats, or had they allowed white Republican Party managers since Reconstruction to assume rather than work for their votes? Was it women's responsibility to remain steadfast to the Republican Party, or to break with it? These questions that polarized black women in Chicago in the 1890s would recur in various incarnations in future elections. Women of the middle and elite classes who were pushing forward a "woman's era" would answer these questions in conflicting ways.

The specific circumstance that fueled this intraracial debate among women in 1894 was the possibility of "split-ticket" voting. In the university trustee contest, voters could mark up to three candidates among the thirteen who were running. This was because in 1894 three of the university trustee positions—among the twelve who regularly served on the board—were up for election. In August the Republican *Inter Ocean* began reporting that many women intended to vote along gender rather than party lines.[92] For example, instead of voting for the three university trustee candidates running on the Republican ticket (two white men and one white woman), many women were reportedly planning to spread their three ballots across the Republican, Democratic, and Prohibition tickets in order to vote exclusively for women candidates (see figure 3).

In their speeches, Wells, Dempsey, and Brown demanded that women vote a straight Republican ticket. Like many white Republican and Democratic women, Dempsey argued that women would "win further recognition"—that is, the full franchise—by showing men their ability to act as partisans.[93] "Woman's era" philosophy, however, also informed Wells, Dempsey, and Brown's opposition to split-ticket voting. Vote splitting in their opinion betrayed women's responsibility to keep men loyal to the Republican Party. In the past, African American women had used persuasion and threats to prevent men from voting for the Democratic Party. They now could also make their case for Republican loyalty through personal example. Black women leaders, however, had to make sure that women understood

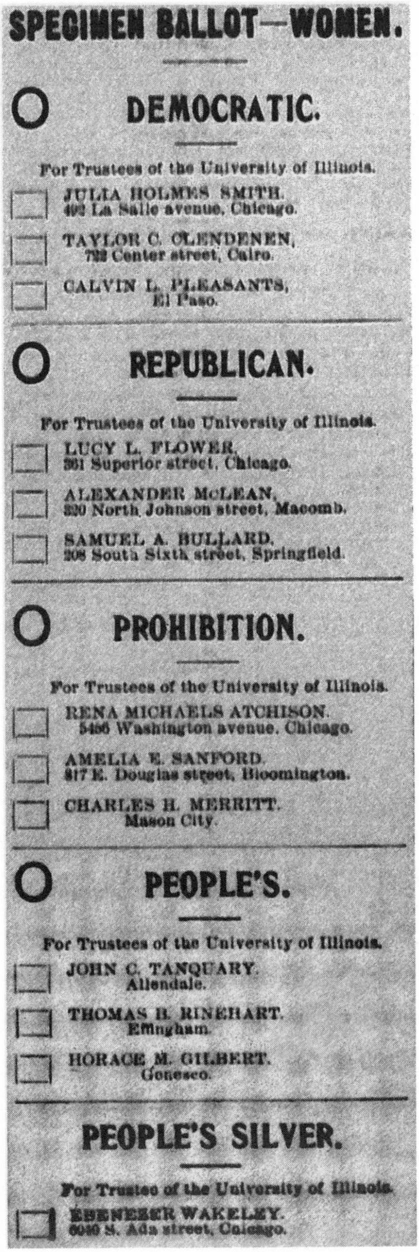

SPECIMEN BALLOT—WOMEN.

DEMOCRATIC.

For Trustees of the University of Illinois.

JULIA HOLMES SMITH.
492 La Salle avenue, Chicago.

TAYLOR C. CLENDENEN,
722 Center street, Cairo.

CALVIN L. PLEASANTS,
El Paso.

REPUBLICAN.

For Trustees of the University of Illinois.

LUCY L. FLOWER,
361 Superior street, Chicago.

ALEXANDER McLEAN,
320 North Johnson street, Macomb.

SAMUEL A. BULLARD,
208 South Sixth street, Springfield.

PROHIBITION.

For Trustees of the University of Illinois.

RENA MICHAELS ATCHISON.
5456 Washington avenue, Chicago.

AMELIA E. SANFORD.
817 E. Douglas street, Bloomington.

CHARLES H. MERRITT.
Mason City.

PEOPLE'S.

For Trustees of the University of Illinois.

JOHN C. TANQUARY.
Allendale.

THOMAS B. RINEHART.
Effingham.

HORACE M. GILBERT.
Genesco.

PEOPLE'S SILVER.

For Trustee of the University of Illinois.

EBENEZER WAKELEY.
6040 S. Ada street, Chicago.

FIGURE 3.

A sample women's ballot that was printed in the Inter Ocean, *November 2, 1894, 2.*

the significance of their errand: that they would in fact set a proper example for black men during their first outing to the polls and vote as a group for all three university trustee candidates running on the Republican ticket. During her Central Music Hall address, Wells reminded "women that they should be loyal to their party." Wells explained, "There were two other women candidates besides Mrs. Flower, and it would not be right for the women to vote for all."[94] Wells made these comments broadly to both black and white women in the audience, but in their various speaking engagements Wells, Dempsey, and Brown made it quite clear that black women had a unique obligation to remain steadfast in their Republican partisanship that distinguished them from their temporary white allies.

In arguing against split-ticket voting, Wells, Dempsey, and Brown imparted sectional and national meaning to their small midwestern contest. Wells entreated her multiple audiences to vote a straight ticket because the Republican Party "had always represented progress and was the party of intelligence and freedom." In her judgment, the party had *already* secured the full voting rights not only of black men but also of women. Wells reminded her audience that the Fifteenth Amendment had enfranchised former slaves, and that the Fourteenth Amendment ensured that "'persons' born in this country or naturalized were citizens."[95] "According to that," Wells asserted, "women have for thirty years possessed the right to vote, for certainly they were 'persons.'"[96] Wells's joint reading of the Fourteenth and Fifteenth Amendments was not a new interpretation; it originated in the Reconstruction-era suffrage movement.

During the 1870s, white suffragists who headed the National Woman Suffrage Association (NWSA)—as part of a strategy for winning woman's suffrage known as the "New Departure"—had similarly argued that if one acquired American citizenship through the provisions of the Fourteenth Amendment, and the Fifteenth Amendment identified voting as a right of citizenship, regardless of "race, color, or previous condition of servitude," then all American citizens were entitled to vote. Suffragists insisted that the Fifteenth Amendment did not *disfranchise* groups—that is, women— not specifically mentioned in the amendment. In 1878, following a series of disappointing Supreme Court battles that severed the nationalizing relationship between the Fourteenth and Fifteenth Amendments, the NWSA dropped the "New Departure" as its principal strategy for securing women's voting rights and began focusing efforts on the passage of a constitutional amendment explicitly enfranchising women. In contrast, Wells continued to demand a broad reading of the Reconstruction Amendments deep into the

1890s. Precisely at a time when the courts and southern states were eroding black Americans' constitutionally recognized rights, Wells sought to emphasize the power and authority of the Fourteenth and Fifteenth Amendments. In this way, she maintained the rhetorical and activist links between black freedom and women's political rights that had once undergirded the woman's suffrage movement.[97]

Like Wells, Dempsey swathed her appeals for Republican loyalty in references to the party's role in the abolition of slavery and commitment to black civil and political rights during radical Reconstruction. At the same gathering that Wells described the enfranchising potential of the Reconstruction Amendments, Dempsey reminded her audience, "Especially in the State of Lincoln, all colored voters, whether men or women would surely stand by the Republican ticket."[98] Dempsey entitled this October 12 speech "New Occasions Make New Duties," a reference to the opening words of James Russell Lowell's poem "The Present Crisis." Dempsey applied Lowell's assertion in this poem, "Time made ancient good uncouth," to women's enfranchisement. As she explained, "These words of the poet, if unexpected by him, constituted a good starter for an appeal for greater political rights for women." Lowell, a Massachusetts abolitionist, wrote "The Present Crisis" in 1845 as a plea for eliminating slavery. Just as Lowell asserted in 1845 that time had rendered slavery "uncouth," so too, Dempsey implied, had women's disfranchisement become "uncouth" almost fifty years later. Dempsey embedded the campaign of 1894 within the Republican Party's historic connection with abolitionism, the Civil War, and Reconstruction. But she also cautioned her audience to stay focused on the current campaign. Again invoking a literary reference, this time to a nineteenth-century Scottish author, Dempsey concluded her remarks with the words of Thomas Carlyle: "Do your duty that lies nearest, knowing it is your duty. The second duty is already clear."[99] Dempsey struck a careful balance between, on the one hand, encouraging a tenacious commitment to the Republican Party among black women and, on the other hand, assuaging those in the audience concerned about women getting too much political power too quickly.

Some may have recognized Dempsey's nuanced literary references, but a great many probably did not. Dempsey's decision to make her point though literature was indicative not only of her middle-class status but also of her intention to make sure that the interracial audience she addressed encountered a highly cultured black woman. African American women contended with a host of negative stereotypes embedded in white society. Originating in the sexual violence of slavery and perpetuated through medical and historical scholarship, the representation of black women as sexual and moral deviants was among the most common of these stereotypes.[100] As Evelyn Brooks Higginbotham explains, variants included "the immoral black female teacher as cause for the weakness of black schools; the immoral black mother as responsible for the degeneracy of the black family; the acquiescence of the black husband to the wife's infidelity; and the widespread belief that black women were unclean."[101] A cartoon published in the *New York World* during the 1892 presidential contest reveals the type of disparaging stereotypes that politically active black women encountered (figure 4). Many African American women combated such character assaults through the measured guarding of public persona.[102] Dempsey's show of refinement and education was a direct challenge to racist partisan assaults on black womanhood (see figures 5 and 6).

The day before the election, Dempsey and Brown stood before an audience of 400 African Americans gathered under the auspices of the First Ward Woman's Colored Republican Club. Dempsey refuted a circular, widely distributed in Chicago's black neighborhoods, which argued that the abolition of slavery was a "side issue" for the Republican Party. According to the *Chicago Tribune*, "Mrs. Dempsey told the colored men and women the Republicans had done all that was ever done for them, and they would remember that and vote with that party." Brown similarly urged the 400 women and men gathered at 486 State Street to vote only for Republican candidates, regardless of gender. As she instructed, "tomorrow you will go to the polls and vote the straight Republican ticket." The significance of this appeal from a former slave, ardently campaigning for the Republican Party and serving as chairman of the First Ward Woman's Colored Republican Club, certainly would not be lost on any audience member weighing whether to vote straight or split the ticket.[103]

Even as women reformers expressed solidarity with black men against racism, they accused men who sold their ballot or voted for Democrats in local elections of race betrayal. Women in Chicago shared this critique of men with other prominent black women reformers across the country. In her 1892 treatise on black womanhood, *A Voice from the South*, Washington, D.C., resident Anna Julia Cooper suggested that little had changed in the gender politics of southern Republican partisanship in the fifteen years since the end of Reconstruction: "It is largely our women in the South to-day who keep the black men solid in the Republican party."[104] As she asserted, "there are not many men . . . who would dare face a wife quivering in every fiber with the consciousness that her husband is a coward who could be paid to desert her deepest and dearest interests." A native North Carolinian and Oberlin graduate, who along with Fannie Barrier Williams was among the handful of black women who addressed the 1893 Congress of Representative Women, Cooper maintained in her 1892 publication the principled partisanship of black womanhood: "You do not find the colored woman selling her birthright for a mess of pottage." Though disfranchised, Cooper maintained, the African American woman "is watching the movements of the contestants none the less and is all the better qualified, perhaps, to weigh and judge and advise because not herself in the excitement of the race."[105]

In 1894 women were not merely influencing men's voting; they were casting their *own* ballots and were, as Cooper put it, very much "caught up in the excitement of the race." In their public appearances, Brown, Wells, and Dempsey emphasized women's duty to dismantle vote-buying schemes. The day before the election, Brown told an audience of 400 women and men gathered under the auspices of the First Ward Woman's Colored Republican Club, "You colored ladies have a chance now to set an example for the men. Just think, we have only this little bit of suffrage and already the politicians are trying to buy our vote and influence us for the Democratic ticket." Emphasizing women's steadfast moral authority, Brown asserted, "They have been buying colored men's votes but they cannot get us women." She concluded, "I don't believe they can buy any colored woman's vote tomorrow for any price."[106] Women's supposed moral superiority over men enabled them to deflect such schemes.

Brown described her own experience with Democratic vote-buying schemes: "I met a man the other day who is prominent in politics. He knew what we colored women were doing and, stopping me on the street, asked me to put on a badge like the one he was wearing and work for the Democratic Party. He said that if I would he would see that I got $300." As Brown explained to her audience, "I told him I wouldn't do it for $5,000. He couldn't get my influence for any consideration." Brown instructed her audience, "If they try to buy your vote tomorrow with a marked ticket take the ticket and $5 too, and take them both to Republican headquarters. They will give you $50 for such a ticket." Brown warned that after blotting the ticket and handing it to the election judge, "wait till he puts it in the box. It doesn't make any difference if he should happen to be a Republican judge. Watch him just the same."[107] That seems to be exactly what they did at the polls the next day. African American women in the First Ward, for instance,

CAMPAIGN NEWS FROM REPUBLICAN HEADQUARTERS.

The Thompson Street Influence Club is now fully organized.

Above: FIGURE 4. *"Campaign News from Republican Headquarters." Scrapbook no. 13, Frances E. Willard / WCTU Scrapbook Collection, Frances E. Willard Memorial Library and Archives, Evanston, Illinois (*Temperance and Prohibition Papers: A Joint Microfilm Publication of the Ohio Historical Society and the Woman's Christian Temperance Union, *ed. Francis X. Blouin Jr. [Columbus: Ohio Historical Society, 1977], reel 32); courtesy of the Frances E. Willard Memorial Library and Archives.*

Opposite, top: FIGURE 5. *Portrait of Ida M. Dempsey. Franklyn Atkinson Henderson collection of photographs of African American old settlers of Chicago [graphic], Chicago History Museum; copy courtesy of the Chicago History Museum.*

Opposite, bottom: FIGURE 6. *Portrait of Ida B. Wells. Andrew Scruggs Lawson,* Women of Distinction: Remarkable in Works and Invincible in Character *(Raleigh, NC: L. A. Scruggs, 1893), 33. Manuscripts and Archives Division, The New York Public Library, Astor, Lenox and Tilden Foundations.*

said that "if they were offered money they would take it and vote the Republican ticket. In this way they thought they would lessen to a small extent the purchasing fund of the Democrats."[108]

In contrast to Brown, Fannie Barrier Williams offered a very different account of how men had misused the ballot since the Fifteenth Amendment's enactment, as well as how women should use their new voting rights to make black ballots valuable: she urged black women voters to cross party lines. Williams used her indignation over her encounters with white women's racism as a launching pad for making this argument. After hearing Fannie Barrier Williams speak at the Congress of Representative Women, several leaders of the Chicago Woman's Club nominated Williams for membership. Founded in 1876, the Chicago Woman's Club was the city's premier women's reform organization. By 1893 the club claimed 620 members, all white. While some members enthusiastically supported Williams's membership, others opposed it. Their vocal demands that Williams withdraw her nomination emerged just as the 1894 election season was heating up. There is no indication that Flower personally opposed Williams's nomination. Still, as a past president of the Chicago Woman's Club, Flower was closely associated with the organization. White Democratic candidate Julia Holmes Smith was also active in the club, as were several leading white Republican and Democratic women.[109]

Although Williams did not specifically mention her battle to desegregate the Chicago Woman's Club, she denounced white women party managers and candidates as duplicitous. In the November 1894 edition of the *Woman's Era*, the organ of the Boston-based New Era Club, Williams warned, "We ought not to put ourselves in the humiliating position of being loved only for the votes we have." Williams asserted, "The sincerity of white women, who have heretofore so scorned our ambitions and held themselves aloof from us in all our struggles for advancement, should be, to a degree questioned."[110] She insisted, "We should never forget that the exclusion of colored women and girls from nearly all places of respectable employment, is due mostly to the meanness of American women, and in every way that we can check this unkindness by the force of our franchise [it] should be religiously done." Williams urged women to use their vote "to force these ambitious women candidates and women party managers to relent their cruel opposition to our girls and women in the matter of employment and the enjoyment of civil privileges."[111]

Williams suggested that in denouncing split-ticket voting and demanding Republican loyalty, black Republican women in the city were merely repeat-

Women's Voting in Chicago in 1894

ing the mistakes that black men, whom she saw as dependable Republican voters, had made since 1870. Describing the campaign rhetoric of Flower's black women supporters to *Woman's Era* readers, Williams lamented, "Our own women . . . have gone into the fight with a party zeal that would be satisfactory to the most exacting 'boss.'" Williams characterized their Republican zeal—what she called "anxiety for the success of a party ticket for party reasons"—as the "folly and neglect of self-interest that have made colored men for the past twenty years vote persistently more for the special interests of white men than for the peculiar interests of the colored race." Rather than let white Republican women assume black women's votes because of the party's antislavery history, black women, Williams advised, should "array themselves, when possible, on the side of the best, whether that best be inside or outside of party lines." As historian August Meier has documented, some black men had in fact urged other men to vote as "independents" at the end of the nineteenth century. For example, the AME *Church Review* explained: "When the vote of the colored man in the South becomes worth something his life will be worth something . . . There is no better way to make his vote valuable than by dividing it up." In 1891 the president of one of North Carolina's leading black colleges anticipated, "The last decade of the century will find [the black man] voting for good men and wise measures, rather than for mere partisans as such."[112]

In one sense, then, Williams's insistence that "our women" should "feel sufficiently independent" in the exercise of their ballot fit with such strategizing to make black ballots potent again. Williams's contribution to this discussion, however, emphasized the political possibilities embedded in women's "finer virtues," as she put it. "Much more ought to be expected of colored women in 1894 in the exercise of their suffrage," she explained, "than was expected of the colored men who first voted under the 15th Amendment." She asked rhetorically, "Must we begin our political duties with no better or higher conceptions of our citizenship than that shown by our men when they were first enfranchised?"[113] The answer of course was no. This was not the last time that politically active black women would rely on "woman's era" philosophy to reject partisan loyalty.

Newspaper coverage in the months leading up to the election indicates, however, that few fulfilled Williams's call to cross party lines or, for that matter, the projections that women planned to vote exclusively for women candidates. The absence of black women campaigning on behalf of the People's Party is not surprising. Despite its large following in the South and West, the People's Party in Illinois was small and weak—so weak that it did not win a

Women's Voting in Chicago in 1894

single race in Illinois in 1894.[114] Additionally, the People's Party—or Populist Party as it was also known—had acquired a reputation of uneven dealings with black male voters in the southern states where the party was well organized. In some southern states the party had put forward Populist-Republican "fusion" candidates who courted black votes, but in other states white Populists terrorized African Americans who did not support the ticket.[115] In the case of the university trustee contest, the People's Party had no claim to the gender vote. All three candidates on the People's Party ticket were men.[116]

The story was quite different with the Prohibition Party. Two women were running on its ticket, Amelia Sanford and Rena Michaels Atchison. Moreover, Sanford's candidacy benefited from her activism in the Woman's Christian Temperance Union (WCTU). With a membership of 160,000 in 1890, the WCTU was the nation's largest women's reform organization.[117] Officially, it was independent from the Prohibition Party, but the WCTU's charismatic president, Frances Willard, encouraged WCTU members to support the Prohibition Party.[118] WCTU organizers in Illinois did the same. In 1894 the WCTU's Illinois chapter harnessed its sizable membership—in 1890 more than 14,000 across the state, and more than 1,200 in Chicago—to campaign for Sanford, Atchison, and other Prohibition Party candidates.[119] This membership included a handful of "colored locals."[120]

Since the antebellum period, churches, fraternal organizations, and abolitionist societies of free black communities had advocated temperance as critical to both worldly and spiritual salvation. Many free blacks perceived liquor as a tool of slavery, something that slaveholders forced upon slaves to prevent rebellion.[121] As Frederick Douglass argued in 1855, "When a slave was drunk, the slaveholder had no fear that he would plan an insurrection; no fear that he would escape to the north."[122] In the years after the Civil War, temperance continued to fit prominently in the self-help and racial uplift ideologies to which so many black women reformers subscribed.[123] Like white temperance activists, many black women perceived liquor consumption to be a special concern to them as women. Drunken husbands threatened the stability of the home and family. Moreover, the politics of "racial destiny," which placed so much weight on healthful homes, invested black women's efforts to eliminate vice with the very survival of the race.[124] In her contribution to an *AME Church Review* symposium on temperance, Frances Ellen Watkins Harper, the suffragist and former abolitionist who held a national position in the WCTU, revealed just how deeply this opposi-

[52]

tion to liquor ran among women reformers. Harper, who significantly had also coined the term "woman's era," compared the crusade to the struggle to end slavery: "We have before us another battle, not one of flashing swords and clashing steel, but of moral warfare, a conflict in which there is room for woman's influence as well as man's power." Harper urged her readers to take a multipronged approach in solving the problems of liquor: "Consecrate, educate, agitate and legislate."[125] It was this last strategy of fighting intemperance through legislation that fit well with women's movement from the electoral sidelines to the ballot box at the end of the nineteenth century.

Despite the Prohibition Party's obvious draw to a group of women committed to using the ballot to eliminate liquor consumption, there are no reports of black women campaigning for the party. This is not surprising given that "colored locals" were short-lived and marginalized from the WCTU networks that campaigned for Prohibition Party candidates in 1894.[126] The Illinois WCTU often slighted its black members—driving saloons out of white neighborhoods into black ones and perpetuating stereotypes that, as one white WCTU leader put it, "beer drinking is the rule and not the exception among the professing Christians of colored churches."[127] It is also not surprising given that WCTU president Frances Willard was engaged in a highly publicized war of words with Wells after Willard gave a published interview in which she stated that drunken black men endangered southern white families.[128] Wells denounced Willard's statement as tantamount to condoning the "fraud, violence, murder . . . rapine, shooting, hanging, and burning" that white southerners meted out in the name of protecting white womanhood.[129]

Some black women did plan to go with the Democrats. At an IWREC meeting in mid-September, Third Ward Club representative Mrs. D. P. Moore explained to the audience, "in canvassing through the different precincts we find a good many Democrats and I understand there is going to be an organization of the women of that party." Under such circumstances, Moore inquired, "We want to know . . . how we are to proceed with the work."[130] A small number of black Democrats had emerged in Chicago in the 1880s. Most were supporters of Chicago's white Democratic mayor Carter Harrison during his various administrations between 1879 and his assassination in 1893. As one historian explains, however, "the Harrison popularity . . . was largely personal and was not translated into an effective or substantial black following in the party."[131] This assessment seems to have held true for women.[132]

The absence of black women campaigning for the Democrats can be explained not only by the party's association with black oppression but also by the legendary corruption and violence of late nineteenth-century Chicago machine politics. The Republican *Inter Ocean* labeled as the "City Hall Gang" a group of Democratic thugs who, with police protection and Mayor Hopkins's support, "slugged their way from polling place to polling place" on registration days. The gang beat, stabbed, and in one instance, abducted male Republican voters. Several of these incidents occurred in the black-populated First and Third Wards. Attempts to "capture" identification books listing legally registered voters and to contest registrants' identities typically resulted in fights at polling sites.[133]

This violence and corruption was often directed specifically at black men. A common method of disfranchisement involved suspect notices of registration fraud. In late October, for instance, Democratic election officials sent suspect notices to every black man living on Armour Avenue and Clark, Dearborn, and State Streets in the Second Ward's Twentieth Precinct. The notice automatically removed a voter from registration lists. Reinstatement required the demonstration of voting qualifications before a board of clerks and judges assembled on "revision night." The disfranchising scheme worked through the issuance of suspect notices to incorrect addresses. The purposeful misdirection of notices ensured that the majority of these men were unaware of their contested status until arriving at the polls on election day and learning that their names had been stricken from registration lists. With revision night long since past, these men were denied recourse for reinstatement and ultimately access to the ballot box. Even those aware of suspect notices lost their franchise. Some were working until after hours. Others who could attend "were kept away revision night because they were afraid of being arrested."[134]

Fear of arrest and violence was certainly justified. On revision night, October 27, Democratic city hall employees issued warrants for the arrest of twenty-five black Republican men of the Second Ward on the charge of illegal registration. Nine were arrested and immediately bailed out by the Second Ward alderman. The "City Hall Gang" promptly notified black Republican voters in the Second Ward of the arrests and promised "similar punishment for all who did not come out openly for the Democratic ticket."[135] Altogether the gang arrested 200 black men in the wards throughout Chicago on these trumped-up charges.[136] The threat of violence was an implicit if not explicit part of this harassment. While the "City Hall Gang" was intimidating black voters in the Second Ward, a Democratic

Women's Voting in Chicago in 1894

police officer warned a group of black Republican men in the Eighteenth Ward that "if they did not vote the Democratic ticket they would be 'taken care of.' "[137]

Schemes and threats aimed at disfranchising black men no doubt weighed on women's decisions about whether to campaign and for which party. Male voters were embedded in a network of relationships that included mothers, sisters, wives, and daughters. Women residing in the Eighteenth Ward would have heard of the Democratic threats to "take care of" black Republican voters. Those in the Second Ward would have been aware of arrests and slur campaigns, and witnessed male relatives receiving suspect notices. Women were among the large audiences assembled at Bethel AME, Bethesda Baptist, and Quinn Chapel AME churches on the night of October 28 to protest Democrats' "southern" and "uncivilized" methods of arresting 200 black Republican men for illegal registration.[138]

Indeed, African American women need not look to the experiences of male relatives to learn the risks and costs of electoral work. They personally encountered multiple assaults on their reputation and right to vote. Describing the high registration of black women in the First Ward, the *Chicago Tribune* predicted that the majority of these women would be disqualified.[139] They also ran into opposition when attempting to register. The most widely reported incident involved Dempsey. A Democratic election judge at Dempsey's Sixth Ward polling site refused to allow her and other women of the ward's Fifth Precinct, many presumably black, to register on October 16.[140] The judge laced this refusal with "a good deal of abusive language."[141] In her regular *Inter Ocean* column, white suffragist and IWREC organizer Mary Krout explained that "[i]nstead of submitting tamely" to the abuse and disfranchisement, Dempsey "jumped upon her bicycle and rode down to the Republican women's headquarters in the Grand Pacific Hotel" to report the incident. Several other women and even a husband also lodged complaints. Republican women's headquarters, in turn, informed the election commission of the judge's misconduct, and the "refractory official named Murphy was promptly disciplined." The women were able to register a week later.[142] Dempsey's willingness to challenge white male authority only underscores her deep commitment to voting and to the Republican Party. Success, no doubt, was sweet for Dempsey and those who had campaigned with her when Flower and the two other Republican candidates, Alexander McLean and Samuel Bullard, emerged victorious. It was even sweeter because at the federal level, Republicans regained control of both Houses of Congress.[143]

[55]

TWO YEARS AFTER THIS victory, Chicago was preparing again for elections, as 1896 was a presidential election year. Republican presidential candidate William McKinley was running against Democratic and Populist candidate William Jennings Bryan. Significant changes had taken place on the local and national political scenes between 1894 and 1896. Frederick Douglass, black America's senior statesman and an untiring advocate of black equality, died in February 1895. Seven months later, a new leader rose to national prominence with a message very different from Douglass's. In September 1895 Booker T. Washington made his famous "Atlanta Compromise" speech at the Atlanta Cotton States and International Exposition in which he discouraged protests against disfranchisement and segregation and instead urged blacks to win white favor through industry and thrift.[144] Along with this unofficial change in leadership, the two years between 1894 and 1896 witnessed an acceleration of legalized disfranchisement and segregation across the South. In 1895 Governor Ben Tillman finally achieved his goal of disfranchising black men in South Carolina, when the state legislature revised the state constitution to include a patchwork of literacy, registration, and poll tax requirements. Further south, Louisiana was also preparing to disfranchise its black voters.[145] On May 18, 1896, the U.S. Supreme Court handed down its *Plessy v. Ferguson* decision that "separate but equal" accommodations were constitutional.[146] With this ruling, the Supreme Court set the stage for the legal segregation of almost every aspect of life, and even death, across the South.

The intervening two years also saw a flurry of black women's organizing, a direct response to this crush of injustices. Although Fannie Barrier Williams had finally managed to desegregate the Chicago Woman's Club in 1895, this spurt in organizing focused on the creation of independent black women's clubs.[147] By 1896 Chicago claimed two nondenominational, permanent black women's clubs: the Ida B. Wells Club and the newly established Phyllis Wheatley Woman's Club. Named after the famous poet and slave, the Phyllis Wheatley Woman's Club conceived of itself "as a neighborhood betterment organization" and initially put a great deal of energy into closing neighborhood saloons.[148] In July 1896 members from both clubs joined black women reformers from throughout the country in Washington, D.C., to form a national movement that endeavored to lift the race out of the quagmire of institutional and extralegal racism through self-help and self-improvement. Believing that " 'a race could rise no higher than its women,' " historian Deborah Gray White explains, the women who gathered in Washington, D.C., "felt that when they improved the condition of

[56]

black women, they necessarily improved the condition of the race."[149] The organization that they established, the National Association of Colored Women (NACW), set upon the task of reforming poor black women's behavior and living environments. The NACW's motto, "Lifting as we climb," demonstrated that although the elite and middle-class women who founded the NACW distinguished themselves from poor black women, they also understood that white racism ensured that their own future was tied up with the progress of less fortunate black women.[150]

Clergy did not initially indicate concern about how the NACW's establishment would affect their own leadership roles within black communities, including their authority within party politics. For example, an 1896 *AME Zion Quarterly Review* article that congratulated the NACW's founders on taking "this much needed step" belied the animosity that clergy would direct at clubwomen in the coming years. Sounding very much like NACW organizers themselves, the *Review* article advised the newly formed women's club movement, "Light high the banner of pure womanhood and encourage a noble, ambitious manhood," and "all darkness will disappear and our most ardent hopes will blossom into living realities."[151] In Chicago, however, male political leaders, whether clergy or the emerging class of professional black politicians, would eventually have to make decisions about how to respond to women's organized political power. Was women's organized political power a threat to black men's leadership roles in party politics? Should women's leadership in party circles be encouraged? In 1896, women's voting power in Chicago remained very restricted; they still had only the right to vote on school-related offices and matters. Women's small share in election returns enabled male leaders in the city to postpone addressing these questions. When male leaders were eventually forced to confront these questions after women's voting rights expanded again in 1913, they would do so in a city that had been radically transformed by the influx of thousands of new southern migrants and an explosion of black institutions, from women's clubs, to fraternal organizations, to churches. In other words, they would have to do so in a city in which black women had a much larger institutional base from which to push forward their political agendas.

Although black male political leaders in Chicago could avoid these hard questions for several more years, there were already indicators at the close of the nineteenth century that the black women's club movement would emerge as a force to contend with in party politics at both the national and local levels. One of the NACW's precursor organizations, the National Federation of Afro-American Women, sent three representatives to a Republican convention in Detroit in 1895.[152] At the National Federation of Afro-American Women's 1896 convention (the last before it merged with a parallel organization to form the NACW), members passed a resolution praising the Republican Party's inclusion of an antilynching plank in its 1896 platform, and sending condolences to the Democratic Party that "in the interest of good morals and good government . . . failed to do so."[153] At the local level in Chicago, members of both the Ida B. Wells Club and the Phyllis Wheatley Woman's Club joined more than 4,000 marchers who participated in a torchlight parade and a mass black Republican rally for the McKinley ticket two days before the election.[154] Marchers were greeted by the large crowd assembled at Chicago's second biggest auditorium, Tattersall Hall, including the "handsomely dressed mistresses of the homes of the colored elite on South Dearborn street and elsewhere."[155]

The all-male lineup of speakers urged the men in the audience to vote for McKinley, extolling the candidate's support for a high protective tariff and the gold standard, and denouncing the Democratic Party's mistreatment of African Americans in the South. At least one of the speakers, however, directly addressed the women in the audience. James Madison Vance, a national black Republican leader from Louisiana, urged women to keep men loyal to the Republican Party: "So, one closing word, dedicated to our women folk. Ah, let their kindly, loving presence illumine any dark corners about these questions and help to a right decision to vote."[156] Vance's concluding remarks sounded similar to the very demands that many women made of themselves and saw as part of fulfilling the "woman's era." In Vance's hands, however, this comment smacked of condescension. In his formulation, women were gentle helpmates against which men defined their manhood, not political partners who had as much invested in how black men cast their ballots as the men themselves. No matter how it was presented, though, the fact remained that women's only recourse in the 1896 presidential election in Chicago was to influence men.

African American women in Chicago used their opportunity to vote in 1894 to engage in wide-ranging conversations about radical Republican politics and women's partisanship. They conducted an intraclass debate about how women should use their new voting rights to enhance black influence within party politics. Southern migrant women's leadership in the campaign helped to impart a sectional flavor to women's campaign rhetoric. This was because migrant women arrived in the state with fresh stories of southern white supremacy that they and their families had personally experienced. These stories included accounts about a new phase of "legalized" disfranchisement that was just beginning to unfold across the South. In response, southern migrants and longtime midwesterners worked together in 1894 to transform a small local contest about university policies into a forum for endorsing a particular strain of Republican Party ideology. This was the Republican Party's battered radical emancipatory tradition. Still, as James Madison Vance reminded the women who had gathered at Tattersall Hall in the fall of 1896, their political power was quite limited. Women in Illinois were not entitled to vote for president in 1896. In elections other than those relating to local school matters, African American women's political influence in Illinois continued to rest in their ability to persuade or pressure men.

Women in Illinois would have to wait another seventeen years before they obtained the right to vote for president in 1913, and another twenty years until they actually cast their first ballots for president in 1916. In the meantime, a new generation of black women came of age in the South. The vast majority watched the "legal" disfranchising revolution that had begun in Mississippi in 1890 come to their own state and then reach its awful completion in Oklahoma in 1910. A small number, however, came of age in southern black communities that managed to retain black men's voting rights in the midst of this white supremacist revolution taking place all around them. The southern political experiences of two women from this new generation and their eventual entrance into Illinois politics after women's voting rights in the state expanded in 1913 are the subjects of the next chapter.

[2]

Because Her Parents Had Never Had the Chance

Southern Migrant Politics during the 1910s

In 1912 Jennie E. Lawrence quit her work as a teacher in the Carolinas to pursue a career in social work in Chicago.[1] At some point between 1904 and 1907, Ella G. Berry left her home in Louisville, Kentucky, for Cincinnati and then for Chicago.[2] By relocating to Illinois in search of professional and economic opportunity, both women also took control of their own political destiny and helped to transfer the center of the struggle for black rights from the South to the Midwest. During the 1910s, both emerged as leading Republican organizers in the predominantly black wards of South Chicago. By tracing Lawrence's and Berry's journeys through the lens of voting rights, this chapter considers how the political knowledge that migrant women acquired before leaving the South shaped their involvement in Chicago's Republican circles after women's voting rights expanded yet again in 1913.

Within a year of Lawrence's 1912 arrival in Illinois, the state legislature increased the number of elections in which women could participate. In June 1913 the state legislature passed the Presidential and Municipal Suffrage Bill, which, as its name suggests, granted women residents of Illinois the right to vote in presidential elections and for many municipal offices.[3] Illinois was among twenty-nine states where women could vote in presidential elections prior to the Nineteenth Amendment's enactment in 1920. Four other states where large numbers of southern blacks relocated also extended the presidential franchise to women during the 1910s: Michigan, Indiana, Ohio, and New York. Upon settling in Chicago in 1913, Detroit or New York City in 1917, or Cleveland in 1919, a migrant woman acquired voting rights and thus joined the rapidly expanding black urban electorates of the Midwest and Northeast.[4]

Scholars have noted that because of their sheer numbers, migrants helped to create black urban constituencies in cities such as Chicago, Detroit, New

York, and Philadelphia large enough to make white politicians take notice of their potential voting power. In this way, migrant women and men paved the way for several black communities in the Midwest and Northeast to gain a foothold in the arena of white male-dominated party politics. By leveraging this potential voting bloc, community leaders sought entrée into midwestern party politics and ultimately the local and national governments that these electoral contests determined. Studies on the Great Migration have paid less attention to the political knowledge and experiences these women and men carried with them and then transplanted into their chosen communities than to the number of potential votes migrants constituted.[5]

Migrant women brought with them the memory of white supremacist measures undertaken in the name of a Democratic "solid south." As children, teenagers, and young adults in the South, they had heard about or personally experienced the violent battles over black men's voting rights. They had watched Democrat-controlled state legislatures strategize a range of measures—the poll tax, the grandfather clause, the literacy and understanding tests—that would disfranchise black men without explicitly using racial terms. They had witnessed "White Only" and "Colored" signs emerge at theaters, water fountains, park entrances, waiting rooms, and any other number of public spaces.[6] They had felt the sting of racial epithets and the pain and anger of limited opportunity.

Southern migrant women's transfer of political knowledge to the Midwest during the 1900s and 1910s was not a new process. Rather, it was a link in a chain that stretched back to the nineteenth century and that would extend several decades into the future. Women who had undertaken the journey during the 1890s had similarly drawn upon southern experiences in shaping midwestern politics. This was evident in the 1894 campaign when canvassers like Wells and Brown imparted sectional meaning to a small midwestern contest. The ongoing relocation of southern women as the new century unfolded reinvigorated the southern orientation of black Republican women's politics in Illinois that earlier arrivals like Wells and Brown had initiated.

Lawrence and Berry each represented slightly different groups of migrants. Lawrence originated from one of the nine additional southern states that had revised their state constitutions to disfranchise black men since the last time that women's voting rights had expanded in Illinois in 1891. Lawrence infused midwestern women's political culture with the passion and immediacy of the intervening disfranchisement battles that had taken place since then. She also served as a "proxy" voter for the communities that she

Southern Migrant Politics during the 1910s

had left behind in the Carolinas. Berry, by contrast, represented a much smaller group of migrant women who originated from regions of the South where African Americans clashed with white supremacists but were able to hold onto the ballot. These women from states like Kentucky and Maryland similarly introduced into their new homes fresh stories of battles with southern white supremacists. But they also linked the Republican networks that they joined in Illinois with those that endured in the communities they left behind.[7]

Once in Chicago, Lawrence and Berry integrated into the city's existing women's political networks through the expanding fraternal and women's club movements. In a much more complicated way, migrant women also entered into local politics through an array of churches that were multiplying in diversity and numbers but declining in political influence. As migrant and longtime Chicago residents worked together in these institutions on a series of elections after 1913, they created a hybrid political knowledge that blended local campaigning with concerns about black rights in the South. This knowledge was overlaid with the optimism of "woman's era" philosophy that gave partially enfranchised women confidence that they could actually take on local bosses in municipal elections and southern white Democrats in federal contests. Regardless of their place of origin, middle-class women canvassers generally agreed that it was women's responsibility to lead men by example in party politics and to correct their mistakes.

How they should lead, however, was a matter of debate, especially within municipal politics. This dispute was part of an ongoing conversation about how African American women's votes would or should affect the party system, a conversation that in 1894 had pitted the likes of Wells against Fannie Barrier Williams. In 1894 Wells had insisted that it was women's responsibility to remain loyal to the Republican Party. Williams, by contrast, urged African American women to "array themselves, when possible, on the side of the best, whether that best be inside or outside of party lines."[8] The arrival of tens of thousands of migrants in Chicago, combined with women's expanded voting rights after 1913, changed the focus of the conversation. The issue at hand was not women's Republican loyalty, though this debate would return in full force in the 1920s. Rather, the question was how women should relate to Chicago's white-controlled Republican machinery: Was it women's responsibility to use their organizational strength to help bolster black influence within white-controlled Republican machinery? Or, in the long term, would the race benefit most if women mobilized Chicago's ever growing black population toward creating an independent black Republi-

[62]

can political base that could compete with the regular machine? At stake was the meaning of black representation and how or if it could be achieved within Chicago's white-controlled client-patronage system.

Southern Origins and Political Lessons

The tens of thousands of women who made their choices to relocate to Chicago during the first two decades of the twentieth century were from different parts of the South, each region with its own idiosyncratic racial, gender, and class politics. Lawrence and Berry were among those migrants who came from the Upper South.[9] Prior to 1910, the vast majority of migrants to Chicago originated from the Upper South, and especially from Wells's one-time home of Tennessee and Berry's native Kentucky. Lawrence's home state of North Carolina, along with Virginia and Maryland, also saw the departure of a large number of black residents for Illinois. Smaller numbers hailed from Washington, D.C., Oklahoma, and West Virginia. While the majority of these migrants represented the impoverished farming and laboring classes "who constituted the overwhelming proportion of black southerners," a significant minority was drawn from the South's nascent black middle class. In fact, middle-class participation was prominent enough for historians to identify this accelerated exodus as the migration of the "talented tenth." This was a reference to W. E. B. Du Bois's call for college-educated elites, approximating 10 percent of the African American population, to serve as community leaders and liaisons with white America.[10]

Lawrence was among this college-educated group. Their numbers nationwide in this period were closer to 1 than 10 percent, and their middle-class status was defined more by education and community leadership than by a level of financial security that indicated middle-class arrival among white Americans.[11] Berry's entrée into the middle-class was much more circuitous and tentative than was the case with Lawrence. It was based not in her education, which ended with high school, but rather in her extensive community work. Indeed, the evidence suggests that migration may have been a critical part of the process by which Berry solidified her foothold in the nascent black middle class. The move enabled her to recraft her public image, from a divorcée to a widow and from a former domestic to a social worker.

Jennie Lawrence was born in Salisbury, North Carolina, in 1886.[12] She was the second surviving child of Annie Henderson Lawrence and Abner

Bernard Lawrence.[13] In the twelve years since Abner had made his fiery Fourth of July speech against Democratic Party candidates, both North Carolina and the Lawrence family had seen a significant number of changes. North Carolina had come under Democratic control since Zebulon Vance's 1876 gubernatorial victory. Following Abner's 1878 ordination and then marriage to Annie, the newlyweds made their way to the Lumberton–Red Springs Area in southeastern North Carolina. There, the newly minted minister took charge of four rural congregations with memberships ranging from ten to sixty-two—Wilson Presbyterian Church, Lumberton Presbyterian Church, Panther's Ford Presbyterian Church, and Red Spring Presbyterian Church. Because of the shortage of trained ministers, it was not unusual for a single minister to organize and run multiple rural churches; this was especially the case among rural black congregations.[14] Within a year, however, the couple had moved again, this time to Mt. Airy along the Virginia border, where Abner continued his ministry and Annie took care of their infant son, John. One year later, Annie gave birth to a second son, William.[15]

Between 1879 and 1888, Abner, Annie, and their growing family lived alternately in either Mt. Airy or Winston. Abner regularly traveled between twenty and seventy miles from his home to minister to the multiple congregations under his charge in Mt. Airy, Winston, Boonville, and Pittsburg.[16] At the same time, Annie worked as the sole teacher of as many as eighty-three students in the church school that the Board of Missions for Freedmen of the Presbyterian Church had established in Mt. Airy.[17] Along with organizing new congregations, the board identified the establishment of such schools as a critical part of missionary work among southern blacks. As the board explained in an 1890 report, educational work "is the right arm of our Church among the Freedmen." Annie was among the 133 black teachers—most of them women and many of them ministers' wives—whom the Board of Missions for Freedmen had sent into the field to educate former slaves and bring them into the Presbyterian fold in the first quarter century after the Civil War.[18] In the last two and a half years of Abner's life, the Lawrences made two additional moves. First, 1889 found them in the city of Abner's birth, Lexington, where Abner was in charge of two congregations. Then, in 1891, the Lawrences relocated to Salisbury in the heart of the Piedmont, where for the first time since his 1878 ordination Abner was not assigned to a church.[19] There he remained until his death in February 1892.[20]

Jennie followed in the footsteps of her father by attending two of the private black schools that had been founded by various white and black

Southern Migrant Politics during the 1910s

churches after the Civil War, Livingstone College in Salisbury and Scotia Seminary in Concord.[21] By the time Jennie entered Scotia Seminary around 1900, the family owned a home just outside of Salisbury's city limits.[22] Though better off than most, Annie still struggled to support the four children and teenagers living in her household: her eighteen-year-old niece, Nellie Henderson, and her three children, nine-year-old Annie F., fourteen-year-old Jennie, and fifteen-year-old Levi. All four were attending school in 1900, and Annie was determined to keep them there.[23] Despite her considerable teaching experience, Annie found employment as a laundress, one of the few occupations available to black women. Annie's widowed mother, Caroline Henderson, who lived with her daughter and four grandchildren at this house on the outskirts of Salisbury, also contributed to the family income by working as a laundress.[24]

With their emphasis on a classical liberal education, Scotia and Livingstone contributed to Du Bois's vision of producing a "talented tenth" among black youth. The AME Zion Church opened Livingstone in 1880 as a coeducational institution that divided into theological, classical, normal, and preparatory departments.[25] Because the abysmal state of black education in the South left many unprepared for college-level work, Livingstone, like many southern black colleges, initially offered a range of precollegiate courses in which students could enroll before moving on to the more advanced curriculum.[26] The Northern Presbyterian Church established Scotia Seminary in 1867 as a sister institution to the all-male Biddle University. Modeled after Mount Holyoke Female Seminary—the all-women's school founded in 1837 in South Hadley, Massachusetts—Scotia was the first major boarding school for black girls and women to be located in a former Confederate state. Like Mount Holyoke, Scotia aimed to offer its students a rigorous academic curriculum. Like Livingstone, Scotia offered instruction from the elementary to the college level. At the higher level, Scotia students could chose from one of two tracks: the four-year grammar program, which included instruction in math, science, history, English, and literature, or the three-year normal and scientific program, which consisted of courses in geometry, astronomy, physics, history, Latin, and rhetoric.[27]

Jennie's education at both AME Zion and Presbyterian institutions was not unusual. African American students regularly crossed denominational lines in their quest for an education. It is unclear what prompted the switch from Livingstone to Scotia—possibly concern over Livingstone's coeducational environment, but more likely the desire that Jennie finish her education in the Presbyterian fold and at the sister institution of her father's alma mater.[28]

[65]

Whatever the reason, this familiarity with both denominations may very well have contributed to the ease with which Lawrence moved among Chicago's various churches when canvassing years later. Her education at Livingstone and Scotia was a testament to Abner and Annie's sheer determination that their children would enjoy the privileges of freedom. The Lawrences were among the minority of black families who were able to educate members beyond the secondary level at the turn of the century. Annie herself had been able to acquire only a common school education.[29] The education of her children beyond the secondary level, though desired, was never a given. It was especially hard won after Abner's death.[30]

Livingstone and Scotia prepared Lawrence to step outside of the very limited roles that the world into which she had been born had prescribed for black women. Annie's teaching in the Presbyterian Church's freedmen schools in the 1880s had demonstrated to her young daughters the important contribution that black women could make in helping the race. Jennie's education at Scotia and Livingstone further instilled in her a belief that she personally could help to lead the race out of the nadir of institutionalized racism. This conviction would guide her political activism as an adult. While emphasizing the importance of domestic duties and motherhood, both schools also prepared their female students for public leadership through a steady diet of racial uplift ideology and Christian egalitarianism. At Livingstone, the black female faculty offered Lawrence additional role models beyond her mother of black female leadership. She was also part of a coeducational environment that emphasized women's responsibility in racial uplift work. On Livingstone's coeducational campus, female students participated and even competed with male students in a variety of extracurricular activities, from debates to running the campus magazine.[31] As the *Star of Zion* reported in 1898, "Livingstone College is doing for women what no other institution is doing, bringing her up to be the equal of her eternal antagonist man, in debate, in public spirit, in morals and thought; and side by side with him she determines to help solve the problems of human life."[32] Young women like Lawrence learned that their own personal displays of temperance and modesty would go a long way toward undermining devastating racist stereotypes of African Americans as licentious, intemperate, and immoral. They also learned that it was women's unique responsibility to instill these values in their homes and to introduce them to poor blacks through educational campaigns.[33]

Scotia, where Lawrence ultimately graduated with high honors, offered similar lessons, but it did so with an all-female student body and under the guidance of a biracial staff. The mostly white faculty at Scotia was a very self-selecting group whose faith fueled their efforts to promote racial equality on the well-groomed campus that stood as an island unto itself just fifteen miles north of racially segregated Charlotte. Lawrence's immersion in this Christian egalitarianism at Scotia would have only bolstered her desire to undermine Jim Crow through teaching and eventually politics.[34] As one observer noted in 1904, Scotia's "aim is to send out teachers and leaders who are 'capable, conscientious, and consecrated.' "[35] Indeed, Scotia served as a training ground for a number of future race women, including Mary McLeod Bethune (1894), who after years of Republican activism emerged as one of the most influential African Americans in national politics during the Democratic administrations of Franklin Delano Roosevelt.[36]

Ella G. Berry was not as fortunate as Lawrence in that she was able to complete her education only through high school. She was born Ella Tucker, the daughter of Matilda Portman and Dave Tucker, in the central Kentucky city of Stanford in November 1876.[37] Although large portions of the state had small slave populations, Berry originated from the Bluegrass region where slavery had thrived since the late eighteenth century. With its rich farmland, the northern half of Lincoln County, where Stanford is located, was home to many slaveholders.[38] Her parents' surnames indicate that they had been born slaves. One of the various wings of Lincoln County's slaveholding Tucker clan most likely had held Dave as chattel and was responsible for his surname. Matilda Portman had most likely spent her young life as one of the nine to ten slaves held by M. C. Portman, a Stanford area farmer.[39]

Matilda's children were born in the years that spanned the transition from slavery to emancipation. Her first child, George, who was born in 1855, also bore the Portman name. Her second child, J. Henry Butcher, was born within months of the Emancipation Proclamation, and her remaining four children, including Ella, were born free during the years of Reconstruction and "redemption." The five different surnames of her six children—Portman, Butcher, Montgomery, Murphy, and Tucker—speak to the complicated history of family formation during slavery and the years after emancipation, during which former slaves searched for loved ones from whom they had been separated and asserted autonomy by choosing their own partners and surnames. Limited sources make it difficult to unpack the twist and turns of Matilda's personal life. What is clear, though, is that despite the absence of a husband in her household, Matilda was very resourceful in making ends meet and even elevating her family financially. In

[67]

1870 Matilda and her two young sons lived in the home of the wealthy white Stanford family for whom Matilda worked as a domestic servant.[40] Within two years, however, Matilda escaped the constant white surveillance that came with being a live-in domestic and acquired a degree of personal and financial autonomy that was desired by so many former slaves when she managed to purchase a small piece of property.[41] Eight years later in 1880, the only man living with Matilda and her children was her eldest son, George. Family members pooled their labor in order to survive and perhaps occasionally to enjoy some modest luxuries. While Matilda took care of her two young daughters, five-year-old Ella and one-year-old Maggie, her four sons, from twenty-five-year-old George to ten-year-old Henry, generated income for the family by working as laborers.[42]

Around the time that Berry turned nine in 1884, her family did what a number of black Kentuckians did between the Civil War and 1900: they migrated to Louisville.[43] Migrants made this move in search of employment, public schooling, and a respite from unchecked racial violence. In many instances, this violence was fueled by white resentment over a broken promise. Kentucky was one of four slaveholding states that had remained loyal to the Union. Many white Kentuckians did so only because the Union initially promised to protect their right to hold slaves. Once President Lincoln issued the Emancipation Proclamation in 1863, white Kentuckians took out their anger on the state's black population. This pattern, of course, emerged across the former Confederacy. But after 1865, the federal government took measures—albeit briefly—to check white power and violence in the former Confederate states. Kentucky, by contrast, had not rebelled; it therefore did not have to go through a period of reconstruction. The state's white population was left free to mistreat black neighbors with minimal or no federal intervention.[44]

In the years after the Civil War, Louisville gained the reputation of being a racially progressive island in this sea of racial violence. This did not mean that Louisville promoted racial equality. Like other parts of the South between the late 1860s and the 1880s, Louisville maintained a racial caste system through "an informal code of exclusion and discrimination." It was understood, for instance, that blacks were unwelcome in white neighborhoods, expected to show deference to whites, ineligible for many jobs, and barred from white-run theaters, restaurants, and hotels. Unlike Birmingham, Houston, Atlanta, and any number of other southern cities and towns, however, Louisville did not experience a single race riot or lynching between 1865 and 1930. Less egregious acts of brutality certainly occurred. Days after

[68]

Congress enacted the 1875 Civil Rights Act, for instance, a white crowd beat two black men who had patronized a white-owned restaurant. But Louisville's white leaders generally discouraged lynchings and mob rule, relying on black leaders to impress upon their community the need to remain in "their place" and the police and courts to discipline those who did not. Many of the city's black leaders—though not all—were willing to take on this accommodationist role in order to keep white fury at a minimum. Confronted with outrageous scenes of brutality at home, rural Kentuckians, and indeed blacks from throughout the South, were attracted to even the precarious racial stability that existed in Louisville.[45]

Ella's childhood in Louisville was not an easy one, economically or otherwise. Matilda and her children had only themselves upon whom to rely for income. Matilda worked variously as a laundress, a domestic, and a cook; her older sons also contributed to the household economy by working as porters.[46] Unlike Lawrence's parents, Matilda had a very minimal education. Shortly before her death she learned to read but never did learn to write.[47] Her daughters would. In Louisville, Ella and Maggie both attended school. Though Berry completed high school, her education did not offer entrée into the city's nascent black middle class. She went through a segregated school system that provided only the barest of resources to black students. She did not go on to attend any of the black colleges associated with the talented tenth.[48]

One bright spot during these years was Ella's involvement in Louisville's vital fraternal movement. Her entrance into this world as a child was one of the most important factors that enabled her to emerge as a prominent community leader in Chicago.[49] In Louisville, she most likely joined the United Brothers of Friendship and Sisters of the Mysterious Ten (UBF). (In Chicago, the UBF was the first fraternal group with which Berry's name was associated after her move.) Founded in Louisville (the Brothers in 1861 and the Sisters in 1878), the UBF went on to establish chapters in other locations, including Chicago. Louisville, however, was the organization's base and center of activity. As a child, Ella would have been part of one of the juvenile orders. As a young adult, she would have contributed to and in turn had access to the social insurance benefits that the UBF offered members. She would also have had the opportunity to pursue the many leadership positions that the organization afforded ordinary black women. As Theda Skocpol, Ariane Liazos, and Marshall Ganz have pointed out, historians have largely ignored the significance of fraternal organizations in black associational life. These "popularly rooted" organizations offered "many

Southern Migrant Politics during the 1910s

people who rarely had authority at work or in formal politics . . . unique opportunities to learn organization skills and serve as group leaders."[50] Ella was just such a person. In Louisville, she began a long climb up the fraternal leadership ladder that would eventually take her to the top.

In the meantime, wage labor and marriage awaited Ella upon completing her schooling. As Jennie Lawrence was making her way through Livingstone and then Scotia in the 1890s, Ella was working as a domestic in Louisville and starting her own family.[51] Around 1896 Ella married William Berry and shortly after gave birth to a daughter, Tillie (Matilda). Theirs was not a happy marriage. By 1900 William had abandoned Ella and Tillie, leading Ella to move back in with her mother and eventually to file for divorce.[52] The trauma of abandonment would have tested Ella's emotional ties to Louisville. The 1902 death of the beloved mother after whom she had named her daughter and who had for so many years served as the emotional and financial glue of the family would have further loosened Berry's links to the city.[53] It was sometime after Matilda's death in 1902 that Berry left Louisville for Cincinnati. Between approximately 1904 and 1907, she made her way to Chicago.

Although personal reasons clearly contributed to Berry's decision to leave Louisville, her departure was most likely inspired by much more than personal heartache. Scholars attribute the exodus of which Lawrence and Berry were a part between the 1890s and early 1910s to a worsening of the already oppressive conditions under which African Americans lived in the South, even in "progressive" Louisville. The transformation of segregation from custom to law spread rapidly across southern cities and states during these years. This move to legally mandate the separation of blacks and whites was a direct response to young African Americans, who, like Berry and Lawrence, had been born free or, like Ida B. Wells, had been emancipated as small children. As Leon Litwack explains, "Jim Crow came to the South in an expanded and more rigid form, partly in response to fears of a new generation of blacks unschooled in racial etiquette and to growing doubts that this generation could be trusted to stay in its place without legal force."[54] For white southerners, sixteen-year-old Wells's attempt in 1883 to ride in a first-class train car and physical ejection was a case in point.[55] Ten years later, Wells was exiled from the South just as the Tennessee Legislature was strengthening existing segregation laws and creating new ones.[56]

Berry and Lawrence, by contrast, experienced the full mushrooming of these laws in Kentucky and North Carolina after 1890. As a child and then a teenager, Berry watched "White Only" and "Colored" signs increasingly mark the landscape of her world every time the Kentucky General Assembly passed another discriminatory act: statutes prohibiting interracial marriage (1893 and 1894) and laws segregating train cars (1890 and 1892), railroad waiting rooms (1894), streetcars (1902), and all private and public schools, including universities (1891 and 1904).[57] For her part, Lawrence was about thirteen in 1899 when the North Carolina General Assembly ratcheted up its enactment of segregation laws. That year, the state assembly mandated the separation of blacks and whites on trains and steamboats. Within two decades, Jim Crow laws regulating North Carolina's schools, streetcars, and hospitals were also in place. These laws continued to grow in terms of both numbers and creativity well after Berry and Lawrence had resettled in Chicago.[58]

The hardening of segregation was accompanied by ongoing brutal acts of racial violence aimed at preventing a new generation of southern blacks from stepping beyond its "place." Although southern blacks had been the targets of racial violence for centuries, the 1890s marked a new era in this odious history. After 1889 the number of lynchings increased in both frequency (a record number of 161 took place in 1892) and barbarity.[59] Lynchings sometimes took place before hundreds and even thousands of people in a carnival-like atmosphere in which the torture was extended over hours.[60] Seventy-five documented lynchings of African Americans by white mobs took place in North Carolina between 1882 and 1930.[61] During the 1890s, white mobs tortured and murdered sixty-six African Americans in Kentucky, double the number of such incidents that occurred between 1880 and 1889.[62] None of these took place in Louisville, but the black community of Louisville in which Berry was embedded was very much a witness to this escalating racial violence. Many, of course, had moved to the border city in order to escape it. In Louisville itself, African Americans encountered detailed reports of these murders in local newspapers—like an 1899 article about an especially sadistic lynching in western Kentucky that the *Louisville Courier-Journal* ran under the headline, "Burned at Stake, Richard Coleman Meets Death at Hands of a Frenzied Mob."[63] Louisville's black community also encountered numerous "legal lynchings," that is, executions following cursory trials before hostile all-white judges and juries. These trials often took place under the threat that if a guilty verdict was not reached, then mob rule would prevail. Under these circumstances, Louisville's white leaders could claim that law and order had won the day, yet ensure "that any black accused of certain crimes received the same punishment as that meted out by the lynch mob."[64] Hearing about local lynchings sowed a seed of anger in

[71]

the minds of young girls that would bloom when they became political actors years later in the North.

Young women like Lawrence and Berry also learned hard political lessons while in the South, lessons that they would carry with them when they relocated northward. They learned to distrust the Democratic Party as the voice of white supremacy. Some acquired this knowledge firsthand as they watched and then tried to personally help black men circumvent Democratic disfranchisement schemes in their respective states. Others were too young to remember the disfranchisement battles that took place across the South between 1890 and 1910, but their families made sure that they knew this history, recounting stories about the white Democratic drives to "legally" disfranchise black men and community efforts to defeat them. The "memory" of disfranchisement battles that these women carried north was a memory that had been entrusted to them by those whom they left behind. Still other young women came from a handful of states where black men had managed to retain the ballot. This third group served as a direct link to the black Republican activism that continued in pocket communities even after Jim Crow legislation had transformed most of the South into a one-party system.

Berry was among this third group, a migrant from a state where African Americans had battled white supremacists but maintained black men's voting rights. Prior to her departure for Louisville, she would have witnessed how black men's retention of the ballot could affect white Republican actions. The most apparent example of this came from the governorship of Republican William O'Connell Bradley between 1895 and 1899. Black men across Kentucky helped to put Republican William O'Connell Bradley in office. During the same years in which Berry married, gave birth to Tillie, and then was abandoned by her husband, the state's first Republican governor used his office to decry racial violence and Jim Crow as no governor in the state had done before. In 1897 Bradley called the Kentucky state legislature into special session to enact an antilynching law, which it did. Throughout his tenure as governor, he urged county officials to prosecute lynch mob participants, and in an important symbolic gesture in 1898, Bradley addressed an antilynching organization in Ohio.[65] He also used one of his annual addresses to the state legislature to demand the repeal of the Separate Coach Law. As a young woman interested in politics, Berry surely followed the rise of a white Republican politician who, amid a sea of white supremacist Democrats, actually represented the black voters who helped to put him in office.[66] Perhaps the Bradley administration even offered Berry some hope as she sorted through the turmoil of her personal life.

In Louisville, Berry also learned to associate the Democratic Party with black oppression. She repeatedly watched the Democratic Party rally voters through appeals to white supremacy. There are seemingly endless examples. Perhaps one that would have stuck out in the mind of a young woman who was interested in politics was the successful Democratic drive to repeal women's school suffrage in 1902. Recall that only a small number of women had obtained the right to participate in such elections in 1894—those who lived in Lexington, Covington, and Newport. Despite the small number of women who could actually exercise this limited suffrage, white Democratic legislators raised the intertwined bogeys of black and Republican domination when black women outvoted white women in the 1901 Lexington school board election. "Democrats," one white Kentucky newspaper reported, "say that few but negro women care to exercise the right of suffrage, and the result of a school board election in" the three cities where women could vote "is a Republican victory in many instances, because the vote of the white women is not polled." As the article continued, "The shortest way [out] of the difficulty, so the Democrats say, is to disfranchise the women."[67] The Kentucky legislature did eliminate all women's voting rights in the state in March 1902 in order to eliminate the black female Republican vote.[68] By then in her midtwenties, Berry's antipathy toward the Democratic Party would have grown as these events unfolded in the pages of the local and national press. Commenting on the irrationality of Kentucky's decision to disfranchise the majority in order to prevent a minority from voting, the *Colored American Magazine* declared, "Some folks are queer."[69] Berry's choice of words may have been harsher, especially given white Democrats' characterization of the black women voters of Lexington as ignorant and sexually promiscuous.[70] As a resident of Louisville, Berry herself could not vote in these school board elections but, like many black women, may very well have perceived the smear campaign against the women of Lexington as an attack on black womanhood more generally.

Because she did not sever her ties to Louisville after she moved to Chicago, Berry's story demonstrates how the transfer of political knowledge sometimes took place over the course of several years and multiple trips. During the 1910s and 1920s, she returned to this city nestled along the Ohio River for extended stays.[71] Family ties ensured these periodic visits: although her sister Maggie and brother John Murphy also relocated to Chicago, her brother J. Henry Butcher remained in Louisville.[72] These trips embedded her once again in Louisville's white supremacy. When she returned for several months in the spring and summer of 1912, for instance, she would have found the city under a Democratic mayoral administration that had been swept into office with the by then familiar though effective refrain that Republican victory meant black domination.[73] These trips would also afford opportunities to connect with women in Louisville who remained deeply engaged in party politics into the 1920s. If she had traveled to Louisville on the eve of the 1920 election, the first since the Nineteenth Amendment's enactment, she would have encountered black women, by one report, "canvassing every street and alley in the city where members of our race may be found, urging women to the necessity of qualifying to vote in the coming elections, both of the state and for the President."[74] Future trips might have led to meetings with Louisville's two black Republican women's clubs that were operating by 1924 (the West-End Republican League of Colored Women and the East-End Colored Women's Political Clubs).[75]

Lawrence, by contrast, was among that group of southern women who witnessed the elimination or near elimination of black voting in their states. Abner Lawrence lived to see the first of these states, Mississippi, enact a new constitution designed to disfranchise black men in 1890. After Abner died in 1892, his wife and children lived to see eight additional states revise their constitutions with the express purpose of disfranchising black men: South Carolina in 1895, Louisiana in 1898, North Carolina in 1900, Alabama and Virginia in 1901, Texas in 1902, Georgia in 1908, Arkansas in 1893 and again in 1908, and Oklahoma in 1910.[76]

Jennie Lawrence spent her teenage years watching North Carolina's Democratic Party conduct a racially inflammatory campaign designed to transform the state into a one-party system and ultimately to disfranchise black men. The impetus was the emergence of a tenuous but successful coalition between the Populist and Republican parties. Between 1894 and 1898, this Republican-Populist "fusion" party won majorities in both chambers of the state assembly, elected a governor and several congressmen, and gained control of the supreme court and the superior courts. African American voters had supported the fusion ticket, and some men were rewarded with or elected to government positions, many of them low ranking, but positions nevertheless. Seeking to regain the ascendancy that they had held since Reconstruction, the Democratic Party used race-baiting to draw white voters away from the fusion party and to break up the coalition. In the press and at a barrage of rallies, white Democratic Party leaders charged that

Southern Migrant Politics during the 1910s

black officeholding reversed the natural racial hierarchy by placing black men in positions of authority over white North Carolinians. This reversal, Democratic demagogues argued, threatened to break down the public order, most menacingly by emboldening black men to act inappropriately toward white women.[77]

Twelve years old, Lawrence was young, but she was old enough to feel the heightened racial tensions and threats of violence that gripped North Carolina during the 1898 election season. She would have heard her mother and neighbors discuss white Democrats' belligerent rhetoric, such as their promise to "crush the party of negro domination beneath a majority so overwhelming that no other party will dare to attempt to establish negro rule here."[78] She would have witnessed their disappointment when the white supremacy campaign paid off and the Democratic Party regained control of state government. She would have heard about the white mob that swept through Wilmington's black district two days after the election, killing indiscriminately, setting buildings ablaze, and forcing ten fusion party men, four black and six white, to resign from the Wilmington board of aldermen so that white Democrats could replace them.[79]

As Lawrence settled into student life at Scotia Seminary on the outskirts of Charlotte, the Democratic Party turned to the next phase of its campaign to ensure its party's dominance in the state. She might have discussed with her Scotia classmates, who, like her, were being educated to serve as future leaders of the race, how African Americans should respond to the North Carolina legislature's 1899 approval of a disfranchisement amendment to the state constitution. Perhaps the young women felt a sense of hope in the interracial cooperation that they were practicing at Scotia when they learned that North Carolina's two white fusion party senators (one Republican and one Populist) had protested the amendment on the floor of the U.S. Senate in January 1900. This sense of hope, however, would have been quickly dashed when—with the help of both paramilitary intimidation and a new election law that discouraged black registration and voting—North Carolina voters ratified the amendment in a statewide election in August.[80] At the tender age of fourteen, Lawrence watched North Carolina's Democratic Party destroy the black manhood voting rights that her parents had worked so hard to protect.

After graduating from Scotia Seminary around 1903 or 1904, Lawrence followed in the footsteps of her mother and embarked on a career teaching in the public and church schools of North and South Carolina until her 1912 relocation to Chicago.[81] Lawrence's employment was part of a larger transformation of teaching into a female-dominated profession that was taking place at the turn of the century. In 1890 the nation's 7,864 African American women teachers constituted a slight majority over the 7,236 black men in the profession. Two decades later, the number of male teachers remained almost constant. In contrast, by 1910 Lawrence was among the 22,547 African American women working in one of the few professions open to them.[82] Like her mother, several of Lawrence's teaching posts were in schools run by the Board of Missions for Freedmen of the Presbyterian Church. Among the first of these was the Salem School in Anderson, South Carolina.[83] Around November 1906 Lawrence joined Reverend J. P. Foster, his wife, and possibly his adult daughter in educating 162 students at this school located in the shadow of the Blue Ridge Mountains.[84] As her parents had experienced, working with the Presbyterian Church's Board of Missions for Freedmen meant frequent moves. Within two years of beginning the South Carolina assignment, Lawrence went back to North Carolina to teach at a Presbyterian Freedman School located in Statesville, about twenty-five miles from Salisbury.[85] There she remained through at least the spring of 1910.[86] By her final year in the South before moving to Chicago, the Board of Missions for Freedmen had reassigned her to a school back in South Carolina—this time further downstate in Aiken, not far from Augusta, Georgia.[87]

As a teenager, she had learned about the lengths to which white Democrats would go to deny black men the ballot. Now as an adult traveling to various posts in North and South Carolina she learned about the lengths to which African American communities would go to try to sidestep disfranchising measures. She may have tried to help through her work as an educator. The struggle to reclaim black men's voting rights intersected with the increasingly feminized schoolhouses that were the province of a new cadre of female teachers, such as Jennie Lawrence. Across the South, local schools, and the churches in which they were often located, harnessed resources toward preparing men to pass the literacy and understanding tests that awaited them at the polls.[88] For instance, with the impending enactment of the new Mississippi constitution in the fall of 1890, a local black newspaper urged preachers and educators to teach literacy. As another paper reported, "Night schools for negro men have already been established in the Delta." Poignantly underestimating the lengths to which white southern Democrats would go to disfranchise black Republican men, this journalist promised readers: "All that these men have to learn is the alphabet. Perfect familiarity with that will enable them to vote."[89] White registration officials had no intention of "passing" the most educated black men who attempted these

Southern Migrant Politics during the 1910s

frequently obscure or completely illogical tests.[90] Historian Glenda Gilmore notes that "the few surviving voter registration books reveal that the black voter was rare" in the North Carolina elections of 1902 and 1904.[91]

The precipitous decline of black male votes masks the endurance of black electoral activism in the wake of these disfranchisement schemes. For instance, existing voter registration books do not document how many communities undertook group journeys to the polls and *attempted* to register men but were turned away by white supremacists. Nor do they document community efforts to prepare men to go to the polls. Shortly after the disfranchising amendment went into effect in 1902, Lawrence, the newly minted teacher, may have shared the belief among some black North Carolinians that literate African Americans would retain the ballot.[92] By the time Lawrence completed her teaching assignment in Anderson, South Carolina, and returned to North Carolina around 1909, however, it was more than evident that this was not the case. While education was critical to racial uplift, it would not defeat North Carolina's literacy test. Even as Lawrence continued her teaching duties in Statesville and in South Carolina again between 1909 and 1912, she may have already turned her sights northward.

It is unlikely that either Lawrence's or Berry's view of the Republican Party was uncomplicated or without nuance. After all, the Republican Party in both Kentucky and North Carolina had its own muddied history of racism. For example, after the disfranchising amendment went into effect in 1902, the Republican Party in North Carolina ejected black leaders from the party.[93] With the exception of William Bradley's governorship, the Republican Party in Kentucky regularly refused to back black candidates and tended to dispense menial patronage positions (jobs as street cleaners and janitors) to black supporters.[94] Rather than abandon the Republican Party, however, Lawrence and Berry attempted to reform it from within after relocating to Chicago. So in addition to bringing a deep distrust of Democrats, they also carried with them a reformist impulse. Once in Chicago, they fought to make the Republican Party represent African Americans. They not only pushed the Republican Party to be responsive to black needs but also demanded that the party support black candidates.

Lawrence personally experienced the politicized atmosphere of North Carolina's black schools in the years immediately after the state's disfranchising amendment went into effect. Other women learned about white Democratic disfranchisement and intimidation schemes from their parents. This was the case for Arkansas native Ella Elm, whose story serves as the opening vignette to this book. "Ella you is a little girl now," she remembered

Southern Migrant Politics during the 1910s

her father telling her, "but when you grow up to twenty-one and can vote don't never vote a democrat ticket." Her father's words echoed in her ears after her 1913 relocation to Illinois and for more than two decades thereafter.[95] By honoring his request, she was in effect voting for him by proxy.

While Lawrence and Berry were among thousands of women who relocated from the Upper South between the 1890s and 1910s, Elm was representative of migrants from the Deep South. Along with Ella Elm's native Arkansas, these states included Mississippi, Alabama, Georgia, Louisiana, Texas, South Carolina, and Florida. The number of migrants from these states began to outstrip those from the Upper South in the 1910s. By 1915 Deep South migrants, many from rural areas, constituted the majority of African Americans arriving in Illinois. This mass exodus from the Deep South continued unabated through World War II, with particularly intense periods between 1916 and 1919 and again between 1924 and 1925.[96]

Like that of many other migrants from the Deep South, Elm's decision to relocate to Illinois in 1913 was influenced by acute unemployment and underemployment in her home state of Arkansas. While Elm did not elaborate on such economic difficulties to the Works Progress Administration (WPA) interviewer who visited her Murphysboro, Illinois, home in the late 1930s, many others did in correspondence with the *Chicago Defender*. For instance, following several advertisements for wartime industrial laborers that ran in the *Defender* during the spring and summer of 1917, one woman described to the editor the difficult conditions she faced in New Orleans: "When you read this you will think it bery strange that being only my self to support that it is so hard, but it is so. everything is gone up but the poor colerd peple wages." As she explained, "they pay so little for so hard work that it is just enough to pay room rent and a little some thing to eat." "Please good peple," she implored when asking about the jobs mentioned in the *Defender*, "dont refuse to help me out in my trouble for I am in gret need of help God will bless you."[97] Similarly, in late April 1917 a Biloxi, Mississippi, wife and mother of three inquired about employment in the Midwest for herself, her husband, and her twenty-one-year-old daughter. Upon securing positions, she promised in the letter, "we will come as we are in a land of starvaten." Though only one woman's voice, this Mississippi woman's letter represented the hopes of many other southern women, both married and unmarried, when she wrote, "I hope that you will healp me as I want to get out of the land of sufring."[98]

The 1914 outbreak of World War I in Europe, coupled with increased anti-immigration legislation, created job openings for African Americans in

Southern Migrant Politics during the 1910s

midwestern industries, but mostly for men.[99] One migrant woman to Illinois explained concisely the very limited employment opportunities African American women faced throughout the nation: "it would not make much diffrent if I would be throughly edacated for I could not get any better work to do, such as house work, washing and ironing and all such work."[100] Most migrant women from the Deep South continued as wage laborers after settling in Illinois, and often in jobs similar to those they had left behind in the South, as domestics, cooks, and laundresses. Wondering why tens of thousands of southern black women were willing to endure the difficulties of relocation when job prospects in the Midwest mirrored those in the South, one historian characterizes these women's northward exodus as an effort to escape the sexual oppression and stereotyping that had plagued generations of African American women in the South. The opportunity to cast a ballot did not necessarily drive southern black women to uproot their lives; more pressing were the exigencies of escaping sexual violence and poverty. Still, as with the waves of southern women who had preceded them, women from the Deep South used the political opportunities afforded them through migration to act as proxy voters for those whom they left behind.[101]

Elm was not alone in this desire to use her vote on behalf of those who could not. In interviewing recent migrants during the 1920s, University of Chicago sociologist Harold Gosnell noted that the ballot was a "symbol of emancipation" and a "guarantee of equality of opportunity" as much for migrant women as it was for men. Southern migrant women in Chicago, he explained, "shared with their men folks an intense interest in politics."[102] One young migrant woman, Mrs. Edwards, indicated her desire to serve as a kind of proxy voter for her family. Edwards explained to interviewers that after arriving in Chicago "[s]he was very anxious to vote 'because her parents had never had the chance.'"[103] Edwards did not say which way she voted, but another migrant woman who had relocated to Chicago from Georgia during the 1910s did. As Gosnell and his colleague Charles Merriam recorded, "She thinks that anyone who has lived in the South should forever hate the Democratic party, 'not because all Democrats are bad, but because the party keeps its foot on the black man.'"[104]

These women interviewees helped to transfer a political culture that defined voting rights as owned collectively by the community from the South to the Midwest. So, too, did Lawrence, Elm, and Berry. During Reconstruction, disfranchised women influenced men's voting and political decisions within southern black communities.[105] As the new century unfolded, African Americans' ability to cast a ballot was increasingly determined more by region and less by gender. The disfranchised, both men and women, resided in the South; the enfranchised, including women, lived outside that region. Lawrence and Elm used the voting rights they acquired by relocating to Illinois on behalf of those who remained in the South. Elm honored her father's wishes to vote against the Democratic Party. Lawrence sought to make the Republican Party an institution that—as it had once been in the South—could be used to promote black interests. Berry connected Chicago's circle of Republican women to the black Republican politics that endured in Kentucky.

Integrating into Midwestern Politics

The Illinois legislature's expansion of women's voting rights in 1913 created opportunity for Elm, Berry, Lawrence, and many others to practice their brand of "proxy" politics, and not just in a handful of small school elections, as had been the case up until 1913. After 1913 they were entitled to vote for a range of municipal offices, and in 1916 they would cast their ballots for president. Migrant women were heavily involved in the series of contentious municipal contests that took place in the Second Ward after 1913. These contests focused on local issues, but for newly arrived migrants, the very act of voting was inflected through the prism of their southern experiences. Migrant women's voting and canvassing was in some ways a rebuke to white southerners who worked so hard to undermine black rights. Southern disfranchisers could not contain women's political ambitions in Chicago. While women's votes in municipal elections may have been symbolic vis-à-vis the South, their participation in presidential elections had the potential to directly affect the lives of southern blacks. In 1916 the South's expatriate daughters used their vote to do battle with southern white Democrats in the arena of national party politics.

Migrant women may have arrived with distinct ideas about voting, but they encountered an unfamiliar political world. Both Lawrence and Berry found help navigating this world from fellow clubwomen. During the 1910s, the expanding women's club movement served as a key setting for middle-class black women to pursue their political ambitions free from the racism of white women and theoretically unencumbered by church patriarchy, though in reality the lines demarcating the reach of clerical authority were not always so distinct. Since the National Association of Colored Women's 1896 formation, the number of women who affiliated with the NACW had mushroomed across the nation. In 1911 the *Crisis* placed this number at

Southern Migrant Politics during the 1910s

45,000.[106] The women's club movement in Illinois kept apace. A plethora of new clubs devoted to a range of social welfare and self-improvement projects formed during these years, and in 1912 Illinois clubwomen sent the largest number of delegates to the NACW's biennial convention in Virginia.[107] Although the NACW was founded as a nonpartisan organization, members' strong partisan tendencies were intermittently on display at both local and national gatherings. In Illinois, the Phyllis Wheatley Club, the Frederick Douglass Woman's Club, the Cornell Charity Club, the Ideal Woman's Club, and the umbrella organization that periodically brought these groups together, the Illinois Federation of Colored Women's Clubs (IFCWC), all held forums in which members discussed woman's suffrage and met with political candidates.[108]

At the national level, members' intention to make good use of the national forum that the NACW offered for partisan ends was evident at the first annual convention in 1896 when those attending passed a resolution praising the Republican Party's inclusion of a clause condemning lynching in its national platform and castigating the Democratic Party's failure to do the same.[109] Meeting in St. Louis in 1904, members similarly passed a resolution congratulating the "National Republican Convention in the adoption of that part of its platform which asserts that any state disfranchising its voters shall be limited in its Congressional representation."[110] NACW leaders did not strictly demand nonpartisanship in NACW-sponsored forums until the late 1920s. Even then the NACW was not always successful in containing strong partisan sentiments.[111] Until the leadership began to explicitly reprimand members for violating the nonpartisan policy and a separate national Republican women's organization took shape in the 1920s—both subjects of the next chapter—the NACW and its many local affiliates remained vital forums for Republican activity.

As Wanda Hendricks and Anne Meis Knupfer have documented, the women who ran these social reform groups also established a whole new host of clubs in the early 1910s that were explicitly focused on electoral politics. Wells-Barnett was the driving force behind two of these.[112] In 1910 Wells-Barnett organized the Women's Second Ward Republican Club, and in 1913 she founded the Alpha Suffrage Club. By 1917 this list also included the Aloha Political Club, the Colored Women's Party of Cook County, the Mary Walker Thompson Political Club, and the Third Ward Political Club, among others. As was the case after the enactment of the Woman's Suffrage Bill in 1891, the formation of several of these political clubs was a direct response to the expansion of women's voting rights in the state in 1913.[113]

[81]

With her educational background, Lawrence easily integrated into Chicago's network of middle-class women who ran these clubs. Very shortly after her 1912 arrival, Lawrence continued her education by entering the Chicago School of Civics and Philanthropy (CSCP). There, she encountered the social reform network that centered around Hull House, the famous settlement house founded in 1889 by Jane Addams and Ellen Gates Starr on Chicago's West Side. In its earliest incarnation in the 1890s, the CSCP was briefly housed at Hull House. The educated cadre of white women who had spent time at Hull House were the driving force behind the CSCP and its twin missions of training professional social workers and conducting social policy research on subjects such as housing, employment, and poverty. Students included a handful of black women like Lawrence who sought to introduce the new profession of social work into Chicago's segregated South Side.[114] After completing her studies at the CSCP, Lawrence accepted a low-paying position as superintendent of the Phyllis Wheatley Home, an institution that Fannie Barrier Williams characterized as the "most important undertaking among colored women" in Chicago.[115] Established in 1908 by the black women's club of the same name, the Phyllis Wheatley Home helped women who were arriving in Illinois without relatives or friends, and frequently with little money, to find housing and jobs.[116] Lawrence put migrant women in contact with volunteer families willing to take them in or, when possible, provided them with temporary lodging at the Phyllis Wheatley Home itself.

FIGURE 8.

Portrait of Ella G. Berry.
Elizabeth Lindsay Davis and
Mrs. S. Joe Brown, The Story of the
Illinois Federation of Colored Women's
Clubs *and* The History of the Order of the
Eastern Star among Colored People, *1E.*
© *1996 Gale, a part of Cengage learn-*
ing, Inc. Reproduced by permission.
www.cengage.com / permissions. Wide-
ner Library, Harvard College Library,
E185.93.12D381997.

During her four-year tenure as superintendent, Lawrence more than dou-
bled the number of girls and women the home could accommodate and
encouraged Chicago's leading social service agencies to address the needs of
black women. Lawrence was committed to ensuring safe working environments for migrant women and gained a reputation for checking in on her
charges while they were on the job.[117]

By one account Lawrence's colleague at the Phyllis Wheatley Home,
Joanna Snowden Porter, mentored Lawrence on the basics of campaign
"detail work and salesmanship." (Snowden Porter was on the home's board
of directors.) A Chicago native and prominent clubwoman, Snowden Porter's insights into the complicated world of machine politics in the city would
have been invaluable to a newcomer like Lawrence.[118] Lawrence, however,
may have also mentored the Chicago native on the state of black politics in
North Carolina.

Berry's involvement in Chicago's associational life also helped her to
integrate into the networks of Republican women that had been established
before her arrival in Chicago. One gets the sense, however, that Berry's
entrée into these middle-class networks was a bit more hard-won than was
the case for Lawrence. Part of this process seems to have entailed recrafting
her public image. In Chicago, she presented herself variously as married or
widowed, but significantly not as a divorcée.[119] Berry's choices here were a
reflection of what Darlene Clark Hine has identified as the "culture of

[83]

dissemblance" among African American women—namely, "the behavior and attitudes of black women that created the appearance of openness and disclosure, but actually shielded the truth of their inner lives and selves from their oppressor." "Because of the interplay of racial animosity, class tensions, gender role differentiation, and regional economic variations," Hine explains, "black women, as a rule, developed and adhered to a cult of secrecy, a culture of dissemblance, to protect the sanctity of inner aspects of their lives."[120] Though divorced, Berry continued to use the title "Mrs." until her death in 1939. She gained the cultural capital and veneer of male protection that came with the title and shielded herself from outside scrutiny about her bad marriage and abandonment by claiming to be married or widowed. Nor is there any mention of her daughter Tillie. Did Tillie die or remain in Kentucky with a relative? The archives are unyielding.[121] Berry's careful shielding of her painful past enabled her "to accrue the psychic space and harness the resources" she needed to pursue the public life of a clubwoman, fraternal leader, and political canvasser.[122]

What Berry lacked by way of education for gaining entrée into Chicago's black reform circles, she more than made up for by throwing herself into community activism. In Chicago, Berry entered into a booming fraternal movement, which in 1905 Fannie Barrier Williams characterized as "[n]ext to the Negro church in importance, as affecting the social life of the people" and as more effective than the churches in enforcing the "lessons of right living, of charity and truthfulness."[123] During the 1910s, Berry was active in the (Louisville-headquartered) United Brothers of Friendship and Sisters of the Mysterious Ten, as well as the Order of the Eastern Star. Eventually she would become heavily involved in the Improved Benevolent and Protective Order of the Elks of the World, or the "black Elks" as they were commonly known.[124] Berry also began to make her mark in the women's club movement, where her name was most closely associated with the Cornell Charity Club.[125]

The ties that Lawrence and Berry established with longtime club and fraternal groups helped them navigate the incredibly complicated and fluid electoral scene that they confronted in Chicago. The crowded field of political actors who shaped this scene included not only clubwomen but also an array of clergy and local bosses. These actors sometimes worked together, but they also regularly clashed in the struggle for control of patronage positions that victory at the polls permitted. The contest for control of government resources was in turn refracted through larger racial and gender hierarchies that were being challenged. Clerical antipathy toward women's

Southern Migrant Politics during the 1910s

growing organized political power, for instance, was one manifestation of how gender and racial struggles influenced elections. African American demands that black men rather than white men represent them in local offices was another. Add to these power struggles substantive debates about which candidate was actually best qualified to occupy a given office (and, for that matter, what qualified meant), and the decision of which candidate to support could be daunting indeed for any newcomer. These complex and often intertwined factors that migrant women encountered as they socialized into Chicago politics, as well as how migrant women responded to them, were evident in the Second Ward contests for city council that took place in the 1910s.

The Contests for Second Ward Alderman

A series of elections for the two city councilmen, or aldermen, that the Second Ward was allotted on Chicago's city council dominated South Side politics during the 1910s. The Second Ward was ground zero for the massive population transfer that was taking place between the South and Chicago. In 1910, 27 percent of the Second Ward was black. Five years later, according to one estimate, African Americans constituted the majority of voters in the ward, and by 1920, the Second Ward was more than 71 percent black.[126] By 1913 and 1914 respectively, Berry and Lawrence were both living in the Second Ward just several blocks from one another.[127] They were among the hundreds of new residents who were quickly making the Second Ward Chicago's most heavily black populated ward. They were also among the thousands of black women who participated in the hotly contested Second Ward alderman contests during the 1910s. Both Berry and Lawrence continued their commitment to the Republican Party in these elections. A decade later, Berry and Lawrence would work together in the same Republican machine. During the 1910s, however, they aligned with competing Republican factions. Tracing their activities during the alderman contests not only demonstrates the incredibly complicated set of factors migrant women confronted when they integrated into local Republican circles. Not surprisingly, it also reveals that, when taking full advantage of their new voting rights in the complex world of Chicago machine politics, migrant women were anything but a monolithic group.

Black men had won various public offices in Illinois since John Jones's 1871 election to the Cook County Board, but none had been elected to the office of city alderman. The office was powerful because the seventy alder-

[85]

men who sat on the city council governed the finances and appointments that in turn determined how the city apportioned a wide range of public services from sanitation to police protection.[128] For several years, South Side leaders had demanded the election of one of their own—someone who would reflect the community's growing racial consciousness and someone who would ensure that the rapidly expanding Second Ward would receive its fair share of city services. As the *Defender* explained in 1910, "We must have a colored alderman not because others were not friendly, but because we should be represented just the same as the Irish, Jews, and Italians."[129] The regular white-controlled Republican machine that dominated Second Ward politics, however, refused to nominate a black aldermanic candidate. In 1910 and 1912, Edward H. Wright, a twenty-five-year veteran of Chicago politics, had run as an independent Republican candidate. Despite a respectable showing, Wright was unable to defeat his machine-backed competitors.[130]

In 1914 the women of Chicago went to the polls with the right to vote for various municipal offices. The addition of women voters to municipal politics created new momentum in the drive to elect a black man to the city council. One of the Second Ward's two alderman positions was up for election. In the Republican primary, incumbent Second Ward alderman Hugh Norris was seeking reelection. Norris, who was white, had the backing of the powerful regular Second Ward Republican machine headed by George Harding and Martin Madden, which once again had refused to nominate a black candidate. His competition was William Cowan, a well-respected black businessman who had never run for office before, but was politically well connected. In the past, Cowan had cooperated with influential South Siders such as Edward Wright and Ferdinand Barnett (Wells-Barnett's husband) to build a black Republican organization that was independent from the city's white-controlled machines.[131]

The 1914 Second Ward alderman contest was not animated by specific policy debates. The candidates and their supporters agreed on the need for improved public services: the influx of new residents had put a heavy strain on the existing infrastructure, from transportation to garbage collection. They disagreed on who could get the job done in city council. For example, the *Defender* made clear its position that a black man's personal investment would make him a more persistent advocate for the ward: "A member of the race can do greater work for the Second Ward and the majority of its voters than any of the candidates in the field." As the *Defender* elaborated, a black council member "would fight for better street car service on 31st and 35th streets, cleaner streets and alleys, ashes emptied oftener, better fire protection, worn streets repaired, and the same proper attention to playgrounds and public bathing front as other sections of the city." "When the interests of the race are at stake," the *Defender* insisted, "there will be a member there to look after our interests, as other nationalities do."[132]

Women's clubs canvassed heavily during this racially charged primary contest but not as a unified group. Middle-class women canvassers generally agreed that it was women's responsibility to lead men by example in the campaign. With the multiple Republican candidates from which to choose in the primary and then the general elections, however, they disagreed on the specifics of what example women voters should set: should they help to elect an independent black Republican candidate or remain loyal to the regular Republican machine and its white candidate? Their use of the same "woman's era" philosophy to justify their different choices demonstrates just how malleable this idea was within the realm of party politics.

Wells-Barnett was the most famous Cowan supporter; the story of her Alpha Suffrage Club crisscrossing the Second Ward registering women voters and urging them to "help put a colored man in the city council" is well known.[133] Less familiar are the individual stories behind some of the other Second Ward women who canvassed for Cowan in the primary. Berry was one of these women. Berry worked for Cowan's election through the newly formed Political Equality League of the Second Ward. Edward Wright founded the Political Equality League with the explicit purpose of creating an organization that could take on the regular Republican machine and fulfill his long-sought-after goal of electing a black alderman in the Second Ward.[134] Why did she support Cowan? Berry's experiences with the Republican Party in the South cannot be discounted when analyzing her reasons for supporting the independent black Republican candidate, especially when other well-respected women in the Second Ward made a different decision. Berry had witnessed the Republican Party in Kentucky refuse to endorse black candidates for local office. Here was an opportunity to reform the Republican Party from within, using her own ballot and canvassing know-how. She was finally in a position to help elect a black Republican to represent her.

When Norris narrowly defeated Cowan in the primary, Cowan's women supporters presented a gendered interpretation of the outcome that both held men accountable and emphasized women's ultimate responsibility to make the election of a black alderman happen.[135] "It's a disgrace that our men did so little to nominate a man of our race for alderman," one woman wrote in a letter published in the *Defender* after the primary. As another letter writer put it, "the women have more race pride than the men." This letter writer, who identified simply as "a suffragette in the second ward," asked men to "shake off the raiment of greed and graft, and stand by the women for the protection of the race" in the general elections. Though men had faltered in the primary, she insisted, women would help them redeem themselves by pushing Cowan to run as an independent candidate in the general elections.[136]

Even as these women chastised men for Cowan's defeat, they were well aware that other women with whom they had collaborated on a number of projects had campaigned heavily for Norris during the Republican primaries. For instance, Ida Dempsey, who had teamed up with Wells-Barnett during the 1894 campaign, canvassed for the white machine-backed candidate. Marie Mitchell, who affiliated with Berry in the Cornell Charity Club, worked through the Second Ward regular Republican machine to organize women voters for Norris's victory. For this group, women voters could best fulfill their role as protectors of the race by bolstering black strength within the established Republican machine, not breaking with it. As Wanda Hendricks astutely notes, here "the concept of the 'race man' went beyond traditional notions of color to include one who could clear a path for African Americans to derive benefits from an oppressive system."[137] Women like Mitchell and Dempsey perceived Norris, though white, as better situated within the city's Republican networks to promote Second Ward needs than a black candidate who was independent of the machine.[138] They were no doubt also looking ahead to the future, positioning themselves and the women of the Second Ward to enter more fully into the power networks of Republican ward machinery.

The historian's search for patterns raises a question of degree: were native or longtime northern women more receptive to working with the regular Republican machine? It is tempting to argue yes, especially when, for example, four of the five women who spoke at one of the last Norris rallies before the primary fit this description.[139] The flipside of this argument is that new arrivals were less attached to the politics of local machinery, at least initially. There may be some truth to both statements, but there is simply not enough evidence to conclude that black women campaigners divided between the candidates in such a clean, well-delineated pattern. Moreover, there are examples of southern-born women campaigning for the white machine-backed candidate, and native northerners working hard to see a black man win the primary.[140] For migrant women who sought patronage positions for

[88]

themselves or family members, canvassing for Norris was a strategic political move. The main discernible patterns are migrant women's consistent support for Republican candidates and their inconsistent integration into local Republican machine politics.

As migrant women sorted through the complicated menu of Republican candidates both inside and outside the machine, black and white, they also navigated a politicized religious landscape that had changed significantly since the last time women's voting rights had expanded in Illinois in 1891. The arrival of thousands of southern black migrants had caused religious institutions in Chicago to enter into a period of enormous transition and flux. For example, Walters AME Zion, where Berry possibly attended, experienced the type of growth in membership that was taking place in established black churches across the city. By 1917 Walters AME Zion's membership had grown by more than 300 percent.[141] A heavily Baptist migrant population resulted in an even greater growth spurt among Baptist churches, and it was no coincidence that by 1930 the city's five largest black congregations were all Baptist. Overall, the approximately twelve black churches that dominated black institutional life in Chicago at the end of the nineteenth century mushroomed into about two dozen or so by 1914 and into more than two hundred by the 1920s. The largest number of these were Baptist.[142]

The very volume of churches that sprang up on the South Side during the 1910s and early 1920s makes the history of black women's political activism through them quite complex. Some generalizations can be drawn as to the role that the churches played in integrating migrant women into Chicago politics. Established churches were often one of the first explicitly partisan institutions that many migrant women encountered upon arriving in Illinois, and sometimes even before departing the South. Newcomers approached congregations not so much as Republicans, Democrats, or independents but rather as individuals and families seeking housing, employment, and communities of worship. Along with women's clubs and the Urban League, established churches, such as Olivet Baptist and Institutional AME, were on the front lines of helping the thousands of migrants who were arriving on the South Side each year, providing them with advice on adjusting to their new city, as well as basic social services.[143]

These established congregations that black migrant women turned to for help settling in and then as potential sites of worship introduced them to the unique contours of Chicago politics. From their years in the South, migrant women were familiar with ministerial leadership in politics, as well as the use of churches for partisan activities. However, they did not know the person-

Southern Migrant Politics during the 1910s

alities, alliances, and policy debates that made up Chicago's complex political world. Nor upon arriving did migrant women for the most part know how Chicago's numerous congregations fit into this maze of machine politics. Sunday services offered a primer in the unique contours of Chicago politics. On a given Sunday during an election season, women trying out one of the mainline congregations witnessed ministers and fellow congregants intensely engaged in local and national party politics. At the invitation of ministers, politicians made their case at the close of services, and clerics themselves used the pulpit to advocate for candidates.[144]

To be sure, migrant men also learned about regional politics by observing the political theater that often took place on Sunday. The role of the churches in introducing migrant women to regional politics, however, was more far-reaching because more women than men were regular churchgoers. A 1901 survey of church affiliation among 398 African American residents "in a lower-class precinct" of Chicago found a "disproportionate number of those who belonged were women."[145] This gender imbalance in one Chicago precinct was a microcosm of black churchgoers nationwide. In 1906 women constituted two-thirds of the more than two million members of the National Baptist Convention, the largest black religious denomination.[146] As one historian explains, African American women arriving in midwestern cities from the South "expected to work and to work hard, for work was part of the definition of what it meant to be a black woman in America, regardless of region."[147] With minimal time to attend political rallies, Sunday services were the political meetings many churchgoing women could attend most regularly.

What political message migrant women encountered or could express as a member of a given church, however, depended very much upon which congregation they attended. The links that individual ministers cultivated with local machines crossed denominational lines. Clergy who usually (though not always) supported the regular Republican machine headed by Martin Madden, William Hale Thompson, and George Harding included Ebenezer Baptist's John Francis Thomas and Olivet Baptist's E. J. Fisher. Such ties changed quickly, however, when a new minister took over a congregation. This was the case, for example, when E. J. Fisher died in 1915 and was replaced with Lacy Kirk Williams. Unlike Fisher, Williams's loyalties were toward the wing of the Republican Party that was headed by ex-governor Frank Lowden and Charles Deneen. A church's political affiliation also shifted quickly under the leadership of the same minister. One of Chicago's most astute political leaders, Archibald Carey, adeptly worked with various

Southern Migrant Politics during the 1910s

wings of the Republican Party, as well as local Democratic politicians, during his tenures as minister at Quinn Chapel AME between 1898 and 1904, Bethel AME between 1904 and 1909, and Institutional AME between 1909 and 1920.[148]

Within the context of church patriarchy, this constantly shifting labyrinth of political alliances between clergy and machines sometimes made the old-line congregations challenging sites for women to organize politically. Further complicating the situation in the 1914 primary were the debates about whether Second Ward voters should remain loyal to the regular Second Ward Republican machine by voting for Norris, or should help a black candidate win the Republican nomination by casting their ballot for Cowan. So long as women's political positions matched those of clergy, church resources could benefit women's political organizing. Such was the case in January 1914 when Bethel AME's pastor W. D. Cook permitted a mass women's rally on behalf of Cowan to take place at the church.[149]

The willingness of ministers to use their authority over women congregants in electoral matters, however, was on stark display at Ebenezer Baptist in the days after Norris, the machine-backed white candidate, won the Republican primary. Ebenezer Baptist's John Francis Thomas, who usually sided with the regular Second Ward Republican machine, joined many of the South Side's leading clergy during the primary to give, as the heavily pro-Cowan *Defender* put it, "helping talks from their pulpits of the duty of the woman voter to her race." Walter AME Zion's head pastor Henry J. Callis was among this group. If not an explicit "helping talk" telling women to vote for the black candidate, Callis's Sunday sermon two weeks before the primary, "The Healing Power of Obedience," probably got the point across all the same. At a rally held at Ebenezer Baptist after the primary, Callis joined Thomas and Quinn Chapel AME's J. C. Anderson in chastising women voters who had voted for a white candidate over a black one. Thomas went the furthest in his censure, promising that "the women members of his church who worked and voted against the nomination of William R. Cowan and voted for the renomination of Alderman Norris would not be permitted to further hold any official positions in his church."[150]

This was certainly not the first time that congregants had differed from clergy when endorsing candidates. Men had done it for years. So what was different now, and why did clergy direct their anger at women specifically? By the 1910s, Chicago's black clergy had started to lose some of the political strength that they had wielded at the end of the nineteenth century. They were no longer the primary or only political brokers between black

Southern Migrant Politics during the 1910s

neighborhoods and white party bosses. Alongside clergy, professional black politicians, secular organizations like the National Association for the Advancement of Colored People (NAACP) and the Urban League, and, most threatening of all, clubwomen also claimed to speak for black communities in political contests. In response, clergy attempted to prevent any further erosion of their political power.

Clubwomen's political power was especially threatening because, even though men controlled clerical positions, they were dependent upon the fundraising abilities of their female-dominated congregations for church revenues. In a 1915 *Crisis* article, Nannie Helen Burroughs succinctly argued, "The Negro Church means the Negro woman." Burroughs, historian Evelyn Brooks Higginbotham explains, was the "dynamic force behind the Woman's Convention" of the National Baptist Convention, USA, during the first half of the twentieth century. Founded in 1900 as its all-female auxiliary, the Woman's Convention served as an autonomous space from which black Baptist women launched a reform movement to undermine sexism and racism. Burroughs elaborated upon her dramatic claim: "Without [the black woman], the race could not properly support five hundred churches in the whole world. Today they have 40,000 churches in the United States. She is not only a great moral and spiritual asset, but she is a great economic asset."[151] If women chose to tie their fundraising to clerical support of certain candidates, they might reconfigure the existing gender balance of power within individual congregations. In his denunciation of Thomas, the always colorful founder and editor of the *Broad Ax*, Julius F. Taylor, pointed to the pivotal role women played in the financial life of the churches. (Taylor was a black Democrat who regularly used the pages of the *Broad Ax* to espouse his political views, including his intense opposition to church involvement in electoral politics.) "If the preachers are going to continue their warfare and rail against the Colored women for simply exercising their political rights," Taylor advised, "then they should withhold their dollar money from the preachers and possibly that would bring them to their senses, for they cannot live in grand style very long unless they regularly receive the dollar money from the women members of their various churches."[152]

Perhaps what is most striking about this 1914 conflict between clergy and politically active women was the clerical effort to control women congregants who had worked outside of church networks to achieve their political goals. In other words, Ebenezer's women congregants who had canvassed for the white machine-backed candidate in the primary had not done so through the church. Thomas would not allow it. Rather, their organiza-

Southern Migrant Politics during the 1910s

tional efforts had relied upon the various women's political clubs that had emerged on the South Side. Thomas's threats made clear that, despite middle-class women's efforts to create clubs that offered them independence from both black men and white women, the establishment of black women's clubs did not completely buffer them from hostile clergy.

Still, there was an important difference when compared to the last time women's enfranchisement expanded in 1891. By 1914 black Chicagoans had significantly more options for religious expression. Women congregants could more readily protest abuses of clerical power with their feet. As Milton Sernett argues, in terms of church affiliation, it was a "buyer's market."[153] While many women congregants may have been introduced to regional politics when they tried out a congregation on a given Sunday, they did not necessarily agree or approve of the political advocacy they encountered. In black Chicago's fluid economy of church attendance, women had the option to go elsewhere. They could move to a congregation where the ministers' politics more closely matched their own, or they could choose a smaller storefront where politicking was rare. Indeed, there is evidence that some women rejected the mainline churches, in part, out of disgust with the constant political exhortations that took place there. Asked by WPA workers about whether storefront churches were an "asset or liability," one woman became "heated in her defense" of the storefronts, which as the name suggests were often informal prayer meetings that were held at stores and private homes. In the process, she spurned any notion that politicking belonged on the pulpit. She also pointed to the class tensions at play between mainline church congregants and storefront participants: "Yes, I go to church to hear a sermon and not political speeches like you hear in the big churches. A lot of people make fun of storefront churches because they belong to some large church. . . . All they want is to say 'I belong to so-and-so's church.'"[154]

Reverend Thomas's hostility against Ebenezer's politically active women congregants in 1914 was far from an isolated incident. Indeed, clerical animosity toward organized women's power would have been familiar to NACW activists, southern and northern alike. Five months after Thomas's threats of retribution, Buffalo clubwoman Mary Talbert raised the issue of the sometimes strained relationship between clergy and clubwomen at the NACW's Ninth Biennial Convention in Ohio. With sixty-eight delegates representing twenty-eight clubs, including the Phyllis Wheatley Club, the Alpha Suffrage Club, and the Cornell Charity Club, women from Illinois and especially Chicago were one of the largest regional groups at the convention.[155] Re-

Southern Migrant Politics during the 1910s

porting in her capacity as chairman of the NACW's executive board, Talbert addressed the topic of bringing more middle-class women into the movement, or, as she put it, "splendid women who have not yet seen the necessity of 'lifting as we climb.' " Ministerial help was part of the answer. As she told the 400 women who had gathered for three days on the grounds of Wilberforce University, "It behooves us as club women to see that we urge our ministry to co-operate with us" in encouraging women of the "favored class" to do their duty of "lifting an entire Negro manhood and womanhood into better life." Talbert acknowledged the gendered politics of church finances that was familiar to her audience: "Often ministers have been particularly antagonistic to this club movement, fearing that it will affect the financial support of the church." In 1899 NACW president Mary Church Terrell had asserted that women's financial strength and otherwise essential role in the day-to-day administration of congregations had earned them the right to ask ministers to "preach at least one sermon" toward arousing "the conscience of some women, who have thus far failed to do her duty to the only national organization we have." "It is proverbial," Terrell wrote in the pages of *National Notes*, "that our women bear the heaviest burdens of the church work, so that it is especially fitting that the church, through the pastor, should come to our assistance, whenever it can consistently and conscientiously do so."[156] Fifteen years later, Talbert took a slightly more conciliatory approach than her colleague, conceding, "We sympathize with the feeling of such ministers, for we know that the average minister does not receive a living salary, much less a working salary." She emphasized club-women's sincere intent: "There can be one motive in all our work—the spirit of Christian love, the expression of racial brotherhood." However, NACW members, she insisted, had to address clerical hostility head on, and not by retreating from their reform work when ministers felt threatened. Quite the contrary, Talbert called upon members to "educate [clergy] to the fact that the time has come when they, too, must join with us in enlarging the work by these organizations of women's clubs."[157] Talbert did not say how this education was going to take place without provoking the type of backlash that occurred at Ebenezer. Declarations of Christian love and racial brotherhood notwithstanding, Talbert was essentially asking ministers to help strengthen a movement that some perceived as having the potential to usurp their authority. Unsettled by women's organized power in 1914, male clergy chastised and threatened women who had supported the white machine-backed candidate Norris.

The white and black men of the Second Ward regular Republican machine employed an entirely different strategy when trying to contain the political strength of women voters as the 1914 alderman contest switched gears from the primary to the general elections: they brokered a deal. The machine, of course, was trying to contain the organized power of a different group of women than Thomas was, those who demanded the election of a black alderman. When Cowan and another young black politician, Charles Griffin, decided to run as independent Republican candidates in the general elections, the regular Republican machine feared Democratic victory. Concerned that the dilution of Republican votes among the three candidates—two black and one white—would ensure the election of a Democratic alderman, the machine sought women's help to prevent such an outcome. In her autobiography, Wells-Barnett described how black and white machine representatives Oscar DePriest and Samuel Ettelson attended an Alpha Suffrage Club meeting to plead Norris's case. The canvassing strength of organized black women in the ward disrupted existing gender and racial hierarchies, resulting in a black man pleading a white candidate's case before a black women's club. Indeed, the meeting exemplified the complicated racial alliances and politics that migrant women navigated in their adopted city. The women of the Alpha Suffrage Club extracted a promise from the regular Second Ward organization: in return for their support of Norris, the Second Ward machine would endorse a black aldermanic candidate the next time a vacancy opened up. Norris's ultimate victory at the polls ensured that, at least for the time being, white men would continue to represent the mostly black Second Ward in the city council. The women who had supported Norris in the primary held a "love feast" to celebrate the victory. Those who by contrast had demanded the election of a black candidate in the primary and who had brokered a deal with the machine in the generals waited for an opening to see if the machine would carry through its promise of nominating an African American.[158]

During the 1914 primary the *Defender* quoted women voters as proclaiming: "The men have made several attempts to elect an alderman. They failed, but we will succeed."[159] It took them longer than they expected, but in 1915 women fulfilled their promise. Through their show of organizational strength and shrewd negotiations, African American women cracked the machine and successfully pushed the white-controlled organization to do what it had never done before: endorse a black man for alderman. In 1915, the Second Ward regular Republican organization backed Oscar DePriest for alderman. One of the two Second Ward alderman seats had opened up when sitting alderman and machine leader George Harding was

Southern Migrant Politics during the 1910s

elected state senator. A native Alabaman who moved to Chicago in 1889 and worked his way up the Second Ward Republican machine, DePriest carried the contentious 1915 Republican primary that pitted him against two other black candidates, Louis Anderson and Charles Griffin. He went on to win the general election in early April by a wide margin (he received 3,700 more votes than his nearest competitor, Democrat Al Russell) to become the first black alderman in Chicago's history. His victory rested, in part, on both the heavy canvassing efforts of the Alpha Suffrage Club and the votes of women, who constituted more than a third of the ballots cast for him.[160] DePriest's victory heralded a new era of black self-representation in the city council.

It was during Oscar DePriest's two unsuccessful runs for reelection as Second Ward alderman in 1918 and 1919 that Jennie Lawrence's name begins to show up in newspaper coverage of local politics.[161] Though it is hard to know exactly when Lawrence began her affiliation with DePriest, it seems likely that it was before her name began to appear in the newspaper in 1919—if not during DePriest's first run for alderman in 1915, then probably by the time his second attempt was under way in 1918. In many ways the 1918 race between DePriest and Robert R. Jackson was reminiscent of the 1914 alderman contest. In the primary, two candidates competed for the Republican nomination, one supported by the regular Second Ward Republican machine, the other not. This time, however, the independent Republican candidate was DePriest. The Second Ward Republican organization refused to back his reelection efforts following a 1917 trial and acquittal on conspiracy and bribery charges. In response, DePriest established an independent Republican organization known as the "People's Movement" and ran in both the primary and general elections. Lawrence became one of the key organizers in the People's Movement. In 1918 there was one other important difference when compared to 1914: both DePriest and Jackson were black. After DePriest's defeat in 1918, he tried again in 1919, this time running against another black candidate, incumbent alderman Louis Anderson. (Louis Anderson became the city's second black alderman in 1917 when DePriest decided not to seek reelection because of the conspiracy and bribery charges.) Again DePriest met defeat in 1919.[162]

Berry's and Lawrence's involvement in the 1918 and 1919 alderman campaigns demonstrates how southern migrant women integrated differently into local Republican circles once in Chicago. Both women worked for the election of a black Republican alderman during these contests. Like Berry, Lawrence's experiences watching the Republican Party in the South

Southern Migrant Politics during the 1910s

eject black leaders may have motivated her commitment to black self-representation. Even as Berry and Lawrence used their voting rights to reform the Republican Party from within, they did so through different avenues and with different candidates. Berry, who had campaigned *against* the regular Republican machine when it put forward a white candidate in 1914, canvassed for the machine when it endorsed a black candidate in 1918. Jackson was a well-respected state senator and Spanish Civil War veteran who, like Berry, was heavily involved in multiple fraternal orders. His supporters perceived him as the clean alternative to DePriest, who, although he had been acquitted of the initial conspiracy and bribery charges, still had several other indictments hanging over his head.[163] The machine rewarded Berry for her efforts with a school census enumerator job after Jackson's victory.[164]

Lawrence, by contrast, worked with the People's Movement, if not in 1918 then in 1919 to help DePriest regain his seat on the city council. It is worth noting that Lawrence's support for DePriest is a bit curious at first glance. The same can be said for some of the other prominent clubwomen who remained loyal to the ex-alderman, perhaps none more so than Elizabeth Lindsay Davis. Davis was one of Chicago's most prominent clubwomen, a founder of numerous women's organizations, including the Phyllis Wheatley Home. Lawrence's and Davis's canvassing for DePriest was curious not only because of the cloud of corruption charges that still loomed over his head but also because Alderman DePriest had voted against measures popular with black women. For example, he voted against a proposal that would have prohibited the sale of liquor in Chicago. Middle-class women reformers demanded saloon closures for a variety of reasons, including their concentration in the South Side. So why did Lawrence, Davis, and other clubwomen work with DePriest? Ella Berry may have perceived DePriest as corrupt, but his women supporters characterized the machine that abandoned their candidate as unprincipled: it was dismissive of DePriest's strong following among black voters when it decided not to endorse his reelection campaigns. Although DePriest had voted against the saloon measure, he had also introduced a civil rights ordinance prohibiting discrimination in public accommodations.[165] African American women were not single-issue voters; they could not afford to be. Rather they made strategic decisions based on the particulars of each campaign. In this case, they prioritized his ultimately unsuccessful action to end racial discrimination in Chicago over any disapproval of other parts of his voting record. This was certainly not the last time that they would have to prioritize issues.

[97]

The same year that Lawrence's name begins to appear in newspaper coverage of the People's Movement, she and her sister Anna professed their faith before the Grace Presbyterian Church Council and were accepted as members of the congregation. Where the Lawrence sisters worshiped prior to 1919 is unclear. In Chicago's "buyer's market," they had a range of choices, especially if they crossed denominational lines. In joining Grace Presbyterian, Jennie and Anna were able to sustain ties with the denomination of their youth. Were there other motivations for attending Grace? They joined in January when yet another DePriest primary campaign was beginning to heat up. Perhaps it was just a coincidence. Or perhaps the Lawrence sisters chose Grace because its politics more closely matched their own when compared to the previous churches with which they affiliated. DePriest was a member of Grace; and while Reverend Moses Jackson did not openly campaign for DePriest, neither did he use Grace's pulpit to rail against DePriest, as clergy at many of the South Side's largest congregations had in 1918 (this included clergy at Bethel AME, Quinn Chapel AME, Institutional AME, Walters AME Zion, Olivet Baptist, and Salem Baptist).[166] In any case, at Grace Presbyterian, the Lawrence sisters became part of a distinctly middle-class and high-powered community of worshipers that, in addition to DePriest, included *Defender* editor Robert S. Abbott and Chicago Urban League organizer George Cleveland Hall, among many others.[167] Though Methodist, even Wells-Barnett had been a member of Grace Presbyterian between 1903 and 1917. It was from Grace Presbyterian, Patricia Schechter explains, that Wells-Barnett "launched her community-building work through 1920."[168] Lawrence also used Grace as a base for her own political activism.

1916 Presidential Election

In the midst of these aldermanic contests, African American women in Illinois prepared for another voting rights first, the opportunity to cast a ballot for U.S. president. In 1914 and again in 1915, African American women organized heavily to make the "Municipal" part of the 1913 Presidential and Municipal Suffrage Bill meaningful to Chicago's growing black community, though, of course, they did not always agree on candidates and strategies. Now they prepared to make the "Presidential" part of the bill meaningful as well. In 1916 Republican Charles Evans Hughes, the former New York governor and Supreme Court justice, was seeking to unseat incumbent Democratic president Woodrow Wilson. Wartime labor shortages and boll weevil–infested cotton crops also turned 1916 into one of the heaviest years of black migration out of the South.[169] The women of Illinois—both long-time residents and the thousands of southern migrants who were streaming into the state that year—were among the estimated 60,000 black women across the nation who were entitled to vote for president in the fall.[170] In campaigning for the Republican presidential candidate in 1916, politically active black women in Chicago established a unity of purpose that eluded them in local Republican politics.

The Republican National Committee appointed several African American women in Harlem and Chicago to conduct the Hughes campaign among these 60,000 women. Ella Berry obtained one of these appointments, officially holding the position of "organizer." Living in the Second Ward, one of the most heavily black-populated political units in the nation, she was well situated to reach black voters. Berry's extensive community activism since before her arrival in Chicago, however, was a far more valuable asset to her canvassing than her address. In the months preceding the election, Berry was herself elected to a large number of positions. She began 1916 by continuing her climb up the fraternal leadership ladder with her election as an officer in one of the local chapters of the Order of the Eastern Star. By February, Berry had been elected as president of the Cornell Charity Club. Come summer she was elected parliamentarian to the Illinois Federation of Colored Women's Clubs, as well as the person who would represent the Michigan Conference of the AME Zion Church to the press. (The AME Zion Church was divided into several regional conferences, Chicago's churches being part of the Michigan Conference.) These positions were embedded within networks of politically active African Americans. Berry's ability to tap into these networks would have given her the contacts and legitimacy that she needed when arriving in various towns across Illinois to establish Hughes Women's Republican Clubs.[171]

While campaigning for Hughes, African American women in Illinois further developed the type of hybrid political knowledge that blended local canvassing know-how with an eye toward undermining the Jim Crow system in the South. On the southern end of this hybrid equation, Berry was not the only one who had come of age in the South. At the Colored Women's Hughes Republican headquarters in Chicago, Berry was joined by Wells-Barnett, whose official title was "speaker," and by Ada Dennison McKinley, who held the title of "secretary."[172] Born in 1868, McKinley spent her entire childhood in Reconstruction era Texas, first in Galveston and then in Corpus Christi. McKinley's young adulthood took place during the years immediately after "redemption" on the outskirts of Houston, where she attended Prairie View College, and in the Texas hill country, where she studied at Tillotson Missionary College and then found employment as a teacher. Married in 1887 to William McKinley, a dentist whom she had met while teaching in Austin, the couple relocated to Chicago at some point in the 1890s after diphtheria tragically took the lives of all three of their children. Like Wells-Barnett, McKinley did not experience the full mushrooming of Jim Crow laws before leaving the South. White Democratic legislators completed the drive to eliminate the black vote in Texas between 1902 and 1905 after the McKinleys' departure. Like Wells-Barnett, though, McKinley would have witnessed enough Democratic efforts to disfranchise black men in the 1870s and 1880s to instill both a deep hatred of the party and a longing for a more activist federal government.[173]

The infusion of southern women's political knowledge into the Hughes campaign effort among black women also took place in the Harlem-based office of the Colored Women's National Republican Committee. Though she was not yet entitled to vote, Alice Thompson Waytes was responsible for the entire Hughes campaign among African American women. Like several of the women whom she oversaw in the Chicago office, Waytes knew firsthand the indignities of southern white supremacy. She spent her childhood and teenage years in South Carolina's capital, Columbia. There she enrolled in the college preparatory program at Benedict College, one of the all-black colleges that the mostly white and northern-based American Baptist Home Mission Society (ABHMS) had founded in the South in the years after the Civil War. After Benedict, Waytes made her way to Raleigh, North Carolina, where by 1901 she had completed the missionary training program at another ABHMS institution, Shaw University.[174] In 1900 Jennie Lawrence watched from afar in Charlotte as Democratic legislators meeting in Raleigh disfranchised black men. For Waytes, the disfranchisement revolution was taking place in her own back yard.

Waytes brought to the Hughes campaign not only firsthand experience with southern white supremacy but also a strong familiarity with Chicago's community of reform-minded women. Sometime after 1901 Waytes relocated to Chicago, where she deepened her religious education by attending Moody Bible Institute. Founded in 1889, the Moody Bible Institute was an evangelical seminary that offered a curriculum deeply embedded in the principles of the Social Gospel, the reform ideology that sought to apply the teachings of Jesus toward solving the many problems of industrial, urban America. Students undertook a two-year missionary training program that

Southern Migrant Politics during the 1910s

offered courses in basic theology and that required them to practice the Social Gospel by conducting evangelical outreach work among the urban poor. In 1904, the same year that she graduated from the Moody Institute, she planted firm roots in Chicago's community of politically active black women with whom she would later work on the Hughes campaign. She also applied her Social Gospel teachings toward solving the problems of black Chicago by helping to establish the Frederick Douglass Center.[175]

Waytes's activities after 1904 are dizzying to follow. Her many moves reveal how the transfer of political knowledge sometimes was a drawn-out process. Ella Berry traveled back and forth between Chicago and Louisville, connecting the politics of her new community to those of her former home. Waytes too moved back and forth between the North and the South creating a web of experiences that linked the changing politics of both regions. With her return to the South, Waytes taught in the highly politicized atmosphere of southern black schools during the first decade of the twentieth century, first in her hometown of Columbia and then at the Florida Baptist Institute in northern Florida.[176] The second decade of the twentieth century found Waytes back in the North, where she held a variety of teaching, social work, and church-related positions in Massachusetts and New York.[177]

Black Republican women's drive to undermine Jim Crow in the fall of 1916 revolved around removing an administration that many black men had helped to put in office four years prior. During the 1912 campaign, the national Democratic Party atypically made overtures to black northern voters. Several black delegations who had met with then New Jersey gover-nor Wilson, for example, reported positively on his promises to veto any legislation "inimical" to black Americans and to fairly distribute patronage positions among black supporters. Though wary, W. E. B. Du Bois argued in a 1912 *Crisis* article that it is "better to elect Woodrow Wilson President of the United States and prove once for all if the Democratic party dares to be Democratic when it comes to black men. It has proven that it can be in many Northern states and cities. Can it be in the nation? We are willing to risk a trial."[178] Du Bois, however, did not speak for either Wells-Barnett or Waytes. Neither was prepared to "risk a trial" with a Democrat. Among themselves, however, they disagreed on what course of action black voters should take with the disorganized Republican Party. Although not one of the estimated 13,488 black women entitled to vote in the presidential contest, Waytes was among a handful of prominent black women who followed Theodore Roosevelt out of the Republican Party and into the Progressive Party in 1912. Waytes personally traveled across the Midwest and Northeast stump-

Southern Migrant Politics during the 1910s

ing for Roosevelt. By contrast, Wells-Barnett's anger over Roosevelt's unfair discharge of a black regiment of soldiers when he was president seethed when she publicly called upon black men to reelect William Taft. Wilson, of course, ultimately won, and more than 100,000 African Americans helped to put the first Democratic president since Cleveland into office.[179]

Four years later, W. E. B. Du Bois concluded that "[t]he Negro voter enters the present campaign with no enthusiasm."[180] Du Bois's assessment did not accurately characterize the views of Hughes's women campaigners, however. Their hybrid political knowledge was overlaid with the optimism of "woman's era" philosophy. Fannie Barrier Williams, who was in charge of publicity at the Colored Women's Hughes Republican headquarters in Chicago, expressed this optimism in 1913 when she described the ballot as "an effective weapon with which to combat prejudice and discrimination of all kinds."[181] So too did Elizabeth Lindsay Davis, who headed campaign headquarters in Chicago, when she heralded women as a "potent factor in the body politic" in 1915.[182] A 1916 *Crisis* cartoon aptly titled "Woman to the Rescue!" offered a dramatic visual representation of the hope invested in black women's voting (see figure 9). The message was clear: armed with the federal constitution, black women would protect future generations from the indignities of white supremacy.

Longtime Chicago residents, Davis and Williams (along with "vice chairman" Irene Goins) constituted the campaign's native northerners. It is worth noting, however, that Davis and Williams had spent time in the South: Williams had taught freed peoples during Reconstruction, and Davis had briefly taught in Louisville, Kentucky, at some point during the 1870s or early 1880s.[183] Neither had come of age in the South or had made the difficult decision to leave all that they knew for the unknown challenges of Chicago. Still, surely they had encountered the rabid white supremacy that was rampant in the 1870s and 1880s during their temporary teaching assignments. Davis's and Williams's experiences further focused the southern orientation of northern women's campaigning. Their belief in women's responsibility to protect the race buoyed their determination to do battle with the profound power of southern white Democrats in the arena of national party politics.

The flipside of this optimism about women's voting was a critique of black men that, in turn, contributed to a gendered interpretation of the presidential election. The *Crisis* cartoon depicted this critique in the image of a black man running away from the battle scene proclaiming: "I don't believe in agitating and fighting. . . . To h[ell] with Citizenship Rights. I want money." Nannie Helen Burroughs also articulated this idea that black men had

FIGURE 9. *"Woman to the Rescue!,"* Crisis, *12, no. 1 (May 1916): 43. Widener Library, Harvard College Library, US10700.18.5 (11–12).*

betrayed the race in a 1915 *Crisis* symposium on suffrage: "The Negro woman . . . needs the ballot to get back, by the wise *use* of it, what the Negro man has lost by the *misuse* of it. She needs it to ransom her race." Burroughs, a D.C. resident who was herself not entitled to vote, was well known to the women who ran the Hughes campaign through her work in the NACW and the National Baptist Convention.[184]

Burroughs's criticism of black men in the *Crisis* article was not new, but it did have a particular resonance in Washington, D.C. She was writing from the city that had felt the racism of the Wilson administration more than any other in the country. It was no coincidence that the Federation of Colored Women's Clubs of the District of Columbia proposed a resolution at the NACW's 1916 convention that sought to put the organization on record as officially endorsing Hughes's candidacy.[185] Woodrow Wilson's presidency did not inaugurate a new era of Democratic interest in protecting black citizenship rights as Du Bois had hoped. Rather, it heralded the arrival of a flood of southern white racist Democrats into the city. As historian Harvard Sitkoff describes, "Dixie Democrats held sway, from the Virginian in the White House to the new Chief Justice, Edward D. White of Louisiana, to the leadership of both House and Senate." They quickly moved to transform the District into a southern city by segregating many federal offices and introducing more racist legislation into Congress "than had been submitted to any previous congress."[186] Burroughs did not directly argue in the *Crisis* symposium that black women needed to use their vote to defeat Wilson in 1916. The article's purpose was to make a case for women's full enfranchisement, not to argue how the limited number of enfranchised black women should cast their ballot in one year's time. However, it is worth speculating how women reformers' critique of black men shaped their interpretation of the 1916 election. Hughes campaigners who, like Burroughs, believed in the redemptive power of women's voting may very well have viewed the 60,000 black women's votes whom they were soliciting as "ransom" to save the race from men's misstep of electing a Democratic president.

A record of Berry's campaign speeches did not make it to the archives, but one can speculate as to what she might have said to a Paris, Illinois, audience of black women in late October that prompted the local *Defender* representative there to describe her address as one that "was full of thought and had its weight."[187] The campaign revolved around the war raging in Europe, American preparedness, and tariffs. Given the antiblack policies of the Wilson administration and the "southification" of the District, however, the election had a particular urgency in the ongoing battle to undermine Jim Crow that would not be lost on daughters of the South. "Our women," the *Defender* insisted, "need to go to the polls and register to give a rebuke to Wilson, who has been the 'father' of the present 'Jim Crow' system at Washington."[188] Berry may have gone further and urged women to fix what men had broken.

Besides his role as Wilson's opponent, what else might Berry have highlighted in making the case for Hughes? What did the national Republican

Party offer black Americans and, even more specifically, black women? How to answer this question was a challenge black women campaigners would face again and again over the next two decades. In the absence of surviving documents, it is impossible to know exactly what Berry and other women canvassers said on the campaign trail. They did not have a great deal with which to work. Hughes did not make civil rights a priority, and the Republican Party platform did not contain a specific plank referring to black civil rights. When a black delegation asked Hughes for "an expression of his attitude toward the colored people of the United States," he responded by abstractly pledging friendship and his belief "in a constitutional government." He avoided any specific policy statement by explaining that he "never thought it was necessary to refer to any Americans by their color."[189] Despite the obvious limitations of his answer, Hughes's constitutional reference would have resonated with specific meaning to migrant women searching for political partners who would help them, as the *Crisis* cartoon depicted, use the federal constitution to destroy the vultures of Jim Crow.

In the past, Republican women had responded to limited options by focusing on exceptions to Republican indifference. This was a strategy that they would employ again in the future. If they chose to pursue this strategy in 1916, the exception could be found with Hughes's mostly positive record as a Supreme Court justice. The Chicago-based *Champion Magazine* pointed to this record in its September 1916 inaugural edition: "It is due to him more than any other man that the notorious Grandfather Clause has been repudiated by the highest judicial body in this country."[190] *New York News* editor George W. Harris predicted elsewhere in the same edition that the election of the man who "helped to write the anti-peonage and the 'anti-grandfather clause' decisions of the Supreme Court" would mark "the beginning of the black race's redemption."[191] Hughes had indeed written the court's 1911 *Bailey v. Alabama* decision declaring Alabama's peonage laws in violation of the Thirteenth Amendment's prohibition of slavery. Hughes was also one of the concurring justices in the 1915 *Guinn v. United States* case that ruled that the grandfather clauses in the Oklahoma and Maryland state constitutions violated the Fifteenth Amendment. In 1914, however, Hughes had written the majority opinion upholding an Oklahoma separate coach car law.[192] The pro-Hughes editors of the *Champion Magazine* chose to gloss over this significant blemish in the candidate's record. Well versed in the politics of limited options, perhaps women campaigners did as well.

Two days after enfranchised citizens went to the polls on November 7, the *New York Age* ran an article under the headline, "Women Help Elect Hughes in Illinois." While Hughes carried Illinois by a wide majority, he narrowly lost the election.[193] In response to Wilson's victory, the *Champion Magazine* warned, the "race is in peril, the greatest peril it has been in since the Civil [W]ar."[194] On the next page, the editors suggested an antidote, although they did not directly put it this way. "The high priestess of achievement," the editors wrote, "is the Negro woman." "Wherever there is progress," they asserted, "there is the Negro woman."[195] In four years time, African American women would have another opportunity to rebuke Wilson with their vote. They had no way of knowing in 1916 that they would also have a great deal more help in their pursuit of race progress within national politics, more than 2.8 million additional black women who finally acquired the right to vote with the enactment of the Nineteenth Amendment.[196] Many of these women were migrants who carried to the polls their desire to use their ballot to elect a federal government that would protect the basic citizenship rights of all Americans in the South.

WHEN SOUTHERN BLACK WOMEN boarded trains for Illinois and other destinations to the north and east, they carried with them a very distinct set of memories of their experiences with white supremacy. They knew firsthand the indignities and inequalities that had befallen southern blacks under the solidly Democratic South. They had also witnessed local white Republican politicians deny southern black communities self-representation.

This firsthand knowledge affected how many migrant women used their ballot. Though ever distant from its emancipationist origins, the Republican Party benefited from this enmity for Democrats that was sown in the minds of young girls and women across the South at the end of the nineteenth century and the beginning of the twentieth. Migrant women often cast their ballots and canvassed for Republican candidates not only for themselves but also for the families and communities they had left behind in the South. They used the voting rights they had acquired to defeat Democratic candidates. They also attempted to use their ballot and organizational strength to reform the Republican Party from within.

Once in their new homes, migrant women adjusted to Chicago's ever-changing political landscape—machine politics, established associational life, and a fluid and diverse church economy. In the process, they integrated differently into Chicago's complicated labyrinth of Republican machine politics. Both Lawrence and Berry, for instance, remained within the Republican fold but worked with different Republican factions as the Second Ward alderman battles raged during the 1910s. While the results of these

[106]

various alderman contests affected the delivery of social services to the South Side in a very real way, black women's participation in these municipal elections during the 1910s was largely symbolic in relation to the South. Municipal officials did not have the power to regulate southern misbehavior. At the national level, by contrast, black women's votes did have such a potential. In 1916 partially enfranchised women in Illinois unsuccessfully attempted to elect a president who they hoped would use federal power to undermine white supremacy and, conversely, to defeat a sitting Democratic president who had used the executive office to extend Jim Crow's reach. They would try again in four years.

During the 1910s, middle-class women's belief in their responsibility to lead the race gave them the confidence that they could and should use their votes to do battle with local party bosses, as well as southern white supremacists within the arena of national politics. In the 1920s, as the next chapter examines, middle-class black women continued to rely upon this "woman's era" philosophy to guide their organizational commitment to the national Republican Party. Other women, however, used this philosophy to argue that African American women should abandon the Republican Party and its increasingly limited interest in black rights.

[3]

Profit from the Mistakes of Men
National Party Politics, 1920–1924

"I wish I had time to go into detail," Chicago clubwoman Margaret Gainer proudly announced in March 1921, "but Illinois believes it has done its part." Gainer was addressing leading black clubwomen from throughout the country who, like her, had worked on behalf of the Colored Women's Department of the Republican National Committee (CWDRNC) in the 1920 election and had traveled to Washington, D.C., in order to celebrate together the inauguration of Warren G. Harding as president. "Not only have we instructed the women in voting," Gainer told an audience which included the likes of Alice Dunbar-Nelson and Mary Church Terrell, "but, through influential effort, have helped elect and appoint men and women of our group to creditable positions." "Personally," she concluded, "I can assure you we did not miss a precinct in Cook county." The 1920 election was the first in which women across the nation held full voting rights. Just over two months before Americans headed to the polls in November 1920, the Nineteenth Amendment fully enfranchising American women became part of the U.S. Constitution. Asked to speak for five minutes about their canvassing experiences during the 1920 presidential campaign, one woman after another stood up to share success stories at the D.C. meeting. The excitement in the air was palpable, and the women had so many stories to relay that, as one reporter put it, "the five-minute limit was not sufficient, and the time-keeper's rap, rap, found each with 'just one more experience' to relate."[1] The mood at this inauguration week meeting was understandably buoyant. Decades of deliberate organizing had paid off. They had made good use of numerous local black women's Republican clubs, like those created in Chicago during the 1910s, to canvass voters in national elections. These women had also made good use of the well-established national networks of the National Association of Colored Women (NACW) to coordinate these disparate local Republican clubs. And all of this toward a success-ful conclusion: the return of Republicans to the White House and both chambers of Congress following eight years of Democratic control. This was a victory, these women believed, that would help push forward their goal of undermining white supremacy through the electoral system.

Almost as soon as women acquired full voting rights, however, fracture lines appeared in the facade of solidarity that black Republican women tenuously maintained among themselves in presidential elections. The bat-tle to enact legislation making lynching a federal crime was the source of these fracture lines. Initially, it appeared that black women's campaign efforts for the Harding-Coolidge ticket in 1920 would be rewarded with the enactment of federal antilynching legislation. This hope that the Republi-can Party would push forward such legislation was short-lived. Precisely at the moment that African American women had finally acquired full voting rights, the Republican Party was increasingly abandoning its black constitu-encies. During the 1920s, white party managers redoubled their efforts to break up the Democratic "solid South" by cultivating the support of south-ern lily-white Republicans and by avoiding policy issues that might dis-courage southern white interest in the party.[2] Between 1920 and 1924, it became clear that federal antilynching legislation was one of the casualties of the Republican Party's drive to break the "solid South." White Republi-can complicity in the defeat of antilynching legislation led politically active black women to a crossroads by the mid-1920s: Should they remain Re-publicans and battle this ongoing trend within the party to attract white southerners at the expense of loyal black constituencies? Or should they abandon the Republican Party altogether?

Black women reformers believed that they were uniquely qualified and obligated as leading women of the race to help black Americans navigate through election seasons. Upon reaching these crossroads, the vast majority of black women reformers continued along a familiar path. They urged black voters to remain loyal to the Republican Party. They also put their trust in black women's institution building and created a national black Republican women's organization. Despite the promise that the new na-tional organization held, black Republican women found themselves mov-ing from an offensive to a defensive position: their drive to elect candidates committed to creating an activist government in the realm of civil rights was quickly eclipsed by a more desperate campaign to keep white Democrats out of the federal government. By 1924, however, other women, who were no less committed to the possibilities of black women's self-help activities, came to a very different conclusion: if it was indeed middle-class women's responsibility to lead the race, then it was their duty to lead African Americans out of the Republican Party.

1920 Campaign

In the first national elections in which American women citizens were fully enfranchised, the Republican Party relied heavily upon NACW leaders to conduct campaign work among black women. This pattern was already evident during the 1916 election, when party managers turned to clubwomen to run the Colored Women's Division of the Hughes campaign. But the numbers of enfranchised black women voters had ballooned since the Hughes campaign by more than 2.8 million.[3] Moreover, according to an NAACP finding publicized to put pressure on the parties, a combination of migration and women's enfranchisement placed the black population of six northern states, including Illinois, and two border states, Kentucky and Maryland, in a position to determine which way the 165 electoral college votes controlled by these states would go.[4] How women's full enfranchisement would affect the partisan balance of power was still unclear. Whether black women's votes would help undermine the solid Democratic South and bring black male voters back into the political fold, as many African Americans hoped and white southerners feared, was also uncertain.

As the number of enfranchised black women voters grew, so did the number of prominent women the Republican National Committee (RNC) recruited to run its Colored Women's Department. The women who ran the Hughes Colored Women's Division in 1916 were all certainly well known, none more so than Wells-Barnett. In 1920 the RNC continued this practice of recruiting leading race women by asking one of the most nationally respected women in black reform circles to stump for Harding, incoming NACW president Hallie Quinn Brown. Men in the Colored Voters' Division of the RNC began recruiting Quinn Brown in the summer of 1920. Just five days before she was set to begin her presidency at the NACW's biennial convention in Tuskegee, Alabama, Philip H. Brown (no relation), the assistant director of publicity in the Colored Voters' Division, implored in a letter, "We need you." Writing with the respect owed to a woman of Quinn Brown's stature and the deference expected from the son of one of Quinn Brown's colleagues, Brown continued, "your many years of brilliant service to the race have brought you the faith and confidence of our people, and in these degenerate days of reprisal against our citizenship, no one can spread the gospel of race rights better than you."[5] With Quinn Brown's official role in the Colored Women's Department still undecided in mid-August, Philip Brown's colleague Charles Hall moved forward with the organizing efforts and asked Quinn Brown for one of the most valuable resources that she had at her disposal: a list of the clubs affiliated with the NACW, along with the names and addresses of club officers.[6]

White party managers certainly benefited a great deal by partnering with NACW leaders in 1920. In return for a minimal investment, in terms of both campaign resources and political promises, they acquired access to the NACW's well-developed networks of clubwomen throughout the nation. What did clubwomen have to gain from such a relationship? They had their own motives. NACW leaders believed that black women's voting would help clean up politics and, more important, restore black civil and political rights. While some clubwomen had begun this purifying process when they voted in select locations prior to the Nineteenth Amendment's enactment, the 1920 election offered the first opportunity for African American women to undertake this project wholesale with full voting rights. As the NACW's executive board reported at the organization's 1920 convention, "It is our ambition that the club women shall purify not merely increase, the volume of the stream of politics, and that their interest in a candidate for office will extend to the ability to hold that office worthily."[7]

The 1920 election also offered an opportunity to stave off challenges to their leadership. At the same time that black women reformers were finally positioned to carry forward their "woman's era" agenda in party politics as fully enfranchised voters, they found their claims to race leadership starting to come under siege from the masculinist politics of the New Negro movement. As Deborah Gray White argues, men of the New Negro movement directly challenged "woman's era" philosophy and "the idea that women stood at the center of the fight for equality."[8] In response to this drive to remasculinize the rhetoric of race leadership, middle-class black women continued to emphasize their own unique responsibilities to instruct men and poor African Americans within party politics.[9] The next several elections would prove whether women's full enfranchisement and efforts to integrate into the party system would in fact lead to any significant changes in civil rights policy. Partnering with white party managers was a good strategic move if they wanted to use party politics to promote black rights and demonstrate the effectiveness of their race leadership within the electoral system.

Middle-class black women focused on the exceptions to Republican in-

[111]

difference to black rights. In 1920 the key exception was a law for which women had been lobbying for decades—federal antilynching legislation. In the twenty-seven years since Wells-Barnett's 1893 Free Speech piece had led to her exile from the South, thousands of women had mobilized to end lynching through the NACW, women's church auxiliaries, and eventually the NAACP. Ignoring Wells-Barnett's demands to make antilynching a top priority for six years, the male-dominated NAACP finally began to do so in 1915. By then leadership struggles for control of the antilynching movement had resulted in Wells-Barnett's marginalization in both the NAACP and NACW.[10] Never easily deterred, Wells-Barnett continued her public protests against lynching during the 1910s through other forums. Moreover, as Patricia Schechter demonstrates, Wells-Barnett's profound intellectual contribution to the movement was evident throughout the drive for a federal antilynching bill. Although not acknowledged, Wells-Barnett's assertion that racism and not rape was the cause of lynching offered a powerful argument around which the larger antilynching movement was able to organize.[11]

Finally, in May 1920 Republican representative Leonidas Dyer of Missouri managed to shepherd an antilynching bill out of committee and onto the House floor. Dyer's Antilynching Bill invoked the equal protection clause of the Fourteenth Amendment to make mob violence a federal crime. Individuals who participated in a lynching, as well as officials who either allowed the crime to occur or failed to prosecute offenders, were subject to imprisonment and fines.[12] Much to the disappointment of antilynching advocates, Congress adjourned before taking action on it. But the synergy created by an active antilynching movement, expanded black constituencies in the North, and responsive representatives from those districts made sure that the momentum for such a bill continued into the presidential election season. Meeting in Chicago for the Republican National Convention in mid-June, delegates drafted a platform that called upon "Congress to consider the most effective means to end lynching in this country."[13] It was the third time that the Republican Party had explicitly mentioned lynching in its national platform. In 1896 and then in 1912, the party had included platforms condemning mob violence. The 1920 plank was the first to recommend some kind of federal involvement in solving the problem. In his nomination acceptance speech Harding reiterated this emphasis on federal intervention and further asserted that "the Federal Government should stamp out lynching and remove that stain from the fair name of America." Still, the plank's wording was ambiguous. Rather than demand federal antilynching legislation or mention the Dyer Bill by name, the party obliquely left it up to Congress to "consider the most effective means" to stop mob violence.[14] White party managers were trying to have it both ways. They promised as little as they thought necessary to maintain black support without antagonizing the southern white voters whom they sought to attract and who considered mob violence a local matter outside the purview of federal jurisdiction.

Middle-class black women worked with both the possibilities and the limitations of this plank. From the independent space of the NACW, they rebuked the party for not going far enough by withholding the organization's official endorsement of the Republican Party in 1920. Meeting in Alabama in mid-July for their biennial convention, delegates listened to outgoing NACW president Mary Talbert read a telegram from Warren Harding in which he extended "best wishes for a successful and interesting convention."[15] The Nineteenth Amendment's ratification was still pending in mid-July. Should the Tennessee state legislature ratify the amendment at a specially convened session the following month (which it did), the addition of tens of thousands of motivated black women voters might tip the balance of power in close elections.[16] White party managers included the NACW among Harding's regular round of greetings with this possibility in mind. As perfunctory as the telegram was, some delegates responded with a motion to endorse the Republican Party. Others rejected any official endorsement— not because of the NACW's nonpartisan policy, which members had ignored in the past but because, as they explained through a play on words, the Republican Party's antilynching position constituted a "splinter" and not a full plank. Those who opposed endorsement won the day, and the motion was voted down. In the end, the convention sent a telegram to Harding thanking him for his note and passed a pointed resolution protesting mob violence. In clearly stated terms, the 700 women who were meeting on the grounds of the Tuskegee Institute resolved, "we pray for an enactment of a Federal statute against lynch law, with severe penalties for the violation thereof, and that such statute be enforced, if need be, by military power of the government."[17]

This NACW debate exposed the first visible cracks in the facade of solidarity that black clubwomen maintained among themselves in presidential elections. It also demonstrated the controversy that ensued when members attempted to use NACW forums for explicitly partisan purposes. At this stage, black clubwomen's discontent with the Republican Party's antilynching plank did not take a partisan form. In other words, delegates who opposed endorsement did not in turn switch to the Democratic Party. Quite the contrary, on the campaign trail, they presented a unified front that emphasized the possibilities rather than the limitations of the Republican Party's antilynching plank. Yet, the fracture lines of antilynching politics were in place, and they would grow. Within two years, some middle-class women would begin to manifest their frustration over the lack of progress on the Dyer Bill in a partisan way: they would begin to defect to the Democrats. The very issue that had caused conflict within the NACW served as a point of cohesion on the campaign trail. As one woman explained, African American women "felt that the Republican platform of 1920 had in it something a little less than a splinter concerning Lynching, but, they had hopes."[18] It was on these "hopes" that African American women focused when they decided to work on behalf of the Harding-Coolidge ticket.

NACW leaders worked vigorously for Republican victory in 1920 under the auspices of the Colored Women's Department of the RNC. Hallie Quinn Brown ultimately accepted a position on the National Speakers Bureau and made no less than fifty-two speeches (forty-two in her home state of Ohio and ten additional ones in other parts of the country).[19] Ohio clubwoman Lethia Fleming headed the Colored Women's Department from RNC offices in Chicago's Auditorium Hotel. Under Fleming's direction, the Colored Women's Department was divided into several levels of organization. Mary Church Terrell, the NACW's first president, directed canvassing work in the eastern states, and Victoria Clay Haley, who had held NACW executive positions during the 1910s, did the same in the western states. Each state in turn had a state leader who then reported to either Terrell or Fleming. In Illinois, this leader was Elizabeth Lindsay Davis.[20] The enormous energy clubwomen put into canvassing for the Harding-Coolidge ticket was evident in the whirlwind activities of Mary Burrell, a leader in the New Jersey Federation of Colored Women's Clubs. Within two months, Burrell helped initiate well over forty Republican meetings and personally gave upward of thirty campaign speeches all over Essex County, New Jersey.[21] The dedication with which they approached this work was especially evident among southern women who faced overt threats as a result of their canvassing activities. In Florida, for instance, Eartha White encountered white women who told her that she "must cease [her] political activities or 'else.'" As White recalled in the months after the election, she "decided to 'else'" and kept right on canvassing Florida's black residents to vote for Republican candidates in November.[22]

Despite the enormous effort that black clubwomen were making on behalf of the national Republican ticket, the RNC demonstrated its tenuous commitment to them when, as Chicago clubwoman Joanna Snowden Porter put it, "our women leaders were unable to use the splendid array of workers who were willing to help swell the landslide of votes . . . because of the fact that funds were not obtainable to pay expenses." Serving on the National Speakers Bureau with Quinn Brown, Snowden Porter was personally aware of the expenses involved in stumping for the Harding-Coolidge ticket and the acute "embarrassment entailed upon the women's department" by this lack of funds. Black Republican clubwomen were able to avert this "crisis" when they "helped raise the funds to carry on the fight for the restoration of the 'peoples' rule.' "[23] In Chicago, for example, Snowden Porter's colleague Bertha Montgomery, who was president of the Permanent Cook County Women's Republican Club, raised at least $1,000 during the campaign season for this purpose.[24] Although Snowden Porter, who was also president of the Northwestern Federation of Colored Women's Clubs, put a positive spin on the financial crisis and subsequent fundraising efforts as an "educational asset" for future organizing, the lack of funds also indicated how limited the RNC's commitment was to mobilizing black women. Regardless of her positive spin, Snowden Porter understood that the struggle to enter and substantially influence white-dominated institutions had never been easy. Cracking the elite power structures of the RNC would certainly be no different. For the time being, they used their newly acquired voting rights and organizational skills to push against this limited commitment and try to expand it. Within a few years, however, they would respond to such Republican snubs quite differently.

As fully enfranchised black women prepared to vote in November, many for the first time, southern white Democrats also prepared for black women's arrival at the polls. In the weeks just prior to the election, readers of Chicago's militant black newspaper the *Whip* learned about the Democratic Party's campaign encouraging southern white women to outvote black women. As the *Whip* explained, "It is feared in all quarters that the colored vote will be so heavy as to break the 'solid ivory South' if white women do not rally in support of the democratic ticket."[25] Such reports would have only intensified the already deep-seated antipathy of many black voters against the Democratic Party and the sense that the Republican Party was the only option. This assertion that women's enfranchisement would lead to "negro domination" had long been the rallying cry of white southerners who opposed woman's suffrage. One Virginia newspaper's claims in

1915 that "twenty-nine counties of Virginia would be condemned by woman suffrage to colored rule and five others would be in serious peril of it with woman suffrage" was typical of this antisuffrage position.[26]

The worry (from the view of white supremacists) or the hope (from the perspective of black suffragists) was not only that the Nineteenth Amendment would enable black women to outvote white women but also that it would reopen national discussions about black men's voting rights. As Congress prepared to vote on what would become the Nineteenth Amendment in 1919, Democratic senator Ellison D. Smith of South Carolina directly addressed this possibility: "I warn every man here today that when the test comes, as it will come, when the clamor for negro rights shall have come, that you Senators from the South voting for [woman's suffrage] have started it here this day." Smith asked rhetorically, "If it was a crime to enfranchise the male half of this race, why is it not a crime to enfranchise the other half?"[27] Upon witnessing a group of black women prepare for a political meeting once the Nineteenth Amendment was enacted, white Democrats in Tennessee concluded that "their efforts to save the South from Negro domination were foiled by the ratification of the amendment."[28]

Numerous reports in the black press indicate that black women's canvassing paid off. African American women registered and then voted in significant numbers in 1920, albeit not always successfully. The *New York Age* described a "large number of colored women qualifying themselves for exercise of the franchise" in Harlem, Brooklyn, and the Bronx, as well as in New Jersey. As the *Age* reporter editorialized, "the women, especially the colored women, are determined to do all in their power to rid the country of the evils wrought by Wilsonism and the Democratic party."[29] Of course, it was black women's votes in the South and the possibility that they might help reintroduce a two-party system there that most concerned southern white Democrats like Senator Smith. As in the North, southern black women made every effort to register and vote, even though they met with heavy resistance. In parts of Alabama, for example, reports emerged of election officials who demanded that individual women be accompanied by two white male supporters (or a single romantic partner) in order to register. "In spite of these unlawful barriers," the *Chicago Defender* told its national audience, "hundreds of women are storming the court house clamoring to register, regardless of Democratic interference."[30] When women in various cities in Georgia were denied the opportunity to register, Savannah native Mary Williams, an RNC organizer who was also a leader in the Georgia State Federation of Colored Women's Clubs, told them that " 'they were entitled to vote, and should storm the polls on election day.' " In the aftermath of the election, Williams described to fellow campaigners women's persistence in the face of white male intimidation: " 'They did as they were told, and although thousands qualified, they were turned away.' "[31] Harding defeated his Democratic candidate by a large margin, and Republicans retained control of both houses of Congress.[32]

Hope and Disappointment between 1920 and 1922

With the battle behind them and Republicans back in office after eight years of Democratic control, black clubwomen began to plan for the future. Meeting in Washington, D.C., in early March 1921 for Harding's inauguration, black women from across the country who had canvassed for Harding shared war stories and congratulated one another for their hard work. In the midst of these celebrations, leaders of the RNC's Colored Women's Department retreated to John Wesley AME Church to map out their next steps. Also there to participate in the deliberations were prominent black Republican leaders Henry Lincoln Johnson, Charles A. Cottrill, and Robert R. Church Jr. The meeting concluded with the proposal to establish a women's director position as part of the permanent staff housed at the Negro Republican Headquarters on Pennsylvania Avenue in Washington, D.C. Meeting participants also planned a fundraising campaign to generate $15,000, $5,000 to cover the salary of the black women's director and $10,000 to apply toward "legislative relief" for black Americans.[33] In a 1921 bulletin, Mary Williams and Rebecca Stiles Taylor (like Williams, Taylor was a leading Georgia clubwoman who had worked for the CWDRNC in 1920) explained this decision to place the women's directorship at Negro Republican Headquarters in terms that emphasized cooperation across gender lines: "There is but one Republican Party of which Negro men have always been a part and to divide the Negro's strength, now that women have been given the ballot is but to weaken the Negro vote and cause more dissention within the race—Solidarity is the word."[34] Placing the women's directorship in what was for all practical purposes the RNC's black "men's division" may have been a sign of solidarity, but it was also a means of keeping women's organizing potential under the purview of male party managers.

African American women, however, also attempted to establish an independent national Republican organization. Around 1919 Monen L. Gray founded the Negro Women's Republican League (NWRL).[35] Gray was a South Carolina native who had worked variously as a seamstress and a

[117]

teacher and who had migrated with her husband and young son to the District of Columbia from Georgia sometime between 1910 and 1920.[36] During the 1920 presidential campaign, the NWRL worked closely with the RNC. Afterward, Gray turned to solidify the NWRL's infrastructure and expand its reach by pushing for a midwestern headquarters in Indiana to function alongside the already operational D.C. headquarters and by calling for a national conference to be held in Denver.[37] Gray appears to have met with some success: a piece of NWRL letterhead from January 1921 listed the names of more than eighty of the most prominent clubwomen from around the country.[38] Nevertheless, the NWRL seems to have been short-lived; all mention of the group drops off in the archives after 1921. In four years, many of the same women who affiliated with the NWRL would try again and succeed in creating a permanent Republican women's organization that was both national in scope and independent from the RNC.

In the aftermath of the 1920 campaign, African American women also turned their sights toward policy. Just five days after the polls closed, Wells-Barnett made it clear at a meeting of the newly formed Metropolitan Center Lyceum in Chicago that African American women expected the Republican Party to fulfill its campaign promise to address mob violence. After pointing out that the presidential elections had been marred by lynchings in Florida and the disfranchisement of black women in various parts of the South, Wells-Barnett "call[ed] upon the Republican Congress which we have helped to put in power . . . to immediately take steps to make lynching a Federal crime." While making this demand, Wells-Barnett specifically turned to Congressman Martin B. Madden, who had just finished addressing the audience and whom black voters in Chicago had reelected for two more years in the House. Wells-Barnett also exhorted Congress to take immediate action to end segregation in the federal government and to reduce congressional representation from those states that disfranchised residents. The second section of the Fourteenth Amendment provided for the reduction of representation in the House in the case of disfranchisement, but Congress had never used this provision to remedy black disfranchisement in the South. Wells-Barnett concluded with a resolution urging "our people in every section of this country to make similar demands of the men that we helped to elect to this Republican Congress" and pledging "to organize our forces to work for the political freedom of our brothers and sisters in the south."[39]

Echoes of Wells-Barnett's demands for policy change could be heard at Republican women's celebratory meetings in Washington, D.C., in March

1921 (though Wells-Barnett herself was not present). Maggie Lena Walker, who headed the important financial institution, the Independent Order of Saint Luke, and who in 1920 had served as an RNC organizer in Virginia, insisted, "Now that black men and women have stood solidly by the Republican Party, we must demand representation."[40]

As the battle for a federal antilynching bill heated up again during the next two years, African American women pressured Republican politicians whom they helped put in office to uphold campaign promises. In August 1922, for example, the NACW sent a delegation representing "14 pivotal" states in the upcoming midterm election to meet with President Harding and Republican senator Samuel Shortridge (see figure 10). This meeting took place at a decisive moment in the battle for federal antilynching legislation: the House had finally passed Dyer's Antilynching Bill in January 1922, and within a few weeks Senator Shortridge would introduce the bill into the Senate. Wells-Barnett represented Illinois in this NACW delegation. Illinois was critical in the 1922 elections because of the large number of representatives who had voted in favor of the Dyer Bill earlier that year and who were up for reelection. All six of the representatives from Chicago (one Democrat and five Republicans), including Madden, who had cast a ballot in support of the Dyer Bill in January were up for reelection.[41] Furthermore, both of Illinois's sitting senators, Medill McCormick and William Brown McKinley, had been elected with black support in 1918 and 1920 respectively.[42] With midterm elections fast approaching, and the bill potentially weeks away from a Senate debate, the NACW delegation asked for Harding's and Shortridge's assistance in pushing the Dyer Antilynching Bill through the Senate. Speaking for the group, Hallie Quinn Brown explained to the president and senator, "We urge it as women because in the last 35 years 83 women have been lynched." Antilynching activists had made this point before, but during 1922 they emphasized even more forcefully that mob violence was a woman's issue because women were lynched. Employing Wells-Barnett's strategy of turning the discourse of civilization on its head, Quinn Brown insisted that the 1,472 lynchings that had taken place over the past thirty-five years "shame our country before the civilized world." In case none of these arguments were convincing enough, Quinn Brown reminded both men of their and their party's promises: the Republican Party's 1920 antilynching plank and Harding's April 1921 instruction to Congress "to wipe the stain of barbaric lynching from the banner of a free and orderly representative democracy." The "Republican party now in power," Quinn Brown insisted, "can carry out these pledges."[43]

FIGURE 10. *Antilynching delegation to President Harding, August 14, 1922. The caption to this photograph identifies the women as (first row, left to right) Mrs. Ida Brown, New Jersey; Miss Mary B. Jackson, Rhode Island; Mrs. Ida W. Barnett, Illinois; Mrs. Mary Parrish, Kentucky; Miss Hallie Q. Brown, Ohio; Mrs. Minnie Scott, Ohio; Mrs. Cora Horne, New York; Mrs. Estelle Davis, Ohio; Mrs. E. G. Rose, Delaware; (second row) Mrs. Lethia Fleming, Ohio; Mrs. Ida Postles, Michigan; Mrs. Peal Winters, California; Mrs. Myrtle F. Cook, Missouri; Mrs. C. Chiles, Kansas; Mrs. Ruth Bennett, Pennsylvania.* Crisis, 24, no. 6 (October 1922): 260. Widener Library, Harvard College Library, US10700.18.5 (23–24).

Black clubwomen also embarked on an aggressive campaign of fundraising and publicity. Leading the charge was former NACW president Mary Talbert and her Anti-Lynching Crusaders, the temporary women's organization that Talbert had helped to establish in the summer of 1922 for the sole purpose of assisting the NAACP's Dyer Bill lobbying effort.[44] The Anti-Lynching Crusaders did not claim a partisan affiliation and welcomed congressional support regardless of party status. Still, the Anti-Lynching Crusaders was noticeably peopled by women, including Talbert, who had worked hard for the Republican Party in 1920 and who justifiably expected Republican support for the bill in return.[45] During 1922, the Anti-Lynching Crusaders sought, as the group's slogan stated, "A Million Women United to Stop Lynching" and aimed to raise a million dollars. Though they did not meet these very ambitious goals, the group provided invaluable financial assistance to the NAACP's Dyer Bill campaign. The more than 700 members and dozens of local Crusader groups across the country also brought the horrors of lynching to the consciousness of quite possibly millions of Americans, white and black. In Illinois, Tennessee native Annie Laurie Anderson, who was also president of the Illinois Federation of Colored Women's Clubs, served as the state organizer.[46]

For the Anti-Lynching Crusaders, converting Americans to the Dyer Bill cause was very much a form of proselytizing, with all its religious implications. Their self-identification as crusaders and references to their drive as the "Ninth Crusade" conjured images of the medieval Christian offensives to drive "infidels" from the Holy Land.[47] In printed prayers that the group sent out by the thousands, the analogy was hard to avoid. Their twentieth-century crusade was intent on reclaiming the American Holy Land, or, as they put it, the nation that God had set apart "to be an example unto all people of the blessings of liberty and law" from the "abyss of moral anarchy and social ruin" toward which lawless mob violence was steering it. In this widely distributed prayer, the women invoked their faith to inspire support for the bill, as well as to indict those who opposed it as un-Christian: "We pray Thee to enlighten the understanding and nerve the hearts of our lawmakers with the political wisdom and moral courage to pass the Dyer Bill" and to "[h]ave mercy upon any of our legislators who may be so embittered with the gall of race hatred and fettered by the bonds of political iniquity as to advocate or apologize for lynching, rapine and murder."[48]

In addition to such flyers, leaders published hundreds of press releases publicizing lynching figures—3,436 between 1899 and 1922, 83 of whom were women—and disputing the common claim that rape was the primary cause of lynching. The most celebrated of these was "The Shame of America," a full-page advertisement that ran in the *New York Times* in November 1922 under the auspices of the NAACP and with Anti-Lynching Crusader funds. "In one day's advertising," the *Crisis* enthused, "at least five million men and women read the facts and thousands of them read them for the first time." Along with the NAACP, the Anti-Lynching Crusaders urged Americans "to pour in upon the Senate a stream of requests for immediate action."[49]

Despite this groundswell of activism, congressional Republicans, who held the majority in both houses, yielded to the Democratic minority in December 1922 and withdrew the bill under the cloud of a filibuster that threatened to end all remaining Senate business. Though Harding had spoken in favor of federal antilynching legislation in the past, he ignored the NAACP's and NACW's pleas for help. Instead, he remained silent at several critical moments during 1922 when a positive word from him might have saved the bill.[50] Candidates and politicians had certainly disappointed before. The defeat of the Dyer Bill in 1922, however, was especially frustrating precisely because it would have been the first major piece of civil rights legislation enacted after the Nineteenth Amendment. African American women had long claimed that their enfranchisement and participation in party politics would be beneficial to the race. The addition of millions of black women to the voting roster, and black Republican women's personal efforts to get as many of these women to the polls as possible, did not lead to a dramatic change in the federal government's commitment to protect black bodies and rights.

With this very disappointing conclusion to a promising and hard-fought effort to enact a federal antilynching bill, black women reformers who had campaigned for Harding in 1920 and who had lobbied their congressmen over the next two years found themselves at a crossroads. How should they respond to the Republican Party's abandonment of the Dyer Bill, both Harding's blatant betrayal and congressional Republicans' decision to withdraw the bill when Democrats embarked on a filibuster? African American women's divergent answers to this question created cracks in the unified front that the shared battle against lynching helped maintain in national politics. The fracturing of this unity became evident during the 1924 presidential election. The majority of politically active women continued to work with the Republican Party. A vocal minority, however, urged black voters to support a Democratic presidential candidate.

1924 Campaign

At the 1920 inaugural celebrations, Mary Talbert had urged black women to "learn to play the game as it should be played and profit from the mistakes of the men."[51] Perhaps they could play the game better in 1924 and learn not only from men's mistakes, but also from their own. One of the key lessons they learned, it seems, was that they had not fully tapped into the canvassing energy and resources of middle-class black women from throughout the country. One group of African American women responded to disappointment by digging in and increasing its institutional base for conducting Republican work.

Over three days in early August 1924, middle-class clubwomen excused themselves from the NACW's fourteenth biennial convention that was taking place in Chicago to attend a series of meetings held at Wendell Phillips High School, Bethel AME Church, and Bethesda Baptist Church. They did so in response to a call they had received from two southern colleagues, Mary (Miller) Williams of Georgia and Mary (Montgomery) Booze of Mississippi, to come together for the express purpose of organizing a national black Republican women's organization. In 1924 both Williams and Booze were Republican National Committeewomen who had attended the Republican National Convention in Cleveland two months prior. Since working as an RNC organizer in the 1920 campaign, Williams, the daughter of a Georgia minister and the widow of a local educator, had gone on to serve as president of the Georgia State Federation of Colored Women's Clubs. Mary Booze was the daughter of Isaiah Montgomery, the founder of the all-black town of Mound Bayou and notoriously the only black member of the 1890 Mississippi constitutional convention. Booze had spent her adult life helping to develop the town that her father had established.[52] Not surprisingly, Illinois clubwomen, eleven in total, were especially well represented at the meetings.[53]

The organization that emerged from these meetings was the National League of Republican Colored Women (NLRCW).[54] It was the second attempt to form an independent national black Republican women's organization, but it was the first one to function effectively for several years. Founding members established the machinery to ensure the NLRCW's survival beyond Chicago: a schedule of yearly meetings, six committees charged with a range of duties from fundraising to publicity, and a nationally based group of prestigious officers. Monen Gray's Negro Women's National Republican

League had also begun to take such steps during the winter of 1920 and 1921. Unlike the NLRCW, however, Gray's group did not have the vibrant Nannie Helen Burroughs at its helm. Burroughs's election as president was among the key factors that enabled the NLRCW to thrive where Gray's organization had failed. The forty-five-year-old mainstay of Washington's elite black community offered the NLRCW a wealth of resources.[55] Burroughs brought years of organizational experience in Republican, Baptist, and civil rights organizations and the vast networks that came with such institution building.[56]

The women who established the NLRCW had several motivations in doing so. At the foundational meeting, Blanche Beatty, a Floridian who had served as an RNC speaker in 1920, explained the importance of removing Republican activities from NACW forums: "in as much as, [t]he National Association was a non-political body—an organization of this kind was a necessity."[57] The occasional use of the NACW for Republican work had proceeded without too much controversy during the first two decades of its existence. The controversy surrounding the antilynching plank in 1920, however, had demonstrated the limits of using the NACW for explicitly partisan work. This was an issue that members would revisit several times in the coming years. The formation of the NLRCW was part of this ongoing discussion of the role of partisan politics in the NACW.[58] NACW leaders did not strictly demand that members stop using the organization's venues, especially *National Notes*, for Republican politics until 1926, when the ranks of black Democratic women were growing.[59] Ironically, the push for the elimination of explicitly Republican activities from NACW venues during 1925 and 1926 did not originate with Democratic members. Rather Republican members concerned that affiliating too closely with any party, even their own, might undermine the NACW's independence finally demanded the suppression of partisan activities in the organization.[60]

In setting up the NLRCW, women reformers created an independent institutional base from which African American women could carry forward their political agendas. This base had already begun to emerge at the local level in the plethora of black women's Republican clubs that operated in cities, counties, and states across the nation. As one woman asserted, however, these local clubs were not linked in such a way that their collective power could be fully realized in federal elections: "We have long needed an organization of this kind as in union there is strength and the various organizations, local in their scope and influence has given our women but a very small place in National Political life."[61] Neither the NACW nor the Colored Women's Department of the RNC fulfilled this role. The NACW did not devote

all of its resources toward Republican canvassing, and the CWDRNC was ultimately under the direction of white party managers. The NLRCW filled in the
organizational gap that had been left open by these other groups.

Three weeks after the NLRCW's establishment, New Yorker Elizabeth Ross
Haynes sent a letter to Burroughs congratulating her on the new organization and offering advice about canvassing strategies for the upcoming elec-
tion. Harding had died while in office in 1923 and was succeeded by Vice
President Calvin Coolidge. With big business prospering after an economic
downturn, Coolidge easily won the Republican Party nomination in 1924.
He shared the ticket with Charles Dawes, an Illinois banker and former
director of the budget. Coolidge and Dawes found themselves up against a
Democratic ticket consisting of compromise candidate John Davis of West
Virginia and his running mate Charles Bryan, the governor of Nebraska
and the brother of former Democratic and Populist presidential candidate
William Jennings Bryan. The two major parties also faced the strongest
third party ticket in some number of years, the Progressive Party, which
placed renegade Republican reformer Robert La Follette at its head and
Burton Wheeler, a Democratic senator from Montana, in the second position.[62] With such a crowded field, and especially the presence of a reform
ticket, Haynes insisted that "our key women must have at their finger tips
just what the Republican Party has to offer the negro as over against the
other two parties. There are some real values in the party platform even as
doubtful about them as we may wish to feel. Such a comparison sent to
leaders would not be amiss."[63]

What did the Republican Party and its presidential candidate have to offer
black Americans in 1924, and particularly black women? What "real values"
might black Republican women point to when canvassing on behalf of the
Coolidge-Dawes ticket? The list was short indeed: a national platform supporting the establishment of an interracial commission that would address
racial tensions surrounding black migration, the passage of protective labor
legislation for children, and the enactment of federal antilynching legislation.[64] African American women's campaign rhetoric was often indistin-
guishable from men's. Referring to Coolidge's statement that black Americans were entitled "to the protection of the Constitution and law," two
leading D.C. women activists, for example, praised his "expressions of fair-
ness to all men regardless of race or creed."[65] Stumping across Oklahoma
and her home state of Missouri, Anna Roberts pointed to the interracial
commission proposal as part of her "message of hope" to black women
voters. By her account, she found audiences receptive, perhaps none more so

than those who had been directly affected by the 1921 Tulsa race riot, one of the nation's bloodiest. As Roberts predicted in the pages of *National Notes*, "There is now a real battle ground for real racial development." "The time is ripe now," she concluded, "for emphasis on the right kind of legislation represented by the rank and file of our colored citizenship."[66]

Black Republican women, however, also crafted their appeals to women voters through the gendered ideology of racial uplift. Even as black women reformers battled racism through public forums, most also believed that the greatest opportunities for women to conduct racial uplift work could be found in the home. Mothers, they asserted, must create the proper home environment for nurturing their children, and as Anna Roberts told her audiences, women could "help themselves and their homes by the use of the ballot."[67] In Chicago, Lillian Browder explained that she "found it easy to interest our women if they were told of the things in governmental affairs that are vital to home-life; upper-most in her mind is a good home with proper environments for the rearing of her children." Black women campaigners like Browder insisted that the enactment of protective labor legislation would safeguard black family life. Browder, for instance, identified state laws "regulating working hours for our women" as among the "governmental affairs" instrumental in creating such good home environments for child rearing.[68] This advocacy of laws regulating women's working conditions helps to explain why the pages of *National Notes* were notably silent about the equal rights amendment that many white women reformers endorsed during the 1920s.[69] First introduced into Congress in 1923, it had the potential to make unconstitutional the gender-based protective labor laws like those that Browder favored.

Black clubwomen were far more vocal, however, about protective labor legislation affecting children, and during the 1924 campaign season the NLRCW identified the proposed child labor amendment as a key canvassing issue for black women.[70] The amendment's authors did not necessarily prepare this bill, which empowered the federal government to regulate the labor of children under eighteen, in order to protect black Americans. Black women reformers, however, saw it as an opportunity to focus attention on forced labor in the South. The amendment could be employed, for instance, to prevent white planters from closing black schools as they regularly did across the South during picking season.[71] Inadvertently, the child labor amendment also reinforced a particular type of family life that black women reformers favored, one in which children were under the constant care of mothers. In this sense, the amendment complemented the mother's education programs that the black women's club movement created to instill middle-class standards among poor women. Support for the amendment, however, did not distinguish the Republican Party from its competitors. Both the Progressive and Democratic parties also included planks favoring initiatives to protect children in the wage labor force, although the Democrats emphasized states' rights in the application of such measures.[72]

The 1924 campaign witnessed significant black support for both the Progressive and Democratic party candidates. Republican women's decision not to join the approximately 500,000 African Americans who ultimately cast their ballot for the Progressive ticket was a missed opportunity to support one of the first presidential candidates in a long while whose views shadowed closely the distinct Republican constitutionalism they championed.[73] Progressive Party presidential candidate Robert La Follette had by far the strongest record on race among the three candidates. As his biographer explains, "La Follette shared with his outspoken wife an unshaken belief that the racism of whites was the root cause of the nation's racial inequality and was especially abhorrent because it blocked access to the opportunities that should be open to all Americans."[74] He had consistently demonstrated his commitment to using federal power to battle racial injustice over the course of his nearly thirty-five years in Congress, from his support of the Lodge Federal Elections Bill as a young representative in 1890 to his public endorsement of the Dyer Antilynching Bill as a seasoned senator in 1924.[75] La Follette's support for legislation that would benefit laborers led W. E. B. Du Bois to call the Progressive Party platform "one of the best programs ever laid down by a political party in America." Chicago orator Roscoe Conklin Simmons characterized La Follette as "the hope of the Negro race."[76]

Black women's opposition to La Follette appears to have been driven by a classic issue surrounding third-party candidacies. Black Republicans, women and men alike, feared that a split in the traditional Republican base would help carry the Democrats to an easy victory.[77] Seeking to poke holes in La Follette's strong record, black Republican women pointed to the Progressive Party's proposed constitutional amendment that would give Congress the power to reenact legislation that the Supreme Court had deemed unconstitutional as a key reason to reject La Follette.[78] Referring to this controversial plank in the pages of *National Notes*, Chicago clubwoman Joanna Snowden Porter characterized black Progressives whom she encountered during her speaking tour across Missouri as "unmindful of the utter confusion which would follow upon the heels of such subscribing to the undermining of the constitution and a chaotic state of American laws, as has never been seen in history."[79] This familiar constitutionally based rhetoric was mirrored in the campaign slogan that black Republican women emphasized as they canvassed towns across Minnesota, a state with a significant La Follette following: "Vote, Elect Coolidge and Dawes, Save the Constitution."[80] La Follette had pushed the controversial plank in order to overturn antilabor decisions.[81] If successful, the proposed amendment could also presumably be used to counter anti–civil rights decisions. Black Republican women did not see it this way. Instead, they viewed the profound change in the notion of the balance of power that the amendment would have caused as a potentially dangerous tool in the hands of southern congressmen. As NAACP attorney James Cobb insisted, "Where would be the end of the vicious legislation affecting our group at the hands of a hostile congress, dominated by southern influence?"[82]

Publicly, black Republican women attempted to poke holes in La Follette's record. Privately among themselves, however, black Republican women were clearly looking beyond the two major parties for inspiration. Characterizing the Progressive Party as "too young and weak to do us any good" in a letter to Burroughs, Detroit activist Lillian Johnson recommended to her colleague that rather than dismiss the Progressive Party altogether, "We should watch and study it." "Who knows," Johnson concluded, "it may be the champion of our cause, since the Republican ranks is being so largely invaded by the Ku Klux Klan element, ostensively to fight Catholism [sic]."[83] Johnson's comment was rife with ambiguities. She was clearly looking for options outside of the Republican Party, but her criticism of white Republican racism was muted. The lily-white element invading the Republican Party in the 1920s was as much, if not more, antiblack as it was anti-Catholic. With so few options, Johnson preferred to focus on white Republicans' anti-Catholic biases rather than fully confront how antiblack lily-whitism might affect her own support for the Republican Party.

An even greater concern among black Republican women was the defection of black women to the Democratic Party itself. The expectation that Republican control of Washington would result in federal antilynching legislation had once kept many black women in the Republican Party. The Republican Party's failure to enact antilynching legislation since regaining control of Washington in 1920 now pushed African American women out of the party. Among the most vocal of these women was Alice Dunbar-Nelson. Born Alice Ruth Moore in New Orleans just two years before the end of Reconstruction, Dunbar-Nelson relocated from her city of birth to Brooklyn in the 1890s and lived in Washington, D.C., with her first husband, renowned poet Paul Laurence Dunbar, before making her home in Delaware around 1902. While her celebrity never matched that of her first husband, Dunbar-Nelson wrote extensively and was an important literary figure in her own right.[84] She expressed her race pride and independent spirit not only in her writing but also in her political activism. In 1920, she was the first African American woman to serve on Delaware's State Republican Committee.[85]

Like other black Republican women activists, Dunbar-Nelson hoped that black women's extensive canvassing efforts for the GOP in 1920 would result in federal antilynching legislation. Although the House passed the Dyer Bill in January 1922, Dunbar-Nelson was deeply disappointed by Republican representatives who voted against the bill, and she did something about it ten months later in the congressional midterm elections. Cooperating closely with NAACP leader James Weldon Johnson, Dunbar-Nelson was "untiring and courageous," as the *Whip* put it, in her efforts to prevent the reelection of Delaware's Republican representative Caleb Layton.[86] Layton was among four Republican congressmen whom the NAACP helped defeat in November 1922 in retaliation for voting against the Dyer Bill.[87] One month after the midterm elections, Republicans withdrew the Dyer Bill from the Senate in the face of a Democratic filibuster. With the midterm elections over, Dunbar-Nelson set her sights on the 1924 election.

Along the way to the 1924 election season, Dunbar-Nelson encountered more disappointment over the Republican Party's handling of antilynching legislation. In his first message to Congress in December 1923, Coolidge had urged the body of legislators to "exercise all its powers of prevention and punishment against the hideous crime of lynching." When it did so two weeks later by reintroducing the Dyer Bill, Coolidge remained silent, ensuring that the bill never made it out of committee and onto the House floor.[88] The Republican Party's 1924 platform was the first Republican platform to specifically call for a federal antilynching bill. The possibility embedded in the platform was severely muted by Coolidge's inaction with regard to the Dyer Bill. In the final weeks of the campaign, Dyer himself came out with a statement that was published in the black press asserting that Coolidge did in fact favor federal antilynching legislation.[89] As respected as Dyer was among black Americans, many were not reassured. Any fleeting sense of confidence was further shattered by the fact that Coolidge was the only presidential candidate who refused to denounce the Klan.[90]

By 1924 Dunbar-Nelson's conversion to the Democratic Party was complete. She served as director of Colored Women at Democratic Party headquarters in New York, the site of the nation's largest community of black Democrats, as well as the political and literary rumblings of what became known variously as the New Negro movement and the Harlem Renaissance.[91] As the director of Colored Women for the Democratic Party, Dunbar-Nelson had to convince black women to break with the party that with few exceptions had garnered the loyalty of black voters for more than half a century. She relied upon the Republican Party's abandonment of the Dyer Bill to make her case.

In a dramatic campaign speech that ran about thirty or forty minutes entitled, "Why I Am a Democrat in 1924," Dunbar-Nelson recalled black women's extensive campaign efforts for the Republican Party in 1920 and then profound disappointment when the men they had helped to put in office permitted the Dyer Antilynching Bill to die in the Senate in 1922: "The women of the race gave to the party in 1920 a tremendous vote of confidence. It was the first opportunity that we had had to express nationally our opinion as to the man who would control the destiny of the race in the White House." In return, Dunbar-Nelson explained, "The women of the race asked one thing." Listing the usual gains expected at the end of a successful campaign, Dunbar-Nelson insisted that black women "did not want office," nor did they "want to sit in the councils of the mighty." One can imagine her pausing at this point in order to emphasize the singularity of black women's demand in 1920: "They only asked that the Dyer Anti-Lynching bill be placed on the Statute Books of the nation." But, as she dramatically reminded her audiences, "The Republican Party killed the Dyer Anti-Lynching Bill after great beating of tom-toms." Here, Dunbar-Nelson shifted blame for the Dyer Bill's defeat from the Democrats to the Republicans and rightly blasted the Republicans for hiding behind the Democrats to cover their own duplicity and inaction. "Cynically," she told her audiences, the Republicans "connived at the historic filibuster, and as usual, passed the buck to their enemies, the Democrats." Had white Republicans wanted to see the bill through in 1922, Dunbar-Nelson insisted, they had more than enough resources and influence at their disposal to do so: majorities in both houses of Congress, a vice president (Coolidge) who presided over the Senate where the filibuster took place, and a president (Harding) who held the "the power of patronage at his back and public sentiment behind him" and who "could have whipped the Senate into line but failed to do so."[92]

Dunbar-Nelson directly challenged her colleagues' association of black women's unique leadership responsibilities with the Republican Party. According to Dunbar-Nelson, women were wasting their time trying to keep men within the Republican fold; rather their efforts should be directed at helping men leave it. "It was to be expected that the men of the race would be loyal to the party which they felt had given them the rights of manhood," she conceded, but "there is such a thing as carrying loyalty too far." It was time now for women to recognize, as she put it, that "[t]he Republican Party is cowardly," and "[n]o woman loves a coward." In scathing language that revealed just how deep her sense of betrayal ran, Dunbar-Nelson denounced the "slime" of white Republicans' "craven hypocrisy," pointing not only to the party's abandonment of the Dyer Bill but also to its unwillingness to promote black women in civil service jobs (after pretending "to the women of the race that their best friends are within its ranks") and its refusal to condemn the Klan ("the colored woman feels that there must be some sinister reason for its fear" of the Klan).[93] Women's moral superiority, in her opinion, pointed not to dogged institution building in the Republican Party but rather to a stark recognition that the Republican Party was bankrupt as far as African Americans were concerned.

Dunbar-Nelson's campaign rhetoric fused black women reformers' mandate to lead the race "through intelligent use of the ballot" with the defiant spirit of the New Negro movement and its injunction against black accommodation of white racism. She not only took on the Republican-focused renditions of "woman's era" philosophy but also challenged the male-focused articulations of New Negro ideology. While New Negro ideology promoted a militant black resistance to racism, it also equated the rehabilitation of the race from the humiliations of the nadir with the assertion of a type of manhood that privileged patriarchy and virile masculinity.[94] Dunbar-Nelson's arguments as to why women should switch to the Democratic Party in 1924 pushed against the hypermasculinity of New Negro ideology by continuing to place women at the center of the fight for black equality in party politics. In the political arena, Dunbar-Nelson suggested, the New Negro was a woman. As she told audiences, "The hour has struck for all loyal colored women to come to the aid of the race by asserting political independence." Independence, not loyalty, was women's greatest potential contribution to party politics. Men had already had their chance to lead in politics and failed; it was women's turn. "The old shackles of political superstition and party tradition," she insisted, "must be stricken from the race, and the emancipation must come through its women."[95] It was incumbent upon women to disturb harmful patterns that men had established and failed to break.

[131]

Within the New Negro movement, "memory" of a glorious African past served as an important source of racial pride, but in Dunbar-Nelson's hands memories of a more recent past that associated Republicans with emancipation and Democrats with slavery were detrimental to black political agency. She dismissed the tramping out of pictures of Lincoln every campaign season ("enough to make that sainted martyr turn over in his grave"). The "New Negro," she proclaimed, "has gotten to the point where he has learned to think instead of merely remembering."[96] In future elections, Dunbar-Nelson would again employ the language of memory and impart gendered meaning to it, arguing that women's differing memories of political emancipation released them from the Republican Party.

Dunbar-Nelson also challenged overly simplistic characterizations of the Democratic Party as exclusively the party of white supremacy. She denounced "[t]hose who would keep the Negro vote solidly Republican [by raising] the bogey of Southern domination." This was a direct attack on Republican men, as well as on Republican women leaders like Jeannette Carter and Emma Thompson, who proclaimed in an open letter published in the *Defender*, "We denounce the Democratic party and swear eternal opposition against it because it is the facile tool of Southern race prejudice and lawlessness."[97] In response to such statements, Dunbar-Nelson emphasized regional differences in the Democratic Party: "There is more in common between a Democrat and a Republican in Mississippi than there is in common between a Democrat in New York and a Democrat in Mississippi."[98] She also pointed to Democratic presidential candidate John Davis's repudiation of the Klan in 1924, as well as to his role as solicitor general in the 1915 *Guinn v. United States* case in which the Supreme Court found the "grandfather" clauses in Oklahoma and Maryland to be unconstitutional. Davis's arguments in *Guinn* as solicitor general, however, masked his own personal approval of disfranchisement and segregation. Dunbar-Nelson would not have been aware of this disjuncture between his professional service and personal views, as he strategically did not publicize it and instead relied upon his record in *Guinn*, as well as other antidiscrimination cases he had successfully argued during his tenure as solicitor general, to attract black votes. Davis's personal views on Jim Crow more closely matched his role years later as lead counsel in the effort to uphold the "separate but equal" doctrine in the series of cases that became known as *Brown v. Board of Education*.[99]

In her various speaking engagements in 1924, Mary Church Terrell blasted Alice Dunbar-Nelson for working with the Smith campaign. Although she did not specifically refer to Dunbar-Nelson, Terrell was clearly thinking of the literary figure when she asserted to audiences, "Do not believe any colored woman, no matter what may be her literary ability," no matter "how much you may admire her intellectual attainments who tells you [that] you should support the Democratic party because it will advance our interests of the Negro as a whole."[100] Terrell was also clearly threatened by the legitimacy that Dunbar-Nelson brought to the Democratic campaign when she publicly mused, "it is hard to understand how any colored woman who . . . is clothed in her right mind can use her influence to put the Democratic party in power."[101]

The majority of politically active black women did not in fact follow Dunbar-Nelson into the Democratic Party in 1924, but their relationship with the Republican Party was increasingly strained and undergoing a transformation. Republican women were well on their way toward shifting from an offensive to a defensive strategy, from attempting to reform the Republican Party from within to merely staving off Democratic victory. This was a shift of degree, as the Democratic Party had long served as a negative reference group for black Republicans, but a shift nonetheless. Like Republican men, black women had few options but to focus on Democratic abuses in making their case for the Republican Party. Writing from Michigan, Lillian Johnson explained to Burroughs in a private correspondence that she urged women "to vote for the Republicans for while they do not give us as much as they should, the Democrats would take away from us, if they were in power long."[102] Like Johnson, Irene Moats's tireless effort traversing the mountainous terrain of West Virginia's sparsely populated Pendleton County in order to reach black voters was also heavily motivated by the desire to prevent the election of a Democratic president. As Moats explained in the pages of *National Notes*, "We had every thing to lose and nothing to gain if by any chance the Democratic party should gain control of the state and the nation." "Our contiguity with the solid South," she insisted, "made the situation here especially critical at this time."[103]

In many ways, black Republican women's reasons for supporting the Coolidge-Dawes ticket were identical to black men's. In 1924 the Democratic Party made increasing overtures to black voters, but the fact remained that the strength of the party lay in the white supremacist South. Dunbar-Nelson was, for the time being, atypical among southern migrants in her support of the Democratic Party's presidential candidate. The deep antipathy toward the Democratic Party that other migrants carried with them from the South continued to inform their opposition to the party, even to northern Democrats. Like their male counterparts, many middle-class women concluded that even though a vote for La Follette would indicate their discontent with the Republican Party, it might also help the Democratic cause. This left the Republican Party, and it offered very little by way of addressing America's racial caste system: an antilynching plank that was not promoted by the party's own candidate, and a protective labor legislation platform that was also endorsed by the other major parties (and that might benefit black women and children, but that was not conceived for that specific purpose). Women and men alike, therefore, asserted less that the Republican Party offered substantial benefits to black voters, and more that voting any other way would result in the worse outcome of Democratic victory.

Even though Republican women and men shared much in 1924, there were differences between why each group worked so hard for Coolidge. Unlike their male counterparts, middle-class black women were at the beginning stages of establishing their own independent national Republican network. An analysis of what organizing an independent network meant to black Republican women helps to explain why they canvassed so hard for the Republican Party in 1924 in such a way that does not simply lead to the conclusion that they were tools of white party bosses. It also raises larger questions about the totality of established power structures. How do marginalized groups make the party system responsive to their needs when those who control the system have no motivation to share their power or use their power in support of certain policies? How can marginalized groups create the necessary leverage to motivate those who hold the power? Can this work be done within the party system, or is extraparty pressure group politics necessary? In differing periods, Americans of diverse backgrounds have attempted to answer these questions through a variety of methods. In the 1920s black women reformers tackled these questions through self-help and institution building.

Women affiliated with the NLRCW believed that with proper long-term organizing, they could demonstrate to those who held power in the various divisions of the Republican Party that they were invaluable partners for reaching the thousands of black voters who had been added to the registration books through women's enfranchisement and migration. This type of logic was evident in the private correspondence of one Boston clubwoman. Referring to the debates among black voters over how to respond to Republican apathy in 1924, Mary Gardiner insisted, "I did not feel that this was the time for our people to split up our votes." The solution, from Gardiner's perspective, was not abandoning the party but working to gain more influence: "We should stay in the Grand Old Party and unite in a permanent organization to do some real effective work."[104] The NLRCW's founders already claimed a permanent status; either Gardiner did not know this or was suggesting that the permanency of the group would be recognized only over time. In either case, the implication was that independent organizing and influence within the party were two sides of the same coin. With more time to organize beyond the merely three months that had transpired between the NLRCW's creation in August 1924 and election day in November 1924, the NLRCW could demonstrate their full canvassing potential and, in turn, acquire the leverage necessary to make the party responsive to their policy demands. At the very least, such organizing would help black Republicans wage a respectable fight to keep Democrats out of the federal government.

Of course, this view that patient institution building directed toward the Republican Party would eventually reap rewards that black men had not been able to bring about in the fifty years since the Fifteenth Amendment's enactment was not one held by all middle-class women. Dunbar-Nelson's Democratic activities are a case in point. Dunbar-Nelson was very much a part of this middle-class reform tradition of self-help, and she too understood it as a strategy that might work within the electoral arena. It was Dunbar-Nelson, after all, who, while celebrating with other black Republican women in 1920, had insisted, "We should have organization, organization and more organization."[105] Her belief in women's institution building may have endured, but her switch from the Republicans to the Democrats made clear that she did not think that building a base for a party that already expected black votes would pay off. She, instead, endeavored to create a space for black women within the Democratic Party.

In 1924 this public dispute between Republican and Democratic women over how to make the party system responsive to their demands took place primarily within class lines, among women reformers who disagreed about how best to apply "woman's era" philosophy to the party system. This intraclass debate over whether women reformers had an obligation to dig still further into the Republican Party or to lead the way toward building within the Democratic Party would only intensify in future elections. The partisan disagreements that took place across class lines would also intensify. In future elections, poor and working-class African American support for the Democratic Party represented a rejection not only of white Republicans but also of black Republican leaders, including women leaders, whose ongoing investment in the Republican Party seemed out of step with the cultural and political expectations of urban black communities.

In the meantime, with such an emphasis on institution building as the hope for reforming the party system, it is no surprise that during the 1924 election season independent black Republican women's organizations affiliated with the NLRCW came into existence at the state level. These organizations were simultaneously locally and nationally oriented. At the local level, they brought together the various black Republican women's clubs that had separately emerged at the ward, city, and county levels during the previous decades. In turn, they connected these local Republican women's clubs to the larger national black Republican women's network that was continuing to take form in the NLRCW. Among the first of these NLRCW state affiliates to form was the Colored Women's Republican Clubs of Illinois (CWRCI). Two weeks before the polls opened in November 1924, 150 clubwomen from throughout Illinois responded to Irene Goins's call to meet in Chicago for the purpose of creating a statewide convention of black Republican women. With the establishment of the CWRCI, Goins and her colleagues pooled the collective resources of the dozens of black Republican women's clubs that had emerged across Illinois during the 1910s and early 1920s.[106] Operating primarily at the ward and county level, several of these clubs had participated in the divisive Second Ward city council elections during the 1910s. The collective potential of their diverse organizational strengths, however, had yet to be fully harnessed in federal elections. Goins sought to realize this potential by creating a statewide black Republican women's organization.

Although the formation of the NACW, the NLRCW, and local affiliates like the CWRCI provided interdenominational structures through which members could mobilize for candidates and legislation outside the direct purview of the churches, the history of black women's partisan institution building is not a secularization story. The overlapping memberships of the NACW and the NLRCW were comprised of women who held deep religious convictions or were active in their respective church movements (the two did not necessarily go together, though they often did).[107] Goins, for instance, was a devout Christian who reported experiencing a personal conversion at the age of thirteen. A member of Chicago's Quinn Chapel AME Church all of her adult life, Goins did not separate her faith from her politics.[108] And she was not alone. For many, their faith informed their politics, whether expressed within a specific church movement or not. This was evident when the Anti-Lynching Crusaders included prayer in their Dyer Bill publicity drive. It was also discernible in the ways that women reformers discussed the Nineteenth Amendment. For example, Reverend Florence Randolph, a NLRCW founding member who was one of the AME Zion's handful of ordained women elders, viewed women's enfranchisement through the lens of holiness doctrine and its notion of sanctification—that is, the state of being free from sin and attendant to the internal voice of Christ.[109] Contributing to a 1920 issue of the *Competitor* in her capacity as head of the NACW's Religious Department, Randolph identified voting as an avenue through which individual women might express their holiness: "With the enfranchisement of women and the great victory our problems became more complex, hence, we must include in our plan a living faith in Him who said, 'All things are possible to him that believeth.' "[110]

NLRCW meetings began with prayer, and politically active women who never preached or aspired to hold ministerial positions expressed their conviction that God could act through individuals in the world.[111] As Estelle Davis reflected in the aftermath of the 1924 campaign, "How little we realized in our club work for the past 25 years that it was God's way of preparing us to assume this greater task of citizenship." Joining the likes of Archibald Carey and Charles Evans Hughes, Davis relied heavily upon existing NACW networks during her twenty-one-city speaking tour across Kansas and Michigan for the RNC. "I often wonder," she mused, "what would have happened without our organized club work which has not only trained us for service, but has created a nation-wide sisterhood through which we know the outstanding women of each state who are able to serve our race in the time of need."[112] Davis's belief that God worked through the NACW's gradual growth over a quarter of a century not only exemplifies how these women employed their faith to interpret events small and large in their lives but also suggests why some campaigned so hard for the Coolidge-Dawes ticket, despite the party's meager offerings. The same trust that God's plan was revealed gradually ("how little we realized . . . that it was God's way of preparing us") could apply to the patient institution building that black women were undertaking in both the NLRCW and the RNC. "Now, the thing that has counted most in my work in Connecticut," one organizer wrote Burroughs in the closing weeks of the 1924 campaign, "is persistence, eternal persistence, and patience, and a faith that will not shrink, though pressed by every foe."[113]

Republican activists did not make a facile assertion that God worked through the Republican Party; nor did they claim to have a monopoly on faith. Their understanding of the relationship between their activism and their faith ran much deeper. It was rooted in a larger vision of how to act in the world that did not distinguish between efforts to eliminate sin (personal and societal) and to push forward social change. This vision was evident in a congratulatory letter that Brooklyn clubwoman Louise Fayerweather sent to Burroughs shortly after the NLRCW's formation. Fayerweather suggested that involvement in the new organization suited a life devoted to sanctification, but that, in order for political activism to have a spiritual quality, it needed to be embedded within a larger commitment to charity. "For a successful movement of this kind," Fayerweather explained, "we must bear in mind the meek and lowly are to be considered, and must be organized [according to] the simple truth that selfishness must be overthrown." The NLRCW, she continued, must be used "to build up for the future generations yet unborn." "With that as our aim," she concluded, "the God of all will sanctify our efforts."[114]

While Fayerweather held a view typical of the black middle class—it was their duty to reach out and guide the black masses—that often had condescending undertones, her advice here offered a theological framework for transforming what was essentially a middle-class canvassing effort into a mass movement. Despite such awareness, NLRCW leaders would miss several key opportunities for reaching poor women voters during the 1920s. Middle-class Republican women's application of "woman's era" philosophy to party politics enabled them to remain politically engaged despite the profound disappointments they encountered on the campaign trail. But their investment in "woman's era" philosophy would also create class blind spots in their organizing that, in some instances, deterred them from canvassing poor African Americans who did not adhere to the behavioral expectations of women's racial uplift ideology and, in other instances, led them to avoid women too closely associated with the masculinist politics espoused by New Negro men.

The history of black women's partisan institution building is also not a story of disengagement from the churches. While the NLRCW's founders did not seek to compromise the independence of their newly established organization by placing it under the authority of male ministers, they were quite interested in utilizing the enormous canvassing resources that ministers had at their fingertips to accomplish their partisan goals.[115] Elizabeth Ross Haynes said as much just three weeks after returning to her home in Harlem from the Chicago meetings that led to the NLRCW's formation.[116] Brainstorming about strategies for registering black women throughout the country, Haynes suggested, "If we could even secure 10 minutes from all the churches on the same Sunday and get the women pledged to register and vote on the dates impressed upon them, some votes could be gotten." Perhaps referring to the seemingly unavoidable strategy of going through ministers to reach a large number of female voters, Haynes confided to Burroughs, "[t]his may seem like the same old story and it is." With the NLRCW just weeks old and members still in the process of setting up the group's organizational machinery, however, Haynes concluded that this was perhaps the best option, for "without money," as she put it, "a big machine may be very unwieldy."[117]

From RNC headquarters in Chicago, Quinn Brown sent letters to black clergy throughout the city in mid-September. As she explained in the letter, "In all matters where racial unity and co-operation are needed, our ministers who are closely in touch with the greatest numbers of people can always wield the largest influence, if they are willing to do so." "We believe you are for Coolidge and Dawes," she continued, "so we are asking you to select women in your congregation to work in their various neighborhoods lining up our colored women for 'Coolidge and Dawes' in their regular precinct and ward organization."[118] This letter campaign asking Chicago clergy to help organize women was replicated in other locations. From West Virginia, for instance, Irene Moats described mailing thousands of "'Ministers letters' [as] suggested by the Chicago drive."[119] In Rhode Island, Bertha Higgins reported, "I had the hearty cooperation of the ministers of our state," and in Minnesota, Rebeque Foree "[m]ade a special plea to our churches in the Twin Cities, through their respective pastors."[120]

The ease with which Quinn Brown approached ministers asking them to help "line up our colored women for 'Coolidge and Dawes'" belied the fact that the churches remained complicated arenas for women to assert public authority and political power. This turn to ministers for help during the electoral season took place against the backdrop of women's ongoing struggle for greater inclusion in church governing bodies. Between 1920 and 1924, the AME Church was embroiled in a heated debate over admitting women as voting members of its main governing body, the General Conference. Writing disapprovingly of the General Conference's rejection of women members at its 1920 meeting in St. Louis, Reverdy Ransom pointed to the blatant power dynamics that lay behind this continued exclusion of women: "since women composed a decisive majority of church members almost everywhere it was feared that the laymen would stand little chance being elected" as delegates if women were entitled to vote. In response to the majority's concern that women might outnumber them in the General

Conference if given the right to vote for delegates, Ransom countered, "The church has nothing to fear but all things good to be hoped for by the accession to membership in the General Conference of our representative women who so largely compose the character, intelligence and consecration which is the salt of the Church today and its hope in the future."[121] Four years later, the General Conference reversed itself and granted women the right to vote for lay delegates.[122]

As one churchwoman put it, the 1924 "General Conference made women equal to men in so far as it pertains to standing, and participating in the affairs of the church," but male clergy intended to maintain their predominant position. This was evident when one churchwoman chastised *Christian Recorder* editor Richard Wright Jr. (also Ransom's former assistant pastor at Chicago's Institutional AME) for an article describing "the kind of 'MEN' that should constitute the next General Conference." She insisted that Wright should make clear to women readers that they were entitled to vote for lay delegates because "these hard working women should know their rights so that they may take advantage of the same, and have a part in the making of laws and otherwise in governing the affairs of the church."[123] Women, however, also found supporters among clergy for their political activities in the 1920s. Deeply frustrated by black party men whom he described as more interested in patronage than race advancement, Presbyterian reverend Francis Grimké of Washington, D.C., for example, expressed hope in "the women, who are now also getting into politics." Women "unlike the men," Grimké hoped, "will think of [politics] mainly not as a means of getting somewhere for themselves personally, but as a means of furthering the interest of the race; of using their political influence definitely for the purpose of wiping out all discriminations on account of race or color." Sounding like black women reformers themselves, Grimké concluded, "In this way, with their persistent energy, push, and organizing ability, they can be of immense value to the race."[124]

Although Republican women had to navigate church politics, working with ministers enabled them to reach the hundreds of migrants who were pouring into local congregations in cities like Chicago where a great deal of politicking took place. There were, however, downsides to this strategy of canvassing through the mainline churches. Canvassers missed poor migrants who did not attend established or even migrant-era mainline churches for any number of reasons, from discomfort with styles of worship to an inability to pay church dues. Beyond the class limitations of this strategy, there was the issue of the clergy's own partisan leanings. Ministers could be helpful so long as they held similar political views. For example, when AME leaders from around the country passed a resolution endorsing Coolidge at their early October convention in Chicago, a door closed for Democratic or Progressive women canvassers to employ AME Church resources.[125] So long as men maintained a monopoly or near-monopoly of clerical positions, they would also serve as gatekeepers to church forums for reaching voters during election season. The support of several male clergy for Democratic candidates four years later, most notably AME bishop Reverdy Ransom, would create new possibilities for women who had left the Republican Party to conduct church-based canvassing work.[126] Still, the decision of whether to open church doors to women canvassers—whether they be Republicans or Democrats—ultimately rested with male clergy.

The limits of middle-class Republican women's canvassing strategies for reaching poor women was also evident in their response to disfranchising measures in the South. While they protested these measures, they also urged southern black women to try to meet local voting requirements. In 1920, for example, the Citizenship Department of the NACW proposed the establishment of "summer courses in citizenship" that would issue a certificate upon completion that would serve as "qualification for the educational test to vote, wherever and whenever such test is required."[127] Well into the 1930s, NACW activists also encouraged women to pay local poll taxes in order to qualify to vote.[128] Clubwomen were well aware of the profound poverty with which the vast majority of southern blacks struggled. Still, they sometimes characterized women who did not pay the poll tax in terms of moral failure, as unwilling rather than unable to pay the tax. Clemmie White, a Tennessee "State Leader" for the CWDRNC, did so during the 1924 campaign. "We discovered much lethargy and indifference also with regard to meeting the poll tax requirements," she reported in the aftermath of the election. From White's perspective, ensuring that women cast their ballots required guidance and persuasion: "We made some improvement in this situation in proportion to our ability to reach the women and talk to them face to face concerning these vital matters."[129]

Following the 1924 election, Amelia Sullivan of Augusta, Georgia, confided to Burroughs, "At first we were the strongest in the state, (that is we had more registered women than other Georgia Cities) but I sometimes think that of all the work we did, it will mean nothing though." Like White, Sullivan's sense of futility was fueled by the difficulty in guaranteeing that canvassing efforts translated into results on election day: "One great drawback is that they fail to pay the tax after registration. The men will not pay and just a few women will." Even though Sullivan seriously questioned the value of their campaign to register black women across Georgia, she hid her frustration from fellow canvassers. As she wrote, "I never say it to our women; because they are already discouraged." Like White, Sullivan, nevertheless, believed in middle-class women's ability to guide less-fortunate women. As she concluded, "I am still determine[d] to do what I can to keep the work up and to encourage our women to qualify."[130] This experiment in persuasion paralleled the misplaced optimism that motivated men to study in order to "pass" the literacy and understanding clauses that began awaiting them at the polls in the 1890s, although by the 1920s women were well aware of the lengths to which white southerners would go in order to prevent African Americans from voting. Middle-class black women's poll tax drive, like their support for the Republican Party in 1924, was a manifestation of the politics of limited options. They denounced disfranchisement schemes and mobilized to elect politicians who would work to eliminate Jim Crow laws. So long as poll taxes, literacy tests, and other such measures remained in effect, however, the only way to add southern women to the potential voting strength of black women across the nation involved working within the rules of the corrupt Jim Crow system. As White's and Sullivan's own accounts suggest, the heavy moralizing that accompanied these efforts did not in any way help poor women afford taxes. Rather, it most likely sowed seeds of misunderstanding and resentment where a greater sense of solidarity might have been cultivated.

Still another missed opportunity for canvassing poor women during the 1924 campaign occurred when clubwomen decided not to cultivate ties with Marcus Garvey's Universal Negro Improvement Association (UNIA). There were exceptions, most notably Wells-Barnett, who addressed the UNIA in 1918 and who along with her husband personally welcomed Garvey to the United States.[131] The majority of black women reformers, however, perceived the UNIA as a threat to their own race leadership claims. Marcus Garvey urged African Americans to "go back to the days of true manhood when women truly reverenced us."[132] He pronounced that "this is the age of men, not pygmies, not serfs and peons and dogs, but men, and we who make up the membership of the Universal Negro Improvement Association reflect the new manhood of the Negro."[133] As Deborah Gray White argues, the UNIA's male-centered rhetoric seemed bent on displacing women from the leadership roles they had asserted under the auspices of "woman's era" philosophy.[134]

Founded in Jamaica in 1914 and transplanted onto American soil in 1916 when Garvey relocated to Harlem, the UNIA emerged as the largest black mass movement prior to the modern civil rights movement. Garvey's calls for black self-determination and self-defense instilled a sense of race pride among its largely poor following that by the mid-1920s claimed 6 million members organized into 1,000 local divisions, about 80 percent of which operated in the United States.[135] While middle-class women reformers were threatened by Garvey's rhetoric, the UNIA had a special appeal to poor black women who typically worked long hours in menial positions and who were regularly the subject of degrading stereotypes. Garvey's call for "self-made black men who would take black women out of white people's kitchens" suggested a possible escape from the drudgery of wage labor. Garvey's depiction of black women as beautiful and worthy of men's admiration presented a welcome counterrepresentation of poor black womanhood and a place on the women's pedestal that was the province of white women.[136] The UNIA also seemed to offer women men's help in undermining negative stereotypes. In fact, with its male-centered philosophy, the UNIA made it men's responsibility to dismantle white notions "that black women have no virtue to be protected." Battling white sexism toward black women, Garveyites insisted, required a turn inward. As one male Garveyite argued, "If we want others to respect our women we have got to show them the way by doing it ourselves; if we want others to protect our women we have got to set them an example by doing it ourselves."[137] In reality promises of protection "often translated into paternalistic privileges."[138] Still, UNIA rhetoric seemed to offer poor women the hope that they would not have to confront inter- and intraracial sexism alone, especially because middle-class women's promises of help were often accompanied by condescending commentary about poor women's deficiencies.

For a small group of women, the UNIA did provide leadership positions. "The UNIA's constitution," historian Ula Taylor explains, "was very different from that of most black organizations in that women were well integrated into the movement structure." The constitution required that each local division of the UNIA elect a female president and vice president alongside a male president and vice president.[139] But the UNIA was by no means egalitarian. Men in the organization conceived of men's and women's roles in the movement and larger society as complementary rather than egalitarian, or, as one historian has put it, "separate and hierarchical."[140] In this context, UNIA women carefully negotiated their leadership roles. Such negotiation was evident in the leadership style of Marcus Garvey's second wife, Amy Jacques Garvey. As Taylor documents, Amy Jacques Garvey often served as a surrogate leader for the UNIA during Marcus Garvey's several arrests, detentions, and imprisonments during the 1920s. Jacques Garvey carefully crafted a public image of herself as a helpmate to Garvey who was committed to assisting her embattled husband promote his nationalist and political ideals. At the same time, Jacques Garvey also used the pages of the organization's newspaper, the *Negro World*, to push for public roles for women, including their participation in party politics.[141]

The majority of clubwomen may not have been interested in establishing ties with women of the UNIA, but UNIA women closely followed black clubwomen's involvement in Republican Party politics in the pages of the *Negro World*. In February 1921, for example, the *Negro World* included an article from the Colored Syndicate Press Bureau reporting on an informal meeting between Monen L. Gray and president-elect Harding's wife.[142] In 1922 the *Negro World* reported on the activities of the Anti-Lynching Crusaders.[143] After Amy Jacques Garvey set up a women's page in the *Negro World* in 1924, reports of black clubwomen's political activism continued to appear in this new section.[144] The aptly titled "Our Women and What They Think" included mention of Mary Booze's election as a Republican national committeewoman in 1924, as well as a Kentucky county Republican convention's appointment of seven black women as precinct committeewomen that year.[145]

With a national subscription base as large as 75,000 in 1921, Amy Jacques Garvey was able to use the pages of the *Negro World* to encourage women readers to participate in party politics and to discourage her male audience from interfering with black women's electoral activism.[146] In June 1924 she did this by addressing a question that had trailed the woman's suffrage movement: "Will the Entrance of Women in Politics Affect Home Life?" Perhaps to demonstrate that coverage of this issue in the women's page was indeed representative of "men and women in different walks of life," Jacques Garvey included one decidedly negative response among the five responses. This reply came from a minister who insisted that women's involvement in politics would cause the "neglect of children" and jeopardize the propagation of the race. Amy Jacques Garvey, however, rejected the minister's views when she introduced the forum with these words: "Despite opposition women are in politics and are influencing and making humane legislations that only the detailed and fine minds of the female sex can conceive." Closely paralleling the views presented by two other forum contributors, Jacques Garvey concluded, "Such legislations uplift the homes, communities and nation; therefore the home has not been neglected but benefited."[147]

Women also campaigned for candidates through UNIA channels. They participated in the massive UNIA political rallies that took place in Harlem in 1924 to generate support not only for the Republican presidential candidate but also for the Democratic candidate for governor of New York.[148] This was Alfred Smith, who in four years time would run for president. In 1924 at least two UNIA women were arrested in Chicago for helping to lead a political parade without a permit. Never as strong in Chicago as in New York, the two UNIA divisions in Chicago were nevertheless quite active.[149] Accompanied by the Garvey band, the parade of eight women and twenty-six men marched through the streets of Chicago passing out literature in support of Nathan S. Taylor, a white candidate who was running in the Republican primary for congressman from Illinois's First Congressional District. Taylor lost in the Republican primary to incumbent Representative Martin Madden, but Taylor's description of the support he received from the UNIA in Chicago demonstrates the importance of Garvey's organization for the involvement of poor blacks in party politics, as well as the enormous campaign boost that the UNIA could offer a candidate: "One of [the UNIA] leaders heard me speak. He was impressed with what I had to say and so he made it possible for me to speak before them. They worked like Trojans for me. They were bold and fearless. They were a material factor in my campaign. I don't know how many were in the organization but it was very powerful and I got every one of their votes. Five thousand is a very conservative estimate of their strength." If Taylor was accurate in his estimate, then the vast majority of the approximately 6,700 votes he won came from Garveyites. Responding to criticisms that he had "bought them off," Taylor explained, "I didn't give them a cent and they didn't ask for a cent either."[150]

Had the NLRCW or its local affiliate, the Colored Women's Republican Clubs of Illinois, attempted to establish ties with Chicago's women Garveyites, they might have been able to transform their primarily middle-class organizations into truly cross-class political institutions. The ongoing arrival of poor southern migrants to the North made such cross-class organization valuable for political canvassing. In terms of Garveyite and clubwomen's views on women's voting, such an alliance seemed to make good sense. Both groups saw electoral activism as a key means by which African American women could help the race. NLRCW leaders would have agreed wholeheartedly with Garveyite Saydee Parham's defense of women's involvement in politics in 1924: "The interest displayed by women in politics is responsible for playgrounds where children may physically develop into healthy men and women, better educational systems where the poor may receive the higher branches of education, [and] better sanitary conditions by which men, women and children are protected from the ravages of disease and an adjustment of economic conditions."[151] Garveyite women were, however, part of a movement in which men contested clubwomen's claims to race leadership.[152] The perceived threat that UNIA men posed to clubwomen's leadership status ultimately tainted clubwomen's ability to focus on what they shared with Garveyite women and deterred them from pursuing a potentially fruitful interclass political alliance.

"EXHILARATING! INSPIRING! RARE RESPONSIBILITY," Myrtle Foster Cook wrote of her role as chairman of the Western Division of the Colored Women's Department of the RNC. She described the "floor after floor" of "reception rooms, committee rooms, offices, bureaus" that the Colored Women's Department had shared with the hundreds of other Republican organizers who worked out of RNC headquarters at the Wrigley Building in Chicago. "To be a cog in the mighty wheel of this campaign organization," she excitedly told *National Notes* readers, "was fruitful opportunity to contribute one's best to the most extensively and effectively organized human effort to educate the general public to their best interests in national government, And such equipment! such encouragement of initiative! such appreciation of efficiency!"[153] For Foster Cook, being a "cog," as she put it, was a sign that she and her cohort had arrived where the RNC was concerned, and that they were receiving the recognition that they deserved for their service to the party. From Brooklyn, her counterpart Maria Lawton, who had headed the Eastern Division of the Colored Women's Department, similarly concluded that "the opportunity afforded the colored women voters proved an outlet for their pent up aspirations and ambitions to be counted as integral parts of the body politic."[154] Others indicated that there was still a ways to go, but that the massive work they had put over during the 1924 campaign was one more step on the road toward greater recognition from the Republican Party. From Arizona, one state organizer predicted, "I think the effort put forth by our women will be helpful, it gives us more prestige and shows the other race that our women are alive to all issues and understand them."[155] Another from Tennessee anticipated, "With thorough organization and accurate information with regard to the issues involved the colored women will in time prove to be one of the most dependable and valuable assets of the Republican Party."[156] The NLRCW's "work will go on," one woman promised Burroughs, "and the good seeds sown will bear fruit later . . . that will blossom in the home and for the nation."[157]

At the close of the campaign, women prepared to direct the momentum generated during the 1924 election season into more permanent structures. In December, Myrtle Foster Cook announced in the pages of *National Notes* that the Colored Women's Republican Clubs of Illinois, which had "organized temporarily during the campaign," had held "a state convention for permanent organization since the election."[158] Foster Cook encouraged black Republican women in other states to follow suit: "It is advisable that in all other states the campaign organization be held intact as at present, and that when expedient arrangement be made for permanent organization." "Since most of our active club women are also our political leaders," she continued, "we suggest that political state conventions be held in conjunction with, and on the day before or the day after, your state federation meetings."[159] Women in other states did not seem to need much prompting, however. In the same *National Notes* issue in which Foster Cook's advice appeared, one woman who had served as a Colored Women's Department organizer in upstate New York reported, "We are now about to launch a permanent organization, to be known as The Up-State Republican Women's Unit."[160] From West Virginia, Irene Moats indicated just how easy it would be to draw upon the organizational framework generated in 1924 in upcoming campaigns: "we have developed a leadership that not only put over the campaign program, but will also be of service in future situations."[161]

Seeking to strengthen its reach, the NLRCW sent out a questionnaire in December 1924 to leading black women across the country asking them a range of questions. Several of the questions were designed to gauge the nature of women's local organizing: "How many political study clubs have the Negro women in your city?" and "What is being done to educate women as to the value of the ballot?" Other questions inquired about women's experiences in the 1924 election: was it difficult to get women voters to register, were there any reports "of vote-selling among women" or of white employers trying to influence black votes, did men who opposed "woman suffrage influence their wives not to vote?" Still other questions were directed at policy: "What do you think the Negro should demand of the incoming administration? . . . of the next Congress?" Answers varied, but Chicagoan Georgiana Whyte's response was echoed over and over again in the completed questionnaires. "Fair and equal opportunity and the enforcement of the Fourteenth Amendment of the Constitution of the U.S." would meet Whyte's expectations, along with "passage of the Dyer Anti-Lynching Bill."[162]

In the midst of celebrations in 1924, women like Myrtle Foster Cook had confused the validation that came with RNC appointments with actual power sharing. By 1926 it was clear that neither the Coolidge administration nor a Republican-dominated Congress was going to deliver on these policy expectations. During 1925 and 1926 Representative Leonidas Dyer and Illinois Senator William McKinley once again attempted to push a federal antilynching bill through Congress.[163] But as *National Notes* reported disapprovingly in June 1926, Coolidge's failure to include the Dyer-McKinley Antilynching Bill on his list of necessary legislation prevented the measure from ever reaching the Senate floor.[164] One month later at the NLRCW's executive committee meeting in Oakland, California, members vented their frustration at the administration they had helped to put in office. Elizabeth Carter of Massachusetts, for example, denounced Coolidge's "absolute indifference" and proposed that the NLRCW "ask of President Coolidge what his plans are for the future, as affecting the Negro group."[165] As they looked to the next presidential election season, black women reformers confronted a similar question themselves: What were their own plans for the future? Should they remain with the Republican Party in 1928 or finally follow their colleague Alice Dunbar-Nelson into the Democratic Party? The majority of white Republican politicians had abandoned the cause of antilynching altogether. Did the Republican Party offer any policy issue around which black women reformers might mobilize and push forward their agenda of establishing a federal government that would protect black citizenship rights? The politics of prohibition offered a temporary respite for Republican women who were deeply disappointed with the Republican Party but not yet ready to abandon it. Middle-class black Republican women's approach to prohibition politics, however, also raised questions about the degree to which they were in touch with the cultural and political expectations of black urban constituencies whom they claimed to represent in party politics.

[4]

The Prohibition Issue as a Smoke Screen
The Failure of Racial Uplift Ideology and the 1928 Election

In the heat of the 1928 presidential contest between New York's Democratic governor Alfred E. Smith and Republican Herbert Hoover, the Colored Women's Department of the Republican National Committee issued a pamphlet entitled, *The Prohibition Issue as a Smoke Screen*. The pamphlet sought to focus the attention of black voters on one of the most contested topics of the 1928 election, whether the Eighteenth Amendment, which prohibited the manufacture and sale of liquor, should be gradually dismantled, repealed altogether, or remain part of the U.S. Constitution. The pamphlet argued that Democrat Alfred Smith's promise to weaken or annul the Volstead Act—the enforcement provision of the Eighteenth Amendment—was merely "a smoke screen to attract voters" to the Democratic Party, including the majority of black voters who had been loyal Republicans for more than six decades. Leading black Republican women feared that black voters would put their desire for a drink or profits ahead of any kind of historical commitment to the Republican Party. Smith knew perfectly well, the pamphlet explained, that he could not fulfill this campaign promise. As the pamphlet pointed out, "There are 195 Democrats in Congress, 126 of whom represent the dry South, and under no circumstances would they vote to modify the Volstead Act." Smith's promise to modify the Volstead Act, black Republican women asserted in the pamphlet, was a "smoke screen" white Democrats were fanning in order to lure black voters who were increasingly dissatisfied with the Republican Party to the Democratic Party. The Democratic Party, these Republican women insisted, did not represent black interests—quite the contrary. Once Democrats regained control of the White House, they would, in the words of the *Prohibition Issue as a Smoke Screen* pamphlet, "complete our disfranchisement, segregation and humiliation."[1]

The 1928 presidential election battle between Hoover and Smith was marked not only by partisan wrangling over the regulation of liquor in America but also by the early stages of a major voting realignment. More than a quarter of the voters in black precincts in Chicago and Harlem, and scores of black voters in other cities, ultimately cast their ballots for the Democratic candidate Alfred Smith in 1928.[2] Over the next several years, the ranks of black Democrats swelled, and in 1936, for the first time, the majority of black voters cast their ballots for a Democratic presidential candidate. Women citizens had acquired full voting rights only eight years before significant numbers of black Democrats materialized during the Hoover-Smith contest. A number of middle-class black women had spent a good portion of those eight years painstakingly creating Republican women's organizations and gaining a small foothold in the machinery of the Republican Party. At the national level, these groups included the National League of Republican Colored Women (NLRCW) and the organization that had issued the *Prohibition as a Smoke Screen* pamphlet, the Colored Women's Department of the Republican National Committee (CWDRNC). While they too were disappointed with the Republican Party's lackluster record on black rights during the 1920s, they were not ready to abandon the party, especially after having spent the past eight years carefully organizing to gain a foothold within Republican networks. Still by 1928, these women were looking restlessly for a reason to support the Republican Party, any meaningful exception to Republican indifference. They found that exception in the Republican Party's prohibition plank.

Pulling back from the local story, this chapter's national focus enables an exploration of the links that black women reformers drew between two entirely new scenarios in the 1920s, the rise of a well-organized movement to repeal a constitutional amendment and the significant drift of black voters to the Democratic Party in national elections. Because of their long-standing interest in both civil rights and prohibition, black women reformers were uniquely positioned to make connections between what historians have typically analyzed as separate phenomena, the repeal movement and the early stages of the voting realignment.[3] They pointed to the implications of the repeal movement for the Reconstruction Amendments. Leading black Republican women argued that, if successful, the Democratic drive to repeal the Eighteenth Amendment would set a dangerous precedent for eliminating the similarly unpopular and unevenly enforced Reconstruction Amendments. In other words, the repealing of one amendment might lead to the repeal of others. These women's efforts to show the connection between these seemingly unrelated amendments that had been ratified in entirely

Failure of Racial Uplift Ideology

different political eras was part of their ongoing project of shedding light on southern abuses and ensuring a stronger federal government that fulfilled its constitutional obligations. In their reading of the Eighteenth Amendment debate, it is possible to see the ways that African American women carried into the 1920s a discourse about federal rights and responsibilities that had animated U.S. politics during the 1860s and 1870s.

They were not entirely successful, however, in applying nineteenth-century strategies to these two new scenarios in the 1920s. Republican women leaders characterized black support for the Democrats in 1928—and by extension Smith's repeal position—as a threat not only to the Reconstruction Amendments but also to their own gendered claims to authority. Since the 1890s, black women reformers, many of whom were active in Republican politics, had grounded their activism in "woman's era" philosophy: they had asserted that they were more morally suited than men to lead the race out of the profound problems that it faced at the end of the nineteenth century. They would do so by instructing their neighbors on the tenets of racial uplift, the nineteenth-century ideology that insisted that African Americans could demonstrate to white Americans their fitness for full citizenship through displays of modest and dignified behavior. This included abstention from liquor. By the 1920s, however, both racial uplift ideology and women's use of it to claim community authority as the architects of the "woman's era" were being challenged from several quarters. Rather than retreat from this ideology, women reformers dug into it even further, letting racial uplift's injunction against drinking spill into their partisan rhetoric.[4] In 1928 black Republican women leaders employed the increasingly outdated language of racial uplift to associate black Democrats with immoral behavior. Black Republican women accused black Democrats—that is, poor black Democrats—of switching parties simply because they wanted a drink. They also insisted that Democratic voters who were willing to put their enjoyment of the vibrant leisure culture of 1920s America before the Reconstruction Amendments had betrayed the race and were in need of middle-class women's guidance.

Their decision to rely on a declining ideology in this context not only belied their embattled position as social reformers and proponents of the "woman's era" but also severely limited their claims to represent African Americans in party politics. At the very least, their interpretation about the motivations of black Democrats caused them to misread the forces driving black abandonment of the Republican Party. It also undercut the potential broad appeal of their cogent constitutional arguments. Even more damag-

Failure of Racial Uplift Ideology

ing, black Republican women's use of increasingly outdated racial uplift ideology to discredit black Democrats compounded the sense that the Republican Party, including its black leaders, was out of touch with the majority of black voters. In other words, the decline of women's racial uplift ideology bled into and contributed to the loss of black Republican women's authority as party leaders just as the Democratic Party was on the rise among black voters.

Temperance, Civil Rights, and Racial Uplift before the Repeal Movement

African American women's analyses of the relationship between prohibition and civil rights began to emerge long before the 1928 presidential elections, though some of their most sophisticated arguments emerged in that context. Two key strategies forged during the late nineteenth and early twentieth centuries would ultimately shape their read of the repeal movement and the early stages of the voting realignment in the 1920s. First, temperance fit prominently in the racial uplift ideology to which so many women reformers subscribed as a means of undermining racist stereotypes. Second, black women reformers employed prohibition politics as part of their ongoing efforts to encourage an activist federal government in the realm of civil rights. They hinted that national debates over legislating and then enforcing prohibition might reopen interest among white politicians in enforcing the Reconstruction Amendments.

Adherents of racial uplift ideology believed that personal displays of temperance, thrift, and modesty, and, even more important, campaigns to instill such values among poor blacks, would help dismantle racist stereotypes of African Americans as licentious, intemperate, and immoral. Even as women adherents of racial uplift ideology sought basic civil rights for all African Americans, they did so, at least in part, by distinguishing themselves from the majority of black Americans. Indeed, their leadership was embedded in claims of difference and class hierarchy.[5] At the core of these claims of difference were assumptions that the mass of black Americans was often guilty of self-injury and, still worse, of race betrayal. Black men in particular, they insisted, needed women's guidance to avoid the economic and political self-injury that resulted from liquor consumption.

While denouncing white representations of African Americans as weak in the face of alcohol, women reformers sometimes depicted black men in very much the same terms. This type of intraracial criticism was evident, for

Failure of Racial Uplift Ideology

instance, in antilynching activist Ida B. Wells-Barnett's various public statements during the 1890s while embroiled in a highly publicized feud with Frances Willard, president of the Woman's Christian Temperance Union (WCTU). In the international press, Wells-Barnett condemned Willard's assertion that the "grog shop" was the "centre of power" in black communities.[6] In the pages of the black press, however, Wells-Barnett argued that "Miss Willard's statements possess the small pro rata of truth of all such sweeping statements. It is well known that the Negro's greatest injury is done to himself." The self-injury to which she referred was partially economic. Wells-Barnett told her readers that "[t]housands of dollars which might flow into honorable channels of trade and build up race enterprises, are spent for liquor to inflame the blood and incite to evil deeds." In her view, it was not only dollars that black communities lost to liquor consumption and traffic; also lost was the potential of an entire generation of men. Drinking gave "judges and juries the excuse for filling the convict camps" with hundreds of men who represented the "flower of the race." Furthermore, liquor trafficking and the profits it offered, she explained, sacrificed "to the Moloch of intemperance hundreds of our young men" who entered this "nefarious" business.[7]

This type of intraracial criticism in the midst of deflecting white racism was also on display in the final report that famed civil rights activist Frances Ellen Watkins Harper filed as National Superintendent of Colored Work for the WCTU in 1890. Harper reproached a leading white WCTU member from Texas for charging that the black "vote was bought by the liquor men, and defeated prohibition in Texas." This was a reference to the 1887 election in which Texas voters rejected a state constitutional amendment prohibiting the manufacture and sale of liquor.[8] In the years leading up to federal prohibition, numerous cities, states, and counties across the nation held "local option" elections, such as this one in Texas, in which residents voted on whether to grant or deny licenses to sell liquor.[9] Even as Harper denounced this accusation, she did not deny that some black men sold their ballot. Instead, Harper challenged the notion that black men were primarily responsible for the downfall of local option campaigns. Responding directly to the charge lodged by the WCTU leader from Texas, Harper asserted, "As prohibition was defeated in several northern states last year, where there was not, I think, a very large number of colored people, perhaps it would have been a more accurate way of stating it to have said 'helped defeat the measure.'" After spreading the blame among both black and white men, Harper then used the public platform of her annual report to shed addi-

Failure of Racial Uplift Ideology

tional light on white complicity in local option failures. She did this by inverting the familiar racist rhetoric that accompanied vote-selling accusations in such a way as to shift the weight of moral responsibility to elite white men: "if it was shabby for an ignorant black man to sell his vote," she asked, "was it not a shabbier thing if an intelligent white man bought it?"[10]

Despite a defensive stance against white supremacists, the belief among many black women reformers that black men were easily misled by the promise of liquor and thus in need of female guidance was evident in black women's approach to local option campaigns. Though a full accounting of black women's involvement in local option campaigns is still needed, it is quite clear that many threw the full weight of their support toward the enactment of local prohibition laws. Some did so under the auspices of the WCTU, others not.[11] Wells-Barnett, for instance, spoke publicly in favor of local option during an ultimately successful battle to make Decatur, Illinois, dry.[12] By vigorously campaigning for local option laws, women reformers demonstrated by example that African Americans favored prohibition legislation and were willing to use their vote, or at least the ability to mobilize men's votes, toward that end. By proselytizing temperance among the working poor, they endeavored to transform black men who drank into respectable "dry" voters. National Association of Colored Women (NACW) activists like Anna Duncan, president of the Alabama State Federation of Colored Women, urged black women to eliminate intemperance in order to eliminate political corruption. Claiming female moral authority in a 1900 *National Notes* piece, Duncan insisted, "We, as women, can do much in our various stations to purify and strengthen the voting population in all the lines of right and justice."[13]

Women reformers' insistence that they would lead the race would shape the trajectory of their approach to prohibition politics for decades to come. A black man who opposed prohibition in the years leading up to the Eighteenth Amendment had betrayed the race and therefore his claim to speak for the race. This interpretive framework changed very little once the Eighteenth Amendment passed and the focus of prohibition politics was on repeal. Under these new circumstances, middle-class black women continued to invoke the language of moral weakness, political self-injury, and race betrayal when discussing African Americans who publicly favored repeal or supported political candidates who did.

Beginning in the 1910s, NACW temperance discussions increasingly began to include an additional subject—federal power. These discussions were a reflection of developments within the larger temperance movement.

Failure of Racial Uplift Ideology

Many prohibitionists had, of course, long advocated the use of federal power to regulate intoxicants. In the late 1890s, however, the larger temperance movement had fallen into some disarray following the death of Frances Willard and the deepening of factionalism within the Prohibition Party.[14] The turmoil that beleaguered the national temperance movement subsided with the emergence of a new powerhouse on the scene of prohibition politics, the Anti-Saloon League of America (ASL). Working closely with the WCTU, the ASL embarked on a full-scale campaign to enact a national prohibition amendment that began in 1913 when two southern Democrats, Senator Morris Sheppard of Texas and Congressman Richmond Hobson of Alabama, introduced the ultimately unsuccessful Hobson-Sheppard Amendment into Congress. The campaign culminated six years later with the passage of the Eighteenth Amendment.[15] Like many Americans, NACW activists followed these developments with great interest.

As the battle for a federal prohibition amendment heated up on the national stage after 1913, NACW activists expressed their strong support for the addition of such an amendment to the Constitution. They did so in primarily nonpartisan terms. That is, during the 1910s, NACW activists did not directly tie their support for the enactment of a prohibition amendment to their personal campaign efforts for the Republican Party as they would in the 1920s. The nonpartisan quality of NACW rhetoric on the Eighteenth Amendment during the 1910s was very much a reflection of national prohibition politics. Recognizing deep divisions in their own parties on the issue during the 1916 elections, both Democratic incumbent Woodrow Wilson and Republican candidate Charles Evans Hughes avoided the topic altogether. While subsequent candidates were not as tight-lipped, neither the Republicans nor the Democrats included an explicit statement about prohibition in their national platforms until 1924.[16]

Unlike presidential candidates, black clubwomen were forthright about their position on prohibition. At the 1914 and 1918 NACW Biennial Conventions, members passed resolutions endorsing the enactment of both prohibition and woman's suffrage amendments.[17] On the opening day of the 1914 convention, Ida Cummings told her receptive audience, "The temperance question is of vital importance to us." Invoking familiar racial uplift rhetoric, Cummings beseeched the more than 400 women gathered before her, "let us work with renewed energy to rid the land of that which is doing so much to drag us down as a race."[18] One year later, *National Notes* similarly urged its readers to advocate national prohibition and "become positive factors in helping to remove the great source of evil to mankind."[19] With heavy bipar-

Failure of Racial Uplift Ideology

tisan support, Congress approved the prohibition amendment in 1917 and sent it to the states for ratification.[20] That year, the Illinois Federation of Colored Women's Clubs was among the local NACW federations that passed a resolution supporting national prohibition.[21] At the national level, women who attended the NACW's 1918 convention sent telegrams to Congress and President Wilson calling for a prohibition amendment. In their resolutions, NACW activists maintained, not unlike many white prohibitionists, that a federal ban of liquor would eliminate an "arch enemy of the home and the nation" and, in 1918, would conserve food supplies necessary for war mobilization.[22] In January 1919 the NACW's temperance goals were fulfilled when the thirty-sixth state, Nebraska, ratified the Eighteenth Amendment and made the criminalization of the "manufacture, sale, or transportation of intoxicating liquors" part of the U.S. Constitution. In late October 1919, over Wilson's veto, Congress passed the National Prohibition Act, popularly known as the Volstead Act. This piece of legislation outlined the specific provisions necessary for federal enforcement of the amendment.[23]

After the Eighteenth Amendment's ratification, black clubwomen pointed out the implications of national prohibition for civil rights. They suggested that concerns over implementing the Volstead Act might raise white interest in enforcing the Reconstruction Amendments and the Nineteenth Amendment in the South. The ten resolutions passed at the NACW's 1920 convention included the following: "We go on record as endorsing and urging the enforcement of the 18th Amendment to the Federal Constitution of the United States as interpreted in the Volstead Act. And we also urge our National Congress to enforce the 14th and 15th Amendments to the Federal Constitution."[24] The 1920 convention minutes do not reveal whether NACW members explored the full implications of their resolutions, although they clearly situated their approach to the Eighteenth Amendment and the Volstead Act within the context of the Reconstruction Amendments. Their pairing of resolutions pointed to the Volstead Act's obvious Reconstruction-era analogs, the Enforcement Acts of 1870 and 1871 and the Civil Rights Bill of 1875.[25] The Enforcement Acts and Civil Rights Bill were designed to put federal muscle behind the Thirteenth, Fourteenth, and Fifteenth Amendments. When white supremacists moved to disfranchise southern black women after the Nineteenth Amendment's enactment, NACW president Hallie Quinn Brown similarly invoked the Eighteenth Amendment when calling for federal intervention on behalf of black women voters. At the 1921 suffrage memorial ceremony on Capitol Hill, Quinn Brown insisted, "the government is spending hundreds of thousands of dollars to enforce the

Failure of Racial Uplift Ideology

Prohibition Amendment and we hereby petition that congress employ the same means to enforce the Nineteenth."[26] This approach toward the Eighteenth Amendment reflected the general optimism that politically active middle-class women held during 1920 and 1921 about the possibility of using their newly acquired ballot to influence politics—that is, women who were beyond the reach of southern white disfranchisement schemes.

Repeal and Civil Rights in the 1920s

African American women reformers began to publicly unravel the profound implications of national prohibition for civil rights during the mid-1920s, when the movements to modify the Volstead Act and repeal the Eighteenth Amendment were already gaining momentum. In the early 1920s, organized opposition to the Eighteenth Amendment was confined to a few local and national groups composed of white men who received their funding from breweries and distilleries. Viewing the Eighteenth Amendment's repeal as unlikely, these groups sought to dismantle national prohibition by modifying the various provisions of the Volstead Act. By 1927, however, the movement had shifted its strategy away from modification and toward outright repeal. The infusion of corporate money into the repeal movement by 1927 ensured the broad circulation of antiprohibition literature.[27]

During the fourteen years of national prohibition, northern white opponents consistently anchored their challenges to the Eighteenth Amendment and the Volstead Act in self-rule arguments developed by white Democrats during the sectional crises of the 1840s to the 1870s. No less than Yale University's president emeritus, Arthur Twining Hadley, defended sectional nullification in a 1925 *Harper's Magazine* article. "Any considerable number of citizens who are habitually law-abiding," Hadley asserted, can nullify a statute "bad enough in itself or dangerous enough in its direct effects to make it worthwhile to block its enforcement" through disobedience. As precedent, Hadley, like so many others, pointed to white disagreements over the regulation of black bodies and rights. Through collective noncompliance, the "people of the North" had nullified the Fugitive Slave Law, while the "people of the South" had nullified the Reconstruction Amendments. Hadley and others clarified that theirs was not a position of lawlessness or rebellion. He maintained that nullification was a "safety valve which helps a self-governing community avoid the alternative between tyranny and revolution." Even though white defiance of the Reconstruction Amendments had resulted in "a legacy of lawlessness and unrest from which the community is still suffer-

Failure of Racial Uplift Ideology

ing," the federal government's brief attempt to enforce these measures, according to Hadley, had been more harmful to the nation by propagating "a legacy of bitterness" between white northerners and southerners. Others recognized that nullification did in fact promote lawlessness and suggested other means for circumventing the Eighteenth Amendment. Among the most common was the call to dismantle federal enforcement legislation and machinery. The *Chicago Tribune* recommended that one house of Congress could void the Volstead Act by refusing appropriations. By 1932 the chosen analogy was ever familiar. Without funding, "The enforcement unit in the department of justice will be closed. Federal agents will be withdrawn, as the army of occupation was withdrawn from the southern states."[28]

Nullification, state autonomy, community customs, carpetbaggers, withdrawal of federal troops—these were the terms that these white northerners used to frame and support their arguments for disobedience and repeal. The nation had never witnessed such a well-orchestrated repeal movement, which is not to say that this was the first time the idea of repealing a constitutional amendment had been floated. As the *Colored American Magazine* reassured its readers in 1901, however, "The occasional southerner who rises to advocate the repeal of the 15th amendment to the federal constitution apparently does not realize the impossibility of his scheme. You can drive around the amendment and over it and through it with a coach and four, but there it stands, and there it will stand so long as the present constitution is printed in the school books."[29] As the nation inched further into the twentieth century, however, the din of southern Democratic voices demanding the Fifteenth Amendment's repeal rose considerably. Leading the charge were congressional Democrats—Thomas Hardwick of Georgia, James Vardaman of Mississippi, and of course Ben Tillman of South Carolina.[30] In the context of the well-organized effort to repeal the Eighteenth Amendment, many black women reformers were not so confident by the 1920s that the Fifteenth Amendment was as safe as the *Colored American Magazine* had suggested in 1901.

As this organized dissent grew, the ground upon which middle-class black women had based their interpretation of the interplay between national prohibition and civil rights shifted. The modification and repeal movements undermined the NACW's efforts to broaden white enthusiasm for federal enforcement generated by the Eighteenth Amendment's ratification. Even more foreboding, women active in the NACW, the black Baptist church, and the Republican Party pointed out that the modification and repeal movements threatened the continued inclusion of the Reconstruction Amend-

Failure of Racial Uplift Ideology

ments in the Constitution. Politically active women adjusted to the new realities of prohibition politics and moved from an offensive to a defensive position. By 1924 they linked the Eighteenth Amendment and Reconstruction Amendments less as a strategy to encourage an activist federal government in the realm of civil rights and more as a countermeasure to prevent the further erosion and, still worse, the elimination of the Reconstruction Amendments.

NACW leaders urged members to work against modification and repeal efforts. In the July 1924 edition of *National Notes*, the New Jersey Federation reported on its successful efforts to do both. Just weeks earlier Congress had completed hearings on modifying national prohibition.[31] "In these days when all America is exercised over the enforcement of the 18th Amendment," New Jersey clubwoman M. E. Burrell wrote, the New Jersey Federation was doing its part to support "an amendment so vital to the industrial, mental and moral welfare of our country" by running "good government" groups for the black women of the state. In these groups and other contacts with local women, the New Jersey Federation, Burrell explained, was advancing a "program, which included respect and observance of the law—all laws—the constitution in its entirety, without special favor to any one law or amendment, fully realizing that the power of constituted authority in America is much endangered by the violation of one amendment as another." Burrell enthused that women throughout New Jersey "are not only taking their part as American citizens, but they are interesting the other women in bettering the condition of her street and her locality by voting for conscientious men to fill the positions of trust."[32] One month after Burrell's article appeared, the NACW held its Fourteenth Biennial Convention in Chicago. National legislative chairman Mazie Mossell Griffin similarly "urged the women of the National to do all in their power to prevent the repeal of the 18th Amendment to the Constitution of the United States, as this would place the 14th and 15th amendments in jeopardy." Toward this end, the Pennsylvania resident "urged the women of the different state clubs to educate their members to the importance of a wise use of the ballot."[33]

Two years later, as the drive to modify the Volstead Act culminated in another set of congressional hearings, the NACW leadership remained vigilant. The Senate subcommittee running the hearings gave reason for celebration when it resoundingly rejected the various modification proposals presented in April 1926. Gathering for their biennial meeting in Oakland just three months after the close of the Senate hearings, NACW leaders knew that the battle over the Eighteenth Amendment was far from over. Already

Failure of Racial Uplift Ideology

the antiprohibition forces were shifting their strategy away from modification toward outright repeal.[34] With such luminaries as Mary McLeod Bethune and Daisy Lampkin in attendance, the executive board passed a resolution to "stand firmly behind law enforcement and the Eighteenth Amendment."[35] That October, the Rhode Island Federation of Colored Women's Clubs "endorse[d] the National Federation's stand for strict enforcement of the Prohibition Amendment."[36] In a 1926 *National Notes* editorial, Myrtle Foster Cook went much further than her cohort by pointing to the implications of the Eighteenth Amendment debates for the Reconstruction Amendments. Following the same line of argument presented by Griffin at the 1924 convention, Foster Cook asked, "Shall the Eighteenth Amendment to the Constitution of the U.S. be enforced or shall it be modified? The question is before the country." The Kansas City, Missouri, resident continued, "Shall the press, the platform, and the pulpit create an atmosphere of respect for constitutional law and order, a spirit of purpose within the people for the observance of law, and a desire for its enforcement?" "If they do," Foster Cook asserted, "then some day the country will remember the Fifteenth Amendment and demand that Negroes everywhere be allowed to vote; and they will remember [the] Fourteenth and Thirteenth and wipe out peonage, and discriminations in the vital and essential rights of black American citizens."[37]

The 1928 Election: Repeal, Partisan Politics, and Realignment

During the 1928 presidential campaign, leading middle-class women placed their interpretation of the relationship between the Eighteenth Amendment and the civil rights amendments at the center of their Republican campaign work. It was the first presidential contest in which the candidates presented distinct positions on prohibition: longtime prohibition opponent and Democratic nominee Alfred Smith vocally favored withdrawal of both the Volstead Act and the Eighteenth Amendment, while Republican Herbert Hoover denounced efforts to repeal or undermine the Eighteenth Amendment.[38] By 1928 black Republican women were casting about for reasons to remain loyal to the Republican Party and, perhaps even more challenging, for arguments they could use to convince black voters to do the same. The liquor issue offered some help on both counts.

By 1928 middle-class black women, who just a few years earlier were hopeful of using the ballot to broaden white Republican enthusiasm for the federal enforcement of the Reconstruction Amendments, were questioning

Failure of Racial Uplift Ideology

whether to even maintain affiliation with the national Republican Party. Even as they created the machinery for canvassing tens of thousands of black voters, white counterparts were redefining the party. The majority of white Republicans relied on federal power to help big business quell a discontented labor force, rather than enforce the Reconstruction and Nineteenth Amendments. Moreover, ever aware that white supremacists had transformed the South into a one-party system, northern white Republicans sought to break up this Democratic "solid South" by cultivating the support of southern lily-white Republicans, as they were often called. These lily-whites were well versed in the politics of southern white supremacy and regularly fought to prevent "black-and-tan" delegations from representing their states at national Republican conventions.[39]

NLRCW activists were far from reluctant in expressing their discontent and sense of restlessness to white party officials, especially leaders of the Women's Department of the RNC with whom they had worked closely in the 1924 presidential contest. At the NLRCW's May 1928 conference, Virginia clubwoman Ora Brown Stokes told an audience that included the secretaries of labor, the interior, and the navy, among other prominent white Republican leaders, about the Republican Party's neglect of black women campaigners during the last presidential campaign. In 1924 Stokes had served as the Virginia state chairman for the Colored Women's Department of the RNC.[40] Describing black women's frustration while canvassing on behalf of the Republican Coolidge-Dawes ticket in Virginia, Stokes told her audience, "we could never could get in touch with the [Virginia Republican] Central Committee," which "met in Murphy's Hotel where no colored persons, except for help is allowed." With "[n]o help from the white Republicans," Stokes explained, "We financed ourselves, worked to get out our own literature," even though there was "nothing sent [to] us to give out." They also reached out to white Republican women in the North "to move the South for us, as we could not do it." Given that the situation in 1924 was "mighty hard," Stokes asked those gathered before her for the NLRCW conference, "I want to know what we can do about it?"[41]

The unsatisfactory answer came from white party official Sallie Hert, who headed the Women's Division of the RNC and served as an RNC vice chairman.[42] Hert avoided the issue of white Republican discrimination toward black party members altogether. Instead, Hert shifted the focus of discussion to white Democratic electoral fraud in Virginia and her own home state of Kentucky, as well as to white women's disinterest in Republican politics in Virginia. Stokes urged black women not to develop "a faint heart" because

Failure of Racial Uplift Ideology

of white Democratic electoral fraud. "In the end you will prevail," she told them, but in the meantime she suggested, "Keep up the organization spirit and confer with" white RNC committeewoman from Virginia, Willie Caldwell.[43] Stokes's response was curt and to the point: "Our Women are already organized."[44] Many black Republican women had spent the past eight years believing that proper long-term organizing would enable them to gain a foothold in national Republican networks, but by 1928 they were facing the stark reality of the limits of women's institution building within the Republican Party of the 1920s. Self-help and personal initiative could go only so far when the Republican Party remained committed to expanding its base among white southerners at the expense of its black constituency. Stokes was unwilling to let Hert's comment that black women had somehow faltered organizationally pass without a stern rebuke.

Stokes was also unwilling to ignore the Republican Party's growing lily-white composition in the South, despite Hert's efforts to redirect the discussion from white Republican racism to white Democratic racism. Virginia's national committee members in 1924 and 1928, Willie Caldwell (the woman Hert suggested Stokes consult) and C. Bascom Slemp, were no less racist than their Democratic counterparts in the state.[45] With her 1895 novel *The Tie That Binds; A Story of the North and the South*, Caldwell was an active contributor to the nostalgic reconciliation literature that, as David Blight explains, helped excise the primacy of slavery and emancipation from white Americans' memory of the Civil War and Reconstruction.[46] For his part, Slemp was the principal architect of policies aimed at transforming the Republican Party in the South into a lily-white party during the Harding administration. In his own state, Slemp prevented black-and-tan delegations from being seated at Republican National Conventions throughout the 1920s, and in 1928 he was again pushing a lily-white agenda as head of the Hoover campaign in the South.[47] To Hert's suggestion that Virginia's Democrats were the main problem, Stokes countered, "It is not the attitude of the Democrats but the attitude of the Republicans that discourages us, or makes us fighting mad."[48]

Stokes was far from alone among NLRCW leaders in her deep disappointment with the Republican Party. Abbreviated minutes from the closed-door sessions at this May 1928 conference indicate that internal debates took place among NLRCW activists over their future involvement with the Republican Party. A list of subjects discussed included "Why Parties?"; "Loyalty—Fighting It Out in the Family"; "General Reactions—Result of Party Inaction"; "What Are the Amendments to the Constitution Good For?" and

Failure of Racial Uplift Ideology

"What of 1928?" By the end of the conference, NLRCW members prepared a slogan for the upcoming 1928 election that was published in the black press.[49] This slogan read, "Oppose in State and National Campaigns Any Candidate Who Will Not Commit Him or Herself on the Enforcement of the 13th, 14th and 15th Amendments."[50] This slogan was far more an affirmation of these women's commitment to inserting into national elections a discourse about federal rights and responsibilities embedded in the unevenly enforced Reconstruction Amendments than it was a declaration of Republican partisanship.

As the campaign continued into the late summer, black Republican women only increased pressure on white party women to address Republican racism. In early August, the NLRCW sent a letter to assistant U.S. attorney general Mabel Willebrandt asking about her role in the unjust prosecution of black Republican leaders and appointees from Mississippi.[51] Willebrandt had recently spoken at an NLRCW meeting, where she encouraged her audience to remain steadfast. In a letter signed by the entire organization, the NLRCW explained to Willebrandt that in their canvassing work "we were confronted with the following question: Is there a definite movement on the part of the National Republican Committee, functioning thru your office, to rid the Republican Party of Negro leadership in the South?" "We ask this question," they explained, "because the impression is abroad that these vigorous investigations in which you are actively engaged are a first move toward ridding the Party of Negroes and endorsing 'Lily-White-ism.' " In this they joined a chorus of black leaders who denounced the prosecutions as part of the Republican Party's effort to attract southern white voters at the expense of its base of black support.[52] "We find it difficult, in the face of this question," they continued, "to offset the insidious propaganda which is being broadcast most effectively by the Democratic Party whose Presidential Candidate has been nationally known for his singularly fair attitude in dealing with our group." They concluded by asking Willebrandt for "an immediate reply," so that the NLRCW would have the facts to discount, they hoped, any false insinuation that Willebrandt was complicit in expelling black leaders from the party.[53] Willebrandt's response did not make it to the archives. Regardless, the correspondence offers a window into the difficult position in which black Republican women found themselves: simultaneously demanding accountability from seemingly indifferent white Republicans, while trying to canvass black voters on behalf of the Republican ticket.

Republican women perceived themselves as engaged in multiple battles. On the one hand, they were struggling against the white Republican racism

Failure of Racial Uplift Ideology

that was exemplified when Hallie Quinn Brown was, as the *Defender* reported, forced to sit in the "buzzards roost" at the RNC convention in Kansas City.[54] On the other hand, they had to contend with the defection of increasing numbers of African Americans to the Democratic Party. Jeannette Carter's concern was genuine when she alerted the Colored Women's Department of the RNC in the fall of 1928 that "the Democratic organization is very active, in the organization of Smith clubs in all the counties" across New Jersey.[55] Carter, founder of the Washington-based National Women's Political Study Club, had traveled across Virginia, Delaware, and New Jersey in September as a field organizer for the Colored Women's Department. In Virginia and Delaware, Carter was relieved to find active black Hoover-Curtis clubs and to meet with groups who sought her advice on how to form additional Hoover-Curtis clubs. Carter, however, was distressed by the lack of organizing taking place in New Jersey among black women, even those involved in the state committee. She was especially alarmed given the black organizing for Smith that she encountered in the state. Still, she ended her report on a somewhat upbeat note: "My opinion is, that New Jersey can yet be saved for Hoover and Curtis, but it will have to be done independently of the State committee."[56]

Among themselves, black Republican women acknowledged that black Democratic votes were protest votes against the Republican Party. In her report summarizing her October speaking tour across Kentucky, Illinois, Pennsylvania, New York, and Maryland on behalf of the Hoover-Curtis ticket, Nannie Helen Burroughs concluded that "people in this election are going to vote *against* things and candidates, and not *for* anything." " 'Vote against,' " she explained, "is the unwritten slogan."[57] Republican women primarily chastised poor African Americans for switching allegiance to the Democrats. They were well aware, however, that prominent women reformers like themselves—women with whom they had worked closely in both the club movement and Republican Party politics—were campaigning for Smith in order to protest Republican indifference.

Among this group of reformers who supported Smith, none were better known than Bessye Bearden and Alice Dunbar-Nelson. Both Bearden and Dunbar-Nelson were vice chairmen of the Smith-for-President Colored League that was headquartered in Harlem.[58] This was not the first foray into Democratic politics for either. In 1924 Dunbar-Nelson served as director of Colored Women at Democratic Party headquarters in New York.[59] Bearden, a native of North Carolina who lived variously in the Northeast and South during her youth and early adulthood, settled permanently in Harlem

Failure of Racial Uplift Ideology

with her husband in 1915. In Harlem, she was active in the NAACP, the Urban League, and the Utopia Neighborhood Club; and in 1920 she succeeded Ferdinand Q Morton as head of Harlem's influential Negro Democratic Club.[60] In the fall of 1928, Bearden conducted a speaking tour of Tennessee and Kentucky that drew large crowds. Of her visit to Memphis, the *Chicago Defender* reported that "many persons had to be turned away who expressed extreme regret." The *Defender*, which was among several leading black papers (including the *Baltimore Afro-American*, the *Boston Guardian*, and the *Norfolk Journal and Guide*) that came out in support of Smith, attempted to soften black readers' perceptions of southern white Democrats by emphasizing Bearden's positive reception among white women.[61] "In Lexington," the *Defender* reported, "over 5,000 white women turned out to greet the speaker and publicly admitted that she presented the best argument for the Democratic party that had been heard there." In Louisville, "a cordon of police had to be called out to keep the crowd moving so that the distinguished speaker with her escort, could make her way through the throng to address the meeting," which like the meeting in Lexington, consisted of a mixed-race audience. The *Defender* article concluded with a statement designed to distance the Democrats' association with white supremacy and, specifically, to address the use of chicken wire fences at the Democratic National Convention earlier in the year to segregate black participants. During Bearden's speaking tour, the *Defender* noted, "No wire cages were built to separate the race and no disturbance whatever was reported because there was no discrimination."[62]

In her speaking engagements, Dunbar-Nelson would have offered a distinctly gendered argument as to why women should leave the Republican Party, one that hinged on the gendered politics of race leadership and memory. She had done so four years earlier in her "Why I Am a Democrat in 1924" speech and then again in a 1927 *Messenger* piece entitled "The Negro Woman and the Ballot." Like her Republican counterparts, Dunbar-Nelson had asserted in her 1924 speech that black women had an obligation to lead the race. Unlike black Republican women, however, Dunbar-Nelson had insisted that clubwomen had an obligation to lead the race out of the Republican fold and into the Democratic Party. By 1927 Dunbar-Nelson implied that black women had failed to do so, or, as she had put it in 1924, "to come to the aid of the race by asserting political independence."[63]

Dunbar-Nelson grounded this negative assessment in 1927 in a selective retelling of suffrage history. "The Negro woman," she wrote in the *Messenger*, had promised that she "was going to be independent" if given the

Failure of Racial Uplift Ideology

vote. According to Dunbar-Nelson, black suffragists based this claim in the belief that black women and men remembered Reconstruction differently. Radical Republicans had enfranchised black men, not women: "No Civil War memories for her, and no deadening sense of gratitude to influence her vote." Dunbar-Nelson elaborated that the black woman had declared that she "owed no party allegiance" and that "[t]he name of Abraham Lincoln was not synonymous with her for blind G.O.P. allegiance." As a result, Dunbar-Nelson explained, the black woman had vowed that if given the ballot, "[s]he would vote men and measures, not parties." Perhaps most importantly, she had promised that women's guiding influence would rehabilitate black men from the debilitating memory of past Republican deeds: "She would show the Negro man how to make his vote a power, and not a joke" and, in the process, "break up the tradition that one could tell a black man's politics by the color of his skin." Dunbar-Nelson's assessment of black women's success in fulfilling their presuffrage promises, as she relayed them, was decidedly bleak. She portrayed black Republican women, who in her mind had betrayed the promise of political independence, as simultaneously passive and aggressive in their devotion to the Republican Party. On the one hand, they were passive followers rather than leaders of men who had "slipped quietly, easily and conservatively into the political party of [their] male relatives" upon receiving the ballot. On the other hand, they were "virulent and zealous" partisans who were "vituperative in campaigns" and "[p]rone to stop speaking to [their] friends who might disagree with [their] findings on the political issues."[64]

To be sure, some black women had rejected loyal partisanship in the years before the Nineteenth Amendment. Recall that in 1894 Fannie Barrier Williams had used the pages of the *Woman's Era* to urge black women "to array themselves, when possible, on the side of the best, whether that best be inside or outside of party lines" and to warn against engaging in the "folly and self-neglect that have made the colored men . . . vote persistently more for the special interests of white men than for the peculiar interests of the colored race."[65] But many others had argued something quite different: that even as they cleaned up party politics, they would demonstrate their worthiness of the ballot through loyal partisanship. Black Republican women had grounded this loyalty in the memory of the Reconstruction Amendments. And they had repeatedly looked for moments to insert discussion of the amendments into campaigns, regardless of whether a given election had anything to do with the federal enforcement of citizenship rights.

While Dunbar-Nelson asserted in 1927 that the "Negro woman has by

Failure of Racial Uplift Ideology

and large been a disappointment in her handling of the ballot," she actually ended her *Messenger* piece on a positive note, insisting that "it is not altogether hopeless." She would have emphasized this appeal for change in her various speaking engagements as a vice chairman of the Smith-for-President Colored League in 1928. It is possible to imagine Dunbar-Nelson telling her audiences, as she did in the *Messenger* one year earlier, that "the Negro woman CAN be roused when something near and dear to her is touched." "Then," she enthused, "she throws off the influence of her male companion and strikes out for herself." In her view, the 1922 congressional campaign when women crossed party lines to defeat Republican and Democratic congressmen alike who helped to kill the Dyer Antilynching Bill exemplified this willingness to be "roused." Employing the rhetoric of home protection and motherhood, she explained, "When the Negro woman finds that the future of her children lies in her own hands—if she can be made to see this—she will strike off the political shackles she has allowed to be hung upon her, and win the economic freedom of her race."[66] No doubt, in 1928 Dunbar-Nelson made it her mission to help black women voters "see this"—that a vote for the Democratic Party was a vote for the future of their children. How the Democratic Party would specifically help African American women gain economic freedom or protect future generations, Dunbar-Nelson did not say in the *Messenger* piece, which in fact did not equate independent voting with Democratic voting. But the connection between Democratic voting and future generations was certainly implied when she lamented that black women's votes had not shattered "the deadly monotony of the blind faith in the 'Party of Massa Linkum.' "[67] A break from the Republican Party would release future generations from this monotony. It was up to women to lead the way.

Black women's support for the Smith campaign extended well beyond the middle-class reform circles in which Bearden and Dunbar-Nelson operated and included the distinctly working-class constituency of the Garvey movement. Although limited primary sources make it difficult to document the actual voices of poor women who constituted the rank and file of the Garvey movement, tracing the activities of individuals whom such women saw as their representatives hints at some of the issues and events that animated the partisan world of poor and working-class Garveyite women in 1928. One of these key representatives was Amy Jacques Garvey. Jacques Garvey's association with the Democratic candidate was cemented, in part, through her husband's vocal support for Smith. Initially, which party Garvey, and by extension Jacques Garvey, would endorse, or whether the UNIA leadership

Failure of Racial Uplift Ideology

would even take a position in the 1928 presidential election, appeared uncertain. In the months leading up to the Republican and Democratic national conventions in June, the *Negro World* ran editorials debating the merits and faults of presidential hopefuls and concluding ultimately that "nationally, the Negro is between the frying pan and the fire."[68] Shortly after the conventions, however, the UNIA came out strongly in favor of Smith. Marcus Garvey insisted in the *Negro World* that "every loyal member of the Universal Negro Improvement Association will campaign and vote for Al Smith."[69] Throughout the fall the *Negro World* ran a series of ads and articles reiterating Garvey's support for Smith that asserted, "Any Negro who votes for Herbert Hoover is disloyal to his race."[70]

In Harlem and Chicago, where the Garvey movement had set down significant roots, Garveyites also held pro-Smith rallies. In mid-October, for instance, the UNIA's Chicago chapter joined forces with Reverdy Ransom, the outspoken AME bishop and editor of the AME *Church Review*, to throw a mass pro-Smith rally that filled the large auditorium of the Wendell Phillips High School. As William Wallace, a UNIA leader in Chicago told the crowd, "Our great emancipator, Abraham Lincoln, was a Republican, but the example he set has been terribly and greatly neglected so far as we are concerned." "Conditions have sadly changed," he asserted, "and it is better for us to vote independently now." "Governor Smith is our friend," Wallace concluded, "and I urge votes for him.' "[71] Ransom concurred: " 'Every vote for Smith is a blow to intolerance and bigotry.' "[72] Ransom was returning to the city where he had spent the years between 1896 and 1904 directing the resources of the AME Church toward setting up social welfare services for residents in Chicago's South Side, first at Bethel AME Church and then at Institutional Church and Settlement House, which he founded in 1900.[73] His reputation as a social reformer and militant activist would have made his decision to abandon the Republican Party in 1928 carry weight among those in the crowd at Wendell Philips who felt disaffected not only by white Republicans but, perhaps more importantly, by the black middle class, whose seemingly dogged investment in the Republican Party appeared illogical.

Just days before the election, white Democratic Party leaders publicly thanked Jacques Garvey "for her leadership among Negro women." Presumably, they meant her Democratic work among African American women. They also acknowledged Marcus Garvey's support. The occasion was a speech that Jacques Garvey was delivering to the Philadelphia division of the UNIA. Philadelphia was one stop on a brief U.S. speaking tour that Jacques Garvey made without her husband at the end of October. Fearing

Failure of Racial Uplift Ideology

that Garvey's presence in the United States might undermine Republican victory, the incumbent administration pressured Canadian officials to detain him, preventing Garvey from accompanying his wife. On this particular evening, hundreds of Garveyites from Pennsylvania, as well as New Jersey and Delaware, gathered at Philadelphia's Mt. Zion AME Church to hear Jacques Garvey describe her and her husband's efforts to drum up support for the UNIA and its brand of black nationalism in Europe. Shortly before Jacques Garvey began her talk, two white delegates from the Smith-for-President Inter-Racial Committee presented her with a bouquet of flowers as a show of appreciation. "This unexpected display of inter-racial good will," the *Negro World* reported, "elicited vociferous applause from the audience."[74]

Hoover's and Smith's distinct positions on the liquor question offered black Republican women a respite from their own mounting disappointment with the Republican Party and an argument for why black Americans should remain loyal to the GOP, or, at the very least, why they should oppose Smith. On a September Saturday in 1928, for example, NLRCW president Nannie Helen Burroughs urged black Baptist women from throughout the nation who had assembled at the Lampton Street Baptist Church in Louisville, Kentucky, to cast their ballots for Herbert Hoover on November 6 because of his solid position against repeal. All week, these women had joined leading Baptist men in Louisville for the annual meeting of the National Baptist Convention. On that fall Saturday, the women separated from their male counterparts, just as they had since founding a women's auxiliary in 1900, to conduct the business of the Woman's Convention.[75]

With less than two months before the elections, Burroughs distilled for her audience the primary issue: "The test in this campaign is a test of the strength of the amendments to the Constituti[o]n." Arguing against Smith's candidacy, she explained the full and foreboding meaning of placing in the executive office an individual who favored the repeal of a constitutional amendment: "If the eighteenth amendment is not strong enough to stand, if we vote men into office who sanction its modification or annulment, we might as well sign the death certificate of the thirteenth, fourteenth and fifteenth amendments." Burroughs urged her audience, "Do not vote any man into power who proposes to tamper with the Constitution of the United States." She added, "do not forget that the party which Governor Smith represents did not help to write your rights into the Constitution and it should not therefore be given an opportunity to tamper with them."[76] During October, Burroughs conducted a speaking tour on behalf of the Colored Women's Department of the RNC that took her to Pennsylvania, Maryland,

Failure of Racial Uplift Ideology

Virginia, West Virginia, Rhode Island, New York, New Jersey, and much of the same territory in Kentucky that Bessye Bearden had canvassed the previous month. There she presumably conveyed a similar message while giving speeches with titles like "The Moral Issues of the Campaign."[77]

Black Republican men also warned that repealing the Eighteenth Amendment threatened the Reconstruction Amendments. For example, Republican Illinois state senator Aldelbert H. Roberts made such an argument before those attending one of the mixed-gender sessions of the National Baptist Convention's 1928 Kentucky conference.[78] Although Republican men and women employed similar campaign rhetoric, some perceived the Eighteenth Amendment's enforcement to be of greater concern to African American women. At the heart of this assertion lay the related convictions that women's most significant roles were those of wife and mother and that liquor threatened the family stability necessary to properly perform these roles. As clubwoman Ione Gibbs insisted in a 1907 article detailing women's racial uplift responsibilities in the domestic sphere, "intemperance, the great evil that menaces both the young and the old, must be kept out of the home."[79] Two decades later, the gendered assumptions that connected prohibition politics with women's ability to perform traditional domestic roles continued to inform black Republican rhetoric on repeal. In a 1928 article, Howard sociologist Kelly Miller insisted, "Intemperance, which is chiefly a masculine vice, falls heaviest upon [a woman] and her dependent children." The family stability that Gibbs and other clubwomen valued, Miller suggested, would be threatened if liquor were made legal again: "When the husband divides his pay envelope between her and the saloon, she is apt to receive the minor share. Family distress and domestic unhappiness are certain to ensue." As a result, he argued, "Every woman who votes against the eighteenth amendment votes against her sex." In Miller's view, however, the potential ramifications of the election for the future of the Reconstruction Amendments placed a much heavier responsibility on black women than white women. "Any colored woman who votes against [the Eighteenth Amendment]," Miller insisted, "votes against both, her race and her sex."[80]

In 1928 the prohibition planks put forth by "dry" Republicans and "wet" Democrats at the national level concealed significant internal disputes that each party had precariously contained for years with platforms that avoided the issue and presidential candidates who artfully dodged it. On the eve of the 1928 elections, Kelly Miller characterized for readers of the black, Chicago-based newspaper, *The Light and Heebie Jeebies*, some of the regional

Failure of Racial Uplift Ideology

differences that were tenuously contained within each major party: "The Democratic party in the South is Protestant and dry, while in the North it is Catholic and wet." The Republican Party was no less divided along regional lines. Republicans in the West, Miller explained, generally favored prohibition and opposed repeal, while those in the East were "wet."[81] Yet even Miller's summary masks a web of Republican and Democratic views on prohibition that were not only defined by allegiances of region, race, class, and gender but also crisscrossed those allegiances. Black Republican women navigated these complicated allegiances with black Democrats, the Republican Party's lily-white orientation, and their own gendered claims to race leadership in mind.

Republican women's support of prohibition was hardly representative of all African Americans. Quite the opposite: the results of an April 1919 election indicate how significant opposition to prohibition ran in black Chicago. The ballot included a measure to begin prohibition in the city early. The Eighteenth Amendment would take effect in January 1920, but if this measure passed, opponents of liquor would not have to wait nine more months before its manufacture and sale became illegal. Chicago's most heavily black populated wards offered little support for embarking on prohibition any earlier than absolutely necessary. In the Second, Third, and Fourth Wards, only 22, 43, and 13 percent of women who cast a ballot in the April election did so in favor of the early introduction of prohibition. Even fewer men cast a ballot in favor of early introduction; the percentages respectively were 16, 26, and 9. In other words, if this limited support for the early enforcement of prohibition was any indicator of black views on the Eighteenth Amendment, then the vast majority of black voters in Chicago objected to it.[82]

Black opposition to prohibition was grounded in several sources. First, the southern white prohibitionist's explicit role in black disfranchisement, the enactment of Jim Crow legislation, and numerous acts of racially motivated violence created resentment among southern blacks. In the South, the drive to disfranchise black men was closely intertwined with local option campaigns. Southern white prohibitions asserted that the "black vote was wet and hopelessly corrupted by liquor interests" and therefore needed to be eliminated if local option elections were to succeed. Indeed, prohibitionists were among the panoply of voices in Mississippi during 1889 and 1890 calling for the disfranchisement of black men through a rewriting of the state constitution. They even addressed the Mississippi constitutional convention that had been called to order for just that purpose in the late summer of

Failure of Racial Uplift Ideology

1890, explaining that the state's thirty-five counties lacking local option "are mostly in the black belt and are kept wet by the negro vote."[83]

Southern white prohibitionists also employed stereotypes of drunken black men who threatened the sexual purity of white womanhood in the service of legislating temperance.[84] This argument, for instance, gained renewed currency in the aftermath of the 1906 Atlanta Race Riot. The riot itself was sparked by newspaper reports of black men sexually assaulting white women. Claims that, as one man from western Georgia put it, "Atlanta would not have had a race riot had it not been for low grogshops, and Negroes full of rum and dope," then drove the local option campaign that resulted in the 1907 State Prohibition Act. A statewide ban of liquor was necessary, white prohibitionists argued, in order to protect white women from such indignities.[85] One local white paper in southwestern Georgia contended that blacks "inflamed with whiskey" were the cause of 95 percent of assaults and attempted assaults.[86] Another, the *Union Recorder* of Milledgeville, declared that barrooms "furnish loafing places for vagabond Negroes, to sell them liquor that inflames their passions, preparing them for any and all sorts of crime." "This reason alone," the *Union Recorder* insisted, "should make the white voters of Baldwin County solid against the reopening of the barroom in this city."[87] These assertions easily merged with disfranchisement arguments that the black vote needed to be eliminated in order to make local option campaigns a success.[88] It is quite possible that many African Americans responded to these assaults on their personal and political liberties by associating alcohol consumption with the defiance of Jim Crow.[89] This would hold true for those who remained under the yoke of southern white supremacy, as well as the tens of thousands of southern blacks who relocated to the Midwest and Northeast precisely because they sought greater expression of personal liberty.

Simple "wet" and "dry" labels also masked intraracial disagreements about black participation in commercialized leisure that were, in turn, shaped by debates over the relationship between behavior and class formation. Many African Americans drank, served, and sold alcohol, placing them on the "wet" side of the Eighteenth Amendment debates. Liquor consumption was a mainstay of commercial leisure districts that emerged in major American cities across the nation during the first two decades of the twentieth century. Migrants who sought to express their personal liberty through liquor consumption had plenty of opportunities to do so in these vibrant districts that awaited them in the urban North. In Chicago, the stretch of State Street between 26th and 39th Streets that was known as "the Stroll"

Failure of Racial Uplift Ideology

offered a veritable menu of amusements: movie theaters, vaudevilles, restaurants, nightclubs, gambling and pool halls, saloons, and, after 1919, "speakeasies." On a given evening, a newcomer to the city might begin on the north end of the Stroll at the Pekin Theater to catch a movie. If she and her companions sought more entertainment, they had their pick of nightclubs from which to choose. They might head a couple blocks south on State Street to drink, dine, gamble, and dance with up to 300 other patrons at the Elite No. 1 Club. If their wallets permitted, the group might then walk a few blocks further south to the Dreamland Café to hear blues and jazz greats such as Alberta Hunter, Joe "King" Oliver, Lil Hardin, and Louis Armstrong. Along the way, they would encounter white Chicagoans who engaged in a kind of racial tourism by visiting establishments along the Stroll. They would hear the sounds of boisterous club goers mixing with bursts of music as doors swung open and shut at the various nightclubs that they passed—the Café Champion, the Elite No. 2 Club, and the DeLuxe Café among others. These sights and sounds served to distance migrant women and men from the world they had left behind in the South.[90]

Migrant participation in this leisure culture was an expression of self-ownership and a rebuke of the mean-spirited claims of southern white prohibitionists. Yet it was also a direct rejection of women reformers' racial uplift demands that migrants, especially women, display modesty in their new surroundings. Clearly, migrant women's definitions of what it meant to be a free person were diverse. While some middle-class women carried northward a belief that racial uplift ideology would ultimately help enhance black freedom, other migrant women who operated outside of such women's reform circles held a very different understanding of how they could not only increase black freedom but also personally enjoy their own liberation from southern white supremacy. Born out of a shared dilemma of how to respond to southern white supremacy, these divergent responses to commercialized leisure in the North created intraracial tensions that spilled into the partisan politics of prohibition.

There were also economic motivations for opposing prohibition. In the years before the Eighteenth Amendment, legal establishments that sold liquor—saloons, dance halls, pool halls—were sources of revenue for a significant number of African Americans.[91] Chicago, for instance, claimed hundreds if not thousands of saloons by the beginning of the twentieth century. With a few exceptions, white-owned saloons, however, ignored state civil rights law and excluded black patrons, sometimes violently. This created an opportunity for enterprising black businessmen, and by 1900 Chi-

Failure of Racial Uplift Ideology

cago claimed forty-eight black-owned saloons. In his study on public drinking, historian Perry Druis explains that in Chicago "the saloonkeeper was an important part of the black business community." Black business directories sometimes included saloon owners in their brief sketches about self-made men—a familiar self-help narrative that ironically was driven by the sale of liquor. The economies of many working-class households were tied to establishments that sold liquor as well. White barrooms may not have welcomed African Americans as patrons, but they were willing to hire them as servers, maids, janitors, and musicians. By one estimate, 12 percent of black men in Chicago were employed in both black- and white-owned saloons and poolrooms in 1914.[92] Working-class African Americans also created their own leisure institutions that helped them to make ends meet. Some periodically turned their homes into makeshift saloons or transformed rented storefronts into nightclubs. Others threw "rent parties" in private homes or apartments, where hosts typically used the modest entrance fee required of guests to cover their monthly rent.[93]

Then there was the revenue generated by the whole microeconomy of vice that revolved around the world of the saloon, pool hall, dance hall, and, after 1919, the "speakeasy." Gambling, prostitution, and, after 1919, the illegal sale of liquor fueled this informal economy that was centered in the predominantly black neighborhoods of cities like Chicago, New York, and Detroit. During the 1900s and 1910s, antiprostitution reform in such cities drove this microeconomy out of white or mixed-race areas and more deeply into segregated black neighborhoods.[94] Middle-class leaders protested the migration of vice into black communities at every stage, asserting that it threatened their ability to ensure proper homes. In 1913, for instance, NACW president Margaret Washington (the wife of Booker T. Washington) denounced the "very common practice of establishing the district of segregated vice near the residence districts of colored citizens" and urged NACW members to "march an army of protest to the City Hall and battle for the strength and purity of your sons and daughters."[95] The Eighteenth Amendment only invigorated the growth of such vice districts in black neighborhoods throughout the nation. Chicago was no exception. During the 1900s and 1910s, the vice district was located on the northern border of the Black Belt in an area known as the Levee District between 18th and 22nd Streets and between Halsted and Federal Streets. Antivice reform pushed this illicit economy several blocks southward to the heart of the Black Belt and, more specifically, to a multiblock radius around the Stroll between 33rd and 35th Streets. There, the Eighteenth Amendment helped to transform this over-

Failure of Racial Uplift Ideology

whelmingly black neighborhood into a center for "the illicit sale of alcohol and sex."[96]

While reformers lamented the concentration of vice districts in black neighborhoods, this informal economy was an important source of revenue for poor African Americans who eked out a marginal existence. This was especially the case for African American women, many of them new arrivals from the South, who encountered very limited job opportunities. Facing chronic under- and unemployment, some dipped in and out of the sex trade to supplement nonexistent or meager wages.[97] Of the black prostitutes he encountered, one Chicago policeman asserted: "If they could just get a job scrubbing floors you wouldn't see them trying to be whores very long. They are for the most part just unfortunate women who have to do anything to get something to eat."[98] Those women who were able to obtain legal employment often found that the only jobs open to them were as domestics or laundresses. In such a limited and underremunerated job market, some chose to sell sex over working as a domestic. "When I see the word *maid*," one black prostitute exclaimed, "why, girl, let me tell you, it just runs through me! I think I'd sooner starve."[99] The exact number of African American women who engaged in prostitution is unknown. Vice reports make it quite clear, though, that black prostitution grew significantly in the years of the Great Migration and even more so once the Depression devastated black communities economically. In his 1933 study *Vice in Chicago*, for example, Vanderbilt University sociologist Walter Reckless reported that fully 45 percent of underworld establishments investigated for prostitution included black sex workers.[100] This was a marked contrast to the racial composition of prostitution in Chicago fifteen years prior when, by most accounts, only a small number of black women worked as prostitutes.[101]

While the actual political doings of the most marginal of black women remain largely obscured by limited primary documents, it is clear that they had a stake in vice policy. An administration's policy on vice, whether at the local or national level, directly affected the economic stability of poor black women and families who relied upon the vice economy for survival: crackdowns on vice, in turn, eliminated income. One widow described how the election of an antivice administration in Chicago destroyed her economically. William "Big Bill" Thompson's third term as mayor of Chicago between 1927 and 1931 was the stuff around which the legends of prohibition gang violence were constructed. The Republican mayor ran an "open town" that permitted illicit prostitution, gambling, and drinking establishments with minimal police interference.[102] This widow recalled the signifi-

Failure of Racial Uplift Ideology

cantly higher wages that she earned under an "open town" administration when she was able to find work as a maid for two prostitutes: "I made good money then, for I had a chance to make tips. I never made less than $25 a week for they catered to the rich men, bankers, and other high-class people." The hotel where she worked, she explained, "was full of those women, and it ran wide open until party politics was changed." In 1931 Democrat Anton Cermack replaced Thompson as mayor of Chicago. Cermack and his successor (Cermack was assassinated in 1933), Edward Kelly, supported a protracted effort to crack down on vice.[103] "It was soon after a cleanup drive was begun that they were raided, so naturally I lost my job," the woman recalled. She continued to work as a maid in a private white home, but earned only $7 dollars a week, which as she put it, "is clear money but I can't do much with it."[104]

Vice syndicates in the South Side, according to Reckless, also permitted poor families or storefront churches to occupy the ground floor of a building in order to disguise the use of upper floors for gambling, prostitution, and liquor-related business.[105] This arrangement not only served to camouflage vice activity but also created a loyal political base. Poor black voters had every reason to support Thompson, whose Republican political machine held ties to the "Second Ward Syndicate" that distributed such favors and created vice-related business opportunities.[106] With Thompson's defeat, many poor families and worshipers presumably lost their free housing and worship space. Without fundamental structural changes in the institutionalized racism and sexism that pushed women and families to the very margins of the economy, poor men and women did not have the same motivation as their middling counterparts to vote for antivice candidates.

Not all working-class and poor women, however, favored a vibrant vice economy by any means. Most notably, the UNIA's opposition to the Eighteenth Amendment was grounded precisely in the recognition that prohibition fueled this vice economy. Garveyite women shared clubwomen's disapproval of liquor. Unlike clubwomen, however, Garveyites argued that the end of prohibition, not its continuation, offered the greatest opportunity for the protection of black homes and rights. In a 1924 editorial in "Our Women and What They Want," a Garveyite who went by the pseudonym "Disgusted" pointed to the ineffectiveness of the Eighteenth Amendment. Disgusted rhetorically asked readers of the women's page: "Does prohibition, as we have it today, prohibit? Does it accomplish the purposes designed in the passage of the bill? Does it give us the long-wished-for dreams in seeing our homes rid of ills occasioned through the demon monster drink? Does it bring to our firesides the sobriety sighed for the joy that comes in homes free from the influence of drink?" "Look about you," Disgusted urged readers, "and let the evidences answer the foregoing questions for you." For Disgusted, the answer to these questions required merely the consideration of how the Eighteenth Amendment had transformed law-abiding communities and individuals into vice districts and criminals: "Homes and districts, that once knew not the woes of licensed drinks, are now the producers and protectors of this illegal and illicit trade. Thousands of men, with loving wives and dear little children, who did not drink nor did they contact others who drank, are now manufacturers of all the forms of 'hootch.'" Facing "rich returns," "the satisfaction of knowing every other fellow is engaged in this same business," and small fines if caught that were "a very small fraction of your gains," those involved in the illicit sale of liquor, Disgusted argued, had "no compunction of conscience" to stop their illegal activities.[107] So long as federal prohibition continued, the vice economy that this writer and other Garveyites so vehemently opposed would threaten the moral and physical safety of home and community.

Four years later, the *Negro World* continued to lament the havoc that the Eighteenth Amendment had wrought on black homes and identified Alfred Smith's candidacy as a means by which African Americans might help extricate their communities from prohibition-fueled vice and violence. As a July 1928 *Negro World* editorial calling for Smith's election argued, "In Harlem, the greatest vice is not 'playing the numbers,' not the cabarets, not the debauchery of young womanhood, but Prohibition." "The corner saloon and the evils it bred" prior to the Eighteenth Amendment, the editorial declared, "were a sacrificial alter compared with the degradations of the apartment-speakeasy." The benefit of the legal saloon was that at least "the confirmed tippler and the quean of the streets were segregated" from hardworking and clean-living families. "In a thousand homes in Harlem" where speakeasies surreptitiously had operated since the Eighteenth Amendment's enactment, such drunkards and prostitutes "rub shoulders with innocent children." "Where there is hooch," the editorial summed up, "the people perish."[108] Here, the *Negro World* was referring to the moral and health risks of alcohol, the latter of which Reverdy Ransom also emphasized months later in his November speech at the pro-Smith UNIA rally in Chicago. As Ransom told the crowd, "Smith does not want to bring whisky back into the country—it has never been taken out—but what he wants is a better grade of it."[109]

The *Negro World* editorial was also referring to the violence that prohibi-

Failure of Racial Uplift Ideology

tion had unleashed on black communities. Black saloons and speakeasies were the subject of crackdowns and brutality meted out by overwhelmingly white police forces charged with enforcing prohibition.[110] Self-defense, in this interpretation, entailed voting for the policy that would alleviate police misconduct. At least one *Negro World* reader, S. R. Hall of Pittsburgh, wrote back enthusiastically lauding the editorial: "I think that every Negro newspaper in America should come out boldly across the front page of their paper and say as you have said." "I have always voted a Republican ticket," Hall explained, "but this country is in such a mess with this prohibition business until it takes only a man like Al Smith to straighten things out."[111]

Republican women justifiably feared that black opposition to prohibition —originating from black patronage of illicit nightclubs, reliance on the informal economy, and outrage over white abuses—created the potential for a voting bloc that included white northern Democrats and black voters. It was this fear that lay behind the *Prohibition Issue as a Smoke Screen* pamphlet's stern warnings about the interdependency of northern and southern white Democrats: "Don't fool yourself, Colored voters! Al Smith may be a fine fellow, but: Al Smith in New York is not Al Smith in the White House. Al Smith is only one man—the standard bearer of a party, the majority of whom are Southern Democrats." Here, the Colored Women's Department of the RNC was calling attention to the fact that as a northern Democrat, Smith was a minority in his own party. Smith, the pamphlet's author(s) suggested, was merely a northern front for southern Democrats. As the pamphlet explained, "If he is elected, the solid South will gain control of the Government."[112]

From the perspective of black Republican women, black opposition to the Eighteenth Amendment threatened much more than black support for the Republican Party. It threatened their very claims to leadership both within the Republican Party and more broadly through the politics of racial uplift. Unlike the average voter, Republican women activists had made a significant personal investment in the machinery of Republican politics, an investment they hoped would offer returns beneficial to black citizens, as well as to their own political capital. By 1928 black Republican women leaders had gained considerable momentum in terms of canvassing skills, and they were in a position to offer interested candidates significant help in reaching black voters. Of course, many were themselves deeply dissatisfied with the lilywhite aspects of their party. Many campaigned for Hoover in 1928 not because they were enthusiastic about what the Republican Party had come to represent at the national level, but rather because they feared a worse

Failure of Racial Uplift Ideology

outcome if southern white Democrats gained control of the presidency. Still they were reluctant to leave the Republican Party because of the cachet and organizational machinery they had so carefully cultivated over the years. For them, the dissolution of black Republican support meant the loss of political influence and raised the prospect that they might have to rebuild. While the Republican Party was bankrupt in its dealings with black Americans, the Democratic Party was not necessarily any better. On the national level, the Democrat Party certainly did not offer anything substantial to black Americans. The prospect of rebuilding must not have been very appealing. This was especially the case when black Republican women perceived themselves to be in a position to cash in, both literally and figuratively, on carefully cultivated relationships with white Republican politicians at the local level.

The very same women who were leading the charge in the Republican Party also faced mounting challenges to their "woman's era" philosophy and its grounding in racial uplift politics. In the nineteenth century, women reformers insisted that men had failed to solve the problems of the race. Now New Negro men reversed the accusation. Women reformers had promised to lead the race out of the nadir, but still three decades after they had proclaimed the beginning of the "woman's era," institutionalized racism remained very much intact.[113] Critics looking for evidence of women reformers' failure to deliver on promises could draw examples from temperance and prohibition politics. As Fannie Barrier Williams, for example, had argued in an 1895 piece entitled, "Opportunities and Responsibilities of Colored Women," "If temperance could be the cardinal virtue of our race nothing would be able to resist our advancement toward the enjoyment of all the equalities of freedom and citizenship of this country."[114] Black support of local option campaigns and the Eighteenth Amendment had neither undermined racist stereotypes nor reversed disfranchisement. Nor from the UNIA's perspective had the Eighteenth Amendment eliminated an "arch enemy of the home," as the NACW had insisted in 1918 that its ratification would accomplish. The Eighteenth Amendment, the UNIA asserted, had merely forced respectable families to live in close proximity to underworld characters.[115] Marcus Garvey was among a panoply of New Negro male leaders who "made race progress dependent on virile masculinity."[116] So when the editors of the *Negro World* denounced Hoover for supporting an amendment that "is vitiating the home-life of Negroes" they did so with a distinctly gendered understanding of home protection in mind, one that emphasized men's responsibility to physically defend black homes from white violence.[117]

Failure of Racial Uplift Ideology

In this context, UNIA opposition to the Eighteenth Amendment was a not so subtle rejection of women reformers' claims that they knew best how to protect the black home.

Black participation in urban leisure culture and the underground economy that typically accompanied it further undermined women reformers' insistence that they knew best how to lead the race. African Americans, and especially black women, who enjoyed the sexually charged atmosphere and liquor-fueled establishments of Chicago's Stroll, for instance, rejected racial uplift's demands of modesty. In so doing, they also expanded the boundaries of acceptable behavior for black women and fed into the "new morality" of the 1920s that celebrated a degree of sexual frankness epitomized in the figure of the blues woman who inhabited the Stoll's nightclubs. Indeed, Victoria Wolcott has demonstrated that the very definition of appropriate behavior, often referred to as respectability, took on new meanings among the working poor in Detroit during the 1920s. African Americans blurred the line between reputable and disreputable behavior when they produced illegal alcohol and ran gambling rings in the backrooms of legitimate businesses, or when women supplemented meager domestic wages by working as prostitutes. The wages generated by such illicit leisure work, Wolcott argues, funded reputable community institutions, including churches, and enabled men and women who were struggling financially to provide for their families. The *Negro World* editorial that endorsed Smith's prohibition stance said as much when it accused church leaders and reformers of benefiting from the illicit sale of alcohol as much as bootleggers did. "The 'Drys,' " the editorial complained, "build reputations advocating and defending prohibition," while churches relied upon the donations of members who participated in the vice economy. "Show us a preacher who would banish a bootlegger from his church," the *Negro World* scoffed, "and we will show you an egg-dealer who abhors laying hens." Such broadened definitions of appropriate behavior and respectability jeopardized the relevance of the moral guidance that black clubwomen offered their communities.[118]

Deborah Gray White demonstrates that in the face of such challenges to their leadership, NACW activists resisted adjusting their reform agenda, choosing instead to hang onto their commitment to racial uplift ideology ever more fervently. As White argues, "Moral purity and socially correct behavior became even more of a crusade than in the pre-war years."[119] With prohibition politics so deeply implicated in women's self-mandate to instill temperance, thrift, and modesty among poor African Americans, it is perhaps no surprise that this retrenchment in women's racial uplift ideology

Failure of Racial Uplift Ideology

spilled into their partisanship. Indeed, these women's dogged commitment to the Eighteenth Amendment in the face of significant black opposition, as well as evidence that prohibition fueled vice in black neighborhoods, needs to be understood as a manifestation of this retrenchment within the realm of party politics. It explains why black women reformers who entered electoral politics to help southern blacks did not advocate the position held by many southerners living all around them in the North when it came to prohibition. Women reformers were not unaware of black disapproval of prohibition. Quite the opposite: black Republican women were acutely aware of the disconnect that existed between themselves and many working-class African Americans on this issue, and they perceived this disconnect as a threat to their leadership status. Their defensive efforts to reassert moral and political authority around prohibition generated a class blind spot in their canvassing that in turn led them to dismiss the views of the very constituencies whom they claimed to represent.

That Republican women's blending of racial uplift rhetoric with their partisanship created a class blind spot in their canvassing was evident when they berated African Americans who would, as they portrayed Democratic voting, put their desire for liquor before the Reconstruction Amendments. In an October letter, Wells-Barnett reported to RNC publicity director Claude Barnett (no relation) on the women's Hoover-Curtis clubs she helped establish in ten Illinois counties. These clubs, she explained, "are doing their bit by showing the unthinking masses that Al Smith cannot carry out his pledge to modify or annul the Volstead Law; and that if he could do so, it would open the door for the Democratic Party to try to repeal or modify other amendments to the Constitution—amendments which vitally affect the Negro more than any other group of our citizens, the 14th & 15th amendments which gave our race liberty and citizenship."[120] Here, Wells-Barnett's cogent constitutional arguments bled seamlessly into her assumption that the majority of African Americans were capricious in their decisions to vote the Democratic ticket, or that such a choice resulted from a weakness for alcohol. The "unthinking masses," Wells-Barnett's letter suggested, needed middle-class Republican women's guidance on at least two counts: they needed instruction on how to behave properly and how to vote properly. As part of this instruction, Wells-Barnett told her audiences, "This time the wolf in sheep's clothing is spending money like water to hire our folks in the Democratic camp." She promised, however, that "very few of them are going to betray our race for 30 pieces of silver, or, for the prospect of a drink of liquor."[121]

[181]

Failure of Racial Uplift Ideology

Myrtle Foster Cook similarly asserted in a letter she distributed to Missouri voters from the Western Division Headquarters of the RNC: "Now some of our foolish voters want to put Democrats in the White House. Misled by *a mess of pottage*. It is positively alarming!"[122] Here was the language of moral weakness, self-injury, and race betrayal that many of these women had employed for decades to oppose black drinking. In 1928 these women applied to black Democrats, women and men, the familiar suffrage and racial uplift critique once reserved for black men that men were willing to sell their hard-won voting rights for a small price.[123] In doing so, however, they muddied the cogency of their constitutional observation with a reformist rhetoric that was in decline and, in turn, undermined the appeal of their constitutional argument for attracting skeptical voters to the Republican Party.

By equating black support for Smith with the political self-injury of vote selling or the moral self-injury of liquor consumption, Republican women downplayed, if not dismissed, the legitimate reasons that scores of black voters cast their lot with Smith in 1928. The evidence suggests that opposition to prohibition did fuel some black support for the Democratic Party in 1928.[124] For the average black voter—as well as several prominent leaders including Alice Dunbar-Nelson, Bessye Bearden, Amy Jacques Garvey, and Reverdy Ransom—the primary issue that drove them toward the Democratic Party in 1928, however, was the sense that the Republican Party had abandoned the race and no longer made any effort to represent black Americans.[125]

Privately, Nannie Helen Burroughs suggested that the liberalization of liquor laws was not the primary issue attracting black voters to the Democratic Party. Burroughs, who had so eloquently articulated the constitutional implications of repeal to the National Baptist Woman's Convention in September, informed her Republican colleagues toward the close of the campaign that "Negroes will not vote for Smith because he is wet." This was a conclusion she had come to following her month-long speaking tour across Kentucky, Illinois, Pennsylvania, Maryland, and New York on behalf of the Hoover-Curtis ticket. As she explained in her final report, the black voters she encountered "want to be sure that they are voting against the Klan, and they know the Klan is against Smith." "They are not for Smith," she clarified, "but they are against the Klan."[126] In other words, black support for the Democratic Party derived from anti-Klan sentiment—the recognition that Smith, the first Catholic to run for president, and African Americans shared

Failure of Racial Uplift Ideology

a common enemy in the KKK—rather than an active antiprohibition agenda. Made in the final weeks of the campaign, Burroughs's observations did not make their way into black Republican women's campaign rhetoric. To eliminate discussion of the Eighteenth Amendment from their canvassing efforts would have undermined a key opportunity to refocus national attention on the Reconstruction Amendments. It might also signal a concession that women's moral expertise in battling intemperance was no longer needed.

In 1928 black Republican women won the battle but lost the war. In the short term, Herbert Hoover won the election, and the Eighteenth Amendment remained part of the Constitution for another five years until the Twenty-first Amendment ended national prohibition by repealing the Eighteenth Amendment. While Republican women achieved their short-term goals, they became increasingly embattled politically. Their reliance on a classed reformist rhetoric that was losing its saliency undercut the potential appeal of their cogent constitutional argument. Indeed, to audiences comprised of those who enjoyed the vibrant leisure culture offered at locations like Chicago's Stroll, middle-class women's use of racial uplift rhetoric must have highlighted the degree to which black women reformers were out of touch with the changing social norms among urban black communities. In 1928 black Republican women were already in the difficult position of defending a party that many African Americans perceived to be, at best, out of touch with the needs of black Americans and, at worst, totally indifferent. To then blend their defense of the Republican Party with a reformist rhetoric that sounded out of step with the cultural transformations that had taken place in urban black communities was to call into question not only the Republican Party's relevance but, even more foreboding, these women's own claims to represent the race within party politics.

They, of course, did not know that they were living through the early stages of a major voting realignment and that by 1936 the majority of enfranchised black voters would vote the Democratic ticket. It is easy to look with the vantage of hindsight and see that Republican women were fighting an uphill battle. Theirs in many ways is a declension story: just at the moment that they had built up a considerable network of Republican resources, this network became increasingly obsolete. Forces beyond their control led black voters out of the Republican Party and into the Democratic Party. "We are between the devil and the deep blue sea," a "dear old man" told Burroughs during her October tour.[127] As black Republican women searched restlessly about for a reason to remain loyal to the Republi-

Failure of Racial Uplift Ideology

cans, this statement aptly characterized their frustrating situation. Alarmed by the drift of black voters to the Democratic Party and not ready to abandon the Republican Party themselves, but close, black Republican women dug in. They had much at stake personally and professionally and had become protective of the political base they had so carefully cultivated.

Failure of Racial Uplift Ideology

[5]

Political Recognition for Themselves and Their Daughters

The Campaigns of Ruth Hanna McCormick, 1927–1930

"Resolved, that we hereby serve notice on Mrs. Ruth Hanna McCormick that we resent the slight thus put upon the Negro women of Illinois whose vote she solicits, by the employment of an outsider to influence that vote, and pledge ourselves to use our influence to urge the Negro women throughout the state to resent the slight thus put upon them."[1] So went a letter that fifty leading black Republican women from throughout Illinois endorsed in early October 1929 and sent to Ruth Hanna McCormick, a white Republican seeking the party's nomination for U.S. senator from Illinois. The "outsider" to whom the letter referred was Mary Church Terrell. McCormick had invited Terrell to head her campaign among black women in Illinois. Terrell was an outsider only in the sense that she lived in Washington, D.C., rather than Chicago. She was very much an insider in the black Republican women's club movement. The women who authored this note knew Terrell— several personally, others certainly by name—from her activism in the National Association of Colored Women (NACW) and the Colored Women's Department of the Republican National Committee (RNC). Some had personally celebrated with Terrell at Harding's inauguration in 1921. Others had worked with her in the late summer of 1924 in Chicago to establish the National League of Republican Colored Women (NLRCW).[2] And just three years prior, Terrell had traveled to Chicago to campaign for another Illinois senator, William McKinley. McKinley's reintroduction of the Dyer Anti-lynching Bill into the Senate in 1926 generated a groundswell of black female support for his 1926 renomination campaign. Several of the same women who drafted the notice to McCormick in 1929 had, by Terrell's own account, "extended every courtesy imaginable" to her during the McKinley campaign.[3] In this context, local women's response to Terrell's hiring seems puzzling. Why did they object to the hiring of a woman with whom they had worked for Republican victory in these and many other instances? Why did they seek the removal of a woman whose national prominence would lend the McCormick campaign instant legitimacy among many black voters? The answer to these questions can be found by examining African American women's motives for supporting Ruth Hanna McCormick's two runs for Congress between 1927 and 1930.

Chapter 3 detailed women reformers' meticulous efforts to create a national network of black Republican women through the NLRCW. Such a network, they insisted, would help create the conditions necessary to push forward their multiple and interlocking agendas: their desire to gain a voice in influential Republican circles, their continued efforts to accomplish specific policy goals, and individual women's ambitions to enhance their own political capital. A similar process took place at the local level. Recall that in the closing weeks of the 1924 presidential contest, NLRCW activist Irene Goins founded the Colored Women's Republican Clubs of Illinois (CWRCI). This chapter returns to local Illinois politics and to the CWRCI. By the time McCormick announced her intention to run for Congress in 1927, CWRCI members had created a well-developed network of politically active women who were in a position to offer deserving candidates considerable help in reaching black voters.

They determined that McCormick was such a candidate. One of the most influential women in Republican politics in the country, and also one of the wealthiest, McCormick was a woman who could significantly advance the political careers of individuals and groups who affiliated with her, if she chose to do so. To be sure, the CWRCI expected McCormick to reward its campaign efforts on her behalf in the realm of policy. Like their colleagues in the NLRCW, CWRCI activists were looking restlessly about for candidates who would ensure stronger federal enforcement of the Constitution in the South. In McCormick they did not find a candidate who would do this via the Eighteenth Amendment in that she did not offer the trenchant anti-repeal position that middle-class black women championed in the presidential contest. So, when canvassing for McCormick, they strategically set aside the Eighteenth Amendment and instead focused on the meaningful constitutional issue that McCormick did endorse: the reduction of southern representation in the House. Alongside policy concerns, however, CWRCI activists bartered their canvassing network for campaign jobs. For some women, campaign jobs might serve as a stepping-stone to more influential positions

Campaigns of Ruth Hanna McCormick

within Republican machinery, both within Chicago and at the national level. Significantly, McCormick's personal ambitions for Congress intersected with the emergence of an independent black Republican political machine within the city in ways that bolstered this possibility. For others, campaign jobs were less a long-term strategy for gaining some power within Republican machinery and more a temporary source of income that could help them and their families weather the financial uncertainty of the Depression. Either way, the potential that a limited number of campaign jobs offered black Republican women in Illinois led to the struggle over Terrell's hiring and, more important, helped generate CWRCI support for McCormick in the face of alternative Republican candidates and the growing presence of black Democrats in Chicago's South Side.

The McCormick congressional campaigns were not the first time that black women in Illinois had bartered their votes and organizing resources with a candidate to achieve specific campaign goals. In 1914, for example, the Alpha Suffrage Club had extracted a promise from the Second Ward Republican Organization to run a black candidate in 1915. The Alpha Suffrage Club was able to exact this promise because of the growth of Chicago's black population and the club's willpower, if not the organizational resources, to mobilize this expanded black population. Fifteen years later, black Republican women used the same bargaining chips in their attempt to force McCormick to appoint one of their own. But there was an important difference of degree: both black Republican women's organizational strength and the black population of Illinois had grown considerably in the intervening years. Between 1910 and 1930, Chicago's black population had grown from 44,103, or 2 percent of the total population, to 233,803, or almost 7 percent of the total. The arrival of southern migrants transformed Chicago's urban black population into the world's second largest, surpassed only by that of greater New York.[4] Yet even as Chicago's black population grew exponentially, residential segregation remained almost complete, enforced by restrictive covenants and violence. African Americans remained concentrated in the "Black Belt," which stretched several blocks further south and west of its 1910 borders, as well as to a few "satellite" neighborhoods.[5] Black Chicagoans constituted a large majority of voters in the Second, Third, and Fourth Wards and a very sizable presence in several other wards.[6] Illinois's black population also expanded during these years, though nowhere near to the degree witnessed in Chicago. In 1929 one McCormick canvasser estimated that 50,000 African Americans of voting age resided outside Cook County.[7]

Campaigns of Ruth Hanna McCormick

This massive population growth in Illinois and especially Chicago shaped the way that the CWRCI leveraged its canvassing resources in the McCormick congressional campaigns. In 1925, well before there was any sign of the conflict to come, Mary Church Terrell, who was then heading the NACW's legislative committee, advised NACW members across the nation to get involved at the very earliest stages of a campaign: when candidates were deciding whether enough support existed to win the primary and general election. "If they believe a certain man will deal justly by their race," Terrell suggested in the pages of *National Notes*, "they might go to him and urge him to become a candidate for governor, or senator (or any other office) for nomination in the primaries of the party . . . assuring him their support and promising to do everything in their power to secure his selection and election." Once a campaign moved into the hands of white party functionaries after the primaries, Terrell warned, the leverage shifted to "the white leaders of a state and upon their attitude toward colored people on general principles." If African American women wanted to gain influence on matters of policy through the electoral system, Terrell insisted, they "must learn to play the political game as they would any other game in which they wish to become proficient and win."[8] Sidestepping white party functionaries and going directly to candidates in the primaries was one means of doing this.

Whether the CWRCI was specifically responding to Terrell's advice is hard to say. What is certain, however, is that the CWRCI did indeed undertake its heaviest canvassing for McCormick during the primary—while the candidate herself controlled and paid for the campaign—and before the general elections when the white-dominated Illinois Republican State Central Committee became responsible for the campaign. In Illinois, more so than any other state except New York, this strategy had some teeth behind it because African Americans constituted a significant portion of voters in Republican primaries in the state. Although only 8.7 percent of the total adult population in Chicago in 1930, African Americans made up approximately one-fifth of the city's Republican primary voters. In general elections, by contrast, this almost solid black Republican vote was diluted among the entire voting population, making the black vote less critical to a candidate's success.[9] Because of the large black population in Illinois and especially Chicago, the CWRCI had a significant bargaining chip "to play the political game," as Terrell put it. The CWRCI's resources and networks for mobilizing black voters could actually help to make or break a candidate in the Republican primaries. The question remained whether the CWRCI

Campaigns of Ruth Hanna McCormick

would be able to cash in this chip for jobs, real power sharing within Republican Party structures, and, most important, meaningful policy change once the primaries passed.

The Two Irenes

Two Irenes served as the backbone of the CWRCI between 1924 and 1935: Irene Goins and Irene McCoy Gaines. Irene Goins, the organization's founder, served as its first president until her death in 1929. Irene McCoy Gaines succeeded Goins to serve as CWRCI president until 1935.[10] The two Irenes had cultivated ties with McCormick at each stage of her political career and well before her first attempt to win a seat in Congress.

Born in Ocala, Florida, about forty miles south of Gainesville, Irene McCoy came to Chicago as a child. Her mother had relocated to Chicago with her infant daughter following her divorce from McCoy's father. McCoy completed elementary and high school in Chicago, but she returned to the South to attend Fisk University in Nashville. After graduating from Fisk in 1910, McCoy moved back to Chicago, where she continued her education at the University of Chicago, taught Sunday School classes at Bethel AME, and found employment as a typist in the law offices of Louis B. Anderson (who in seven years time would succeed Oscar DePriest as Second Ward alderman).[11]

Just nineteen in 1911, the still unmarried McCoy obtained work at the Progressive Party's national headquarters in Chicago.[12] Here, she would have made the acquaintance of the McCormicks, Ruth Hanna McCormick and her husband Medill McCormick, who headed the Progressive Party's western campaign.[13] A daughter of privilege, Ruth Hanna McCormick had spent her life in the company of politically powerful Republican men, first her father, Marcus Alonzo Hanna, and then her first husband, Medill McCormick. Mark Hanna was a Cleveland businessman who had made his fortune in coal and who used his wealth and friendship with former congressman and Ohio governor William McKinley to transform himself into one of the most powerful men in the Republican Party at the turn of the twentieth century. He was chairman of the RNC from 1896 to 1904. McKinley's presidential campaign manager in 1896 and again in 1900, Hanna helped to usher in a new era in campaigning. Using the enormous sums of money that he solicited from corporate America, Hanna ran the first presidential campaign to advertise a candidate much like a product. Complex campaign issues took a backseat to simplified campaign slogans; partisan rhetoric was overshadowed by an emphasis on the candidate's personality.[14] Hanna himself served as a U.S. senator between 1897 and his death in 1904. In addition to inheriting Mark Hanna's political acumen, Ruth Hanna McCormick inherited his large fortune. Just months before Mark Hanna's death, she married Medill McCormick, heir to the *Chicago Tribune* fortune. With their enormous combined wealth, the two embarked on a political partnership that lasted until Medill's suicide in 1925. Together they temporarily parted ways with the Republican Party to campaign for Theodore Roosevelt in 1912, the campaign they worked on with the young Gaines. They also put Medill in the Illinois State House of Representatives on the Progressive ticket in both 1912 and 1914. Back with the Republican Party, the McCormicks ran two successful campaigns in 1916 and 1918 that respectively put Medill in the U.S. House of Representatives and then the U.S. Senate. A final campaign effort was unsuccessful: Illinois governor Charles Deneen defeated Medill in the Republican primary race for the Senate in 1924.[15]

Gaines's work with McCormick in the Progressive Party was the beginning of a long political affiliation. The young race woman and McCormick, who was twelve years Gaines's senior, crossed paths repeatedly during the 1910s and 1920s, each while pursuing her own agenda. In 1914, for example, McCoy marched alongside McCormick, who was then serving as head of the congressional committee of the National American Woman Suffrage Association (NAWSA), in a suffrage parade down Michigan Avenue that garnered an estimated 200,000 spectators. McCormick's show of solidarity with McCoy and the two companies of black women who marched as part of McCormick's Progressive division in this Chicago parade was a far cry from the treatment that Wells-Barnett had encountered one year earlier at a suffrage parade in Washington, D.C.[16] There, Wells-Barnett was angered to tears when the Illinois Equal Suffrage Association conceded to the NAWSA's demand that black women march separately so as not to upset southern white delegates who were participating in the parade. Wells-Barnett famously transformed her pain into a public protest of NAWSA racism by slipping in among the all-white Illinois delegation once the parade got under way.[17] Though McCormick did not comment publicly on the March 1913 parade, which she herself was unable to attend, her decision to march alongside several black women in 1914 suggested that she had taken note of Wells-Barnett's protest.[18] With her husband planning a reelection campaign for the Illinois State House of Representatives, such a symbolic gesture was more than pure altruism: it was good politics. A show of interracial soli-

darity, especially after Wells-Barnett's successful exposure of white suffragists' racism, was an especially important move for a prominent NAWSA leader
who did not want to alienate black women voters from her husband.

For Gaines, participation in the parade was very much part of her lifelong
commitment to battling racism. Like Wells-Barnett's insertion of herself into
the parade one year earlier, Gaines's physical presence in the parade was a
claim upon black women's rightful place within the woman's suffrage movement and to the full citizenship rights that the movement demanded. It was
also good politics. The then twenty-one-year-old Gaines was engaged in her
own political climb, not for power's sake, but rather for the sake of what such
power could offer by way of her antiracist agenda. In this instance, she
deepened her contact with an influential NAWSA leader and the wife of an
Illinois state assemblyman.

The most important political relationships that Irene McCoy Gaines
developed during these years, however, were those with her husband and
with fellow clubwoman Irene Goins. Five months after marching down
Michigan Avenue in the 1914 suffrage parade, McCoy married attorney
Harris B. Gaines. Gaines was a Kentucky native who had relocated to
Chicago with his parents and who had worked as a plasterer in his father's
contracting business until pursuing his law degree at DePaul University.
Harris Gaines shared his wife's passion for justice and belief in the possibility
of using the party system to achieve it. When he began practicing law in
1914, he also began building inroads into Chicago's political machinery by
organizing for the Charles Deneen faction of the Republican Party.[19] Eight
years later, he tried his own hand at running for office. He was unsuccessful
in his bid for assemblyman from the First Senatorial District, but this was
not the last time that either Harris or Irene would run for office.[20] In the
midst of Harris's 1922 campaign, Irene Gaines networked with McCormick
by joining the Republican Woman's Cook County Campaign Committee,
an organization that McCormick established that year in order to assist
Republican candidates win seats in Congress. (From her years of club work,
Gaines already knew the other African American women whom McCormick asked to participate on the committee, including Ada McKinley, Elizabeth Lindsay Davis, and Blanche Gilmer.)[21]

Around 1920 or 1921, Gaines became acquainted with Irene Goins.[22]
Goins was a dynamic organizer who regularly crossed class and racial lines
in pursuit of political goals. Born in 1877 in Missouri, Goins spent much of
her youth in Springfield, Illinois, before relocating to Chicago as a young
adult. She was one of the first black women in the Midwest actively engaged

Campaigns of Ruth Hanna McCormick

in the labor movement. In 1913 she worked on the campaign for an eight-hour day with the Women's Trade Union League and the International Glove Workers Union. She organized black women stockyard workers during the war, and between 1917 and 1922 she served on the executive council of the Women's Trade Union League of Chicago. She was equally active in electoral politics, presumably viewing labor and electoral politics as connected arenas for pursuing racial justice. Both were white-dominated arenas that Goins sought to make not only receptive but also responsive to black women's involvement. In 1916 she campaigned for presidential candidate Charles Evans Hughes as part of the Colored Women's Hughes Republican Headquarters in Chicago. In 1923 she founded and served as the first president of the Douglass chapter of the League of Women Voters. In 1924 she served as the Illinois state chairman for the Colored Women's Department of the RNC. That year, she was elected president of the NACW's local affiliate, the Illinois Federation of Colored Women's Clubs.[23]

By one account, the elder Irene took Gaines "under her wing."[24] Gaines would most certainly have been among the 150 women who responded to Goins's 1924 call to meet in Chicago to create a statewide convention of black Republican women. There, Gaines would have joined her mentor and other politically active women from throughout Illinois in establishing the CWRCI. In her insistence that this political machine she was creating be grounded in both local and national politics, Goins asked Myrtle Foster Cook of the Colored Women's Department of the RNC to address the group. In her effort to build bridges with powerful white Republican women and black men, Goins also invited both Second Ward Republican committeeman Edward H. Wright and Republican national committeewoman Ruth Hanna McCormick to address the group.[25]

By then, McCormick had used her political pedigree and connections to transform herself into a political force in her own right within national and local Republican circles. Historians have noted that McCormick represented one side of a debate that raged among white Republican women as the battle over the Nineteenth Amendment came to a close over how best to integrate white women into the party's power structures. Several of her colleagues demanded equal representation in national Republican Party structures through the establishment of parallel organizations and positions for women. McCormick, by contrast, warned that these measures might merely segregate women within the party without actually offering them real power. Despite her misgivings about separatist organizing, McCormick was a master at it. She served as chairman of the newly created Republican

Campaigns of Ruth Hanna McCormick

Women's National Executive Committee during 1918 and 1919 (which was renamed the Women's Division of the RNC in 1919). In 1920 she agreed to sit on the Republican National Executive Committee after the Republican National Convention voted to add seven women to the previously all-male committee. After the RNC changed its delegate allotment system in 1923, McCormick was among the 118 white women and two black women (Booze and Williams) who were selected as delegates to the 1924 Republican National Convention. McCormick served as Republican national committeewoman from Illinois again four years later at the 1928 national convention in Kansas City.[26] It was in this context of past interactions with one of the most influential women in national Republican politics that the sitting and future president of the CWRCI approached the 1928 election season.

McCormick's Candidacy for the House, 1927–1928

In 1928 Illinois voters would cast their ballot for two congressmen-at-large. Along with Ruth Hanna McCormick, Henry Rathbone and Richard Yates were running in the Republican primaries for these two at-large seats. The two Republican candidates among these three who brought in the largest number of votes would advance to the general elections in the fall as the Republican nominees for the at-large seats.[27] Both Henry Rathbone and Richard Yates were incumbent congressmen. The CWRCI chose not to campaign for either of these candidates. Significantly, Yates, who had sought black votes in the past, was among seventy-four representatives who did not enter a vote in the 1922 House vote that sent the Dyer Antilynching Bill forward to the Senate, where it died.[28] Rathbone seemed to have a more positive reputation. In early 1927, the *Defender* described Rathbone as "[o]ne of the best friends of our Race in congress."[29] Perhaps most famously, Rathbone's parents were in the box with Lincoln at Ford's Theater on the evening he was assassinated. Rathbone also publicly styled himself as a supporter of black education, giving yearly talks at Howard University and speaking on the House floor "heartily in favor" of congressional appropriations for the university. If CWRCI activists had looked into the *Congressional Record*, however, they would have seen that despite his public rhetoric, Rathbone had failed to enter a vote when the House voted on funding for Howard in 1924 and then again 1928.[30]

McCormick's platform did not make her an obvious candidate to garner the CWRCI's support. McCormick did not include an explicit civil rights plank in her platform. In fact, McCormick downplayed policy altogether,

Campaigns of Ruth Hanna McCormick

emphasizing instead her character as a selling point to voters. She had learned from the very best, her own father, how to market a candidate by personalizing a campaign and simplifying political messages, and she put these strategies into practice in her own run for office during 1928. To the extent that McCormick did discuss policy, she focused on her support for U.S. involvement in the Kellogg-Briand Pact, an international treaty outlawing war, as well as for the enactment of a federal bill that would help stabilize falling farm prices. Neither the outlawry of war nor farm subsidies were historical rallying points for middle-class black women.[31]

McCormick also presented a prohibition plank that fell short of the anti-repeal platform that many of McCormick's black female supporters would champion just a few months later in the Hoover campaign. McCormick held that the federal government ought to either repeal or fully enforce prohibition.[32] In her insistence that the federal government must enforce the Eighteenth Amendment so long as it remained part of the Constitution, McCormick offered some acknowledgment of the constitutional and federal enforcement concerns that animated black women reformers. But this was not the trenchant antirepeal position that Wells-Barnett and Burroughs employed in their campaign efforts on behalf of Hoover—that repealing the Eighteenth Amendment was the first step in a slippery slope that might lead to the repeal of the Reconstruction Amendments. The cwrci, which also campaigned for Hoover, clearly did not pick candidates on single issues. Its simultaneous support of Hoover and McCormick might hint at shades of disagreement among black clubwomen that were not apparent in the national campaign rhetoric. In other words, the unified front contained within the campaign literature of the rnc's Colored Women's Department may have belied disagreement even among clubwomen about the benefits of national prohibition. More likely, this lineup of cwrci endorsed candidates was a demonstration of women reformers making strategic choices among an inconsistent field of candidates.

What was the strategic benefit of endorsing McCormick? In a form letter that she sent black women throughout the state, Goins insisted that black women should support the candidate, in part, because of her track record as "a true friend to our race."[33] By 1928 "a true friend" among white Republicans had largely devolved into someone who was not an avowed enemy of black citizenship rights. To the extent that Ruth Hanna McCormick had a track record on race, it had been established through her husband and indirectly through her work on his many campaigns. Medill McCormick's record with regard to black rights was mixed. In the midst of heated de-

Campaigns of Ruth Hanna McCormick

bate over the racial composition of the Progressive Party in August 1912, McCormick sided with those Progressives, including Roosevelt himself, who insisted that the Progressive Party remain a "white man's party."[34] McCormick disappointed again ten years later as chair of a Select Senate Committee on Haiti and Santo Domingo. In a position to demand American withdrawal from the island, a goal clubwomen including Nannie Helen Burroughs and Mary Church Terrell championed, McCormick instead concluded that "we ought to stay there for twenty years."[35] Medill McCormick's stronger antilynching stance helped to make up for these missteps. He had spoken publicly on behalf of the Dyer Bill in 1922; and, as James Weldon Johnson reported in the *Crisis*, McCormick was among eighteen Republican Senators who remained in the Senate chambers during the unsuccessful battle to bring the Dyer Bill to a vote in late September 1922 (he did not break ranks, though, when congressional Republicans decided not to fight the filibuster during the following session).[36] If Medill McCormick's support for the Dyer Bill was any indicator of how his widow might act given the chance to help push a future antilynching bill through Congress, then, at the very least, it seemed unlikely that she would actively work against the race. Perhaps she might even emerge as the congressional advocate of black citizenship rights that black Republican women so desperately sought. The CWRCI was willing to give McCormick a try.

For some women, "true friendship" clearly also had an economic component to it. Many CWRCI activists wanted to reap the political rewards that they had rightly earned through years of service, if not to the candidate, then to her husband. Several black women reformers had worked to help McCormick win his 1918 race for the Senate. Ella Berry and Bertha Montgomery, for example, had served on the interracial Republican Women's Loyalty Campaign Committee that was established to help McCormick win women's votes.[37] And it seems that the McCormicks had a decent record of rewarding black supporters with government jobs. Most notably, Medill McCormick had helped Elmer Myers, Susie Myers's husband obtain a job in the Post Office.[38] Furthermore, the powerful Thompson machine, which was in control of state patronage jobs, initially endorsed McCormick (Thompson withdrew support toward the end of the primary).[39] McCormick herself was one of the most powerful women in national Republican circles. She was also one of Chicago's wealthiest women.[40] She was spending an enormous amount of money from her personal wealth to win the primary, and unemployed or underemployed women sought the economic and patronage benefits that came with paid canvassing work.

Margaret O. Gainer, the Chicago clubwoman who in 1920 had proudly told black Republican women gathered in Washington, D.C., to celebrate Harding's inauguration that "we did not miss a precinct in Cook county," wrote to McCormick in October 1927.[41] Without explicitly broaching the issue of remuneration, Gainer inquired, "May I pledge myself to work for you and thus help to elect you to this office?" Gainer indicated her credentials as a member of the Republican Women's Council, the National Women's Republican Committee, the Illinois Women's State Republican Club, the Illinois League of Women Voters, the Loyal Women's Association of the AME Church, the Bethel AME Sunday School, the Women's Church Federation, the National State and City Federations of Colored Women's Clubs, and the Woman's City Club.[42] Though she did not mention it, Gainer's credentials also included campaign work on behalf of Medill McCormick. Gainer was among the members of the Women's Second Ward Republican Club who had canvassed for Medill McCormick during his successful 1918 run for the Senate.[43] Gainer understandably sought to cash in the favors and political capital she had built over several years for a leadership position within the McCormick campaign machinery, especially a paid position.

Gainer was subtle in her inquiry about a canvassing job, but other women were much more overt in their desire to obtain paid work with the campaign. In a decade that saw the intense commercialization of many aspects of American life, as well as a severe economic downturn, a "true friend" to the race, as Goins put it, could easily be construed as a candidate who offered campaign jobs. Even before McCormick announced her intention to run for U.S. congressman-at-large, African Americans inquired about obtaining paid positions within the McCormick campaign organization. McCormick was still deciding whether and for which office to run in June 1927 when Major Singleton, a public school teacher in southern Illinois, recommended his wife for McCormick's campaign manager among African American voters. "In case you make the race for governor of Ill and need a good live woman for your Negro campaign manager, one who understand how to put over such big propositions," he promised, "I am sure you will make no mistake in corresponding with Mrs. Lucy B. C. Singleton, who is well and favorably know from one end of the state to the other" and whose electoral experience would "successfully land the candidate with telling effect."[44] Similarly, in early November 1927 Etta McPherson of Madison responded to a McCormick campaign letter addressed to her brother announcing the candidacy and inquiring about partisan sentiment in the county. Her brother was out of town, McPherson explained, but more im-

Campaigns of Ruth Hanna McCormick

portant, she was the "one who leads in this priscint as a race woman." McPherson asserted that "the Republican partie feel like that you would be the one for the office." McPherson concluded, "would be glad to help you and you know what it takes to do the proper work in a Campaign Let me hear from you soon."[45]

Although the majority of CWRCI members, including Gainer, worked as volunteers on the McCormick primary campaign, a handful translated their long-standing Republican activism into paid positions. In this respect, club-women's belief in the possibilities of long-term organizing for gaining entry into white-dominated Republican networks had paid off, quite literally. At least it did at the individual level. Individual women traded their access to black women voters, something they had carefully cultivated over the years, for greater political capital within Republican machinery and, of course, for direct economic capital. In February, for example, the campaign hired Margaret Byrd at a rate of $50 a week, plus $40 a week for expenses, to address black audiences across the state. Byrd, an Arkansas native living in Springfield, had served as president of both the Springfield Colored Women's Club and its umbrella affiliate, the Colored Women's Federated Clubs of the Central District. Like many politically active black women, she shared her interest in party politics with her husband. A state auditor who hailed from Ohio, Major Robert A. Byrd was active in local Republican politics. In 1924 he was director of the Colored Speakers' Bureau for the Illinois Republican State Central Committee.[46]

Between the end of February and early April 1928, Margaret Byrd visited no less than twenty cities across the state, sometimes for only a day.[47] Arriving in Mounds at the southern tip of the state in late February, for instance, Byrd addressed one group of clubwomen in the morning, another in the evening, and a third the following day. As might be expected of a paid canvasser who was earning the equivalent of $500 a week in year 2000 dollars, Byrd enthusiastically wrote to headquarters, "Thus far I find the women very decided in their preference for Mrs McCormick."[48] One month and many speeches later, Byrd was 200 miles to the northeast in Danville. As with Byrd's visits to other communities, Goins drew upon the CWRCI's well-developed network to make sure that Byrd had access to women involved in the Danville area's CWRCI affiliate, the Vermillion County Colored Women's Republican Club. Lillian Wheeler, who was president of this club and who also served as CWRCI first vice president-at-large, made arrangements for Byrd to speak to this "all enthusiastic" club.[49] The next day, Byrd addressed a packed house of the Colored Women's Republican Club of Decatur. Only a month old, the

Colored Women's Republican Club of Decatur already claimed a member-ship of 500. More than 56 members, some spilling into the kitchen, gathered in the home of club president and founder Jessie Slaughter to hear Byrd's presentation at the regular Friday meeting.[50]

With a tight race in East St. Louis, the McCormick campaign paid Pinkie B. Reeves and Irene L. Yancy $50 each to canvass the city's large black population during the final month of the primary contest—an enormous fee for one month's work, which was an undoubtedly welcome boost to the Yancy and Reeves household economies.[51] This was especially the case given that most black women earned considerably less than the average American income of approximately $2,000.[52] Yancy, a Tennessee native who was married to a factory foreman and who herself worked as an agent for a dress manufacturer, was well positioned to mobilize the Republican women's networks to which she had access as first vice president of the CWRCI.[53] A mother of five, Pinkie B. Reeves was also embedded within local Republican women's networks in such a way that she could reach a large number of black women voters within a very a short time. Reeves held the position of state organizer in the CWRCI; locally in East St. Louis she was heavily involved in a CWRCI affiliated club that boasted nearly 800 members (the Central Colored Women's Republican Club, Number One, of East St. Louis and St. Clair County). As might be expected of a paid worker, Reeves's correspondence with McCormick both praised the candidate and assured McCormick that she was getting her money's worth. Having heard McCormick speak at the Illinois Republican Conventions in Chicago and Springfield in 1927, Reeves explained to McCormick, "I have the facts to tell my people about you."[54] This Reeves frequently did at her own home, which she transformed into McCormick campaign headquarters during the spring of 1928. As she described to McCormick, "I worked day and night organizing precinct clubs and holding meetings in the evening for your interest."[55] With this accounting, Reeves was certainly looking to the future and the possibility of funneling her short but well-compensated stint into future employment with McCormick in the general elections and after.

Both McCormick and Rathbone won the Republican primary in April and advanced to the general election in November, where they faced Demo-cratic candidates Charles Brown and C. D. Joplin.[56] In the days immediately before and after the primary, Reeves was one among several black women who wrote to McCormick seeking employment and patronage in exchange for service rendered during the primary campaign. As Reeves promised the candidate, "I am going to work harder to help get you elected than I did to

Campaigns of Ruth Hanna McCormick

get you nominated."[57] Six days before the primary, Marry Rucker of Spring-field described to McCormick what she could offer the candidate: "I am sending you some names of some friends of mine [who] have promised to vote for you and I will do all in my power to get them [to] vote that way. I am a member of the colored womens club so I can do quite a lot of good." With a husband who had been unemployed for more than five months, Rucker explained in no uncertain terms that she was "trying to get some one elected who will help me to get him a job."[58] Six days after the primary, Jennie McClain of Rock Island made her case for patronage appointments by first reporting, "I worked very faithfully on 10th of Apr. here and were all glad to say Rock Island Col'd Women came out boldly and voted for your nomination." Referring to the state's two competing Republican machines, Mc-Clain continued, "Now we were not compensated like Small workers and Emersons's but did our full bit for your success." Trusting, as she put it, that "we will not be forgotten or over-looked," McClain got to the point: "As we have one or two young men and women up this way that hoped to get a position of some note after the Nov. election. They need to be recognized according to their efficiency and ability."[59] Black women's letters to the candidate reveal the economic motives that led many to canvass for the candidate and that gave a very specific meaning to political "friendship." McClain's letter also suggests that the "ethos of mutuality" that had shaped black women's view of the vote as collectively owned during Reconstruction and that had guided their desire to serve as proxy voters well into the twentieth century extended from voting to patronage politics: women sought patronage positions not only for themselves but also for others in their community who were deserving or in need.

This scramble for patronage and employment took place in the trans-formed campaign structure of the general elections. As one of the two official Republican candidates for an at-large seat in the House, the McCormick campaign came under the purview of the Republican State Central Committee.[60] Mary Church Terrell had urged women to focus on the primary to ensure that their chosen candidate made it into the generals precisely because once a campaign transitioned from the primary to the generals, black voters were subject to "the white leaders of a state and upon their attitude toward colored people on general principles."[61] This certainly held true in Illinois, with one significant exception. In September, Irene McCoy Gaines obtained a key appointment within the Women's Division of the Republican State Central Committee that was now responsible for McCormick's campaign, as well as the campaigns of other Republican candidates.

Campaigns of Ruth Hanna McCormick

She was in charge of Republican women's activities in the First Congressional District. What McCormick's role was in this appointment, if any, is unclear. Given McCormick's influential connections with Republican Party women within both the state and the nation, it seems reasonable to speculate that Gaines's networking with McCormick over the years was a factor that helped her acquire this appointment. The other factor, of course, was the organizational resources of the CWRCI to reach the sizable black population in the First Congressional District, roughly 58 percent.[62]

As the Republican committeewoman for Illinois's First Congressional District, Gaines was in a position to promote African American women within the committee's expansive campaign structure. Whether she did is unclear, but it is hard to believe that she did not. Within the First Congressional District, she oversaw a two-tiered campaign structure of county chairwomen and precinct committeewomen. The white women in charge of the twenty-four other congressional districts held the same authority within their respective districts. "Under this plan of organization," the *Chicago Daily News* predicted in September, "the republicans will have 6,500 woman workers on duty from now until Nov."[63] Within the First Congressional District, CWRCI members were most likely among the ranks of these women workers "on duty."

There is minimal reporting in the black press on the CWRCI's activities during the general elections, though what does exist makes it clear that the CWRCI continued its relationship with McCormick.[64] McCormick, it seems, continued to wage a campaign of personality, discussing the Kellogg-Briand Pact and the stabilization of farm prices when she decided to address policy issues.[65] While African American women focused on the constitutional issues surrounding repeal of the Eighteenth Amendment in the presidential contest under way, there is no mention of them making similar arguments in connection with McCormick's campaign. This was understandable given McCormick's deliberately nebulous position on repealing the Eighteenth Amendment.

When the Eighteenth Amendment did not serve as a constitutional vehicle for bringing attention to the Reconstruction Amendments, some women turned to the issue of congressional reapportionment. They demanded a recalibration of the number of representatives that each state was entitled to send to the House of Representatives based on changes in the state voting populations. Writing from her home in Washington, D.C., for her regular column in the *Chicago Defender*, "Up to Date," Mary Church Terrell, suggested: "It is well known that congress violated the Constitution which

Campaigns of Ruth Hanna McCormick

provides that there shall be a new congressional apportionment after the census has been taken because it failed to do so after the 1920 returns were in."[66] Addressing black disfranchisement more directly, the *Defender* reported on a questionnaire that had been sent to more than 900 candidates across the country: "Do you hold that all provisions of the Constitution should be impartially enforced? If so, will you introduce or vote for a bill to carry into effect the second section of the 14th Amendment?"[67] The second section of the Fourteenth Amendment provided for the reduction of representation in the House in the case of disfranchisement, but it had never been applied to the widespread disfranchisement of African Americans in the South. McCormick's answer, if she sent one, was not reported.[68] When pressed by black voters on the issue of constitutional enforcement at a mass rally, however, McCormick reportedly "raised her right hand and pledged herself to fight for enforcement of the 14th and 15th amendments."[69] The black women who had helped her win the primary and were again working for her victory would follow up on this promise.

In the November general elections, McCormick and Yates won the two open at-large seats. (Yates became the second nominee following Rathbone's death in July.)[70] Early returns indicated that both McCormick and Yates had carried Cook County by more than 700,000 votes each, marginally ahead of their Democratic opponents Charles Brown and C. D. Joplin.[71] Eventually McCormick received a total of 1,711,651 votes, a significant portion of which came from downstate counties.[72] There were other winners. With the backing of the Thompson machine, Oscar DePriest was elected representative to the House from Illinois's First Congressional District in 1928, making him the first black congressman since 1901.[73] Five black men, all Republicans, won seats in the Illinois legislature. Among these was Irene McCoy Gaines's husband Harris Gaines.[74]

McCormick appears to have used her political influence to assist some black women who had campaigned for her in 1928. She helped obtain appointments not only for Ada McKinley but also for other far less prominent women.[75] There was a flow of letters, for instance, among McCormick, her staff, and the warden's office at the Southern Illinois Penitentiary for about ten months regarding employment for Susie Williams, a woman canvasser from Mounds. By April 1930 Williams was employed as a probation officer for Pulaski County.[76] Another exchange of letters focused on the Southern Illinois Penitentiary as well, but for different reasons. Rosa Davy, a widowed laundress in Metropolis, who had had campaigned for McCormick, wrote to McCormick for help getting her son paroled. Her son, she explained, had been wrongly imprisoned because of a white neighbor who "swore a line on him, made like he knocked her down with a shot gun butt." In response to McCormick's inquiry, the Department of Public Welfare promised to bring the case to the attention of the parole board.[77] Not everyone was happy, though. Hattie J. Wells of Champaign wrote to complain that the women of Coles County "have received no recognition in appointments."[78]

How would black women's support for McCormick pay off in terms of policy now that McCormick was a U.S. representative? Black women supporters may very well have liked the candidate on a personal level, but they did not allow McCormick's campaign of personality to cloud their focus on matters of policy. Among the telegrams and letters that flooded McCormick's office in the days immediately after her victory was a letter from prominent clubwoman Elizabeth Lindsay Davis. In her congratulations, Davis emphasized ties of interracial womanhood: "Your victory is one more step upward for Illinois women, who are interested in better government." While Davis invoked ties of shared womanhood, she reminded McCormick that black womanhood had given her an opportunity to act upon campaign promises that would benefit black voters specifically. "I was very much pleased with your speech at the eighth armory Nov., 4th," Davis explained, referring to the mass black Republican rally that took place two days before the elections.[79] This was possibly the meeting where McCormick had made her pledge to work toward the enforcement of the Fourteenth and Fifteenth Ammendments.[80] Davis continued, "I wish more members of congress would have the courage to express themselves as you did and as all good Americans should."[81] Davis took McCormick's promise regarding the Reconstruction Amendments quite seriously. Whether McCormick would take it seriously within the halls of Congress was yet to be seen.

McCormick's Senate Race, 1929–1930

In September 1929 Ruth Hanna McCormick, the newly elected representative-at-large from Illinois, announced her intention of seeking a seat in the Senate.[82] If McCormick won, then she would become the first woman elected to the U.S. Senate.[83] In many ways, the McCormick Senate race, which ran from September 1929 to November 1930, was the high point of CWRCI activism. "[L]earn to play the game as it should be played and profit from the mistakes of the men," Mary Talbert had advised black Republican women at the 1921 inaugural celebration in Washington, D.C.[84] A decade later, the CWRCI was playing the game of politics quite well. In the previous campaign, the CWRCI had demonstrated its ability to mobilize African American voters throughout the state. Some CWRCI affiliates had even been able to barter their access to networks of Republican clubwomen for paid campaign positions. Whereas the allotment and tenure of paid campaign work had tended to be piecemeal, this time the organization won a spot for its president as head of McCormick's well-funded black women's division. The CWRCI also "played the game of politics" by strategically aligning with Oscar DePriest, the first black congressman in twenty-seven years, and his powerful Third Ward political machine. Paid campaign positions helped middle-class women stay afloat financially. Machine alliances helped build political careers. Both also required a degree of loyalty to candidate and party that shaped campaign rhetoric. CWRCI activists pointed to the ways in which McCormick had worked to enforce the Fourteenth Amendment. By contrast, they characterized McCormick's opponents, Republican and Democratic alike, as disinterested in black rights, strategically eliding over counterevidence.

The CWRCI, with new president Irene McCoy Gaines at its helm, had several reasons for supporting McCormick again this time around. (Gaines succeeded Goins, who died in March 1929.)[85] During her brief time in the House, McCormick kept some of her campaign promises to represent her black supporters there. First, the newly elected McCormick had successfully maneuvered behind the scenes to squash southern congressmen's threats to block Oscar DePriest's seating in the House. This was no small gesture given the symbolism of DePriest's election. DePriest had been elected to represent the First Congressional District. African Americans from throughout the country, however, viewed him as their representative in Congress.[86] "Numerous telegrams and letters . . . reaching me daily," DePriest explained in a statement published in the *Defender* shortly after his victory, "impress me with the responsibility that is on me to represent twelve to fifteen million loyal American citizens who for the past 27 years have been without representation in the congress of the United States."[87] Many would have seen McCormick's actions as a defense of African Americans' right to representation by one of their own.

Even more important, during her brief time in Congress, McCormick had upheld her promise to work toward the enforcement of the Fourteenth Amendment. Since 1920, Massachusetts representative George Tinkham had introduced several unsuccessful bills that used the second section of the Fourteenth Amendment to cut down House representation in those states that disfranchised black voters.[88] Tinkham's efforts intertwined with con-

Campaigns of Ruth Hanna McCormick

gressional debates about adjusting the size and distribution of House seats so that the House more closely represented changes in the U.S. population. As McCormick's first session as a sitting congresswoman came to a close in June 1929, the House scrambled to pass a reapportionment bill before the completion of the 1930 census. Tinkham once again tried to put some teeth behind the Fourteenth Amendment by adding an amendment to the proposed Census and Reapportionment Bill mandating that future censuses count the number of disfranchised citizens of voting age.[89] McCormick was among the minority of representatives who sided with Tinkham during the numerous twists and turns of the debate that ultimately resulted in the passage of a Census and Reapportionment Bill without the Tinkham amendment.[90] At their new headquarters in the London Guarantee Building in mid-October, Gaines and Terrell displayed McCormick's voting record for a visiting *Bee* reporter. Looking back to McCormick's previous campaign for the House, they described how McCormick had "raised her right hand and pledged herself to fight for enforcement of the 14th and 15th amendments" at a rally for black voters in 1928. By supporting the Tinkham amendment, McCormick workers insisted to the *Bee* reporter, the candidate had "fulfilled that pledge." To be sure, these were paid campaign workers whose job was to present a positive image of McCormick, but they were also women who were committed to ending disfranchisement in the South. McCormick was a candidate whose congressional record indicated that she would help them reach this goal.[91]

McCormick's Republican opponent in the primary, incumbent Senator Charles Deneen, also had a civil rights record. As governor in 1905, Deneen signed into law the Illinois Mob Violence Act, which set a $1,000 fine for individuals convicted of participating in a lynch mob and provided a mechanism for the removal of sheriffs who failed to protect prisoners in their custody from mob violence. Though not Deneen's brainchild, the Mob Violence Act had been passed during his administration, associating his governorship with one of the few antilynching laws in the nation. Deneen's decision to then enforce the act in 1909 by dismissing a sheriff who did not prevent a lynching in downstate Illinois solidified his civil rights record in the minds of many black voters in the state.[92] The ongoing relevance of events that took place in 1909 for a political contest two decades later was evident in a letter that a white attorney practicing in Cairo wrote McCormick in early January 1930. The "strong sentiment among the colored voters of the county in favor of Senator Deneen," he reported, "I think, is a result of his action while Governor in removing the sheriff that suffered a colored man in

Campaigns of Ruth Hanna McCormick

his custody to be taken by a mob and lynched."[93] The ongoing relevance of
Deneen's actions in 1909 was also obvious when one realizes that Wells-
Barnett was in the final stages of writing her autobiography as the Senate
primary was heating up in January 1930. In chapter thirty-six, written sometime between 1928 and 1930, Wells-Barnett attributed the absence of additional lynchings in the state since 1909 to Deneen's example: "Every sheriff,
whenever there seem to be any signs of the kind, immediately telegraphs the
governor for troops. And to Governor Deneen belongs the credit."[94]

Not surprisingly, some women had ties to both candidates, complicating
their role in the McCormick-Deneen contest. Irene McCoy Gaines had
worked with Ruth McCormick on and off through the 1910s and 1920s. Her
husband, Harris Gaines, however, had built his political career by aligning
with the Deneen forces, eventually winning a seat in the Illinois General
Assembly in 1928 as a Deneenite.[95] This was the same electoral season
Gaines had campaigned for McCormick as second in command of the
CWRCI. Hardly a sign of marital discord, the pair's alliances with current
political foes was shrewd politics. With ties to both groups, they were well
positioned to navigate the twists and turns of local Republican machinery.
Wells-Barnett and her husband, Ferdinand, also had strong ties to Deneen.
The couple had worked with Deneen since 1896 when ironically Deneen,
who was then state's attorney for Cook County, was forced to appoint Barnett as assistant state's attorney.[96] Briefly involved in the McCormick senatorial campaign at its earliest stages, Wells-Barnett eventually redirected her
energy away from the McCormick contest and toward her own run for the
Republican nomination for state senator.[97]

While Wells-Barnett withdrew from the primary battle between McCormick and Deneen, CWRCI activists did not. Individually and as a group, they
had to choose whether to support McCormick, the junior congresswoman
who had kept her promise to help enforce the Reconstruction Amendments,
or to endorse Deneen, the seasoned machine politician who had signed and
enforced a state antilynching bill two decades before. Ultimately, the CWRCI
went with McCormick. Her civil rights record was a key pull. But it was
not the only factor influencing this decision. It could not have been, given
Deneen's competing record, especially his work with an issue that was as
close to black women's hearts as antilynching. The shifting labyrinth of
machine politics in Chicago and personal finances also intervened in this
decision.

The McCormick campaign was embedded in the factional machine politics of Chicago. Choosing McCormick over Deneen was a strategic decision

Campaigns of Ruth Hanna McCormick

that took into account past and future alliances.[98] A critical factor here was the growing power of Oscar DePriest. Some CWRCI leaders had past ties to Deneen. Many more had worked with DePriest or sought to work with one of the most powerful black men in the city. With the blessing of Mayor William Thompson, DePriest had gained control of the Third Ward Republican Organization (TWRO) through his appointment as Third Ward committeeman in 1927. DePriest used the TWRO to propel himself into Congress in 1928.[99] The CWRCI also helped along the way. With his political star on the rise in 1929, DePriest came out strongly for McCormick and against his old rival Deneen. It was around this time that Harris Gaines split from Deneen for good and came into the DePriest camp.[100] This defection made it possible for Irene Gaines to fully harness CWRCI resources toward the McCormick campaign. And she had good reasons for wanting to do so: if the CWRCI sought to strengthen its alliance with DePriest and his TWRO, then campaigning on behalf of DePriest's candidate in the Senate contest was a good strategic move.

Within this context of past and future alliances, the CWRCI had, of course, already banked considerable political capital by helping McCormick and her late husband. CWRCI activists expected McCormick to fulfill her promises with regard to the Reconstruction Amendments once in office. They also expected McCormick to recognize their hard work in the way that politicians in Chicago rewarded loyalty, through jobs and political appointments. Such tangible rewards might enhance the political visibility and influence of the CWRCI. They might help individual women forward their political careers. They would certainly offer income to women who were especially vulnerable to the diminishing employment opportunities of Depression-era America.

Just how protective the women of the CWRCI were of the political capital they had so carefully cultivated was evident in the conflict over Mary Church Terrell's hiring. Describing her involvement in the campaign in her 1940 autobiography, *A Colored Woman in a White World*, Terrell recalled, "When Mrs. Ruth Hanna McCormick asked me to assist in her campaign for election to the United States Senate I jumped at the chance." Terrell's enthusiasm remained palpable a decade later: "In the wildest flight of a lurid imagination I had never dared to presume to dream that the opportunity of assisting the very first woman in the country who had courage enough to try to break into the United States Senate on her own merit would come to me."[101] By at least one account, however, it seems that Terrell not only dreamed about but also actually lobbied for such a chance by asking newly elected congressman Oscar DePriest to help her obtain a position in the McCormick campaign—and with good reason.[102] No woman had ever been elected to the Senate.[103] There was a real possibility that McCormick might be the first. What opportunities might await those women who helped elect the first woman to the U.S. Senate? African American women faced very finite opportunities for political advancement within the upper echelons of government. Terrell actively sought them out. But she was not the only one.

The flood of discontent over Terrell's leadership emerged in the fall of 1929, shortly after Terrell distributed a thousand campaign letters to black Republican women throughout Illinois. Terrell signed her McCormick endorsement, "Chairman of the Executive Committee." A Gaines correspondence to Hallie Quinn Brown detailed how Illinois women essentially chastised Gaines for allowing Terrell to lead the campaign among African American women: "I was called down by many as President of the Colored Women's State Republican Organization for allowing myself to be used as her assistant."[104] White campaign leaders also received numerous calls and letters demanding a change in leadership. For instance, Hattie J. Wells, treasurer of the cwrci, phoned fellow Champaign resident and white McCormick leader Eleanor Bainum over the matter. Bainum relayed to McCormick, "Wells says the colored women are all your friends, and want to work and organize for you, but they wish to do it under their own leadership."[105] While the cwrci was certainly part of the national network of black Republican women—through its affiliation with both the National League of Republican Colored Women and the rnc's Colored Women's Department—there were also limits to this Republican sisterhood.

Local black women made sure that McCormick understood that their support was earned rather than assumed, regardless of past favors. At the forefront of the protest were Bertha Montgomery, president of the Second Ward Colored Women's Republican Club, and Susie Myers, who together convened an "indignation meeting" in early October. McCormick and Terrell may very well have been surprised by Myers's actions, especially since Myers's husband was the beneficiary of Medill McCormick's patronage.[106] They may also have been caught off guard because Myers and Terrell worked together three years prior. Myers had headed campaign work among black women for the 1926 McKinley campaign, a campaign for which Terrell briefly relocated to Chicago to help out.[107] There was, of course, a critical difference between the McKinley and McCormick campaigns: McKinley had hired a local woman to head the campaign, while

Campaigns of Ruth Hanna McCormick

McCormick had hired from outside the state. Because of this history with the candidate and Terrell, Myers's discontent, perhaps more than others', demonstrated the contingency of black women's support.

The women who protested Terrell's presence demanded the hiring of one of their own to head the McCormick campaign among black women. As Montgomery told the fifty women who represented six black Republican women's clubs at the "indignation meeting," "It is our opinion that there is a woman some where in the state of Illinois who is capable of directing Mrs. McCormick's campaign for senator, and we therefore protest against her bringing a woman from another state."[108] Wells-Barnett, who had not yet pulled away from the contest, concurred: "Anyone who knows me knows well that I would be among the first to protest against the bringing of a woman from another state to lead the women of Illinois in a political campaign."[109] At the close of the meeting, participants unanimously adopted a resolution, which they then mailed directly to McCormick and made available to the black press. "[T]he Negro women who have loyally supported Mrs. McCormick every time she has asked," the resolution explained, "had the right to expect political recognition for themselves and their daughters, which they have not received at her hands." Because McCormick had denied this recognition, the resolution continued, "we hereby serve notice on Mrs. Ruth Hanna McCormick that we resent the slight thus put upon the Negro women of Illinois whose vote she solicits, by the employment of an outsider to influence that vote, and pledge ourselves to use our influence to urge the Negro women throughout the state to resent the slight thus put upon them."[110] In addition, they sent McCormick a protest petition with almost a thousand signatures.[111]

These women's message to McCormick was pretty explicit: they could help her win, but they also could help defeat her. One of the participants drove home this point by recalling a similar situation: in 1924 Medill McCormick had imported Walter H. Cohen of New Orleans to head his senatorial renomination campaign over the objections of local race leaders. She pointedly concluded, "and McCormick lost."[112] If Ruth McCormick stood by her unwise hiring of Terrell, this woman clearly implied, she was facing the same political fate as her late husband, and by no less than the same opponent, Deneen. Deneen, a *Whip* article explained in the midst of the conflict, "has many strong followers amongst our voters and it seems that the Deneenites are laughing up their sleeves at the friction and bitterness among the McCormick women." As the *Whip* insisted, "The women cannot be discounted in Illinois." The *Whip* pointed to women's key role in the

Campaigns of Ruth Hanna McCormick

"record breaking vote" that helped sweep Herman Bundesen into the coroner's office in 1928.[113] The women themselves had demonstrated as much when they very publicly invoked their "right to expect political recognition for themselves and their daughters."

At the October "indignation meeting," speakers emphasized that their objections were politically motivated and not personal. The *Chicago Defender* reported, "Mrs. Grace Outlaw insisted that nothing be done to hurt Mrs. Terrell's feelings, inasmuch as her being here was by invitation and not of her own volition." Similarly, Bertha Montgomery argued, "The fact that it is Mrs. Terrell is incidental. . . . Our protest would be registered if the individual were anyone else from another state."[114] Nor, Montgomery added, "were the women behind the movement seeking to injure Mrs. McCormick's chances of winning."[115] Despite such pronouncements, these protests were designed to send exactly the message that African American women voters could in fact hurt McCormick's chances of winning. Furthermore, the tensions between Terrell and several Illinois leaders clearly did become personal at some point. In a private correspondence to her friend and colleague Hallie Quinn Brown, Irene Gaines detailed one confrontation in which Terrell "became most violent and abusive to each of us and to Mrs. Joan Snowden, who had frankly told her that the women of Illinois would welcome her coming in to help them put over the campaign, or as a volunteer for Mrs. McCormick, or as a speaker, but that they would not stand for an outsider to come as the head of the Woman's Division as long as there are so many capable women leaders in Illinois." Gaines relayed that Terrell, or "Lady Terrell," as Gaines referred to her throughout the letter, "accused us on the staff of agreeing with Mrs. Snowden and other women, and she was especially nasty to me, saying that I could have prevented and stopped the women in their protest if I had wanted to; that I must have wanted her job for myself." Gaines inquired, "Did you have any idea that she is like this? I have always thought her to be so cultured and refined."[116]

The tone of the conflict became so personal precisely because so much was at stake, not the least of which were paid campaign jobs. McCormick ultimately spent $252,672 of her personal fortune on the primary contest. McCormick's was one of most expensive congressional primary campaigns to date, and her expenditures were more than ten times the nearly $25,000 that Deneen spent.[117] Whoever ran the campaign among black women was in a position to help other women obtain jobs funded by McCormick's vast campaign purse and quite possibly future patronage positions. African Americans had felt the effects of the economic downturn even before the

Campaigns of Ruth Hanna McCormick

stock market crash of October. South Side residents had been losing jobs and facing unusually depressed wages for months. Black Chicagoans were boycotting and picketing stores that did not hire African Americans. This was in response to the *Chicago Whip*'s call for a campaign under the slogan of "Do not spend your money where you can not work." Just two weeks before the "indignation meeting," the protracted picketing of Woolworth stores located in the South Side had paid off. A new Woolworth opened with black female employees.[118] It was in this context of growing unemployment and militant actions to secure jobs that black Republican women staged a protest of their own against a woman many had helped to place in Congress the previous year. When these women invoked their "right to expect political recognition for themselves and their daughters," they were invoking their right to a limited number of available campaign jobs.

McCormick conceded to the women's demands at a meeting Oscar De-Priest helped convene sometime toward the end of October or the beginning of November 1929.[119] The CWRCI had forced McCormick's hand, and by November CWRCI president Irene McCoy Gaines headed McCormick's Colored Women's Division (see figure 11). Officially Gaines's title was chairman of state work. The political machine that black Republican women had created in the CWRCI enabled them to negotiate under what terms they would offer their political services. From an office in the London Guarantee Building, Gaines headed a staff that included three other women at the height of the primary.[120] Gaines worked most closely with Jennie Lawrence, who held the position of chairman of Cook County Work, which for all practical purposes meant Chicago. It is not clear how involved Lawrence was in the CWRCI prior to the McCormick campaign, though she did remain active in the organization afterward. (Lawrence was hardly alone. During 1929 and 1930 at least seventeen new black Republican women's clubs joined the CWRCI.)[121] Lawrence's entry into the McCormick campaign was by way of her affiliation with Oscar DePriest and the TWRO. Two other women completed the office: Joanna Snowden Porter, an active CWRCI member who was hired as chairman of publicity, and Alice Sutton, who worked as secretary of the women's division.[122] LeRoy Hardin, chairman of the Colored Men's Division, alerted McCormick to the funding discrepancy between the separate men's and women's departments constituting this Colored Voters' Division. "You will note," Hardin wrote to McCormick, "that the women's department is requiring over $1/2$ of the budget, wherein the men's department is taking less than $1/3$." The men's department consisted of only two paid employees, Hardin and his secretary, Lorraine Johnson.[123] If

Campaigns of Ruth Hanna McCormick

FIGURE 11. *Ruth Hanna McCormick meets with black women supporters in November 1929. McCormick is seated at the center of the table. Irene McCoy Gaines is seated to the left of McCormick, and Mary Church Terrell is to McCormick's right. The woman seated at the table second from the left may be Jennie Lawrence. Ella Berry is standing, second from the left. Chicago Bee, November 10, 1929, clipping from folder 8, box 1, IMGP; copy courtesy of the Chicago History Museum.*

nothing else, the discrepancy was an acknowledgment of the CWRCI's canvassing power, at least when compared to black men's.

African American women desperate for employment turned to Gaines's office for help. As Lawrence described, "We are called upon every day to give someone employment, as thousands of our people have been let out of jobs in the past few weeks." In one instance, she reported, "I was successful last week in placing two young women in the Lane Bryant Department Store as stock girls, and in placing two women in private homes."[124] Lawrence had been finding unemployed women jobs since her work with the Phyllis Wheatley Home. Now, she sought paid campaign work for them. Black women had demanded the hiring of local women to serve as their advocates within the McCormick machinery. Lawrence followed through. She subtly pressured McCormick's white campaign managers, by calling attention to the competition: "As the time draws nearer, the workers are growing anxious to be placed on the payroll. Deneen has engaged a number of women to canvas from door to door in the black belt and it is making it hard for our workers who can only give part time."[125] In the final month of the primary contest, the McCormick campaign did pay for an additional

[211]

123 black women canvassers throughout the state at a cost of just over $13,000.[126] How much Lawrence's pressure played in this last-minute hiring is unclear; however, she did use her inside position within the McCormick machinery to promote the economic interests of other black women, in essence extending the "ethos of mutuality" that had informed her voting since she arrived in Chicago to the stiff competition for campaign jobs.

Terrell remained an important link in the campaign as state speaker, fulfilling the role performed by Byrd in 1928. Terrell's indignation and anger over the demotion did not deter her from embarking on an extensive and enthusiastic speaking tour throughout Illinois. Like the women of the CWRCI, Terrell saw the McCormick campaign as an opportunity to advance her own influence within national Republican politics by working with one of the party's most influential women. Though no longer leading the campaign, Terrell's speaking position was still an influential and visible one. She also earned a sizable paycheck of just over $3,500 for her seven months of employment by the McCormick campaign.[127] Her goals for working for McCormick remained intact, even though her ego was bruised. On arranging Terrell's speaking itinerary across Cook County for January, Lawrence reported that "It was not an easy task, for many of the women still resent her being here."[128] With their demands met, Gaines and Lawrence were willing to soothe the resentment that still lingered among some and return to the work of the campaign. Lawrence and Gaines worked closely with Terrell to coordinate her speaking tour. As it had been with the Byrd tour, their ties to the CWRCI established network were essential to securing lodging and speaking venues in each of the towns that Terrell visited.[129]

Lawrence was the biggest earner among black women who acquired paid positions within the McCormick campaign. For her job as chairman of Cook County Work, she earned $50 a week for eighteen weeks, a total salary of $900.[130] (By contrast, Gaines and Sutton earned $35 and $25 a week for twenty-five weeks. Snowden Porter was employed for sixteen weeks at a rate of $15 a week plus expenses.)[131] With African American women especially vulnerable to unemployment as the Depression deepened, this salary would have been especially welcome for a single woman like Lawrence. Lawrence's complete employment history in the ten-odd years since she left her job as superintendent of the Phyllis Wheatley Home is unclear. In the early 1920s, she obtained employment at the Southside Property Owners Association that Oscar DePriest headed, and given her close ties with DePriest, it is likely that she worked intermittently as a paid canvasser during various campaigns.[132]

Campaigns of Ruth Hanna McCormick

As she had done since at least 1920, Lawrence stretched her income by relying on rent sharing. Although she continued to live in the Third Ward, she had left the apartment she had rented on East 33rd Street, an area that transformed into the city's notorious vice district during the 1910s and 1920s.[133] The daughter of a Presbyterian minister and teacher who would have encountered a vibrant WCTU chapter while attending Livingstone, Lawrence was most likely among the panoply of voices who protested the migration of vice into the South Side.[134] She certainly would have demanded temperate behavior among her charges while at the Phyllis Wheatley Home. Even as she battled the vice economy and perhaps tried to "save" prostitutes through the services offered at the Phyllis Wheatley Home, it is possible to imagine that she herself did not want to live so close to the vice district that flourished between 33rd and 35th.[135] By 1930 she had moved a little more than a mile directly south to 42nd and Michigan Avenue. Her uncle Levi Henderson, with whom she had shared the apartment on East 33rd Street, moved with her. Levi worked as a janitor. Four women boarders also contributed to the household economy. Like Jennie and Levi, these women, who worked as seamstresses, cooks, and in retail, were lucky in 1930 to have employment.[136] The significant salary Lawrence earned in the McCormick campaign ensured financial stability for this household of six. While individual women won campaign and patronage jobs, the economic benefits of such positions clearly extended beyond the individual.

It is perhaps no surprise that Lawrence was the highest earner given her potential to bring a sizable number of voters to the McCormick campaign. Jennie Lawrence was among the 55,306 African Americans who made the Third Ward the most highly black populated ward in the city (79.9 percent).[137] Even more important, Lawrence had transformed herself into a key political broker in Third Ward politics, who was well positioned to fuse the organizational resources of the TWRO and the CWRCI. Lawrence canvassed for DePriest during his successful congressional run in 1928, and in his recommendation to McCormick, DePriest characterized her as "his most outstanding woman worker in the Third Ward."[138] Presumably he was referring to her work for him not just in 1928 but over the years. During the McCormick primary campaign, Lawrence attended TWRO meetings no less than eleven times. There, in addition to the occasional speech, she recruited women to form and join Ruth Hanna McCormick Clubs.[139] In her movement back and forth between TWRO meetings and the McCormick campaign headquarters that she shared with Irene Gaines, Lawrence deepened the links and overlapping memberships between the CWRCI and the TWRO.

[213]

Each was a political machine in its own right with networks of supporters who could help propel a candidate into office and who expected patronage and policy accountability in return.

Lawrence, Gaines, and Terrell canvassed a range of black institutions. They took advantage of their multiple ties to middle-class women's clubs to distribute literature and give campaign speeches—the American Rose Art and Charity Club, the Marquette Woman's Social Club, the Gaudeamus Club, and the Phyllis Wheatley Club were just a few of the many local women's clubs they canvassed in Chicago.[140] Occasionally they clashed with Deneen supporters also active in the club movement. Such was the case at the March meeting of the Colored Women's Clubs of the Central District. As Gaines reported, "There were two strong Deneen women present who tried to get a place on the program but were blocked in their efforts to do so by my women."[141] Gaines also addressed the Douglass League of Women Voters, a group in which she had occupied a range of offices.[142] Even though the number of dues-paying members had declined by about half (from 100 to about 50) since Goins founded the organization in 1923, Gaines attracted a crowd of about 200 to the talk she gave at a tea on behalf of McCormick.[143] The significant overlap in leadership between the cwrci and these various women's clubs enabled McCormick supporters to strategically shut down competition when necessary and transform explicitly nonpartisan venues such as the Douglass League of Women Voters into forums for partisan speeches.[144]

Lawrence, Gaines, and Terrell also reached out to black institutions with more of a cross-class membership than existed in the women's clubs: labor organizations, fraternal groups, and churches. The memberships of these institutions overlapped at times, but not always. Several leading clergy, for instance, initially opposed the labor organizing of the Brotherhood of Sleeping Car Porters (bscp). These various institutions did, however, attract a broad cross section of black Chicago. The women who were leading the McCormick campaign had made inroads into these groups over the course of several years, and they put such ties to good use in 1930. The history of the bscp in Chicago is a case in point. Black clubwomen's organizing, as Beth Tompkins Bates demonstrates, was instrumental to the eventual erosion of community resistance to the bscp. While the majority of the city's black male-run institutions, from the press to the pulpit, initially rejected the bscp, Ida Wells-Barnett, Irene Goins, and Irene McCoy Gaines utilized the networks of the women's club movement to spread the bscp's message: that the battle for workers' rights was synonymous with the struggle for black citizen-

Campaigns of Ruth Hanna McCormick

ship rights. Gaines even asked to sit on the Chicago Citizens' Committee for the BSCP when it formed in 1927.[145]

The decline of community resistance to the BSCP was evident at the well-attended five-day national labor conference that the BSCP held in Chicago in late January 1930.[146] So too was the fusion of party politics and the BSCP's emerging style of protest politics. The BSCP sought to break away from the traditional patronage politics that put African Americans in supplicant positions to white politicians.[147] Still, traditional party politicking took place amid planning for future direct action.[148] Jennie Lawrence used the conference as an opportunity to network for McCormick and arrange speaking engagements.[149] Some of McCormick's labor views would have been welcome at the conference. As Gaines told black audiences elsewhere, McCormick's platform held that "immigration should be rigidly restricted for the protection of labor."[150] DePriest made a very similar argument on the first day of the conference, promising to help organized labor by "pushing a congressional measure to prohibit all immigration for the period of 10 years."[151] Many African Americans welcomed the 1924 Immigration Act for, as the *Negro World* put it, curtailing the "flood of European immigrants who for years have stood in the way of industrial advancement of colored wage-earners."[152] In the difficult economic environment of 1930, McCormick's anti-immigration policy was again perceived as a salve to stiff job competition.

Gaines and Lawrence also included fraternal groups among their meetings to attend.[153] These organizations served as important sites of party politics during the 1920s, especially in northern cities where southern migrants had recently relocated. For instance, leaders of the Improved Benevolent and Protective Order of the Elks of the World, or the "black Elks" as they were known, regularly campaigned for Republican candidates during the 1920s.[154] In 1928 the black Elks urged the voters of Illinois to help DePriest earn a seat in Congress.[155] And the person who headed their women's division during this time was none other than Ella Berry.[156] The fraternal involvement that Berry had begun as a child in Kentucky and continued after her relocation to Chicago had brought her all the way to the top of the fraternal world in the 1920s. The black Elks, like other black fraternal organizations, offered real leadership opportunities for women. They also welcomed a mixture of working and elite classes that was atypical of early twentieth-century black organizations, which tended to be more class stratified.[157] For this reason, fraternal groups were rich sites for enlisting a cross section of voters. In 1930 Berry was campaigning for McCor-

Campaigns of Ruth Hanna McCormick

mick, having recently completed her third term as Grand Daughter Ruler of the Daughters of the Improved Benevolent and Protective Order of the Elks, the highest office available to a woman in the organization.[158] She was well positioned to reach thousands of local Elks and urge them to vote for McCormick.[159]

By far the most common sites that Lawrence, Gaines, and Terrell canvassed were the churches of the black wards and satellite communities. The days when clergy served as the primary interlocutors between black voters and white primary bosses were gone. Black politicians, such as Oscar De-Priest, had taken on this role, and within just a few months DePriest would break from the Thompson machine altogether. In the pages of the *Defender*, lay women and men accused ministers of, as one editorial put it, being "primarily concerned about two things: An elaborate salary and an imposing church building situated in some conspicuous spot."[160] Despite a relative decline in clerical authority within the community, male clergy still controlled access to their congregations. Lawrence, Gaines, and Terrell reached out to ministers in order to secure opportunities to address these sometimes very large congregations. Lawrence and Gaines held luncheons to interest ministers.[161] Terrell explained her deliberate strategy of canvassing a community by first making contact with church leaders: "I am sure I have already won hundreds of votes for you—*Ministers are my specialty*, because they wield such a powerful influence" (emphasis added).[162] As a former NACW president, Terrell knew better than most the history of clerical hostility toward the organization. Making sure that her value in the campaign was not called into question again, Terrell strategically glossed over this history when she enthused to McCormick: "It is easy for me to secure permission to speak when the ministers realize that I am the first president of the National Association of Colored Women, that I have represented colored women abroad twice and I have been working for my group for many years."[163] No doubt, her prominence did help her secure audiences. Still, clubwomen's embattled position as social reformers made Terrell less of a threat to clergy than she had been in the early years of the club movement when the impact of women's independent organizing on clerical authority was still an unknown.

Overall, what Wallace Best describes as the "fracturing of strict class compositions" in many of Chicago's black churches between 1915 and 1930 enabled Lawrence, Gaines, and Terrell to reach a mixed-class, often largely migrant voting population when they canvassed among mainline congregations.[164] Black Baptist churches constituted about 45 percent of the con-

Campaigns of Ruth Hanna McCormick

gregations in the city, while black Methodists composed just under 12 percent.[165] It might have made more sense to canvass broadly among Baptist churches, given their numerical ascendancy. McCormick canvassers, however, spoke evenly among mainline Baptist and Methodist congregations.[166] Strategically, they focused less on denominational size and more on individual church membership size—that is, they sought out large congregations. Each of the large congregations they canvassed—Ebenezer Baptist, Salem Baptist, Bethel AME, and Walters AME Zion—had transformed into the type of mixed-class institutions that Best describes emerging in Chicago as a result of the influx of southern migrants.[167] Among these, Ebenezer was by far the largest, with well over 2,000 members by 1930.[168] The other 2,000-plus congregation they addressed was Metropolitan Community Church. Metropolitan was part of Chicago's burgeoning Community Church Movement that welcomed "all classes of people irrespective of nationality, creed, or economic status."[169] Its base of membership was even more class diverse than the mainline congregations that had been transformed by the arrival of southern migrants.[170] The McCormick campaign had access to Metropolitan because of the church's foundational ties with DePriest, who had arranged a space for Metropolitan's first service when a faction split from Bethel AME in 1920.[171] Factional alliances presumably determined McCormick's and Gaines's access to other congregations as well. It is hard to know how campaign rhetoric landed on audiences. Attendance at these various political speeches did not necessarily translate into votes for McCormick at the polls. What is clear, though, is that women campaigners strategically used church attendance—which remained largely female but had become increasingly cross-class within individual congregations—to make their case for their candidate.

Even though Lawrence, Gaines, and Terrell had each entered electoral politics in order to help their northern communities, as well as the ones they had left behind in the South, they were not entirely successful in connecting with southerners who lived all around them in the North. McCormick campaigners missed an important opportunity for reaching poor black Chicagoans, many of them migrants, when they decided not to canvass the Holiness, Spiritualist, and Baptist storefronts that dotted the South Side. Participants at these "storefront" churches were typically poor and largely female. By 1930, with the Depression deepening, many black women had turned to the storefronts because they could not afford to worship at the mainline congregations. As one woman summarized, "I'm a lone woman and I have a hard enough time keeping a roof over my head without paying

Campaigns of Ruth Hanna McCormick

dues here and there."[172] At churches like Olivet Baptist and Quinn Chapel AME, membership dues only increased as thousands of migrants poured into the South Side during the 1920s. The creation of social programs to aid these new arrivals and the purchase of larger buildings that could accommodate swelling congregations drove several of the established churches into heavy debt.[173] The small storefronts, by contrast, had minimal overhead; they rented inexpensive business space or met in private homes, and they did not offer the costly social services available at many of the large congregations.[174] Low overhead translated into minimal financial pressure for worshipers. "Most of the people who attend the store-front churches," one woman explained to Works Progress Administration interviewers, "are not able to keep up the dues in the big churches and to keep from being embarrassed they attend the store-front churches."After all, she concluded, "They have to worship God somewhere." Of her own dissociation from Chicago's mainstream black congregations, this woman explained, "I am a member of a church but I don't attend very regularly, because they want too much money."[175]

Most storefront churches were very small, which did not make them practical sites for conducting mass canvassing work. A few of these congregations, however, had sizable followings, for example, Lucy Smith's All Nations Pentecostal Church, suggesting that congregation size was not the sole factor shaping Lawrence, Gaines, and Terrell's decision to bypass storefronts, small and large, that dotted the South Side.[176] Also at play in this decision were regional and class tensions. As Wallace Best demonstrates, migrants in particular were drawn to these institutions largely out of a desire to express a southern regional consciousness that was articulated through particular rituals and styles of worship.[177] Uncomfortable with the formality and condescending attitudes they sometimes encountered at Chicago's mainline churches, southern migrants created and turned to existing storefronts in order to exert the openly emotional style of worship they had practiced in the South.[178] For middle-class women like Lawrence and Gaines, though migrants themselves, these emotional styles of worship also would have had a class connotation. Banking on outward displays of modesty more than income as markers of their own upward mobility and distinctiveness from poor African Americans, Gaines, Lawrence, and Terrell would have disapproved of the style of worship that was practiced at such storefronts.[179] Like Republican women's approach to prohibition, Gaines, Lawrence, and Terrell's personal investment in the behavioral code associated with women's racial uplift ideology generated a class blind spot in their canvassing that ironically led them to neglect many of the very people whom they had entered party politics to help and represent.[180]

The Depression affected the campaign in other ways. Middle-class women canvassers obtained paid campaign positions, in part, to meet their own financial needs. Poor women also turned to party politics to help fulfill their economic needs. Unable to obtain coveted campaign positions, poor women took advantage of the only type of financial assistance that local machine politics offered them, gifts in exchange for their votes. Second Ward canvasser Rosa Gordon Newton wrote to Lawrence about her frustration over the Deneen machine's gifting: "The Deneen organization has a general meeting Monday night and a special meeting for ladies on Friday night. Last Friday night the women were presented with bath towels, at another time with nice creton aprons, and I hear this Friday night they are to get something else nice; that it would probably be candy."[181] Newton invited several Second Ward women to attend the Ruth Hanna McCormick Club that she was attempting to set up. In response, she explained to Lawrence, "Some of these women stated that they cannot attend two political meetings, as they have other meetings for different purposes; that they go Friday nights because they are given something." Somewhat condescendingly, Newton continued, "I live in the second ward, and many of the people there have lately come from the South, and they do not know what it is all about, and it is not surprising that they are so easily led by a small gift."[182] Not only did many of these newcomers, like Lawrence herself, probably arrive with significant political knowledge and experience, but they also most certainly understood the implication of accepting those gifts. Whether they actually voted for Deneen in exchange for these gifts is hard to know. But these gifts, some practical, others fanciful, were a small part of the informal economy that enabled poor African Americans to enjoy some small pleasures during desperate economic times.

In the context of such a tight race against an opponent who was popular among black voters, Gaines, Terrell, and Lawrence went on the offensive. Gaines strategically distanced herself and her husband from Deneen by criticizing the senator on a range of issues, from corruption to inaction in the Senate. In a speech that must have run about twenty to thirty minutes, Gaines accused Deneen of being behind DePriest's indictment for "election fraud, graft and vice conditions in the second and third wards."[183] As Gaines told her audiences, these charges, which were dropped in 1929, were "made for the express purposes of keeping a black man out of Congress." She linked the Deneen camp with the notorious election day murder of Octavius

Granady, a black lawyer who was running in the 1928 Republican primary for ward committeeman in the Twentieth Ward.[184] Gaines also characterized Deneen as someone who had a history of using his office to help African Americans only when he was forced to do so. Gaines invoked the story of Ferdinand Barnett's appointment as assistant state's attorney as evidence. Eliding over Deneen's response to the 1909 Cairo incident, Gaines pointed to the 1908 Springfield Riot as further evidence of Deneen's reluctance to use elected power to assist African Americans: "Governor Deneen sat in the executive mansion unmoved and said not a word until he was requested and urged by outstanding citizens of the State to send troops to Springfield from Chicago to control the mob."[185]

Toward the end of the primary contest, the Deneen camp added further credence to Gaines's claims by slighting one of its own. Georgia Jones Ellis, a Deneen-backed candidate for state representative from the Fifth Senatorial District, complained in the pages of the *Defender* that the organization had "double-crossed" her. Ellis, an attorney who had affiliated with Deneen for fifteen years, was also one of three black women running in the 1930 Republican primaries. She complained that the Deneen camp was distributing sample ballots in the Third Ward without a cross in front of her name—this despite the fact that the ballots had x marks next to the name of a white female candidate whom Deneen was endorsing. Ellis's main criticisms were directed at the president of the Third Ward Deneen organization.[186] But readers could infer that Deneen himself was also to blame.

Significantly, Gaines and Terrell denounced Deneen for displaying indifference toward enforcing the Reconstruction Amendments in the South. Doing so enabled them not only to highlight McCormick's positive record here but also to keep the Reconstruction Amendments front and center in a prominent electoral contest. Terrell distilled her views on Deneen for her listeners: "There is only one thing colored people of the state need to know about Senator Deneen. He does not believe that colored people should enjoy the right of citizenship guaranteed them by the Constitution."[187] As proof, Terrell pointed to Deneen's treatment of the 1929 *Chicago Tribune* questionnaire sent to U.S. senators and representatives inquiring whether the member believed in the enforcement of the Fourteenth and Fifteenth Amendments. Deneen was among the majority of congressmen who ignored the inquiry. "Only one conclusion can be drawn from Senator Deneen's failure to reply to the Tribune questionnaire," Terrell asserted: "He does not believe that the 14th and 15th amendments should be enforced. It was to his interest to put himself on record as favoring these two provisions of

Campaigns of Ruth Hanna McCormick

the Constitution. Since he failed to do so, it is evident he is opposed to their enforcement." Deneen's decision not to reply, Terrell explained, "is only the more reprehensible because colored people are said to have cast about 75,000 of the votes which sent him to the United States Senate."[188] Terrell emphasized the responsibility midwestern enfranchised African American women and men held toward southern blacks when casting the Republican primary ballot in April: "How can any self-respecting colored man or colored woman vote to send back to the United States Senate a man who is so unjust as is Mrs. McCormick's opponent to thousands of people to whom he is bound by the ties of bloo[d]?"[189] The intended message was that a vote for Deneen was the equivalent of a vote for Jim Crow.

McCormick did prevail in the Republican primaries. In the Second, Third, and Fourth Wards, where African Americans were a majority, she earned three times as many votes as Deneen.[190] Gaines was in a sense a double winner, in that her husband won the Republican nomination for state representative from the First District. DePriest was also a "double winner," as the *Defender* put it. He was renominated to run for U.S. representative from the First Congressional District. He maintained his ascendancy in the Third Ward by winning again the office of Third Ward committeeman by a six-to-one majority. The three black women who had run in the Republican primaries for the Illinois State Assembly did not fare as well: all three, Georgia Jones Ellis, Ida Wells-Barnett, and Mary G. Clark, lost.[191]

Once McCormick had defeated Deneen to become the Republican Party nominee for senator from Illinois, she had to face James Hamilton Lewis and Lottie Holman O'Neil, the white Democratic and Independent nominees. Machine alliances also shifted dramatically. Thompson, who had supported McCormick in the primary, withdrew his endorsement in the general election, lending it instead to Democrat James Hamilton Lewis. DePriest, who was beholden to Thompson for facilitating his political ascendance as Third Ward committeeman and then as congressman, defied the Thompson machine by continuing to endorse McCormick. This was a bold move that signaled his political independence from the white boss machinery.[192] The cwrci was well positioned to reap the rewards of DePriest's maneuver if it proved successful.

This may explain why the cwrci continued to campaign for McCormick despite Gaines's new status as an unpaid volunteer. In a letter right after the close of the cwrci's sixth annual convention, Gaines wrote one of McCormick's white campaign managers that the convention "voted endorsement of Mrs. McCormick's platform and candidacy, and offered our services as a

Campaigns of Ruth Hanna McCormick

state body to assist in the Fall campaign."[193] Nannie Burroughs even traveled from Washington, D.C., to speak at a McCormick rally alongside DePriest and Lawrence.[194] In the face of such generous support, however, the Republican State Central Committee did not send Gaines promised campaign funds to support black women's canvassing activities. "I am offering my services as a volunteer to take care of Colored women's work until such time as the necessary appropriations are made for our work," Gaines graciously responded.[195] In 1926 Terrell had warned that once a campaign moved into the hands of party functionaries after the primaries, the leverage shifted to "the white leaders of a state and upon their attitude toward colored people on general principles."[196] Her prediction seemed to be coming true here. A black woman continued to remain in charge of women's activities in the First Congressional District. Grace Knighten, president of the ladies auxiliary to the Regular Second Ward Republican Club, replaced Gaines in this Republican State Central Committee office.[197] Still neither Gaines nor Knighten were able to reverse the decision on funding, despite the large number of black women they were able to mobilize across the state. Black votes were not as critical in the general election as they had been in the Republican primary, now that they were diluted among the more general population. The Republican State Central Committee may have offered leading black women some legitimation by appointing one after another to head women's activities in the First Congressional District, but these appointments did not seem to have translated into real power sharing.

Jennie Lawrence continued to campaign for McCormick through both the CWRCI and the DePriest machine. By September 1930 Lawrence headed the CWRCI's finance committee.[198] Along with DePriest's secretary, Morris Lewis, Lawrence edited a campaign magazine in October entitled *The Plain Truth*. There they reprinted articles reporting on James Hamilton Lewis's remark at a 1920 campaign rally that "this is a white man's government."[199] "The election of James Hamilton Lewis to the Senate of the United States," they warned, "would be a distinct contribution to the Southern Democratic Bloc and would strengthen the Democratic party, controlled by Southern Democrats in the Senate and House and therefore would be detrimental to the race."[200] Lawrence and her colleague used the pages of *The Plain Truth* to cast not only James Hamilton Lewis as a white supremacist but also northern Democrats more generally. *The Plain Truth* included a statement in half-inch font sure to catch the eye of anyone who did not want to bother reading the articles: "No Difference between Northern and Southern Democrats."[201] Lawrence was presumably under the

Campaigns of Ruth Hanna McCormick

employ of the DePriest machine, especially given the Republican State Central Committee's stinginess toward black women. Without knowing anything about Lawrence's background, it would be easy conclude that she was merely a gun for hire—that her warnings about James Hamilton Lewis were just politics as usual, meaningless rhetoric. Her acumen for machine politics, however, did not necessarily negate her distrust of Democrats or, as Burroughs had similarly argued in 1928, how northern Democrats would align with the southern wing of the party once they were in Congress. This was a distrust she had developed early on as the daughter of a Reconstruction-era Republican politician and a teacher of freed people, and then as a teacher herself in the post-Reconstruction South. Rhetoric about "a white man's government" coming from a Democrat, even a northern Democrat, would have sounded all too familiar to southern diasporic ears. Here was the defensive position of keeping Democrats out of office that had come to dominate Republican women's rhetoric.

With some notable exceptions, such an aggressive campaign against Illinois Democrats would not have been necessary prior to 1928. The political landscape of Chicago was undergoing changes that Republican canvassers could not ignore. Though still relatively small when compared to Harlem, the black Democratic presence in Chicago was growing. In the aftermath of the April primaries, one precinct captain in the Third Ward "reported five times more Democratic votes in his precinct than in previous years."[202] Thompson, who had garnered significant black support through the years, was now endorsing a Democrat. Other white Democrats courted black votes. Most notably, in 1928 Fifth Ward committeeman Michael Igoe began working with black men and women in the ward to build a black Democratic organization.[203] The result was the Fifth Ward West-End Democratic Club (also called the National Negro Democratic Organization). Three women served as club officers, and a women's auxiliary was also up and running by 1929.[204] In 1930, reports of black Democrats, including women, peppered the pages of the *Defender*. At the very least, black Democratic women's groups were operating in the Third, Fourth, and Fifth Wards.[205]

Prohibition was once again a major issue in an electoral campaign, and James Lewis's strong opposition to prohibition may have attracted some black voters to the Democratic camp in the general elections. The November Illinois ballot contained a triple referendum that would significantly weaken enforcement of the Eighteenth Amendment in Illinois. The candidates and newspapers were abuzz with discussion about where candidates stood on the three questions presented to Illinois voters in the referendum:

should the Eighteenth Amendment be repealed, should the Volstead Act be modified, and should the Illinois State Prohibition Act be repealed?[206] Anecdotal evidence indicated that black opposition to prohibition had not declined since the 1928 presidential contest. If anything, it had probably only increased. Some black voters, including middle-class women, would clearly answer yes to each question.

To mark the end of ten years of prohibition in January 1930, the *Defender* ran excerpts from thirty-two interviews with black Chicagoans about their views of prohibition. Almost uniformly the thirty-two denounced the Eighteenth Amendment as a failure that had merely benefited bootleggers and made liquor plentiful and sometimes poisonous. J. C. Austin, who pastored Pilgrim Baptist, one of Chicago's largest congregations, equivocated the most. Prohibition, he argued, had helped reduce mob violence in the South. He conceded, however, that nationally prohibition was more of "a political game" than a program pursued "with the purpose of enforcing a great law." The five women interviewed pointed especially to the harm that prohibition had done to family and youth. "Nowadays you see school girls doing things they never did before, getting into all kinds of trouble, and most of the time liquor has led to their downfall," explained Marie Moore who was identified simply as a housewife. Prior to prohibition, she asserted, "young children didn't drink, but now that they have taken liquor away and made its sale illegal anybody can get it." Louise Douglass, a thirty-year-old drugstore clerk similarly maintained that the Eighteenth Amendment "has done more harm to young folks in schools and colleges than saloons ever did." "Young girls from 14 up are seen drinking," she lamented. "This bad liquor," she continued, "has deprived many families of the necessities of life." Still another woman who was identified simply as a mother complained, "I think prohibition is terrible because it has caused many girls and young boys to be ruined." Like Moore, this woman reflected back on the years prior to the Eighteenth Amendment: "Young folks didn't drink like this when I was younger. But now everywhere you go people offer you a drink of bad liquor, which may make you blind or even kill you."[207] If any of these women had ever thought that prohibition might benefit racial uplift goals, they had clearly been disabused of this idea over the course of ten years. If they still believed in the tenets of this embattled ideology, then the defeat of prohibition rather than its continuation was key to protecting the race from impropriety.

Indeed, the results of the referendum in the heavily black-populated Second, Third, and Fourth Wards indicated overwhelming opposition to prohibition in 1930. On the first referendum question, 85 percent of voters in the Second, Third, and Fourth Wards combined cast ballots in favor of repealing the Eighteenth Amendment. On the second question, 86 percent in these wards voted for the modification of the Volstead Act. And on the third, 85 percent voted to repeal the Illinois Prohibition Act.[208] How exactly this antiprohibition sentiment translated into the Senate race is hard to say. Speculation is possible though. McCormick's deliberately middle-ground platform—that technically she was dry but would support whatever the voters decided—was not a position that won over adherents; it only appeased them. Lewis's vocal opposition to an unpopular law, by contrast, was designed to bolster his base of support. Perhaps some of the approximately 85 percent of black voters in Chicago who voted against prohibition were drawn to Lewis's candidacy because of his trenchant repeal platform.[209]

Twenty-four percent of Chicago's black voters helped Democrat James Lewis prevail on November 6.[210] Even though McCormick lost, she received 76 percent of the black vote across the state and "carried the Second, Third and Fourth Wards by large margins."[211] Charles Branham describes McCormick's strong showing in the predominantly black wards as vindication of Oscar DePriest's break with the Thompson machine. It was also a measure of the hard work that McCormick's canvassers had put over. But this measured victory took place amid large-scale Democratic success: Lewis's election to the Senate was one of several county and municipal offices that went to the Democrats. Many more would follow in 1932.[212]

AFRICAN AMERICAN WOMEN IN Illinois faced an incredibly complicated set of issues during the Illinois congressional campaigns of 1928 and 1930. They encountered several candidates with records in support of civil rights. This was testament to the fact that Chicago was a place where African American voters wielded some real political power. They faced shifting machine alliances, the emergence of an independent black political machine, and the rise of the Democratic Party in Chicago. They also struggled with a faltering economy in which black women often suffered most. Black Republican women were not always consistent actors. This was witnessed in the CWRCI's decision to support McCormick despite her middle-ground position on prohibition. They also did not act as a monolithic group. This was evident, for instance, in the fact that even as the CWRCI focused energy on the McCormick candidacy, other women worked with the Deneen machine.

The CWRCI steered through this complex maze of political and economic issues while also attempting to forward both group and individual agendas that were deeply intertwined. With an eye toward using their voting and canvassing power for the larger benefit of the race, CWRCI activists repeatedly injected discussion of the Reconstruction Amendments in the McCormick campaigns. They did achieve a small measure of success, though far short of what they desired. It is unlikely that McCormick would have supported the Tinkham amendment to the Census and Reapportionment Bill if she did not have the weight of black votes behind her election to the House. The CWRCI's canvassing efforts helped to generate these votes. Would McCormick have extended her civil rights record beyond its modest beginnings, or was the Tinkham amendment the extent of her willingness to represent her black supporters? Although the CWRCI was betting on the former, it never had the opportunity to find out.

CWRCI activists also used the McCormick campaigns to advance their own political careers and economic needs. Some women did successfully barter their access to CWRCI canvassing networks for paid campaign positions. Had McCormick actually won the 1930 contest to become the first woman elected to the U.S. Senate, then perhaps further rewards were in store: modest patronage, if not posts within the upper echelons of government. The drive for paid canvassing jobs carried with it an unresolved tension between collective political action and self-interest. On the one hand, the "ethos of mutuality" that led women to use their vote on behalf of others was also visible in their efforts to obtain paid campaign and patronage jobs. Women inquired about patronage positions not only for themselves but also for neighbors and family members. They used income generated by canvassing work to help immediate, extended, or constructed families survive hard economic times. On the other hand, the economic exchange that was at the heart of paid campaign work had the potential to undermine "woman's era" philosophy's injunction against putting economic self-interest ahead of race progress.

Women reformers had complained that party money, specifically Democratic Party money, had compromised men's political compass, causing them to vote for the highest bidder rather than for candidates and policies that would most benefit the race. Paid campaign positions were not graft, and this was not the first time women had accepted paid campaign work. Still, in exchange for a salary or the promise of patronage, middle-class women lost some of the political independence that came with volunteerism. What might Jennie Lawrence have said about McCormick's position on the Eighteenth Amendment if, for instance, she were not directly under McCormick's or DePriest's employ? Would CWRCI activists have ap-

Campaigns of Ruth Hanna McCormick

proached Deneen's civil rights record differently if they were not earning income from the McCormick campaign, or if they were not interested in obtaining patronage jobs in the future? Black women reformers had promised that women would do better than men once they got the vote, that they would not let economic temptations interfere with principled electoral activism. Women reformers were disappointed when they encountered poor women, like those described in Rosa Gordon Newton's note, who seemed to be doing just that by accepting gifts from the Deneen machine. Whether such women did in fact vote for Deneen is unclear, but it is probably not unreasonable to assume that some did. While critical of poor women's use of campaign money to fulfill economic needs, black women reformers did not seem to consider how their own economic exchanges with candidates shaped their political decisions, including their decision to remain loyal Republicans in the face of the party's deep retreat from its historical commitment to black citizenship rights.

Paid campaign work and the promise of patronage may have helped some women overcome their sense of restlessness with the Republican Party. The previous chapter detailed the deep disappointment that women affiliated with the NLRCW felt about the lily-white elements of the party. Rather than withdraw from Republican politics, NLRCW activists decided to redouble their efforts. The rise of Oscar DePriest as an independent black political force in Chicago gave the women of Illinois a good reason to do so. So too did the possibility of helping to elect the first woman senator. For other women, these were not good enough reasons to remain with the Republican Party, and for the first time they put the same kind of organizing strength that had been directed toward the Republican Party toward forming black Democratic women's groups.

Campaigns of Ruth Hanna McCormick

Conclusion

"Oh say, Lovie did you hear about Jennie E. Lawrence?" asked "Wire-Tappings" in late October 1932. A regular *Defender* column that announced the comings and goings of social life on the South Side, "Wire-Tappings" was written as if the author was directly interacting with a reader. Adhering to this format, the author responded to an imagined lack of recognition: "You do know her, too. She lives at 4439 Calumet Ave., and is one of the biggest political figures in Chicago." The purpose of Lawrence's mention was to share news of her health: "She has been sick in the hospital with an ailment of her foot. At one time they thought they would have to amputate it. Well, she has recovered sufficiently to return to her home." Ten days after this article appeared, Chicago and the nation would go to the polls again. Politics, it seems, was never far from Lawrence's mind, so much so that "Wire-Tappings" cautioned, "I think that she retards her own progress by worrying about the campaign." The columnist apparently had this information secondhand: "She told a friend of mine that this is the first campaign in many years during which she had not visited every ward and community in Chicago and Cook county, where our people live. You know that she has headed the women's division of the Third ward regular Republican organization of which Congressman DePriest is committeeman. Jennie is a fluent speaker and has always been in demand."[1]

In an odd way, it was perhaps fitting that 1932 was the first year that Lawrence, one of Chicago's most active Republican women campaigners, was unable to make her regular canvassing rounds. Like Lawrence herself, the Republican Party's health among black voters was in decline. For nineteen years, Lawrence had attempted to use her ballot to elect officials who would protect black citizenship rights. Her desire to use the electoral system, and the Republican Party specifically, for this purpose was shaped by her early experiences in the Carolinas. As the daughter of a Reconstruction-era Republican politician and a teacher of freed peoples, Lawrence had learned from her parents about white Democrats' dismantling of Reconstruction in North Carolina. She had seen her mother struggle to educate freed peoples during the nadir of the 1880s. As a teenager, Lawrence watched as a disfranchising amendment to the North Carolina state constitution took effect. Like her mother before her, she had taught in the politicized atmosphere of Presbyterian freedman schools in North and South Carolina. When in 1912 Lawrence relocated to Chicago, she carried to her new home the political knowledge that she had learned as a child and young woman in the South: the lengths to which white Democrats would go to prevent African Americans from voting, and the lengths to which African Americans would go to fight for their basic citizenship rights. Lawrence infused her anger toward Democratic white supremacy into her Republican canvassing work in Chicago's heavily black-populated wards, acting as a kind of political proxy for the disfranchised women and men whom she had left behind in the South.

Lawrence of course was not alone. She joined other black women, many southern migrants, who similarly sought to use women's expanding franchise to create a federal government that would protect black citizenship rights. With so few Republican candidates who actually made any meaningful commitment to using federal power to protect black rights, this turn to the electoral system to accomplish such a goal required the adoption of distinct strategies. First, black Republican women looked for moments in electoral contests to insert discussions of southern abuses and the unrealized promises of the Reconstruction Amendments. In the 1890s African American women in Chicago used a relatively small local contest that had nothing to do with the Reconstruction Amendments to bring attention to southern abuses of black citizenship rights. During the struggle to enact federal prohibition during the 1910s, black women reformers hinted that national debates over legislating and then enforcing prohibition might reopen interest among white politicians in enforcing the Reconstruction Amendments. When the battle over prohibition quickly turned from enactment to repeal, they pointed to the implications of repeal for the future of the Reconstruction Amendments. A second strategy entailed consciously focusing on the exceptions to Republican indifference. This was not easy, and throughout their journey with the Republican Party, African American women attempted to undermine the white Republican racism that made working with the party frustrating. Even while they sought to reform the Republican Party from within, they campaigned for candidates who aimed to use federal power to uphold the provisions of the Fourteenth Amendment. During the 1920s, these efforts revolved around the battles to enact federal antilynching legislation and to legislate reapportionment in the House to reflect the disfranchisement of southern blacks. Occasionally, Republican women had to choose between strategies and issues, as was the case during Ruth

[229]

Hanna McCormick's run for Senate. There, campaigners prioritized Mc-Cormick's support for House reapportionment, and indeed well-paying campaign jobs, over McCormick's less than ideal position on prohibition.

Had Lawrence been well enough to campaign in 1932, she would have had a much harder time making her case that, as the broadside Lawrence edited two years prior said, there is "no difference between northern and southern Democrats."[2] This much was clear by the experiences that her colleagues were having on the campaign trail. The Republican women's club that Susie Myers headed, the *Defender* reported, was "making an extensive fight in the interest of the Republican candidates who at this time need all the help available."[3] The *Defender* explained in a separate article that the rise of black Democrats in the First Ward, which comprised a large portion of the First Congressional District, threatened Oscar DePriest's reelection to Congress. As the *Defender* insisted, "There may be differences of opinion as to some other candidates, but there should be no difference of opinion with the Race voters of the First congressional district on the all-important questions of sending the only member of the Race we have now in the nation's capital back to congress."[4] In a private letter to Nannie Helen Burroughs, Chicago clubwoman Elizabeth Lindsay Davis also expressed her concern about the election just days away in terms that emphasized her belief in women's responsibility to lead the race. Referring to Burroughs's appointment to the Hoover-Curtis Campaign League Advisory Committee, Davis told her National League of Republican Colored Women (NLRCW) colleague, "There never was a time when we needed the help and the influence of strong women like yourself to open the eyes of our misguided people, who are blindly following false leaders to a realization of their great peril." "A Democratic victory at this time," Davis concluded, "will mean calamity to the Nation from which it will take long years to recover."[5]

If Lawrence had been well enough to canvass in 1932, she also would have encountered new challenges in reaching women voters through the mainline churches. Clerical patriarchy had often made women's canvassing through mainline congregations fraught with difficulties. Clergy were not above lashing out at women congregants who disagreed with them politically or whose growing club strength appeared to threaten church finances. Women canvassers who steered through clerical animosity, as well as the constantly shifting labyrinth of political alliances between clergy and political machines, in order to address female-dominated congregations faced a new dilemma in the early 1930s. They found themselves cut off from women congregants not because of clerical intervention, but because of the shame

[230]

Conclusion

associated with poverty caused many women to stop attending mainline congregations altogether. Beginning in the mid-1930s, Works Progress Administration (WPA) interviewers recorded numerous, almost identical accounts of black women explaining that they had stopped attending church because they were concerned about their appearance. "The main reason I haven't been to church" in a year, one woman told an interviewer, "is because I don't have sufficient clothes to wear." Another woman similarly relayed: "I don't attend church as often as I used to. You know I am not fixed like I want to be—haven't the clothes I need." Yet another described her gradual and unwelcome dissociation from her church: "At one time I was active in church, but now I can't dress well, so I don't go to church, only at night, because I haven't got anything to wear."[6] The embarrassment these women felt must have only deepened their sense that radical change was needed in order to alleviate the economic crisis.

It was not just the urban poor who found themselves marginalized from the political life that took place in Chicago's black mainline churches. Financial difficulties caused Lawrence herself to be distanced from Grace's politically influential network of congregants. In 1932 the Grace Presbyterian Church Council suspended Lawrence because of her failure to pay dues. An examination of the Grace Presbyterian Church Council minutes reveals that Lawrence was far from atypical. Even Grace, a church that had the reputation for serving Chicago's black middle classes and elites, was facing a growing problem of nonattendance by the early 1930s. In May 1932—one month after Lawrence's suspension—church elders took up the issue at a council meeting. One elder recommended, "We should find out why the members are not coming to church." But he did not have to wait long or go far to get an answer—a resounding one at that. The session moderator immediately responded by noting that "a number of people in the church are not doing as well financially as they were before." Elder H. C. Caldwell concurred: "Lots of people will not come out because they have no money." Elder S. G. Bowen recounted a recent conversation with a woman congregant: "I met a member who desired to come to church but said that she was financially unable. I urged her to come and she promised to do [so]."[7] Encouragement could not replace financial security. As black Chicagoans struggled to survive, they began to change the political landscape.

Amid financial crisis and deep frustration with the Republican Party, the voices of Democratic women canvassers increasingly joined those of seasoned Republican campaigners like Lawrence. Black Democratic women had been active in Chicago in 1928 and 1930. In 1932 Chicagoan Mary

[231]

Conclusion

Reynolds served as a committeewoman on the National Colored Democratic Association.[8] That year, Democrats like Reynolds helped elect Franklin D. Roosevelt to the first of four administrations. Twenty-one percent of black Chicagoans—slightly less than had lent their support to Alfred Smith in 1928—cast a ballot for Roosevelt in 1932.[9] Though "at the height of his political power," DePriest edged out his white Democratic opponent Harry Baker by only about 6,000 votes.[10] Referring to the Democratic landslide that had taken place in Chicago and across the country in 1932, the *Defender* reported: "Congressman DePriest was one of the few members of his party to survive the onrush of the mighty Democratic wave which swept Roosevelt and Garner toward the White House."[11] A week after the election, Nannie Helen Burroughs reflected on the Democratic tidal wave in a letter to a colleague in Ohio: "So far as the election is concerned political revolutions are good for a democracy like this. If the republican party has any sense left it will put in every day during the next four years rebuilding its ship of state. The party will have to be born again, but it can come back."[12] In the minds of many black voters, the party never came back. And one year later, as Burroughs was already beginning to organize women for the 1936 presidential election, she described her frustration to the president of the Indiana Federation of Colored Women's Clubs. "If we can get any sense into the heads of these dumb antiquated Republicans, we might be able to get somewhere," she wrote Bessie Jones. But, as Burroughs conceded to her friend and colleague, she did not put too much stock in any real change, and instead hoped for a third option: "The truth of the matter is I think that both parties will be scrapped and a new American party formed. The Democratic party is too 'Lilly White' and the Republicans are too ante-bellum."[13]

Although DePriest had struggled for reelection in 1932, the turning point in Chicago actually took place two years later in 1934. That year, voters in Illinois's First Congressional District elected Arthur Mitchell, the first black Democratic congressman in U.S. history. Mitchell's narrow defeat of DePriest is a story that because of its symbolic importance in the history of the voting realignment has been recounted many times.[14] Not as well known are the behind-the-scenes changes that made this victory possible. Though just four years younger than Lawrence, Rachel Bright represented the new guard of black women political organizers in the Third Ward. A Democrat, Bright's appointment as Third Ward committeewoman made her the first black committeewoman in the city. In the final month before the election, Bright worked with Fourth Ward canvasser Marvelyne Carpenter to es-

Conclusion

tablish the Negro Women's Division of the Illinois Democratic Women's Club.[15] The emergence of this organization did not replace the Colored Women's Republican Clubs of Illinois (CWRCI) or make Jennie Lawrence's work in the Third Ward obsolete, but it did make Republican women's canvassing significantly more challenging. It became that much more challenging in 1935 when many leading Republican women in the city, including Ella Berry and Susie Myers, lent their support to the reelection of Democratic mayor Edward Kelly.[16]

The origins of the voting realignment were many. The realignment had begun to take root well before Franklin Roosevelt created the modern welfare state by introducing the federal relief programs of the "New Deal" in 1933, and before black voters in Illinois's First Congressional District elected the first black Democratic congressman in 1934. In many ways, women's reasons for supporting and then leaving the Republican Party in the years before the New Deal paralleled men's reasons: women and men alike shared a deep frustration with white Republican inaction and racism. Although politically active black women and men shared much in the late 1920s and early 1930s, Republican women's break from the party often had a gendered overlay to it.

Even before New Deal programs gave African American voters tangible policy reasons to support the Democratic Party, middle-class black women viewed the abandonment of the Republican Party in distinctly gendered and, indeed, gendered class terms. This interpretation revolved around intraclass disagreement about the relationship between women's race leadership, on the one hand, and the value of partisan loyalty, on the other. From the 1870s through the 1920s, many black women reformers held that it was women's responsibility to keep men loyal to the Republican Party. Women reformers believed that their supposed moral superiority over men and, as women joined the ranks of voters, over women of low social standing required them to instruct these groups on Democratic malfeasance. Republican loyalty, they insisted, would eventually reap rewards. This belief that women must guide the race toward Republican loyalty, of course, was not the only argument circulating about women's unique responsibilities within party politics. A minority of women tapped into this very same ideology of female moral superiority to make a very different claim. Some of the gendered origins of the voting realignment can be found in this alternative claim: that if indeed it was women's responsibility to lead the race, then they must lead the race out of the Republican Party. This argument could be

[233]

heard as early as the 1890s, if not before, but it was Alice Dunbar-Nelson who articulated it most forcefully throughout the 1920s after the Dyer Anti-lynching Bill died in the Senate.

Gendered components of what would eventually cascade into a voting realignment were also evident in the realm of policy in the years before New Deal programs went into effect. Although women and men fervently worked together to pass antilynching legislation, African American women had claimed antilynching as an issue of particular concern to them. During the early 1920s, a shared focus on passing federal antilynching legislation offered cohesion to Republican women who competed for leadership positions and disagreed on other policy issues. White Republican soft-pedaling around and then outright abandonment of the Dyer Antilynching Bill created cracks in the unified front that the battle against lynching had helped to maintain among black Republican women. Initially, Republican soft-pedaling did not push women out of the Republican fold, though internally within the National Association of Colored Women (NACW) members disagreed with how to respond to the Republican Party's weak antilynching platform in 1920. While some NACW members sought to endorse the Republican Party in 1920, others refused to give the Republican Party's watered-down platform the organization's stamp of approval. The death of the Dyer Bill in the Senate in 1922 transformed this anger into revolt. Again, Dunbar-Nelson led the way.

The decline of women's racial uplift politics in the 1920s, while not a source of the realignment, intersected with the drift of black voters to the Democratic Party. Republican women leaders' reliance on the embattled rhetoric of racial uplift undermined their claims to represent the race in party politics. This was evident during the battle to repeal prohibition. While black Republican women forwarded cogent arguments about the constitutional implications of repeal, their simultaneous reliance on this increasingly outdated ideology to generate support for Herbert Hoover, or to chastise those who opposed him and his anti-repeal position, made them appear out of touch with the views of many black Americans.

Black opposition to prohibition that had been evident in the 1928 presidential election became even more vocal in subsequent years. In 1930 the overwhelming majority of voters in Chicago's most heavily black populated wards passed a triple referendum that significantly reduced enforcement in the state. Two years later, as the country geared up for another presidential election, the *Defender* was replete with letters from African Americans from throughout the country who rejected the Eighteenth Amendment as a "gi-

Conclusion

gantic racket" that had "ruined respect for law enforcement" and who were calling for its repeal so that, among other reasons, revenue that went to bootleggers could go toward legitimate jobs.[17]

On July 2, "What Do You Say about It?" (a recurring *Defender* column) published reactions to the question that the column had posed to readers on June 25, two days before the Democratic National Convention opened in Chicago: "Will you change your vote from the Republican party to the Democratic party in the event the latter adopts a non-straddling platform in favor of the repeal of the 18th amendment?" The respondents demonstrated a range of opinions, as well as the growth of radical politics within black communities. Among the seven letters published, two respondents explained that they could care less about prohibition and planned to go with the Communist Party out of disgust with both of the major parties. Two (one possibly a woman) wrote that they could not force themselves to vote a Democratic ticket. One favored repeal, but was unsure about whether he would favor the Democrats or the Communists. Two answered yes. As one of the two who answered affirmatively wrote, "I will change my vote if the Democrats come out flat-footed for repeal of the 18th amendment. We have about had enough of pussyfooting on this issue." Referring to the Republican Party's convoluted prohibition platform, this respondent wrote, "You can't tell what they stand for." If this sample was in any way representative of the black voting population, then about a third of black voters may have been drawn to the explicit repeal plank that the Democratic Party eventually adopted at its convention.[18] In December 1933 the Twenty-first Amendment repealing prohibition was ratified.[19] Prohibition was ultimately one small factor in a large set of forces pushing African Americans out of the Republican Party and into the Democratic fold.

African American women who had been searching restlessly for candidates who favored using federal power to enforce the Reconstruction Amendments began to see possibilities in the Franklin Roosevelt administration. Perhaps most famously, Mary McLeod Bethune, a founding member of the NLRCW in 1924 who had consistently campaigned for Republican candidates all the way through the 1932 election, became an unapologetic "New Dealer" after Roosevelt's inauguration in 1933.[20] Three years after Bethune changed parties, the nation prepared for another presidential election, this time a contest between incumbent President Roosevelt and Republican candidate Alfred Landon. In the intervening three years, the Roosevelt administration had initiated a range of New Deal programs designed to alleviate the massive unemployment and poverty that had besieged the nation. The Roosevelt administration also appointed a number of black administrators. In 1935 Bethune became the second black member of the Advisory Committee of the National Youth Administration (NYA), which was designed to provide employment and student aid for Americans between the ages of sixteen and twenty-five. Bethune quickly transformed the NYA into a program that substantially aided black youth through its Office of Minority Affairs, a division that Bethune helped to create and directed.[21] Historians have demonstrated that white administrators often applied New Deal programs inequitably, favoring white Americans over minority groups. Even in the progressive NYA, programs were segregated. African American leaders protested such discrimination.[22] Still, the New Deal assistance that African Americans had been able to claim by 1936 inspired many black women reformers to abandon the Republican organizations and structures that they had so carefully built up over the course of a decade.

In the final month before the 1936 election, Crystal Bird Fauset, who was heading campaign activities among African American women for the Women's Division of the Democratic National Committee, asked leading black women around the country why they supported Roosevelt's reelection that year.[23] Respondents pointed to specific programs in explaining their decision to vote for a Democratic president, many for the first time: Social Security, the Works Progress Administration, and especially the National Youth Administration. Daisy Lampkin, who like Bethune was a founding member of the NLRCW, argued, "It is hard to believe that any average citizen could be so blind to the immediate future of his country as to vote for any other than Franklin D. Roosevelt." The establishment of Social Security, Lampkin wrote, enabled "the aged to face the sunset without fear of privation or need." Lampkin asserted that "[t]he gratitude of deserving men and women who have had their self-respect restored by getting work under the [Works Progress Administration] is alone enough to urge the re-election of the man who had the vision and then the courage to help the forgotten man."[24] Belle Collins of Lincoln, Nebraska, similarly cited the WPA as the reason for her willingness to overcome her association of the Democratic Party with southern white supremacy. "It is needless to say," Collins wrote Fauset, "I have never voted the Democratic ticket before, for thousands of Negro women are saying the same, and we know why." But, as she continued: "The Negro Democrats had a meeting this week in Lincoln which was well attended by W.P.A. workers (women and men). We realize the significance of this campaign, so far as we are concerned, so we are boosting the Roosevelt ticket."[25]

Conclusion

Several specifically expressed their approval of the work of the NYA. Mrs. John Hope Senior of Atlanta wrote, "One achievement, alone, the conservation of American youth—a generation that will be the guardians of American welfare tomorrow—this achievement of conserving American youth is alone sufficient, in my opinion, to entitle him to re-election."[26] Addie Hunton of Brooklyn similarly explained, "the thing of deepest significance, it seems to me, is the recognition by the President of the United States of the potential strength and efficiency of the youth of the country." "My pride of race and achievement would, it seems to me, be lacking," she continued, "if I did not appreciate that for the first time, the youth of our group have been taken into full consideration in this program, and that in considerable numbers, all over the country, our men and women of specific talent and ability have been called to participate in this effort of our government to build a new era wherein for every man, regardless of race or class there shall be the common necessities of life—roof, raiment and food, with a modicum of leisure and laughter."[27]

The women who responded to Fauset's inquiry made it clear that they saw in these New Deal programs a reinvigorated use of federal power that could be harnessed not only toward ending the Depression but also toward fulfilling the Fourteenth Amendment's guarantee of equal protection before the law. For example, Mary Louise Cornell of Jersey City wrote, "In supporting the re-election of President Roosevelt, Negroes will be showing their gratitude to the man who has not only proven himself the greatest savior of humanity modern times has yet produced, but has caused that part of the American Constitution which makes all men equal regardless of race, creed or color, real, in a sense never before realized by the Negro of this country."[28] Mazie Mossell Griffin, who had served on the NACW's legislative council for over a decade, described in religious terms African Americans' frustrating search for candidates who would uphold the Constitution: "For years we have prayed for a Messiah who would lead the people out of the wilderness, poverty, and degradation rampant, and no one seemed to care." These prayers had met with disappointment: "Legislative enactment after legislative enactment was laid aside and scoffed at." Pointing to the constitutional and federal enforcement potential in Roosevelt's candidacy, she concluded that his reelection "will not only give us hope for the future, but our assurance of equal protection in accordance with the law, with fair play and a square deal assured."[29] Many black women leaders had supported Republican candidates who made any indication of their intention of using federal power to protect black rights, often stretching the search for exceptions to

Republican indifference to its very limits. They had, as Griffin indicated, also prayed for much more. They were ready when Roosevelt's Democratic administration seemed to answer some of these prayers. Formerly Republican women turned away from Republican Party and toward the Democrats as the party who might use federal power to put some teeth behind the Reconstruction Amendments.

The realignment was anything but a "clean" process. Women and men split their vote and switched back and forth between the Republicans and the Democrats. Among the respondents to Fauset's 1936 inquiry was Illinois Association of Colored Women president Nannie Reed. Reed was a South Carolinian who had relocated to Chicago during the 1910s and initially, like many other migrant women, had became involved in Republican politics.[30] In 1926 Mary Church Terrell had reported at the NACW annual convention that "[t]houghtful women have told me that while they are always Republicans in a national election, they vote for the men who are candidates for the various offices in their respective states according to the merits of the men."[31] Reed did the opposite, working for the Democratic ticket in national elections, while remaining loyal to the Republican Party at the local level. This was a testament to the strength of black Republican politics in Chicago. In 1928 Reed and her colleague Grace Outlaw worked together in running the Women's Division of the Smith for President Colored League in Chicago. In 1928 Outlaw simultaneously worked for Republican victory at the local level by heading the Second Ward Ruth Hanna McCormick Club. In 1930 Reed served on the executive board of the CWRCI.[32] By 1936, however, Reed was no longer splitting her ticket or her resources. Explaining to Fauset her reasons for supporting Roosevelt's election to a second term, Reed wrote, "President Roosevelt has put into practical action the things that others have spoken about so glibly from platform and press, but have failed so signally in doing."[33]

While many African American women who were leaders in Republican politics during the first three decades of the twentieth century turned toward the Democratic Party by 1936, others remained steadfast in their support for the Republican Party until the end of their lives. The women who worked together on McCormick's 1930 senate campaign—Jennie Lawrence, Irene Gaines, and Mary Church Terrell—were representative of this group. Jennie Lawrence only lived two years after Roosevelt's 1936 reelection but remained Republican until her death in 1938.[34] Mary Church Terrell campaigned for Republican candidates until 1952. That year, in the last presidential campaign in which she participated before her death in 1954, Terrell for the first time endorsed a Democratic presidential candidate, Illinois governor Adlai Stevenson.[35] Gaines, by contrast, never renounced her affiliation with the Republican Party, though she did maintain a critical stance toward it. In 1952 she campaigned for Stevenson's successful Republican opponent, General Dwight D. Eisenhower. Gaines also ran unsuccessfully for local offices on the Republican ticket: in 1940 for a seat in the Illinois General Assembly, and in 1950 for a position on the Board of County Commissioners.[36] It was only posthumously that Gaines's name was associated with the Democratic Party. Six months after Gaines died of a heart attack in April 1964, and one month before the presidential election between Democrat Lyndon B. Johnson and Republican Barry Goldwater, Gaines's son, Harry Gaines, contributed a piece to the *Defender*. "As the eldest son of the late Irene McCoy Gaines," he wrote, "I have recently and frequently been asked what part my mother would have played in the current presidential election campaign." "Although my mother had been active in the Republican party for many years," he explained, "she long ago established herself as an 'independent' Republican." "I know," he concluded, "that if she were alive she would be strenuously campaigning for the election of Johnson and Humphrey."[37]

From one perspective, black women's Republican organizing is a declension story. Just as they had built up effective Republican organizations, forces beyond their control drew black voters toward the Democratic Party. Some formerly Republican leaders responded by embracing the possibilities that the New Deal held for forwarding the struggle for black rights. Others could not overcome the deep psychological animosity that they held toward the Democratic Party, an animosity that they had carried with them from the South to the North, and from their youth to the final years of their lives. Few women who had been active in electoral politics during the early decades of the twentieth century lived to see the passage of either the Civil Rights Act of 1964 or the Voting Rights Act of 1965. Even fewer lived to see the emergence of the New Right in the Republican Party during the late 1960s and 1970s. How women who had come of age in the early years of the twentieth century might respond to these developments, one can only speculate, as did Gaines's son. It is worth asking what, if anything, did African American women's turn to the electoral system during the nadir of black life accomplish? It would be easy to conclude that Republican women were merely tools of the Republican Party, regularly trumped out at elections to

[239]

wave the "bloody flag." Indeed, the Republican Party did try to use them. But to dismiss so easily their seemingly tireless efforts to break into an elite white power structure is to accept the terms that party leaders ascribed to them.

Ultimately, the process itself—that is, the process of challenging the racialized gender barriers of white party structures—was their most important contribution. They turned to the electoral system to push for federal legislation that would enforce the provisions of the Reconstruction Amendments. Politically active black women favored candidates and legislation that were often unsuccessful. In the process, they disagreed among themselves about candidates and even parties, creating a rich dialogue about what black women's political organizing meant for the future of the race and America. With hindsight, it is easy to see that individual women and groups made mistakes, and that class differences often divided rather than united women. Still, the generation that experienced both the enfranchisement of women and the disfranchisement of African Americans repeatedly asserted black women's rightful claim to participate in the electoral system. They also kept alive a discourse about rights and responsibilities in which many white Americans had ceased to engage. From this perspective, theirs is not a declension story but rather a link in the chain of the long civil rights movement.

Notes

Abbreviations

The following abbreviations are used in the notes.

CABP   Claude A. Barnett Papers, Chicago Historical Society
HMFP   Hanna-McCormick Family Papers, Manuscripts Division, Library
            of Congress, Washington, D.C.
HQBP   Hallie Q. Brown Papers, Hallie Q. Brown Memorial Library,
            Central State University, Wilberforce, Ohio
IMGP   Irene McCoy Gaines Papers, Chicago Historical Society
IWP   Illinois Writers Project: "Negro in Illinois" Papers, Vivian G. Harsh
            Research Collection of Afro-American History and Literature,
            Carter G. Woodson Regional Public Library, Chicago
MCTP   Mary Church Terrell Papers, Moorland-Spingarn Research Center,
            Howard University, Washington, D.C.
NACWP   *Records of the National Association of Colored Women's Clubs,*
            1895–1992, Part 1: Minutes of National Conventions, Publications,
            and President's Office Correspondence, ed. Lillian Serece Williams
            and Randolph Boehm (Bethesda, Md.: University Publications of
            America), microfilm
NHBP   Nannie Helen Burroughs Papers, Manuscript Division, Library of
            Congress, Washington, D.C.
WDNCP   Women's Division of the Democratic National Committee Papers,
            1933–1944, Franklin D. Roosevelt Library, Hyde Park, New York

Introduction

1 "Mr. Elmnm and Ella Elmnm," [n.d.], box 10, folder 28, IWP.
2 Ibid.
3 Between 1880 and 1920, an average of 73 percent of black men and women employed
   in the state worked in agriculture. Close to 90 percent of women not engaged in farm
   labor earned a very modest income as either domestics or laundresses. Fon Louise
   Gordon, *Caste and Class*, 64–69, 84–85.
4 I have not been able to locate documentation of Ella Elm's birth date. I have situated
   Elm within the chronology of Arkansas's disfranchisement battles according to the

year Ella married Texas Elm in 1913. If Ella was at least eighteen in the year of her marriage, then, at a minimum, she would have been thirteen by 1908.

5 Niswonger, *Arkansas Democratic Politics*, 17–21; Fon Louise Gordon, *Caste and Class*, 26–30; Perman, *Struggle for Mastery*, 62–66; Moneyhon, *Arkansas and the New South*, 91.

6 "Mr. Elmnm and Ella Elmnm," IWP. The records of the Illinois Writers Project indicate that Ella and Texas lived in downstate Illinois without indicating the exact name of the community in which the couple resided. Ella and Texas were married in Murphysboro, so their farm may have been located near this southern Illinois city, but I have been unable to find any additional mention of them in either Jackson County records or the U.S. Census. Flug, "Illinois Writers Project: Finding Aid to the Manuscript Collection," 14–15.

7 Mary L. Ayler to Ruth Hanna McCormick, March 27, 1928, box 36, HMFP; Frank B. Jackson to Ruth Hanna McCormick, December 12, 1929, box 69, HMFP.

8 "Mr. Elmnm and Ella Elmnm," IWP.

9 Ladd, "Participation in American Elections," 109.

10 In preparing this discussion of black women's involvement in Reconstruction politics, I benefited enormously from the research of Elsa Barkley Brown.

11 Elsa Barkley Brown, "To Catch the Vision of Freedom," 73–74, 80–81; Saville, *The Work of Reconstruction*, 163–64, 167–70; Eric Foner, *Reconstruction*, 290–91.

12 "She Is a Politician," *New York Times*, October 18, 1895, 8; Dinkin, *Before Equal Suffrage*, 79–80, 148, n. 48.

13 Elsa Barkley Brown, "To Catch the Vision of Freedom," 66–73, 82–84, 87.

14 Avary, *Dixie after the War*, 282–83.

15 Elsa Barkley Brown, "To Catch the Vision of Freedom," 85.

16 Eric Foner, *Reconstruction*, 342, 440; Elsa Barkley Brown, "To Catch the Vision of Freedom," 81, 82, 85.

17 Saville, *The Work of Reconstruction*, 179–80.

18 Elsa Barkley Brown, "To Catch the Vision of Freedom," 80–81; Holt, *Black over White*, 34–35. Julie Saville documents one black Republican leader in South Carolina vocally opposing women's voting. Saville, *The Work of Reconstruction*, 155.

19 Sterling, *The Trouble They Seen*, 470.

20 Ibid.; Elsa Barkley Brown, "To Catch the Vision of Freedom," 82–84; Saville, *The Work of Reconstruction*, 169–70.

21 Du Bois, *Black Reconstruction in America*, 30.

22 Eric Foner, *Reconstruction*, 529–31, 550.

23 Litwack, *Trouble in Mind*, 392.

24 Woodward, *Strange Career of Jim Crow*, 82–93; Perman, *Struggle for Mastery*, 31–32, 66, 125, 174.

25 Historical Census Browser, <http://fisher.lib.virginia.edu/collections/stats/histcen sus/index.html>; Spear, *Black Chicago*, 12.

26 Spear, *Black Chicago*, 190–91; Drake and Cayton, *Black Metropolis*, 348–49.

27 These nine Republican National Conventions held in Chicago between 1877 and

1936 took place in 1880, 1884, 1888, 1904, 1908, 1912, 1916, 1920, and 1932. Sautter, "Political Conventions," <http://www.encyclopedia.chicagohistory.org>; Republican National Committee, *Republican Campaign Text-Book, 1900*, 453; Republican National Committee, *Republican Campaign Text-Book, 1920*, cover page; Republican National Committee, *Republican Campaign Text-Book, 1924*, cover page; Republican National Committee, *Republican Campaign Text-Book, 1928*, cover page; Republican National Committee, *Text-Book of the Republican Party, 1932*, 1; Republican National Committee, *Text-Book of the Republican Party, 1936*, cover page.

28 Gilmore, *Gender and Jim Crow*, 147–49, 151–52, 172.

29 See chapter 1 for a full discussion of black women's use of this strategy in 1894.

30 White, *Too Heavy a Load*, 36–37. Also see Carby's *Reconstructing Womanhood* for a discussion of black women's literary expressions of "woman's era" philosophy.

31 White, *Too Heavy a Load*, 27–28, 36–39; Mitchell, *Righteous Propagation*, 12, 80, 141–42, 152, 168–69, 172.

32 Mitchell, *Righteous Propagation*, 9–10, 12, 141–42, 168–69, 172; White, *Too Heavy a Load*, 26–36. For a full discussion of the complexities of racial uplift ideology, see Kevin K. Gaines's *Uplifting the Race*.

33 Mitchell, *Righteous Propagation*, 13, 137; White, *Too Heavy a Load*, 26–27.

34 Mitchell, *Righteous Propagation*, 137, 171; Gilmore, *Gender and Jim Crow*, 147–53.

35 Elsa Barkley Brown, "Womanist Consciousness," 186–87; Layli Phillips, "Womanism," xxvi–xxvii.

36 *Minutes of the General Assembly of the Presbyterian Church* (1876). Lawrence had earned his license to preach in 1867, a step typical of upperclassmen. Inez Moore Parker, *The Rise and Decline of the Program of Education*, 76.

37 "The Fourth in Charlotte—Great Display among the Colored People," *Charlotte Observer*, July 6, 1876, 4; "4th of July," *Charlotte Democrat*, July 10, 1876, 3; "Pandemonium Broke Loose!," *Charlotte Observer*, June 25, 1876, 4; "Fourth of July Discussion," *Charlotte Observer*, July 7, 1876, 4; "The Republican State Convention," *Charlotte Observer*, July 11, 1876, 4; "Local Ripples," *Charlotte Observer*, July 12, 1876, 4; "From Raleigh," *Charlotte Observer*, July 13, 1876, 1; "The Republican Nominations," *Charlotte Observer*, July 13, 1876, 4; "The Republican Convention," *Charlotte Observer*, July 14, 1876, 4.

38 Robert W. Winson, *It's a Far Cry* (New York: Henry Holt, 1937), 87, and *Wilmington Morning Star*, July 17, 1876, both as quoted in Frenise A. Logan, *The Negro in North Carolina*, 10, n. 28; McKinney, *Zeb Vance*, 110.

39 "The Colored Tilden and Vance Club—Enthusiastic Meeting and Good Speeches," *Charlotte Observer*, October 31, 1876, 4; "The Colored Club to Go Mounted," *Charlotte Observer*, November 1, 1876, 4; "The Right Spirit," *Charlotte Observer*, November 2, 1876, 4; "Meeting of the Colored Club," *Charlotte Observer*, November 4, 1876, 4; "The Last Club Meeting," *Charlotte Observer*, November 7, 1876, 4.

40 Greenwood, *Bittersweet Legacy*, 72–73.

41 "Local Ripples," *Charlotte Observer*, November 7, 1876, 4; "What Providence Did,"

Charlotte Observer, November 9, 1876, 4; "The Colored Club Meeting," *Charlotte Observer*, November 11, 1876, 4.

42 "They Must Forget Him," *Charlotte Observer*, October 31, 1876, 4.

43 "Where They Derive Support," *Charlotte Observer*, November 1, 1876, 4.

44 "Local Ripples," *Charlotte Observer*, November 1, 1876, 4.

45 "The Colored Men," *Charlotte Observer*, November 9, 1876, 2; "Intimidation on Account of Political Faith," *Charlotte Observer*, November 15, 1876, 4. This incident took place in Concord about twenty miles outside of Charlotte.

46 Frenise A. Logan, *The Negro in North Carolina*, 10; Greenwood, *Bittersweet Legacy*, 75.

47 Marriage License of Abner Bernard Lawrence and Annie B. Henderson, 1878, Rowan County Record of Deeds, Salisbury, North Carolina; Bureau of the Census, *United States Manuscript Census*, Surry County, North Carolina, 1880; Bureau of the Census, *United States Manuscript Census*, Rowan County, North Carolina, 1900.

Chapter 1

1 "Women at the Polls," *Chicago Tribune*, November 7, 1894, 11.

2 Anthony and Harper, *History of Woman Suffrage*, 4:600, 604. Shortly after the Woman's Suffrage Bill passed in 1891, women residing in rural areas and small, unincorporated cities were able to vote in school bond, county superintendent, and school board elections. Women in Chicago, East St. Louis, and Cicero had to wait until the 1892 university trustee contest to cast their first ballots. Their participation in the 1892 election, however, was decidedly dismal—for instance, only about 1,200 ballots cast in Cook County. Absent was the vibrant partisan canvassing that emerged in the 1894 electoral season. Instead, in 1892 white suffrage and, to a lesser extent, temperance organizations pursued nonpartisan measures to encourage women voters and prevent election officials from turning them away at the polls. Anthony and Harper, *History of Woman Suffrage*, 4:600, 604; "The Woman's Vote," *Inter Ocean*, November 9, 1892, 2; "Registration, Men and Women," *Inter Ocean*, October 17, 1892, 4.

3 Tello, "Flower, Lucy Louisa Coues," 275.

4 "Women at the Polls," *Chicago Tribune*, November 7, 1894, 11; "Women Did Nobly," *Inter Ocean*, November 9, 1894, 2.

5 "Women Vote in Force," *Chicago Times*, November 7, 1894, 8.

6 I say "at least" because it is entirely possible that several more of these Republican activists were originally southerners. I conducted census research in an effort to identify the states of birth of those individuals who were listed in newspaper reports as having participated in black women's Republican clubs. Many of these women, however, had such common names that a search produced multiple results or, in some instances, none at all. (Africans Americans have been notoriously underreported in the U.S. census.) For example, women active in the Twenty-third and First Wards had common names like Mary Davis, Daisy Wells, Mary Clark, and F. O. Smith.

7 One of these women, Ida B. Wells, departed the South in 1893. All that is known

about the second woman, Fannie Brown, was that she was a former slave. An exact date of Brown's relocation to Chicago does not appear in newspaper reports.

8 Branham, "Transformation of Black Political Leadership," 2–3; Best, *Passionately Human, No Less Divine*, 44; Fisher, "Negro Churches in Illinois," 554–57; Spear, *Black Chicago*, 12; Drake and Cayton, *Black Metropolis*, 31–32, 39.

9 Drake and Cayton, *Black Metropolis*, 44–53; Spear, *Black Chicago*, 12; Drake, *Churches and Voluntary Associations*, 72–73.

10 "The Colored Voters," *Inter Ocean*, February 11, 1876, IWP; Painter, *Exodusters*, 220–21. The *Inter Ocean* announced a "grand Republican ratification meeting" at Olivet Baptist Church in 1876. While it seems likely that women participated, there is no specific mention of them. "Announcements," *Inter Ocean*, October 14, 1876, 8; "Announcements," *Inter Ocean*, October 23, 1876, 8.

11 "Announcements," *Inter Ocean*, October 27, 1876, 8; "Announcements," *Inter Ocean*, November 2, 1876, 8.

12 "Editorial," *Inter Ocean*, April 1875, IWP; "Announcements," *Inter Ocean*, April 2, 1877, IWP.

13 "Torchlight Celebration," *Inter Ocean*, October 17, 1872, 6; "The Republican Processions," *Chicago Tribune*, October 17, 1872, 8.

14 "The Colored Troops Fight Nobly," *Inter Ocean*, November 11, 1870, 4; "The Local Campaign," *Inter Ocean*, November 11, 1872, 6; "The Third Ward," *Inter Ocean*, February 12, 1876, IWP.

15 Pegram, *Partisans and Progressives*, 8–9.

16 Ibid., 155.

17 Ibid., 10; Branham, "Transformation of Black Political Leadership," 10, 17–18.

18 Drake and Cayton, *Black Metropolis*, 50; Philip S. Foner, *The Autobiographies*, 5–6; Philip S. Foner, *History of the Labor Movement*, 106. In the late 1890s, Parsons participated in Eugene Debs's Social Democracy. In 1905 she was the second woman to join the Industrial Workers of the World. During 1914 and 1915, Parsons led demonstrations of the unemployed and homeless in San Francisco and Chicago, respectively. During the late 1920s and 1930s, she engaged in Communist politics through the International Labor Defense and the Communist Party. Ashbaugh, *Lucy Parsons*, 7, 200, 217–18; Kelley, "Parsons, Lucy (1853–1942)," 910.

19 Philip S. Foner, *American Socialism*, 78.

20 Philip S. Foner and Ronald L. Lewis, *The Black Worker*, 15.

21 Philip S. Foner, *American Socialism*, 63; Philip S. Foner and Ronald L. Lewis, *The Black Worker*, 15, 20–21; John Hope Franklin and Alfred A. Moss Jr., *From Slavery to Freedom*, 281–82. Branham, "Transformation of Black Political Leadership," 37. Not until A. Philip Randolph organized the Brotherhood of Sleeping Car Porters and Maids in 1925 would black labor unionism finally surpass the limited successes African Americans had with the Knights of Labor in the 1880s. Philip S. Foner and Ronald L. Lewis, *The Black Worker*, 9–13; John Hope Franklin and Alfred A. Moss Jr., *From Slavery to Freedom*, 382.

22 Kevin K. Gaines, *Uplifting the Race*, 31; Higginbotham, *Righteous Discontent*, 19; Neverdon-Morton, *Afro-American Women of the South*, 3–4; Eric Foner, *Reconstruction*, 97–102.

23 Patton, "Williams, Fannie Barrier," 977; Harris, "Davis, Elizabeth Lindsay," 212; Hendricks, "Davis, Elizabeth Lindsay," 306–7.

24 Philip T. K. Daniel, "A History of Discrimination," 149; Philip T. K. Daniel, "A History of the Segregation-Discrimination Dilemma," 126–27.

25 "Is All for Illinois," *Inter Ocean*, November 11, 1894, 15; "University of Illinois Reference File" and "Negro Matriculation List, 1887–1937," Record Series 2/9/16, University Archives, University of Illinois at Urbana-Champaign; *1929 University of Illinois Directory*, Record Series 26/4/801, University Archives.

26 "Woman's Kingdom," *Inter Ocean*, November 2, 1894.

27 I. Marie Johnson, "Women in Chicago Politics," *Light and Heebie Jeebies* 3 (November 1927).

28 Clipping, "Illinois Women," *Woman's Journal*, box 2, scrapbook 4, Flower and Coues Family Scrapbooks, Chicago Historical Society.

29 Wheeler, *New Women of the New South*, xv, 113–18; Wheeler, "Short History," 13; Kraditor, *Ideas of the Woman Suffrage Movement*, 165. Kraditor notes that as early as 1867 Massachusetts abolitionist Henry Blackwell made a similar argument that the enfranchisement of women would ensure white supremacy in the South. Kraditor, *Ideas of the Woman Suffrage Movement*, 168–69. It should be noted that even as the NAWSA made these racist assertions, it never totally abandoned natural rights arguments for the vote. Wheeler, "Short History," 12.

30 Editorial, *Woman's Era* 1, no. 9 (December 1894). In a 1915 article, Josephine St. Pierre Ruffin, one of the founders of the black women's club that put out the *Woman's Era*, reported that she had voted forty-one times in school board elections since the Massachusetts legislature granted women this right in 1879. Women's school suffrage in Massachusetts was not universal, however. It entailed several restrictions, including a poll tax, an age requirement, and an educational test, that were revised several times in subsequent years. Terborg-Penn, *African American Women in the Struggle for the Vote*, 138; Anthony and Harper, *History of Woman Suffrage*, 4:745–46.

31 "A Beautiful Valley Described as Seen by the Freeman Correspondent," *Indianapolis Freeman*, September 29, 1894; "The Ida B. Wells Club Pass Resolutions," *Indianapolis Freeman*, October 27, 1894, 2.

32 In the summer of 1894, Mrs. Olden joined thirteen black men as delegates to the (Arapahoe) County Republican Convention. All fourteen of the delegates, including Mrs. Olden, were part of the apparently mixed-gender black Republican club of Denver. Along with her delegate status, Olden served as third vice president of the Republican State League of Colorado. Olden was a southern migrant from Tennessee who had resettled in Colorado in 1893. Elizabeth Piper Ensley, "Colorado, Election Day," *Woman's Era* 1, no. 9 (December 1894): 17–18; "A Colored Lady," *Indianapolis Freeman*, November 3, 1894.

33 In 1894 the Kentucky General Assembly granted women who were residents of Lexington, Covington, and Newport the right to vote for members of school boards. Anthony and Harper, *History of Woman Suffrage*, 4:674.

34 "It Is a Bad Experiment," *Lexington Press-Transcript*, October 2, 1895.

35 "The Women, God Bless Them, Victorious," *Lexington Press-Transcript*, November 6, 1895.

36 "Colored Women and Suffrage," *Woman's Era* 2, no. 7 (November 1895): 11.

37 "Women in the Campaign," *Inter Ocean*, August 17, 1894, 6.

38 "To March to Polls," *Chicago Tribune*, September 25, 1894, 2.

39 "Women Do Good Work," *Chicago Tribune*, September 21, 1894, 3; Davis, *Story of Illinois Federation*, 26–27.

40 Unlike other committee members who each represented an electoral district, Dempsey and Wells occupied two of the only five delegates-at-large positions. "The Political Field," *Inter Ocean*, August 17, 1894, 12; "Republican Women," *Inter Ocean*, August 24, 1894, 3; "Women Do Good Work," *Chicago Tribune*, September 21, 1894, 3; "Women at the Polls," *Chicago Tribune*, October 7, 1894, 33.

41 Bureau of the Census, *United States Manuscript Census*, Cook County, Illinois, 1900, 1910, 1920.

42 Robb, *The Negro in Chicago*, 1:227; Knupfer, *Toward a Tenderer Humanity*, 44, 100, 147.

43 Bureau of the Census, *United States Manuscript Census*, Cook County, Illinois, 1910, 1920.

44 Decosta-Willis, *Memphis Diary of Ida B. Wells*, 110; Wells-Barnett, *Crusade for Justice*, xvi, 7–8, 15–18, 22–24, 35–37, 401; Schechter, *Ida B. Wells-Barnett*, 41, 47–48.

45 Wells-Barnett, *Crusade for Justice*, 18–20 (quote from 20); Decosta-Willis, *Memphis Diary of Ida B. Wells*, 56; Rayford Logan, *Betrayal of the Negro*, 21, 56.

46 Wells-Barnett, *Crusade for Justice*, 9.

47 *Nashville Banner*, November 11, 1890, as cited in Cartwright, *Triumph of Jim Crow*, 244, n. 38.

48 Cartwright, *Triumph of Jim Crow*, 42, 201, 203, 227, 234–36, 238, 242, 247–48, 256–57; Schechter, *Ida B. Wells-Barnett*, 71.

49 Wells-Barnett, *Crusade for Justice*, 65–66; Bederman, *Manliness and Civilization*, 55–56.

50 Bederman, *Manliness and Civilization*, 56; Wells-Barnett, *Crusade for Justice*, 86–113, 122.

51 Wells-Barnett, *Crusade for Justice*, 47–52, 63.

52 "Colored Women's Votes Not for Sale," *Chicago Tribune*, November 6, 1894, 2. The postmaster position at Chicago's U.S. Post Office was part of the state's Republican machinery. Since 1883, Illinois Republican senators in Congress had seen to the appointment of a postmaster loyal to their party, even when Democrats controlled city hall. Republican postmasters served even during Democratic municipal administrations because the postmaster office was a federal appointment. A postmaster would be recommended by U.S. senators and then appointed by the president. Harold Gosnell points out that in the fifty years between 1883 and 1933, the constant

[247]

presence of at least one Republican senator in Washington ensured the continuous appointment of Republican postmasters back in Chicago. Gosnell, *Negro Politicians*, 302, 305–8.

53 "To Work in Mrs. Flower's Interest," *Chicago Tribune*, October 6, 1894, 3; "Women Out in Force," *Chicago Tribune*, October 12, 1894, 5; "Republican Women," *Inter Ocean*, October 18, 1894, 2; "In the Third Ward," *Inter Ocean*, October 19, 1894, 2; "Immense Meeting in Lincoln Hall," *Chicago Tribune*, October 19, 1894, 2; "Women Meet in the Marquette Club," *Chicago Tribune*, October 20, 1894, 3; "Welcome to Women," *Inter Ocean*, October 20, 1894, 2; "Mrs. Flower Makes a Strong Speech," *Chicago Tribune*, October 26, 1894, 2; "Republican Women," *Inter Ocean*, October 25, 1894, 2.

54 "Women Out in Force," *Chicago Tribune*, October 12, 1894, 5.

55 Ibid.

56 Bederman, *Manliness and Civilization*, 37.

57 Ibid., 31, 33–39; Massa, "Black Women in the 'White City,' " 333–35; Fannie Barrier Williams, "Intellectual Progress of the Colored Women," 700.

58 "No Color Line for Republican Women," *Chicago Tribune*, September 27, 1894, 2.

59 "Republican Women," *Inter Ocean*, October 6, 1894, 6.

60 "Republican Women," *Inter Ocean*, October 12, 1894, 3; "Colored Republican Women," *Chicago Tribune*, October 16, 1894, 2.

61 "Republican Women," *Inter Ocean*, October 6, 1894, 6; "As Done in Colorado," *Chicago Tribune*, October 11, 1894, 12.

62 "Miss Wells on Negro Lynching," *Inter Ocean*, August 28, 1894, 2; Wells-Barnett, *Crusade for Justice*, 297–98; Schechter, *Ida B. Wells-Barnett*, 186–87.

63 "Will Vote Straight," *Inter Ocean*, November 4, 1894, 3.

64 "Our Colored Citizens," *Inter Ocean*, October 16, 1894, 2; "Meetings of Colored Republicans," *Chicago Tribune*, October 23, 1894, 2; "The Colored Men," *Inter Ocean*, October 23, 1894, 3; "Churches Take It Up," *Inter Ocean*, October 29, 1894, 8; "Other Meetings," *Inter Ocean*, November 2, 1894, 2; "Grand Republican Rallies," *Inter Ocean*, November 2, 1894, 2; "Will Vote Straight," *Inter Ocean*, November 4, 1894, 3.

65 "Our Colored Citizens," *Inter Ocean*, October 16, 1894, 2.

66 "Colored Men in Line," *Chicago Tribune*, October 16, 1894, 2.

67 "Churches Take It Up," *Inter Ocean*, October 29, 1894, 8; "Will Vote Straight," *Inter Ocean*, November 4, 1894, 3.

68 Best, *Passionately Human, No Less Divine*, 3.

69 Fisher, "Negro Churches in Illinois," 559–60, 562, 564; Best, *Passionately Human, No Less Divine*, 36, 57, 184–85.

70 Individual Methodist churches were subject to the decisions of their national legislative bodies, called general conferences, on such matters as ordination rights. This concentrated governing structure enabled Methodist women to undertake a more direct challenge—with more widespread results—of men's leadership monopoly than was possible in the diffused polity of the Baptist denominations. The governing struc-

ture of the Baptist churches greatly facilitated men's opposition to the ordination of female ministers. Each Baptist church had (and has) full autonomy over matters relating to faith and practice among its congregants. As a result, women's ordination struggles among Baptist congregations occurred at the local and individual church level. One woman's victory in her local congregation did not change the policies of other congregations. In essence, each struggle over ordination rights was a new one. Lincoln and Mamiya, *Black Church in the African American Experience*, 68, 287; Collier-Thomas, *Daughters of Thunder*, 28.

71   Collier-Thomas, *Daughters of Thunder*, 22, 26–27.

72   The formal language of this resolution, which the General Conference ultimately passed, was: "Whereas, we have in our Church some female ministers who have been holding pastoral charges much to the detriment of the Church; therefore be it Resolved, That they are hereby prohibited from assignment to a special charge, and simply labor as evangelists." "The General Conference," *Christian Recorder* 22, no. 23 (June 5, 1884): 2.

73   Ibid.; Higginbotham, *Righteous Discontent*, 132.

74   Dodson, *Engendering Church*, 94–95; Collier-Thomas, *Daughters of Thunder*, 22, 26–27.

75   C. Hatfield Dickerson, "Woman Suffrage," *AME Church Review* 4, no. 1 (July 1887): 198–99. I thank Tisa Wenger for sharing this article and the other articles cited in this paragraph.

76   Reverend R. Seymour, "Ought Women to Be Admitted to Membership in the Legislative Bodies of the Church," *Christian Recorder* 28, no. 46 (November 6, 1890): 5.

77   Rev. John M. Brown, "The Ordination of Women," *AME Church Review* 2, no. 3 (January 1886): 354–61; Jones, "The 'Woman Question,'" 218–19.

78   Alice Felts, "Women's Rights," *Christian Recorder* 29, no. 14 (December 10, 1891): 2.

79   "Will Vote Straight," *Inter Ocean*, November 4, 1894, 3.

80   "Women Do Good Work," *Chicago Tribune*, September 21, 1894, 3; Branham, "Transformation of Black Political Leadership," 12–14.

81   "Political Notes and Meetings," *Inter Ocean*, September 14, 1894, 2; "Women Do Good Work," *Chicago Tribune*, September 21, 1894, 3; "Republican Women," *Inter Ocean*, October 12, 1894, 3; "Colored Republican Women," *Chicago Tribune*, October 16, 1894, 2.

82   McMath, *American Populism*, 181, 186; Cashman, *America in the Gilded Age*, 222, 225, 258–61.

83   Editorial, *AME Church Review* 11, no. 2 (October 1894): 309.

84   For examples of white women's campaign rhetoric, see "Women Out in Force," *Chicago Tribune*, October 12, 1894, 5, and "Loyal to the Party," *Inter Ocean*, October 12, 1894, 1. One notable exception was IWREC executive committee member Mary Krout's October 12 speech at the Central Music Hall. Krout mentioned the Republican Party's antislavery origins and denounced the disfranchisement of "one proscribed class" in the South. "Loyal to the Party," *Inter Ocean*, October 12, 1894, 1.

85   The women of Omaha, Nebraska's small black community organized a Colored

Woman's McKinley and Hobart Republican Club and became "enthusiastic disciples of the protection and sound money doctrine" in order to influence the votes of men. As the woman's columnist for Omaha's black newspaper explained, "they are adopting these principles, and advocating their adoption, because of the virtues found therein rather than because the platform is headed with the magic word 'Republican.' " Ella L. Mahammit, "Woman's Column," *Enterprise*, September 5, October 31, 1896.

86 "Will Vote Stright," *Inter Ocean*, November 4, 1894, 3.

87 Perman, *Struggle for Mastery*, 43–44.

88 Kousser, *Shaping of Southern Politics*, 29–30; Perman, *Struggle for Mastery*, 37–44, 46; Crofts, "Black Response," 41–43, 47–49, 56–59, 61–62; Bullock, *A History of Negro Education*, 86–87; Margo, "Race Differences," 14.

89 Rayford Logan, *Betrayal of the Negro*, 87.

90 Perman, *Struggle for Mastery*, 12–18, 31, 35, 46–47, 75, 83, 87–88, 93–99.

91 "Our Colored Citizens," *Inter Ocean*, October 16, 1894, 2.

92 "Republican State Committee," *Inter Ocean*, August 29, 1894, 2.

93 "Women Meet in the Marquette Club," *Chicago Tribune*, October 20, 1894, 3. Also, if the IWREC did not canvass for a straight ticket, the Republican State Central Committee (RSCC) threatened to withhold financial support and ultimately take control of the campaign out of their hands. The IWREC reassured the RSCC of women's unwavering partisanship and complied with the RSCC's request to drop "educational" from its title so that "no word but that of Republican will be understood throughout the State outside of Chicago." In September, the IWREC was renamed the Illinois Women's Republican Committee. "The Political Field," *Inter Ocean*, August 31, 1894, 8; "Republican State Committee," *Inter Ocean*, August 29, 1894, 2; "Republican Women," *Inter Ocean*, September 4, 1894, 4; "The Political Field," *Inter Ocean*, August 30, 1894, 2.

94 "Women Out in Force," *Chicago Tribune*, October 12, 1894, 5.

95 The newspaper reporting of the speech is a bit confusing. The full reporting of Wells's speech is as follows: "Miss Wells referred to the amendment of the Constitution enfranchising former slaves. This clause, she said, declared that 'persons' born in this country or naturalized were citizens. 'According to that women have for thirty years possessed the right to vote, for certainly they were 'persons.' " This passage conflates the Fourteenth and Fifteenth Amendments. Wells first refers to the "amendment of the constitution enfranchising former slaves," or the Fifteenth Amendment. She then points to a clause in this amendment that declares "that 'persons' born in this country or naturalized were citizens." The clause to which she is referring is contained not in the Fifteenth Amendment, but rather in the Fourteenth Amendment. It is unclear whether the *Tribune* reporter or Wells conflated the amendments. I have interpreted Wells's speech as making reference to both the Fourteenth and Fifteenth Amendments.

96 "Women Out in Force," *Chicago Tribune*, October 12, 1894, 5.

97 DuBois, "Outgrowing the Compact of the Fathers," 853, 855, 861; Sneider, *Suffragists in an Imperial Age*, chaps. 2 and 3; Stanton, Anthony, and Gage, *History of Woman Suffrage*, 2:407–520.

98 "Loyal to the Party," *Inter Ocean*, October 12, 1894, 2.

99 "Women Out in Force," *Chicago Tribune*, October 12, 1894, 5; "Loyal to the Party," *Inter Ocean*, October 12, 1894, 1.

100 White, *Ar'n't I a Woman?*, 29, 30; Gilman, "Black Bodies, White Bodies," 231–32, 237–38; Morton, *Disfigured Images*, 27–28.

101 Higginbotham, *Righteous Discontent*, 190. Higginbotham's observations here are based on the work of Guy-Sheftall, *Daughters of Sorrow*.

102 Higginbotham, *Righteous Discontent*, 190–94.

103 "Colored Women's Votes Not for Sale," *Chicago Tribune*, November 6, 1894, 2.

104 Cooper, *A Voice from the South*, 115; Hutchinson, "Cooper, Anna Julia Haywood (1858–1964)," 277–78.

105 Lemert, "Anna Julia Cooper," 5, n. 6; Cooper, *A Voice from the South*, 114–15.

106 "Colored Women's Votes Not for Sale," *Chicago Tribune*, November 6, 1894, 2.

107 Ibid.

108 "Women at the Polls," *Chicago Tribune*, November 7, 1894, 11.

109 Flanagan, *Seeing with Their Hearts*, 31–32; "Work of the Women," *Chicago Tribune*, November 5, 1894, 3; "Color Line in a Club," *Chicago Tribune*, November 14, 1894, 2; "She Needs Not Pity," *Inter Ocean*, November 16, 1894, 7; Knupfer, *Toward a Tenderer Humanity*, 23, 163–64, n. 52; "A Representative Woman," box 2, scrapbook 4, Flower and Coues Family Scrapbooks; "At The Women's Club," box 2, scrapbook 4, Flower and Coues Family Scrapbooks; "Mrs. Altgeld Will Vote Straight," *Inter Ocean*, September 16, 1894, 5.

110 Fannie Barrier Williams, "Women in Politics," *Woman's Era* 1, no. 8 (November 1894): 12–13.

111 Ibid.

112 *AME Church Review* 11, no. 4 (April 1895): 525–26, as quoted in Meier, "The Negro and the Democratic Party," 181, n. 40; J. C. Price, "The Negro in the Last Decade of the Century," *Independent*, January 1, 1891, 5, as quoted in Meier, "The Negro and the Democratic Party," 180, n. 34; Meier, "The Negro and the Democratic Party," 175–82.

113 Williams, "Women in Politics," *Woman's Era* 1, no. 8 (November 1894): 12–13.

114 The Populist Party in Illinois consisted of a fragile coalition of populists, craft unionists, single-taxers, socialists, and Bellamyite nationalists that fell apart before election day. McMath, *American Populism*, 190–92.

115 For a discussion of the Populist Party's uneven efforts at interracial organizing in the South, see Shaw, *The Wool-Hat Boys*; Gaither, *Blacks and the Populist Revolt*; McMath, *American Populism*, especially pp. 171–75; and Woodward, *Tom Watson*, especially chaps. 13 and 20.

116 "Women at the Polls," *Chicago Tribune*, October 7, 1894, 33.

117 Bohlmann, "Drunken Husbands," 160; Wolloch, *Women and the American Experience*, 293; Gustafson, *Women and the Republican Party*, 64. Democratic trustee candidate Julia Holmes Smith was also a WCTU member. An Illinois WCTU member would continue to appear among Prohibition Party candidates for university trustee in every election until 1910. Bohlmann, "Drunken Husbands," 160–61.

118 Edwards, *Angels in the Machinery*, 42; Gustafson, *Women and the Republican Party*, 55, 64–66. In fact, Willard's use of her WCTU office to generate support for the Prohibition Party caused a split within the Union. In 1884 Republican WCTU members who opposed Willard's overt partisanship broke from the union and formed the Nonpartisan Woman's Christian Temperance Union. Gustafson, *Women and the Republican Party*, 55, 64–70.

119 Bohlmann, "Drunken Husbands," 116–17, 160–63. In addition to the Prohibition Party's temperance politics, many white women were attracted to the party's support for woman's suffrage, inclusion of women as full members, and especially in Illinois, promotion of white women to leadership positions. The Prohibition Party in Illinois nominated eleven women as delegates to the party's 1888 national convention. (By contrast, several other state sections sent only one.) Edwards, *Angels in the Machinery*, 48.

120 Bohlmann, "Drunken Husbands," 144–47. The exact number of black WCTU members in Illinois and nationwide is unknown. WCTU historian Ruth Bordin holds that "there were never many blacks in the Union." For her part, Glenda Gilmore asserts that "the WCTU represented the principal interdenominational voluntary association among black women" until the formation of the NACW in 1896. These two accounts are not necessarily mutually exclusive and suggest that a modest number of black women affiliated with the WCTU. Prior to 1896 most black women conducted temperance work within their own church, rather than in an interdenominational context. Bordin, *Woman and Temperance*, 83; Gilmore, " 'A Melting Time,' " 163; Schechter, "Temperance Work," 1156.

121 Gilmore, " 'A Melting Time,' " 154; Schechter, "Temperance Work," 1154; Herd, "The Paradox of Temperance," 356.

122 Frederick Douglass, *My Bondage and My Freedom* (New York: Miller, Orton and Mulligan, 1855), 253, 256, as quoted in Herd, "The Paradox of Temperance," 356, n. 9.

123 Herd, "The Paradox of Temperance," 363; Schechter, "Temperance Work," 1155; Higginbotham, *Righteous Discontent*, 193. See also Kevin K. Gaines, *Uplifting the Race*.

124 Mitchell, *Righteous Propagation*, 12, 80, 148–49.

125 White, *Too Heavy a Load*, 37; Foster, "Harper, Frances Ellen Watkins (1825–1911)," 535; Johnson, "Early, Sarah Jane Woodson (1825–1907)," 377; Frances E. W. Harper, "Symposium—Temperance," *AME Church Review* 7, no. 4 (April 1891): 374. Since the 1870s, in fact, black suffragists, such as Sojourner Truth and Mary McCurdy, had maintained that women's enfranchisement would help outlaw alcohol. This in turn, they asserted, would deter white politicians from using liquor to sway black men's votes. Terborg-Penn, *African American Women in the Struggle for the Vote*, 48–51.

126 Black leaders *had* flirted with the Prohibition Party in the 1880s, when several black newspapers and public speakers endorsed the party. This flirtation, however, was over by the close of the decade. In fact, the future pastor of Chicago's Bethel AME Church, Reverend D. A. Graham, was a candidate on the Prohibition ticket in Michigan in 1888. Perhaps most notable among those leaders who had endorsed the Prohibition Party was T. Thomas Fortune, the influential editor of the *New York Freeman*. During 1887 Fortune served as a lecturer for the National Prohibition Bureau. According to Fortune, the Prohibition Party's legislative efforts would help eliminate southern lawlessness that, in his view, was exacerbated by alcohol. Fortune also saw a vote for the Prohibition Party as a means to show Republicans that they could not take black votes for granted. Drake, *Churches and Voluntary Associations*, 105; Thornbrough, *T. Thomas Fortune*, 91–93.

127 Bohlmann, "Drunken Husbands," 138, 145–47; Schechter, "Temperance Work," 1155–56; *Ninth Annual Report of the Woman's Christian Temperance Union of Illinois, for the Year Ending September 20th, 1882*, 23, as cited in Bohlmann, "Drunken Husbands," 145.

128 Frances Willard, "The Race Problem: Miss Willard on the Political Puzzle of the South," *The Voice*, October 23, 1890, 8. Black women active in the WCTU also denounced such displays of racism within the union. Harper herself criticized the WCTU's practice of segregating black women into "colored locals" and southern white women's inability, as she put it, "to make in their minds the discrimination between social equality and Christian affiliation." In her 1891 symposium piece, Harper advised readers that when white temperance women "draw the line at color, draw your line at self-respect and fight without them." This is exactly what black women delegates threatened to do in 1893 when they walked out of the national WCTU convention in St. Louis, reentering only when their white counterparts removed the segregated seating arrangements. Frances E. W. Harper, "The Woman's Christian Temperance Union and the Colored Woman," *AME Church Review* 4, no. 3 (1888): 315; Schechter, "Temperance Work," 1155; Frances E. W. Harper, "Symposium—Temperance," *AME Church Review* 7, no. 4 (April 1891): 375; Gilmore, " 'A Melting Time,' " 169.

129 Wells-Barnett, *Crusade for Justice*, 111–13. For examples of the *Inter Ocean's* coverage of these exchanges, see "Ida B. Wells Abroad," *Inter Ocean*, July 7, 1894, 13; "Work of Ida B. Wells," *Inter Ocean*, August 13, 1894, 7; Ida B. Wells, "Mr. Moody and Miss Willard," *Fraternity*, May 1894, *Temperance and Prohibition Papers* (1977), scrapbook 69, frame #395; Lady Henry Sumerset, "White and Black in America: An Interview with Miss Willard," *Westminster Gazette*, May 21, 1894, 3; Ida B. Wells, letter to the editor, *Westminster Gazette*, May 22, 1894, 2; Schechter, *Ida B. Wells-Barnett*, 92, 99–102.

130 "Women Do Good Work," *Chicago Tribune*, September 21, 1894, 3.

131 Branham, "Transformation of Black Political Leadership," 72–73.

132 In early September, white Democratic women met to form a committee like the IWREC for the purpose of helping elect trustee candidate Dr. Julia Holmes Smith and other Democratic hopefuls. There is no mention of black women attending this

[253]

founding meeting of the Democratic Women's Campaign Committee. (Unlike Republican women, Democratic women did not form separate women's clubs. Instead, they attended the regular men's ward meetings.) "Democratic Women to Assemble," *Inter Ocean*, September 7, 1894, 7; "Democratic Women Meet," *Inter Ocean*, September 11, 1894, 4; "Mrs. Altgeld Will Vote Straight," *Inter Ocean*, September 16, 1894, 5; "Appoint Ward 'Captains,'" *Inter Ocean*, September 19, 1894, 7; "To Get Woman Votes," *Chicago Tribune*, October 2, 1894, 2; "Women at the Polls," *Chicago Tribune*, October 7, 1894, 33; "Was a Biting Frost," *Inter Ocean*, November 3, 1894, 2; "Women Wind Up Their Campaign," *Chicago Tribune*, November 4, 1894, 3.

133 "Last Day for Votes," *Inter Ocean*, October 22, 1894, 1, 4; "This Is the Last Day," *Inter Ocean*, October 23, 1894, 1; "323,090 on the List," *Inter Ocean*, October 24, 1894, 1–2.

134 "Democratic Suspect Notice Tricks," *Inter Ocean*, October 27, 1894, 2; "Eakins Is Left Off," *Inter Ocean*, November 3, 1894, 3; "Scoundrelism in the Second," *Inter Ocean*, October 28, 1894, 2.

135 "Scoundrelism in the Second," *Inter Ocean*, October 28, 1894, 2.

136 "Churches Take It Up," *Inter Ocean*, October 29, 1894, 8.

137 "Celebrates His Reinstatement," *Inter Ocean*, October 28, 1894, 2.

138 "Churches Take It Up," *Inter Ocean*, October 29, 1894, 8.

139 "Do More This Time," *Chicago Tribune*, October 24, 1894, 2. More often than not, however, the *Chicago Tribune* and *Inter Ocean* lauded the appearance and behavior of black Republican women in the 1894 election. The *Tribune* described members of the Ida B. Wells Club who attended the IWREC's third meeting as "all well dressed and intelligent." African American women, the *Tribune* explained, approached "voting seriously and went about registering in a business-like way." Registrants included "the women of culture in the South Side." But even these laudatory reports of registration and voting reveal the necessity of guarding the presentation of public selves. "Women Do Good Work," *Chicago Tribune*, September 21, 1894, 3; "Treated as Queens," *Chicago Tribune*, October 17, 1894, 1; "How the Women Did Their Work," *Chicago Tribune*, October 17, 1894, 1.

140 Election judges also denied white women's registration in several precincts. Reflecting back on the election in her regular *Inter Ocean* column, Mary Krout explained, "We have heard a great deal of the illegal suppression of votes south of Mason and Dixon's line, but if the whole story of the recent election in Illinois were told, we should learn that the same lawlessness had been countenanced here by election officials, with the difference that the voters where white women instead of black men." "Woman's Kingdom," *Inter Ocean*, November 17, 1894, 16.

141 "It Asks the Election Board for Help," *Chicago Tribune*, October 17, 1894, 2. Other reports of judges refusing women's registration that do not mention race emerge in the white press's coverage of registration. For instance, an October 26 *Chicago Tribune* article explained that "in sections of the State outside of Cook County an effort is being made through cheap trickery to disfranchise the women who wish to vote. Apparently no amount of circularizing by Chairmen Tanner and Phelps will induce

some election officials in the country districts to give women an opportunity to register and vote in accordance with the law." "Advise What to Do," *Chicago Tribune*, October 26, 1894, 3.

142   "Woman's Kingdom," *Inter Ocean*, October 20, 1894, 16; "The Day in the Ward," *Inter Ocean*, October 17, 1894, 2; "How the Women Did Their Work," *Chicago Tribune*, October 17, 1894, 1.

143   Fite, "Election of 1896," 1793.

144   Booker T. Washington, *Up From Slavery*, 148.

145   Rayford Logan, *Betrayal of the Negro*, 82, 89; John Hope Franklin and Alfred A. Moss Jr., *From Slavery to Freedom*, 259–60; Kousser, *Shaping of Southern Politics*, 147.

146   Lofgren, *The Plessy Case*, 3.

147   Knupfer, *Toward a Tenderer Humanity*, 163–64, n. 52.

148   Davis, *Story of Illinois Federation*, 16.

149   White, *Too Heavy a Load*, 22–24.

150   Ibid., 54, 69–70. Also present from Chicago were leaders of Quinn Chapel AME's youth group. Hendricks, *Gender, Race, and Politics*, xii, 20; Salem, "National Association of Colored Women," 845; Davis, *Story of Illinois Federation*, 2.

151   "The Woman's National Federation," *AME Zion Quarterly Review* 2, nos. 3–4 (July–October 1896): 28–30.

152   Terborg-Penn, *African American Women in the Struggle for the Vote*, 88–89. The other of these organizations that merged into the NACW was the National League of Colored Women. Both groups had just recently formed in 1895. Salem, "National Association of Colored Women," 843–45.

153   "A History of the Club Movement among the Colored Women of the United States," 1896, 50, *NACWP*.

154   "Colored Men's Parade," *Inter Ocean*, October 30, 1896, 4.

155   "Arnett's Noble Plea," *Inter Ocean*, October 31, 1896, 5.

156   J. Clay Smith Jr., *Emancipation*, 286–87; "Colored Men's Parade," *Inter Ocean*, October 30, 1896, 4; "Political Notes," *Inter Ocean*, October 24, 1896, 2; "Arnett's Noble Plea," *Inter Ocean*, October 31, 1896, 5.

Chapter 2

1   "J. Lawrence, Loyal Political Organizer," in Robb, *The Negro in Chicago*, 2:278.

2   Berry's 1939 obituary mentions that she had been a resident of Chicago for more than thirty-five years, which would place her in Chicago around 1904. The 1907 Chicago city directory lists an "Elmora" G. Berry, which I believe to be her because it also lists her as the widow of William. The *Chicago Defender* begins to mention her in 1912. The first unambiguous mention of Berry in the city directory is in its 1913 edition. "Ella G. Berry, Former Elk Leader, Dies," *Chicago Defender*, September 16, 1939; *Lakeside Annual Directory of the City of Chicago, 1907*, 294; "In Chicago and Its Suburbs," *Chicago Defender*, June 15, 1912, 3; *Lakeside Annual Directory of the City of Chicago, 1913*, 177.

3   Hendricks, *Gender, Race, and Politics*, 86–87.

4   Keyssar, *Right to Vote*, 401–2. Women in Michigan acquired the right to vote for president in 1917 and then the full franchise in 1918. Women in New York obtained the full franchise in 1917. Ohio granted women the right to vote in presidential elections in 1919. Keyssar, *Right to Vote*, 401–2.

5   For a contemporary examination of how the expansion of the black population in Chicago enabled that community to acquire leverage in municipal party politics, see Gosnell, "Chicago 'Black Belt' as a Political Battleground"; and Gosnell, "How Negroes Vote in Chicago." Also see Spear, *Black Chicago*; Grossman's *Land of Hope*; the essays in Trotter's edited collection, *The Great Migration in Historical Perspective*; and Kimberly L. Phillips's *AlabamaNorth*.

6   For a discussion of the emergence of legalized segregation, see Woodward's *Strange Career of Jim Crow*; and Litwack, *Trouble in Mind*, especially chap. 5. For an in-depth discussion of the disfranchisement revolution undertaken through "legal" measures, see Perman's *Struggle for Mastery*.

7   In spite of several unsuccessful efforts by white residents of Frankfurt to disfranchise black neighbors, African American men in Kentucky retained their right to vote and were active Republicans—and, in a few instances, Democrats—through the late nineteenth century and into the twentieth. In contrast, white Democrats in Maryland successfully passed disfranchising schemes between 1900 and 1912. However, Margaret Law Callcott documents high voter registration and turnouts among African American men in Maryland between 1870 and 1912. Wright, *A History of Blacks in Kentucky*, 2:90–102; Callcott, *The Negro in Maryland Politics*, viii, 101–38, 155–63.

8   Williams, "Women in Politics," *Woman's Era* 1, no. 8 (November 1894): 12–13.

9   Historians have offered several periodizations for the Great Migration, often locating its beginning between 1910 and 1915 and ending between 1925 and 1930.

10 Grossman, *Land of Hope*, 32–33, 148–49.

11 Higginbotham, *Righteous Discontent*, 40–41.

12 Jennie E. Lawrence, Certificate of Death, Cook County Bureau of Vital Statistics.

13 Bureau of the Census, *United States Manuscript Census*, Rowan County, North Carolina, 1900.

14 Marriage License of Abner Bernard Lawrence and Annie B. Henderson, 1878, Rowan County Record of Deeds, Salisbury, North Carolina; Inez Moore Parker, *The Rise and Decline of the Program of Education*, 76; *Minutes of the General Assembly of the Presbyterian Church* (1878), 248–49.

15 Bureau of the Census, *United States Manuscript Census*, Surry County, North Carolina, 1880. The 1880 census indicates that an eleven-year-old boy was also living with the Lawrence family in Mt. Airy. The census lists him as a servant. I have not been able to find any information about the circumstances that led to his inclusion in the Lawrence household.

16 *Minutes of the General Assembly of the Presbyterian Church* (1879), 752; (1880), 206; (1881),

722; (1882), 253; (1883), 837; (1884), 255; (1885), 1116; (1886), 269; (1887), 298; (1888), 313; (1889), 316.

17 *Twentieth Annual Report of the Presbyterian Board of Missions for Freedmen, May 1885*, 33; *Twenty-second Annual Report of the Presbyterian Board of Missions for Freedmen, May 1887*, 39; *Twenty-third Annual Report of the Presbyterian Board of Missions for Freedmen, May 1888*, 33; *Twenty-fourth Annual Report of the Board of Missions for Freedmen, May 1889*, 39.

18 *Twenty-fifth Annual Report of the Board of Missions for Freedmen, May 1890*, 4–5.

19 *Minutes of the General Assembly of the Presbyterian Church* (1889), 316; (1890), 316; (1891), 315.

20 *Minutes of the General Assembly of the Presbyterian Church* (1892), 229.

21 J. Lawrence, "Loyal Political Organizer," in Robb, *The Negro in Chicago*, 2:278.

22 Because I was unable to locate a record of the exact dates that Lawrence attended Scotia, I have estimated the year Lawrence would have entered either Scotia's four-year grammar program or its three-year normal and scientific program. If Jennie was born in 1886, then she would have been about fourteen in 1900.

23 Bureau of the Census, *United States Manuscript Census*, Rowan County, North Carolina, 1880.

24 Bureau of the Census, *United States Manuscript Census*, Rowan County, North Carolina, 1900.

25 Holmes, *Evolution of the Negro College*, 146; Clyde W. Hall, *Black Vocational, Technical, and Industrial Arts Education*, 84; Gilmore, *Gender and Jim Crow*, 40. Livingstone was initially founded as the Zion Wesley Institute in Concord just outside of Charlotte. After purchasing property in Salisbury and relocating the institution there in 1885, administrators also changed the school's name to Livingstone College. Holmes, *Evolution of the Negro College*, 146.

26 Anderson, *Education of Blacks in the South*, 242–43.

27 Elaine M. Smith, "Scotia Seminary," 1016–17. In 1930 Scotia Women's College, as it had been renamed in 1916, merged with Barber Memorial College of Alabama to become Barber-Scotia College.

28 Glenda Gilmore documents parental concern about sending young women to study alongside male students at Livingstone. Gilmore, *Gender and Jim Crow*, 40–42. Jennie's education at both AME Zion and Presbyterian institutions might also have been an indicator of her family's mixed religious background. Abner was obviously Presbyterian, but Annie may have been a member of the AME Zion Church. Annie Henderson and Abner Lawrence were married by an AME Zion minister at Zion Chapel in Salisbury. Their choice of an AME Zion minister just as Abner was finishing his training at Biddle may have been a nod to Annie's AME Zion background. Marriage License of Abner Bernard Lawrence and Annie B. Henderson.

29 Annie B. Lawrence, Certificate of Death, Record of Noble-Kelsey Funeral Home, Salisbury, North Carolina.

30 *Minutes of the General Assembly of the Presbyterian Church* (1892), 229.

31 Gilmore, *Gender and Jim Crow*, 40–43. Gilmore notes that not all AME Zion adherents favored educating men and women together at Livingstone. Methodist parents who objected often sent their daughters to the all-female Scotia Seminary, even though it was a Presbyterian institution. Well aware of parental concerns about coeducation, the faculty at Livingstone enforced strict rules limiting contact between male and female students at social events. Gilmore, *Gender and Jim Crow*, 40–42. Lawrence most likely completed her preparatory courses at Livingstone.

32 *Star of Zion*, June 9, 1898, 1, as cited in Gilmore, *Gender and Jim Crow*, 42. Livingstone was able to undertake this experiment in coeducation at a time when many white North Carolinians vehemently opposed sending men and women to the same colleges because it was financed by an independent black church. Gilmore, *Gender and Jim Crow*, 37, 39–40.

33 Gilmore, *Gender and Jim Crow*, 31. See Kevin K. Gaines's *Uplifting the Race*.

34 Elaine M. Smith, "Scotia Seminary," 1016–17.

35 W. T. B. Williams, "Typical Negro Schools and Colleges in North Carolina," *Southern Workman* 23, no. 4 (April 1904): 237, 242; Anderson, *Education of Blacks in the South*, 85–86, 106, 118.

36 Gilmore, *Gender and Jim Crow*, 11, 18; Elaine M. Smith, "Bethune, Mary McLeod (1875–1966)," 113. Along with Lawrence and Bethune, Scotia graduates included Sarah Dudley Pettey (1883), who used the pages of the *Star of Zion* and speaking tours with her husband to advocate woman's suffrage, black rights, and gender equity within the AME Zion Church; Lucy Hughes Brown (1885), who became South Carolina's first black woman physician and who helped to establish a training school for black nurses in Charleston; and Carrie E. Bullock, who among many other contributions to the nursing profession, headed the National Association of Colored Graduate Nurses in the late 1920s. Gilmore, "Pettey, Sarah E. C. Dudley (1869–1906)," 918; Jerrido, "Brown, Lucy Hughes (1863–1911)," 182; Armfield, "Bullock, Carrie E. (d. 1961)," 189.

37 Ella G. Berry, Certificate of Death, Cook County Bureau of Vital Statistics; Bureau of the Census, *United States Manuscript Census*, Lincoln County, Kentucky, 1880; Jefferson County, Kentucky, 1900. Berry seems to have recrafted her public image in several ways upon relocating to Illinois. She distanced herself from her divorce by claiming to be a widow by 1930. According to the 1920 and 1930 Censuses, she also claimed to be a decade younger. Bureau of the Census, *United States Manuscript Census*, Cook County, Illinois, 1920, 1930. Matilda's name occasionally shows up in the records spelled with an h, that is, Mathilda. She adopted the surname "Butcher" by 1870. Bureau of the Census, *United States Manuscript Census*, Lincoln County, Kentucky 1870.

38 Wright, *Life behind a Veil*, 16; Leach, "Lincoln County," 557; Lucas, *A History of Blacks in Kentucky*, 1:xv–xviii, xx, 108.

39 Bureau of the Census, *Slave Schedule*, Lincoln County, Kentucky, 1850, 1860.

40   Bureau of the Census, *United States Manuscript Census*, Lincoln County, Kentucky, 1870.

41   Lincoln County Tax Book for 1872, no. 2, Colored List, microfilm.

42   Bureau of the Census, *United States Manuscript Census*, Lincoln County, Kentucky, 1880.

43   Matilda first shows up in the Louisville city directory in 1884. She is boarding at 535 East Street. Matilda's two young daughters, nine-year-old Ella and five-year-old Maggie, would have been living with her (though as young children they were not listed in the directory). Matilda's fifteen-year-old son, Logan, also appears in the 1884 directory, though he does not appear to be living with his mother. It seems that in order to pool their resources, the family migrated from Stanford to Louisville in stages over the 1880s and 1890s. While Logan had followed his mother to Louisville in 1884, Matilda's other sons, Henry and John, do not appear in the Louisville city directory until 1887 and 1891 respectively. Matilda's eldest son, George Portman, does not appear to be living with the family in any of the city directories during the 1890s and 1900s. *Caron's Directory of the City of Louisville*, 1884, 1887, 1891.

44   Wright, *Life behind a Veil*, 15–17, 44–46; Wright, *Racial Violence*, 2–3, 19. The Emancipation Proclamation actually did not free the slaves of Kentucky, because it only applied to rebel states. It was the Thirteenth Amendment in December of 1865 that finally freed the slaves of Kentucky. But, as George Wright points out, "the proclamation transformed the war of secession into a war of emancipation," and this is what mattered in the minds of both white and black Kentuckians. White violence against former slaves in many parts of Kentucky was such a problem after the Civil War, in fact, that the federal government finally established a Freedmen's Bureau in the state in order to offer some small measure of assistance. This made Kentucky the only loyal Union state to be assigned a Freedmen's Bureau. Wright, *Life behind a Veil*, 15–17; Wright, *Racial Violence*, 2, 20.

45   Litwack, *Trouble in Mind*, 229–30; Wright, *Life behind a Veil*, 2–7, 57–58.

46   *Caron's Directory of the City of Louisville*, 1884, 1886, 1887, 1888, 1889, 1890, 1891, 1892, 1893, 1894.

47   Bureau of the Census, *United States Manuscript Census*, Lincoln County, Kentucky, 1870, 1880; Jefferson County, Kentucky, 1900. The 1870 census indicates that as an adult Matilda had at least attended a common school for some unrecorded period of time.

48   Davis, *Story of Illinois Federation*, 76; Bureau of the Census, *United States Manuscript Census*, Jefferson County, Kentucky, 1900; Wright, *Life behind a Veil*, 66–67.

49   According to a 1928 *Defender* article covering Berry's bid for reelection as granddaughter ruler of the "black Elks," Berry had "been in fraternal work since childhood." "Daughter Elks Join Brothers in Convention," *Chicago Defender*, September 1, 1928, 1.

50   "In Chicago and Its Suburbs," *Chicago Defender*, December 6, 1913, 5; Skocpol, Liazos, and Ganz, *What a Mighty Power We Can Be*, 13–14, 18, 49–50, 59, 69–79, 81–87.

51 The 1896 Louisville city directory lists Ella Tucker, by then twenty or twenty-one years of age, living in the house of her mother and working as a domestic. The 1902 Louisville city directory lists her sister Maggie Tucker as working as a domestic. *Caron's Directory of the City of Louisville*, 1896, 1902.

52 Bureau of the Census, *United States Manuscript Census*, Jefferson County, Kentucky, 1900; Jefferson County Circuit Court Records, case file 31830, 1902, microfilm.

53 Index to Deaths, Cabinet for Human Resources, Vital Statistics, Jefferson County, Book 11, p. 219, microfilm.

54 Litwack, *Trouble in Mind*, 230.

55 Wells-Barnett, *Crusade for Justice*, 18–19; Schechter, *Ida B. Wells-Barnett*, 43–44.

56 Mack, "Law, Society, Identity, and the Making of the Jim Crow South," 399; Perman, *Struggle for Mastery*, 264–65; "Jim Crow Laws: Tennessee," <http://www.jimcrow history.org>.

57 Wright, *Life behind a Veil*, 63; Wright, *A History of Blacks in Kentucky*, 2:43, 136. "Jim Crow Laws: Kentucky," <http://www.jimcrowhistory.org>. Although the General Assembly enacted a statute in 1902 requiring segregation on streetcars, Louisville's black community managed to prevent the passage of a municipal version of this bill during the 1900s and 1910s. The custom of segregating city streetcars, however, endured without a municipal law. Wright, *Life behind a Veil*, 54–55, 174, 191–92, 243, 248–49.

58 John Hope Franklin and Alfred A. Moss Jr., *From Slavery to Freedom*, 508; Woodward, *Strange Career of Jim Crow*, 97, 102; "Jim Crow Laws: North Carolina," <http://www.jimcrowhistory.org>.

59 Bederman, *Manliness and Civilization*, 47.

60 Litwack, *Trouble in Mind*, 284–87.

61 Tolnay and Beck, *A Festival of Violence*, 37.

62 The actual number of lynchings that took place during these years was most likely higher. Wright notes that he took a very conservative approach in tabulating these numbers. Wright, *Racial Violence*, 70, n. 16.

63 Wright, *Racial Violence*, 94–95.

64 In chapter 2 of his study, *Racial Violence*, George Wright cites numerous sensational-ized articles that were published in the *Louisville Courier-Journal*. Elsewhere in the study, Wright notes, "While the vast majority of lynchings took place in western Kentucky, the greatest number of legal lynchings—30 percent—occurred in Louisville and Jefferson County or Lexington and Fayette County." As he explains, "This is not surprising as whites in urban areas were determined to prevent lynchings and took pride in maintaining law and order." Wright, *Racial Violence*, 12–13, 221–23, 228–30, 233–44, 325–28; Wright, *Life behind a Veil*, 2; Litwack, *Trouble in Mind*, 248.

65 Wright, *Racial Violence*, 177–83; Wright, *A History of Blacks in Kentucky*, 2:90–91.

66 In 1922 Elizabeth Lindsay Davis described Berry as someone who "was always very pronounced in her suffragist tendencies." Davis, *Story of Illinois Federation*, 76.

67 "Klair's Bill," *Lexington Morning Herald*, January 15, 1902, 1.

68 Knott, "Woman Suffrage Movement in Kentucky," 226–31.

69 "The Political Horoscope," *Colored American Magazine*, March 29, 1902, 4; Knott, "Woman Suffrage Movement in Kentucky," 226–27.

70 "A Card by Mrs. Beauchamp," *Lexington Morning Democrat*, January 24, 1902, 2.

71 At least two of these trips, one that took place in 1912 and another in 1927, were mentioned in the *Chicago Defender*. "In Chicago and Its Suburbs," *Chicago Defender*, June 15, 1912, 4; "Kentucky," *Chicago Defender*, December 3, 1927, 4.

72 "Ella G. Berry, Former Elk Leader Dies," *Chicago Defender*, September 16, 1939, 1–2.

73. Wright, *Life behind a Veil*, 190.

74 "Women in Kentucky Active in Politics," *Chicago Whip*, September 11, 1920, 1.

75 Mary V. Parrish to Nannie Helen Burroughs, October 23, 1924, box 23, NHBP; Fannie R. Givens to Nannie Helen Burroughs, October 20, 1924, box 9, NHBP.

76 Kousser, *Shaping of Southern Politics*, 150–51, 165, 169, 180, 205–6, 221–22; Woodward, *Strange Career of Jim Crow*, 84; Perman, *Struggle for Mastery*, 32, 66, 125, 174.

77 Perman, *Struggle for Mastery*, 150–53, 156, 159.

78 Ibid., 159, 349, n. 19.

79 Ibid., 158, 162. Gilmore, *Gender and Jim Crow*, 105–7, 110–14; Prather, *We Have Taken a City*, 111–35; Honey, "Class, Race, and Power in the New South," 176.

80 Perman, *Struggle for Mastery*, 151, 165–68, 171; Edmonds, *The Negro and Fusion Politics in North Carolina*, 198, 205, 209–10.

81 "J. Lawrence, Loyal Political Organizer," in Robb, *The Negro in Chicago*, 2:278.

82 Higginbotham, *Righteous Discontent*, 41–42. Glenda Gilmore documents similar figures for North Carolina, Lawrence's home state. As Gilmore explains, "In 1902, the number of black women teachers and black men teachers was almost the same: 1,325 women and 1,190 men. The percentage of black women teachers exactly matched that of white women teachers: 52 percent. By 1919, 78 percent of black teachers were women, and 83 percent of the white teachers were women." Gilmore, *Gender and Jim Crow*, 157.

83 Lawrence first appears among the teachers listed in the annual reports of the Presbyterian Church's Board of Missions for Freedmen in 1906.

84 *Forty-second Annual Report of the Board of Missions for Freedmen, March 31, 1906, to April 1, 1907*, 28.

85 *Forty-fourth Annual Report of the Board of Missions for Freedmen, March 31, 1908, to April 1, 1909*, 39.

86 *Forty-fifth Annual Report of the Board of Missions for Freedmen, March 31, 1909, to April 1, 1910*, 39.

87 *Forty-seventh Annual Report of the Board of Missions for Freedmen, March 31st, 1911 to April 1st, 1912*, 35.

88 Gilmore, *Gender and Jim Crow*, 158; Montgomery, *Under Their Own Vine and Fig Tree*, 148.

89 This article on the establishment of night schools for African American men in Mississippi was published in the *Jackson Clarion-Ledger* of October 9, 1890. The call for

[261]

teachers and preachers to teach literacy appeared in the *Meridian Fair Play* of October 23, 1890. McMillen, *Dark Journey*, 53, 336, n. 69.

90   McMillen, *Dark Journey*, 53.

91   Gilmore, *Gender and Jim Crow*, 120–26.

92   Ibid., 125–26, 153.

93   Ibid., 129–30.

94   Wright, *Life behind a Veil*, 185–88.

95   "Mr. Elmnm and Ella Elmnm," box 10, folder 18, IWP.

96   Hine, "Black Migration to the Urban Midwest," 127–28; Spear, *Black Chicago*, 129.

97   Scott, "Additional Letters," 426.

98   Ibid.

99   Spear, *Black Chicago*, 131; Hine, "Black Migration to the Urban Midwest," 128.

100 Scott, "Additional Letters," 426.

101 Hine, "Rape and the Inner Lives of Black Women in the Middle West," 292–97.

102 Gosnell, *Negro Politicians*, 18–19.

103 Merriam and Gosnell, *Non-Voting*, 83.

104 Ibid., 139.

105 Elsa Barkley Brown, "To Catch the Vision of Freedom," 73–74, 79–85.

106 Tulia Kay Brown, "National Association of Colored Women," 62.

107 "News Notes of the Nation's Capital," *Chicago Defender*, August 10, 1912, 6. For an in-depth examination of these clubs' activities, see Knupfer's *Toward a Tenderer Humanity* and Hendricks's *Gender, Race, and Politics*.

108 Knupfer, *Toward a Tenderer Humanity*, 49–52; Hendricks, *Gender, Race, and Politics*, xii, 23–26, 38; Davis, *Story of Illinois Federation*, 2. The Ideal Woman's Club of Englewood actually began as the Woman's Republican Club of the First and Second District before changing its name. "Report of the Ideal Woman's Club," 1899, *NACWP*.

109 See chapter 1. NACW 1896 Convention Notes, 50, *NACWP*.

110 "Fourth Convention of the National Association of Colored Women, July 11 to 16, Inclusive, 1904, St. Louis, Mo.," 25, *NACWP*.

111 For example, the 1939 NACW convention was plagued by conflict between Republican and Democratic members about the use of the NACW for partisan purposes. "Politics Brings Tense Situation to NACWC," *Boston Chronicle*, July 29, 1939, scrapbook, IMGP.

112 In 1895 Wells married Ferdinand L. Barnett, thus the change in name.

113 Knupfer, *Toward a Tenderer Humanity*, 52; Hendricks, *Gender, Race, and Politics*, 89–90.

114 The CSCP was named such in 1908 and later renamed the School of Social Service. Along with Lawrence, black CSCP students included settlement house founder Fannie Hagen Emanuel, who took classes there in 1908; fellow Scotia alumna and nursing pioneer Carrie Bullock, who enrolled in courses around 1919; and labor, antipoverty, and fair-housing activist Thyra Edwards, who attended the CSCP during the summer of 1920. Goodwin, *Gender and the Politics of Welfare Reform*, 14, 91; Rycraft, "Abbott,

Edith," 4–5; Fish, "Breckinridge, Sophonisba Preston," 115; Weddle, "Bullock, Carrie E.," 128. Bullock took classes at the School of Civics and Philanthropy in the 1920s; Dodge, "Emanuel, Fannie Hagen," 248–49; Gertz, "Edwards, Thyra J." 244–47.

115 Fannie Barrier Williams, "Colored Women of Chicago," *Southern Workman*, October 1914, 565.

116 Davis, *Story of the Illinois Federation*, 95–96; "Phyllis Wheatley Woman's Club," in Robb, *The Negro in Chicago*, 2:130–31. Various sources give different dates ranging from 1906 to 1908 as year that the Phyllis Wheatley Home was established.

117 "J. Lawrence, Loyal Political Organizer," in Robb, *The Negro in Chicago*, 2:278. Elizabeth Lindsay Davis's 1922 profile of Lawrence for *Story of the Illinois Federation* records a five-year tenure. Davis, *Story of Illinois Federation*, 55.

118 "J. Lawrence, Loyal Political Organizer," in Robb, *The Negro in Chicago*, 2:278; Harris, "Davis, Elizabeth Lindsay," 212–13; "Phyllis Wheatley Home," *Chicago Defender*, February 9, 1918, 2; Davis, *Story of Illinois Federation*, 16, 53. Both Davis and Snowden Porter joined Lawrence at the foundational meeting of the Chicago Urban League in 1916. Irene Goins, whose Republican work is examined in the next chapter, was also in attendance at this foundational meeting.

119 The 1913, 1916, and 1917 Chicago city directories list Berry as a widow. In the 1920 and 1930 censuses, Berry is identified as married and widowed, respectively. With her brother serving as the informant, the coroner listed Berry as divorced and her ex-husband, William Berry, as still living in 1939. *Lakeside Annual Directory of the City of Chicago, 1913*, 177; *Lakeside Annual Directory of the City of Chicago, 1916*, 202; *Lakeside Annual Directory of the City of Chicago, 1917*, 197; Bureau of the Census, *United States Manuscript Census*, Cook County, Illinois, 1920, 1930; Ella G. Berry, Certificate of Death, Cook County Bureau of Vital Statistics.

120 Hine, "Rape and the Inner Lives of Black Women in the Middle West," 292.

121 I have not been able to find any additional trace of Tillie in the extant vital statistic records in either Kentucky or Illinois.

122 Hine, "Rape and the Inner Lives of Black Women in the Middle West," 294.

123 Fannie Barrier Williams, "Social Bonds in the Black Belt of Chicago," *Charities and the Commons*, October 7, 1905, 42.

124 "In Chicago And Its Suburbs," *Chicago Defender*, December 6, 1913, 5; "Personals," *Chicago Defender*, August 21, 1915, 4; "Fraternal News," *Chicago Defender*, January 1, 1916, 5.

125 "Cornell Charity Club," *Chicago Defender*, January 31, 1914, 5; "Eureka Fine Art Club," *Chicago Defender*, September 26, 1914, 6.

126 Gosnell, *Negro Politicians*, 74, 76.

127 *Lakeside Annual Directory of the City of Chicago, 1913*, 177; *Lakeside Annual Directory of the City of Chicago, 1914*, 949.

128 Branham, "Transformation of Black Political Leadership," 5, 10; Gosnell, *Negro Politicians*, 73–74. This number of seventy city council members remained in place until 1921. Gosnell, *Negro Politicians*, 73.

129 *Chicago Defender*, February 5, 1910, as quoted by Branham, "Transformation of Black Political Leadership," 84.

130 Gosnell, *Negro Politicians*, 74; Branham, "Transformation of Black Political Leadership," 56, 82, 84.

131 Branham, "Transformation of Black Political Leadership," 58–59.

132 "Is the Second Ward a Plantation?," *Chicago Defender*, April 4, 1914, 1.

133 Hendricks, *Gender, Race, and Politics*, 101, 103; Gosnell, *Negro Politicians*, 74; Wells-Barnett, *Crusade for Justice*, 345–47.

134 Berry was a member of the Political Equality League's executive committee. "Political Equality League Meets," *Chicago Defender*, June 20, 1914, 1; "A Letter from William R. Cowan," *Chicago Defender*, March 27, 1915, 4.

135 Norris received 3,222 votes to Cowan's 2,700. "W. R. Cowan Defeated for Alderman in the 2nd Ward," *Chicago Defender*, February 28, 1914, 1.

136 "Women Want W. R. Cowan to Run as Independent," *Chicago Defender*, February 28, 1914, 2; "W. R. Cowan Defeated for Alderman in the 2nd Ward," *Chicago Defender*, February 28, 1914, 1.

137 Hendricks, *Gender, Race, and Politics*, 103.

138 Ibid., 102–3. "The Hot Aldermanic Contest in the 2nd Ward Is Drawing to a Close and Alderman George F. Harding Predicts the Re-Nomination of Alderman Hugh Norris," *Broad Ax*, February 21, 1914, 2; "Cornell Charity Club," *Chicago Defender*, February 26, 1916, 4.

139 "The Hot Aldermanic," *Broad Ax*, February 21, 1914, 2. These four women were Mrs. Morris Lewis, Mrs. Ida M. Dempsey, Blanche Shaw, and Cordelia West. Lewis, Dempsey, and Shaw originated from Pennsylvania, Indiana, and Illinois respectively. Cordelia West had relocated to Chicago from Indiana, but may have been born in Kentucky. Bureau of the Census, *United States Manuscript Census*, Cook County, Illinois, 1910, 1920; Davis, *Story of Illinois Federation*, 60.

140 It appears that Marie Mitchell, who led the drive to reelect Norris, was southern born. It is not clear when she arrived in Chicago. On the other side, Elizabeth Lindsay Davis worked for Cowan's victory. Bureau of the Census, *United States Manuscript Census*, Cook County, Illinois, 1910; "Race to Set Precedent by Nominating W. R. Cowan—Give a Clean Man a Chance," *Chicago Defender*, February 21, 1914, 7.

141 Chicago Commission on Race Relations, *Negro in Chicago*, 94. Berry's funeral services were held at Walters AME Zion. "Ella G. Berry, Former Elk Leader, Dies," *Chicago Defender*, September 16, 1939, 1.

142 Best, *Passionately Human, No Less Divine*, 44–46.

143 Grossman, *Land of Hope*, 94; Spear, *Black Chicago*, 178.

144 Gosnell, *Negro Politicians*, 96.

145 Spear, *Black Chicago*, 93.

146 Higginbotham, *Righteous Discontent*, 6–7.

147 Hine, "Black Migration to the Urban Midwest," 139.

148 Branham, "Transformation of Black Political Leadership," 17–18, 26, 65–70; Sernett,

Bound for the Promised Land, 166–71; "Notes on Olivet Baptist Church, Chicago," box 18, folder 21, IWP.

149   "Women Voters, Attention!" *Broad Ax*, January 24, 1914, 11; Sernett, *Bound for the Promised Land*, 165.

150   "Walters AME Zion Church," *Chicago Defender*, February 7, 1914, 20; "Women to Show Loyalty by Casting First Ballot for Cowan, for Alderman," *Chicago Defender*, February 21, 1914, 1; *Broad Ax*, March 7, 1914, 1.

151   Nannie Helen Burroughs, "Black Women and Reform," *Crisis* 10, no. 4 (August 1915): 187; Higginbotham, *Righteous Discontent*, 7, 8, 158–59, 221–35.

152   *Broad Ax*, March 7, 1914, 1; Branham, "Transformation of Black Political Leadership," 71.

153   Sernett, *Bound for the Promised Land*, 164.

154   Drake, *Churches and Voluntary Associations*, 300.

155   NACW Convention Minutes, Wilberforce University, Ohio, 1914, 21–23, *NACWP*.

156   Mary Church Terrell, "An Especial Appeal From the President of the Association," *National Notes* 3, no. 1 (June 1899): 2.

157   "N.A. Colored Women's Convention," *National Notes* 17, no. 2 (November–December 1914): 2–3.

158   "The Aldermanic Contest in the Various Wards throughout Chicago on Tuesday Brought Forth Many Surprises to the Politician," *Broad Ax*, April 11, 1914, 1; Wells-Barnett, *Crusade for Justice*, 246–47; Gosnell, *Negro Politicians*, 74; Branham, "Transformation of Black Political Leadership," 88; "Many Colored Ladies Residing in the 35th Precinct of the Second Ward Hold a Love Feast in Honor of the Re-election of Alderman Hugh Norris," *Broad Ax*, April 18, 1914, 2.

159   "Women to Show Loyalty by Casting First Ballot for Cowan, for Alderman," *Chicago Defender*, February 21, 1914, 1.

160   Hendricks, *Gender, Race, and Politics*, 105–10; Wells-Barnett, *Crusade for Justice*, 347; Gosnell, *Negro Politicians*, 170–72; Branham, "Transformation of Black Political Leadership," 86, 88–89; "Alpha Suffrage Club," *Chicago Defender*, April 3, 1915, 3; "Alpha Suffrage Club," *Chicago Defender*, April 17, 1915, 3.

161   "Thompson and Anderson are Republican Winners," *Chicago Defender*, March 1, 1919, 1. "The Meeting in the Interest of Dr. Le Roy N. Bundy at the Peoples Movement Club Was Fairly Well Attended," *Broad Ax*, May 3, 1919, 4; "Cases against Former Ald. DePriest Dismissed," *Chicago Defender*, June 21, 1919, 14; "The Peoples' Movement within the Republican Party in the Second Ward Will Give a Grand Picnic at Justice Park, Willow Springs, Illinois, Monday, June 30th," *Broad Ax*, June 28, 1919, 4; "Celebrate First Anniversary," *Chicago Defender*, December 20, 1919, 16; "Miss Jennie Lawrence Ill," *Chicago Defender*, December 20, 1919, 12.

162   Branham, "Transformation of Black Political Leadership," 106–8, 114, 119; Gosnell, *Negro Politicians*, 75–76, 174–75; Spear, *Black Chicago*, 189–90; " 'Bob' Jackson Wins," *Chicago Defender*, April 6, 1918, 1.

163   Gosnell, *Negro Politicians*, 67–69, 111, 175.

164   Chicago Commission on Race Relations, *Negro in Chicago*, 654; "School Census Held Up; Jobs Await Election," *Chicago Tribune*, April 24, 1918, 10; "500 Workers to Start School Census Oct. 7," *Chicago Tribune*, September 27, 1918, 17. Governor Frank Lowden appointed her as an investigator for the Commission on Race Relations in 1919. She also obtained an appointment in the Home Visitation Department of the Illinois Public Welfare Service at some point before 1927. Davis, *Story of Illinois Federation*, 76; Irene McCoy Gaines, "Negro Woman in Politics," 207; "Gets State Job," *Chicago Defender*, August, 6, 1927, 2.

165   Harris, "Davis, Elizabeth Lindsay," 212–13; Gosnell, *Negro Politicians*, 175; "The People's Movement," *Chicago Defender*, March 23, 1918, 15; Branham, "Transformation of Black Political Leadership," 97–98.

166   Grace Presbyterian Church Records, vol. 1, Chicago Historical Society. DePriest did not remain at Grace throughout his career. He joined the Congregational Church around 1928. Gosnell, *Negro Politicians*, 98; "Jackson Wins Over DePriest," *Chicago Defender*, March 2, 1918, 1, 2; " 'Bob' Jackson Wins," *Chicago Defender*, April 6, 1918, 1.

167   Hall had unsuccessfully run on the Progressive ticket for county commissioner in 1914. Other prominent politicians who were Grace Presbyterian members included veterans and sometime Republican candidates John R. Marshall and Franklin A. Dennison, and the lawyer who in 1924 would become Chicago's first black elected judge, Albert B. George. "Celebrate the Journey," Grace Presbyterian Church Records; Drake, *Churches and Voluntary Associations*, 108; Gosnell, *Negro Politicians*, 84, 86–87, 99–101, 109, 112, 208–9 ; Strickland, *History of the Chicago Urban League*, 28.

168   Grace Presbyterian Church Records, vol. 1; Schechter, *Ida B. Wells-Barnett*, 187.

169   Chicago Commission on Race Relations, *Negro in Chicago*, 79, 81, 83.

170   "Chicago Women to Help Hughes Win," *New York Age*, October 12, 1916, 1; "Colored Women Voters Aiding Hughes," *Indianapolis Freeman*, October 14, 1916, 8. Other states where women were entitled to vote for president in 1916 included Washington, California, Oregon, Kansas, and Arizona.

171   "Women's Headquarters," *Chicago Defender*, October 21, 1916, 9; "Prominent Woman Is Appointed to National Republican Committee," *Chicago Defender*, October 28, 1916, 2; "Fraternal News," *Chicago Defender*, October 21, 1916, 5; "Cornell Charity Club," *Chicago Defender*, February 26, 1916, 4; "Illinois Women in Session," *Champion Magazine* 1, no. 2 (October 1916): 18; "Michigan Conference," *Chicago Defender*, June 24, 1916, 7; Walls, *African Methodist Episcopal Zion Church*, 222–23; "Prairie State Events," *Chicago Defender*, October 21, 1916, 8; October 28, 1916, 8.

172   "Chicago Women to Help Hughes Win," *New York Age*, October 12, 1916, 1.

173   Lampkin, "McKinley, Ada Sophia Dennison," 571; Perman, *Struggle for Mastery*, 271–72, 275–80; Barr, *Reconstruction to Reform*, 194–99.

174   Bureau of the Census, *United States Manuscript Census*, Borough Manhattan, New York City, 1920; Higginbotham, *Righteous Discontent*, 21; "Miss Waytes to Speak at Montauk Theatre," *New York Age*, August 24, 1916, 1; "Prominent Woman Is Appointed to

National Republican Committee," *Chicago Defender*, October 28, 1916, 2; "Prominent among Women Leaders," *Norfolk Journal and Guide*, November 18, 1916, 2.

175 Hanson, *Mary McLeod Bethune*, 43; "Prominent Woman Is Appointed to National Republican Committee," *Chicago Defender*, October 28, 1916, 2; "Prominent among Women Leaders," *Norfolk Journal and Guide*, November 18, 1916, 2.

176 "Prominent Woman Is Appointed to National Republican Committee," *Chicago Defender*, October 28, 1916, 2. The *Norfolk Journal and Guide* indicates that Waytes taught at the "Live Oak Institute," but this must have been the Florida Baptist Institute that was located in Live Oak, Florida. "Prominent among Women Leaders," *Norfolk Journal and Guide*, November 18, 1916, 2; Department of the Interior, Bureau of Education, *Negro Education*, 1917, 2:177.

177 In 1910 the Church Federation Society of New York appointed her as superintendent of the organization's work among Bible schools. According to an article in the *Norfolk Journal and Guide*, Waytes relocated one year later to Massachusetts, where she served as the pastor of the Shilo Baptist Church. After briefly preaching in the West, Waytes returned to New York to work with prisoners. "Prominent among Women Leaders," *Norfolk Journal and Guide*, November 18, 1916, 2; "Woman's Suffrage," *Crisis* 4, no. 5 (September 1912): 215.

178 "Political," *Crisis* 4, no. 5 (September 1912): 216. "The Last Word in Politics," *Crisis* 5 (November 1912): 29; Sherman, *Republican Party and Black America*, 109–11.

179 Blanche Harris of Newark and Irene Gaines of Chicago also worked for the Progressive Party. "Political," *Crisis* 5, no. 1 (November 1912): 7; "Prominent among Women Leaders," *Norfolk Journal and Guide*, November 18, 1916, 2; "The Eastern Women Show Their Usefulness in Politics," *Competitor* 3, no. 2 (April 1921): 27; "Shooting of Roosevelt Has No Political Significance," *Chicago Defender*, October 19, 1912, 8; "Our Brilliant Ladies Recognized," December 23, 1911, newspaper clipping, IMGP; Sherman, *Republican Party and Black America*, 111.

180 W. E. B. Du Bois, "The Presidential Campaign," *Crisis* 12, no. 6 (October 1916): 268; Sherman, *Republican Party and Black America*, 120. As Du Bois explained in this 1916 article, "Under ordinary circumstances the Negro must expect from [Hughes], as chief executive, the neglect indifference and misunderstanding that he has had from recent Republican presidents. Nevertheless, he is practically the only candidate for whom we can vote." Du Bois praised the Socialist candidate, but concluded that "the vote for the third party is at least temporarily thrown away." Du Bois, "The Presidential Campaign," *Crisis* 12, no. 6 (October 1916): 268.

181 Williams, "Colored Women of Chicago," *Southern Workman*, October 1914, 566.

182 Elizabeth Lindsay Davis, "Votes for Philanthropy," *Crisis* 10, no. 4 (August 1915): 191; "Chicago Women to Help Hughes Win," *New York Age*, October 12, 1916, 1.

183 "Chicago Women to Help Hughes Win," *New York Age*, October 12, 1916, 1; Fannie Barrier Williams was born in Brockport, New York, and eventually made her way to Chicago in 1887. Elizabeth Lindsay Davis was born in Peoria County, Illinois, and

relocated to Chicago around the late 1880s or early 1890s. There is a discrepancy in the location of Goins's birth. According to Davis, she was born in Quincy, Illinois, but an obituary claims that she was born in Missouri. In either case, she was a northerner by birth. She moved to Chicago around 1895. See chapter 5 for a more extensive discussion about Goins's political activism; Patton, "Williams, Fannie Barrier," 977–78; Harris, "Davis, Elizabeth Lindsay," 212; Hendricks, "Davis, Elizabeth Lindsay," 306–7; Davis, *Story of Illinois Federation*, 7; Obituary, box 1, folder 8, IMGP.

184 Residents of Washington, D.C., did not, in fact, obtain the right to vote in presidential elections until the enactment of the Twenty-third Amendment in 1961.

185 "Minutes of the Tenth Biennial Convention of the National Association of Colored Women, August 7–10, 1916, Bethel A.M.E. Church, Baltimore, Maryland," 27, *NACWP*.

186 Sitkoff, *A New Deal for Blacks*, 20; Wolgemuth, "Woodrow Wilson and Federal Segregation," 161.

187 "Prairie State Events," *Chicago Defender*, October 21, 1916, 8.

188 "Women, Register!" *Chicago Defender*, October 7, 1916, 3.

189 "Hughes Makes His Declaration," *Champion Magazine* 1, no. 2 (October 1916): 13.

190 "Justice Hughes," *Champion Magazine* 1, no. 1 (September 1916): 5.

191 George W. Harris, "Colored Citizens and the Present Campaign," *Champion Magazine* 1, no. 1 (September 1916): 19–20; Harlan and Smock, *Booker T. Washington Papers*, 2:498, n. 2.

192 Pete Daniel, "Up from Slavery," 665–66; *Guinn v. United States*, 238 U.S. 347 (1915); John Hope Franklin and Alfred A. Moss Jr., *From Slavery to Freedom*, 319; Sherman, *Republican Party and Black America*, 121.

193 Link and Leary, "Election of 1916," 3:2269; Arthur M. Schlesinger Jr., "The Votes in the 1916 Election," in Schlesinger, *History of American Presidential Elections*, 3:2345.

194 "The Race Is in Danger," *Champion Magazine* 1, no. 4 (December 1916): 170.

195 "The Negro Woman," *Champion Magazine* 1, no. 4 (December 1916): 170–71.

196 "Women Organize G.O.P. Clubs for National Ticket," *Broad Ax*, October 9, 1920, 1.

Chapter 3

1 "Politicians! Politicians! Constructively So!," *Competitor* 3, no. 2 (April 1921): 28–29.

2 Hicks, *Republican Ascendancy*, 50, 66, 69–73, 232; Sherman, *Republican Party and Black America*, 83–85, 153–60, 230, 237–40.

3 "Chicago Women to Help Hughes Win," *New York Age*, November 12, 1916, 1; "Women Organize G.O.P. Clubs for National Ticket," *Broad Ax*, October 9, 1920, 1.

4 "Says Negro Vote May Swing Election," *Chicago Whip*, September 25, 1920, 1.

5 Philip H. Brown to Hallie Quinn Brown, July 6, 1920, HQBP; Philip H. Brown to Hallie Quinn Brown, August 7, 1920, HQBP.

6 Charles E. Hall to Hallie Quinn Brown, August 11, 1920, HQBP.

7 "Minutes of the Twelfth Biennial Convention of the National Association of Colored Women, July 12th to 16th, 1920, Held At Tuskegee Institute, Alabama," 40, *NACWP*.

8 White, *Too Heavy a Load*, 140.

9 Deborah Gray White traces the arc of "woman's era" philosophy from its height in the 1890s to the New Negro movement challenges in the 1920s. Ibid. For a discussion of the demise of this "woman's era" philosophy, see chapter 4.

10 Higginbotham, *Righteous Discontent*; Schechter, *Ida B. Wells-Barnett*, 135–37, 141–42, 144–45. As Schechter points out, Wells-Barnett was not even invited to participate in the inaugural meeting of the NAACP's Chicago Branch in 1911. Schechter, *Ida B. Wells-Barnett*, 142.

11 Schechter, *Ida B. Wells-Barnett*, 124.

12 Zangrando, *NAACP Crusade against Lynching*, 43; Sherman, *Republican Party and Black America*, 181.

13 "Republican Platform, 1920," in Schlesinger, *History of American Presidential Elections, 1789–1968*, 3:2413.

14 Sherman, *Republican Party and Black America*, 178–81.

15 "Club Women Close Meeting," *Chicago Defender*, July 24, 1920, 2; "Minutes of the Twelfth Biennial Convention of the National Association of Colored Women, July 12th to 16th, 1920, Held at Tuskegee Institute, Alabama," 34–35, 54, *NACWP*.

16 A. Elizabeth Taylor, "Tennessee: The Thirty-Sixth State."

17 "Women Wouldn't Endorse Harding," *Afro-American Ledger*, July 23, 1920, 1; "Club Women Close Meeting," *Chicago Defender*, July 24, 1920, 2; "Minutes of the Twelfth Biennial Convention of the National Association of Colored Women, July 12th to 16th, 1920, Held at Tuskegee Institute, Alabama," 55, *NACWP*.

18 "Why I Am A Democrat in 1924," series III, 4, box 22, folder 418, Alice Dunbar-Nelson Papers, University of Delaware Library, Special Collections, Newark.

19 "Politicians! Politicians! Constructively So!," *Competitor* 3, no. 2 (April 1921): 28–29.

20 Terrell discusses this appointment in chapter 31 of *A Colored Woman in a White World*. "Women Have Gracefully and Efficiently Made Their Debut in Politics," *Competitor* 3, no. 1 (January–February 1921): 23–26; "The Women's Republican Organization in the Recent Campaign," *Competitor* 3, no. 1 (January–February 1921): 27–32; Davis, *Lifting as They Climb*, 33–36. Other black Chicago clubwomen who held prominent positions in the Colored Women's Department of the RNC included Joanna Snowden Porter and Margaret Gainer (who joined Elizabeth Lindsey Davis as part of the National Speakers Bureau) and Mrs. E. L. Holcomb (who served as a National Organizer). "The Women's Republican Organization in the Recent Campaign," *Competitor* 3, no. 1 (January–February 1921): 27.

21 "In the Political Arena," *Competitor* 3, no. 4 (June 1921): 34; Davis, *Lifting as They Climb*, 199.

22 "Politicians! Politicians! Constructively So!," *Competitor* 3, no. 2 (April 1921): 29.

23 "Contributed by Mrs. Joanna Snowden-Porter, President of the North-Western Federation of Women's Clubs," *Broad Ax*, December 25, 1920, 3.

24 "Mrs. Bertha Montgomery," *Broad Ax*, November 13, 1920, 2.

25 "Urge White Women to Outvote Colored at Polls," *Chicago Whip*, October 2, 1920, 6; Spear, *Black Chicago*, 193.

26 This quotation comes from the newspaper coverage of the Virginia Assembly debates over the woman's suffrage resolution. Lebsock, "Woman Suffrage and White Supremacy," 70–72, 79; Green, *Southern Strategies*, 36–39.

27 *Congressional Record*, 66 Cong., 1 sess., vol. 58, pt. 1: 619, as cited in Flexner and Fitzpatrick, *Century of Struggle*, 295.

28 "Women Organized for Polls; Southerners Angered," *Chicago Whip*, September 4, 1920, 2.

29 "What Is Shown by the Registration," *New York Age*, October 9, 1920, 1.

30 "Drive Women from Polls in South," *Chicago Defender*, October 30, 1920, 1.

31 "Club Life!," *Competitor* 3, no. 1 (January–February 1921): 33; "Politicians! Politicians! Constructively So!," *Competitor* 3, no. 2 (April 1921): 28; Davis, *Lifting as They Climb*, 267.

32 McCoy, "Election of 1920," 2384.

33 "Politicians! Politicians! Constructively So!," *Competitor* 3, no. 2 (April 1921): 29.

34 "Western Group of National Political Leaders," [n.d.], box 102–13, folder 259, MCTP.

35 In *A Colored Woman in a White World*, Terrell mentions her own ambitions to transform the Women's Republican League of Washington, an organization for which she served as president, into a national organization. Terrell, *A Colored Woman in A White World*, 308.

36 Bureau of the Census, *United States Manuscript Census*, Greenville County, South Carolina, 1900; Clarke County, Georgia, 1910; District of Columbia, 1920.

37 M. L. Gray to Hallie Quinn Brown, January 11, 1921, HQBP.

38 For example, among those listed as Honorary Executive Committee members were Mary McLeod Bethune, Charlotte Hawkins-Brown, Hallie Quinn Brown, Irene Goins, Mary Waring, Victoria Clay Halley, Mary (Mrs. George) Williams, Ora Stokes, and Ida Cummings.

39 "Important Resolutions by Metropolitan Center Lyceum after Address by Congressman Martin B. Madden," *Broad Ax*, November 20, 1920, 9; Gosnell, *Negro Politicians*, 55, 78.

40 "Politicians! Politicians! Constructively So!," *Competitor* 3, no. 2 (April 1921): 28–29.

41 Schechter, *Ida B. Wells-Barnett*, 165–66. The seventh representative from Chicago, James Mann, died in November 1922. Not a single representative from Illinois, either Republican or Democrat, voted against the Dyer Bill in 1922, though nine out of twenty-six from the state, two Democrats and seven Republicans, did not enter a vote. *Congressional Record*, 67th Cong., 2nd sess., 1922, 62, pt. 2: 1795–96; "G.O.P. Members of Congress in City Run Close," *Chicago Tribune*, November 8, 1922, 5.

42   See, for example, "The Medill McCormick for United States Senator Republican Women's Loyalty Campaign Committee . . . ," *Broad Ax*, August 10, 1918, 1; and "McKinley Declares for Equal Rights," *Chicago Whip*, September 4, 1920, 7.

43   Jessie Fauset, "The 13th Biennial of the N.A.C.W.," *Crisis* 4, no. 6 (October 1922): 260; Zangrando, *NAACP Crusade against Lynching*, 67; *Congressional Record*, 67th Cong., 2nd sess., 1922, 62, pt. 2: 1795–96; "Defeat of Congressmen," *Crisis* 24, no. 5 (October 1922): 265; Sherman, *Republican Party and Black America*, 180–84. For an analysis of Wells-Barnett's manipulation of the discourse of civilization, see chapter 2 of Bederman's *Manliness and Civilization*.

44   Davis, *Lifting as They Climb*, 36–37; *Woman's Voice* 4, no. 3 (January 1923), as quoted in Lerner, *Black Women in White America*, 212–14.

45   For example, in addition to its national executive committee, the organizational structure of the Anti-Lynching Crusaders included state directors. Among the state directors listed in a March 1923 *Crisis* article, those representing Ohio, Wisconsin, Iowa, Georgia, Tennessee, Florida, and Delaware had also served in the Colored Women's Department of the RNC in 1920 in the positions of national director (Fleming), national organizer, or state leader. (In the case of Blanche Armwood Beatty, she had held the position of RNC state leader for Louisiana in 1920, but she had apparently relocated to Florida in the intervening years and, as a result, was serving as state director of the Florida Anti-Lynching Crusaders. In the case of Alice Dunbar-Nelson, she was among this group of women who had represented her state in both the Colored Women's Department of the RNC in 1920 and the Anti-Lynching Crusaders in 1922. Unlike her colleagues who held a similar resume, however, by 1922 she was working for the Democratic Party.) "The Ninth Crusade," *Crisis* 25, no. 5 (March 1923): 213–17; "Women Have Gracefully and Efficiently Made Their Debut in Politics," *Competitor* 3, no. 1 (January–February 1921): 23–26; "The Women's Republican Organization in the Recent Campaign," *Competitor* 3, no. 1 (January–February 1921): 27–32; "Politicians! Politicians! Constructively So!," *Competitor* 3, no. 2 (April 1921): 28–29.

46   "The Ninth Crusade," *Crisis* 25, no. 5 (March 1923): 214; Davis, *Story of Illinois Federation*, 4, 14, 48; Bureau of the Census, *United States Manuscript Census*, Perry County, Illinois, 1930.

47   Schechter, *Ida B. Wells-Barnett*, 122.

48   "The Anti-Lynching Crusaders," *Crisis* 25, no. 1 (November 1922): 8; "The Ninth Crusade," *Crisis* 25, no. 5 (March 1923): 213–17.

49   *Woman's Voice* 4, no. 3 (January 1923), as quoted in Lerner, *Black Women in White America*, 212–14; "The Shame of America," *New York Times*, November 23, 1922; "The Ninth Crusade," *Crisis* 25, no. 5 (March 1923): 213.

50   "Group of N.A.C.W. Representatives Appearing before President Harding, August 14, 1922, in Behalf of the Dyer Anti-Lynching Bill," *National Notes* 25, no. 9 (June 1923): 1; Sherman, *Republican Party and Black America*, 184–96.

51   "Politicians! Politicians! Constructively So!," *Competitor* 3, no. 2 (April 1921): 29.

52 "Minutes of the Temporary Organization of the National League of Republican Colored Women," [n.d.], box 309, NHBP; Davis, *Lifting as They Climb*, 129–30, 196, 267–68; Wharton, *Negro in Mississippi*, 211–12.

53 The eleven women from Illinois were Ida Wells-Barnett, Blanche Gilmer, Susie Myers, Bessie Graves Smith, Mrs. Webb, Mrs. Cross, Lena Hall, Bell Graves, Corine Rollins, Victoria Clay Rowland, and a Mrs. Jones. "Minutes of the Temporary Organization of the National League of Republican Colored Women"; "Bethel AME Church, Chicago, Illinois, August 9, 1924 8:00 P.M.," box 309, NHBP; "Minutes, Chicago Illinois August 9, 1924 9.20 A.M.," box 309, NHBP; Irene McCoy Gaines, "Negro Woman in Politics," 88.

54 For the foundational treatment of the history of the NLRCW, see Higginbotham, "In Politics to Stay."

55 "Minutes of the Temporary Organization of the National League of Republican Colored Women"; "Bethel AME Church, Chicago, Illinois, August 9, 1924 8:00 P.M."; "Minutes, Chicago Illinois August 9, 1924 9.20 A.M."

56 Higginbotham, *Righteous Discontent*, 6, 8, 158–59, 221–25; Higginbotham, "Burroughs, Nannie Helen (1879–1961)," 202; "The Women's Republican Organization in the Recent Campaign," *Competitor* 3, no. 1 (January–February 1921): 27; "The Glorious Task of 'Lifting as We Climb,'" *Competitor* 3, no. 1 (January–February 1921): 42.

57 "Minutes of the Temporary Organization of the National League of Republican Colored Women."

58 Another instance in which the NACW leadership discussed the role of partisanship in the organization took place in 1922. At the thirteenth biennial, the NACW's executive board specifically met with Monen Gray to make clear that the Negro Women's Republican League was not a NACW affiliate. Gray's organization was, in fact, listed as an affiliating group in 1920, and organizers allowed Louise M. Dodson, a white RNC representative, to address the 1922 convention. "Minutes of the Thirteenth Biennial Convention of the National Association of Colored Women, August 6–12, 1922, Held at Richmond Virginia," 19–20, 43, *NACWP*; "Minutes of the Twelfth Biennial Convention of the National Association of Colored Women, July 12th to 16th, 1920, Held at Tuskegee Institute, Alabama," 44, *NACWP*; Freeman, *A Room at a Time*, 101.

59 When the NACW did finally begin to enforce its nonpartisan policy more vigorously, its theoretically nonpartisan lobbying efforts for specific pieces of legislation continued to dovetail nicely with the NLRCW's explicitly partisan support of legislation and candidates.

60 "Meeting of the Executive Committee of the National League of Republican Colored Women, Oakland, California, August 6, 1926," box 309, NHBP; Mazie Griffin to Nannie Helen Burroughs, [n.d.], box 9, NHBP. In NACW and NLRCW forums, members complained about Myrtle Foster Cook's use of *National Notes* to report on the Republican campaign effort. As editor of *National Notes* and head of the Western

Notes to Pages 123–24

Division of the Colored Women's Department of the RNC in 1924, her use of *National Notes* to inform members about Republican campaign work seemed like the perfect marriage of overlapping activist commitments. But several of her colleagues in both the NACW and the NLRCW did not see it this way. Minutes from a 1926 NLRCW meeting recorded executive committee members' "general disapproval" of "the way in which the 'National Association Notes' . . . was used to promote partisan (Republican) politics in 1924." In a scathing letter to Burroughs, NLRCW Executive Member Mazie Mossell Griffin insisted, "If its not stopped now the politicians will help us in the future to elect especially our Pres[ident] as it will be a great interest to them." While women like Griffin pointed to policy and principle, the debate over partisanship in the NACW also unfolded against a backdrop of competition for limited leadership positions, and quite possibly a sense of rivalry that may have emerged in 1924 between NLRCW leaders and those who headed the RNC Colored Women's Department. Perhaps the most direct comments on how leadership rivalries contributed to this debate over partisanship appear in Griffin's letter to Burroughs. Alluding to a sense of competition between the NLRCW and the Colored Women's Department of the RNC, Griffin complained bitterly about "the methods used by Mrs. Cook to build up another organization thru the use of *National Notes*" and described Foster Cook's use of NACW resources for the RNC as a "new method of selling us out" (here, Griffin employed the familiar language of selling out that was usually reserved for male politicians). Griffin also suggested that Foster Cook had undermined her work as head of the NACW's legislative department during 1923 and 1924: "I am glad they showed themselves that's why I was not supported in the last year of my administration." Mazzie Griffin to Nannie Helen Burroughs, [n.d.], box 9, NHBP; "Meeting of the Executive Committee of the National League of Republican Colored Women, Oakland, California, August 6, 1926," box 309, NHBP; "National Legislative Headquarters," *National Notes* 25, no. 7 (April 1923): 6; "Minutes of the Fourteenth Biennial Convention of the National Association of Colored Women, August 3–8, 1924, Held at Chicago, Illinois," 19, *NACWP*.

61 Mrs. Charles W. French to Nannie Helen Burroughs, October 20, 1924, box 9, NHBP.

62 Hicks, *Republican Ascendancy*, 80, 83–84, 90, 97–99.

63 Elizabeth Ross Haynes to Nannie Helen Burroughs, August 29, 1924, box 11, NHBP.

64 "Republican Platform, 1924," in Schlesinger, *History of American Presidential Elections*, 3:2512, 2515–16; Burner, "Election of 1924," 2466.

65 Jeannette Carter, founder of the Washington-based National Women's Political Study Club and her colleague Emma Thompson made this statement in a letter that was published in the *Chicago Defender*. Carter was fulfilling her duties as publicity chairman of the Eastern Division of the Colored Women's Department of the RNC by ensuring that the letter made its way into the pages of the nation's most widely read black newspaper. "Political Organization among Colored Women," [n.d.], box 12-1, folder 7, Jeannette Carter Papers, Moorland-Spingarn Research Center, Howard University, Washington, D.C.; "Women's Political Study Club Praises G.O.P. Stand," *Chicago*

Defender, September 20, 1924: 7; "Committee," [1928], box 12-1, folder 8, Carter Papers; *Republican Campaign Text-Book: 1924*, 33, as quoted in Sherman, *Republican Party and Black America*, 212.

66   "Campaign Experiences in Okla. and Missouri," *National Notes* 27, no. 3 (December 1924): 8; John Hope Franklin and Alfred A. Moss Jr., *From Slavery to Freedom*, 352.

67   "Campaign Experiences in Okla. and Missouri," *National Notes* 27, no. 3 (December 1924): 8.

68   Lillian I. Browder, "Ward and Precinct Work in Chicago," *National Notes* 27, no. 4 (January 1925): 14.

69   Initially, in 1923, at least one NACW affiliate endorsed the amendment after it was introduced into Congress that year. Such endorsements, however, were not forthcoming in the pages of *National Notes* in subsequent years. "Resolutions Endorsed by the Tri-State Legislative Ass'n," *National Notes* 25, no. 7 (April 1923): 6.

70   "Conference on Legislative Program Held under Direction of Legislative Department of National League of Republican Colored Women, Philadelphia, Pa., October 26–27," [1924], box 309, NHBP.

71   Grossman, *Land of Hope*, 246–51.

72   "Republican Platform, 1924," in Schlesinger, *History of American Presidential Elections*, 3:2504, 2520.

73   Lewis, *Fight for Equality*, 241–42. Socialist Lucille Randolph (the wife of A. Philip Randolph) ran a well-received though ultimately unsuccessful campaign in Harlem for the U.S. House of Representatives on the Progressive ticket in 1924. "Mrs. Lucille Randolph Running for Congress," *Chicago Defender*, October 4, 1924, 7.

74   Unger, *Fighting Bob La Follette*, 228.

75   Ibid., 89–90.

76   Lewis, *Fight for Equality*, 241; Unger, *Fighting Bob La Follette*, 291. Simmons's departure from the Republican Party was dramatic. Just months before the election, he had delivered a talk on "why Negroes should be loyal to the Republican Party" at one of the NLRCW's founding meetings in Chicago. "Minutes of the Subsequent Meeting of the National League of Republican Colored Women, Monday Morning, Aug. 11, 1924," box 309, NHBP.

77   La Follette actually ended up pulling more votes away from the Democrats. Unger, *Fighting Bob La Follette*, 297.

78   Ibid., 288, 290.

79   Joanna Snowden Porter, "Minnesota," *National Notes* 27, no. 4 (January 1925): 12.

80   "Minnesota," *National Notes* 27, no. 3 (December 1924): 8.

81   Unger, *Fighting Bob La Follette*, 290.

82   "James A. Cobb Says Conditions in This Country Could Be Worse," *Chicago Defender*, October 18, 1924, 2.

83   Lillian E. Johnson to Nannie Helen Burroughs, October 26, 1924, box 14, NHBP.

84   Hull, "Dunbar-Nelson, Alice Ruth Moore (1875–1935)," 359–62.

85   Kevin K. Gaines, *Uplifting the Race*, 210–11.

86 "Two Dyer Bill Opponents Not Re-elected," *Chicago Whip*, November 18, 1922, 1; Alice Dunbar-Nelson, "Politics in Delaware," *Opportunity: A Journal of Negro Life* 2, no. 23 (November 1924): 339.

87 Zangrando, *NAACP Crusade against Lynching*, 74.

88 "Republican Platform, 1924," in Schlesinger, *History of American Presidential Elections*, 3:2515–16; Sherman, *Republican Party and Black America*, 201–2, 205–7.

89 "Dyer Declares Coolidge Is for Federal Anti-Lynch Legislation," *Chicago Defender*, October 18, 1924, 7.

90 Sherman, *Republican Party and Black America*, 201–2.

91 Hull, *Works of Alice Dunbar Nelson*, 1:lix; Sherman, *Republican Party and Black America*, 210–12; Osofsky, *Harlem*, 169.

92 "Why I Am a Democrat in 1924," series III.4, box 22, folder 418, Dunbar-Nelson Papers.

93 Ibid.

94 White, *Too Heavy a Load*, 122–25.

95 "Why I Am a Democrat in 1924," Dunbar-Nelson Papers.

96 Ibid.

97 "Women's Political Study Club Praises G.O.P. Stand," *Chicago Defender*, September 20, 1924, 7.

98 "Why I Am a Democrat in 1924," Dunbar-Nelson Papers.

99 Harbaugh, *Lawyer's Lawyer*, 93–98, 229–30, 483–84, 492–95, 503, 508.

100 Partial Text [n.d.], box 102–3, folder 48, MCTP.

101 Ibid.

102 Lillian E. Johnson to Nannie Helen Burroughs, October 26, 1924, box 14, NHBP.

103 "West Virginia," *National Notes* 27, no. 3 (December 1924): 3.

104 "Mary E. Gardiner to My Dear Co-worker," January 15, 1925, box 9, NHBP.

105 "Politicians! Politicians! Constructively So!" *Competitor* 3, no. 2 (April 1921): 29.

106 Irene McCoy Gaines, "Negro Woman in Politics," 88. Clubs that emerged during the 1920s included the Cook County Woman's Permanent Republican Club; the Women's Republican Club of City, County and State; the Woman's National Republican Club; the Fourth Ward Woman's Republican Club; the Fifth Ward Woman's Republican Club; the Third Ward Woman's Republican Club; the Associated Republican Women's Club; and the Independent Woman's Republican Club. Gaines, "Negro Woman in Politics," 88; Mrs. Iola W. Greene to Ruth Hanna McCormick, April 15, 1928, box 37, HMFP; Leroy M. Hardin to Mr. and Mrs. Hudson, April 3, 1928, box 37, HMFP; "Mrs. Bertha Montgomery," *Broad Ax*, November 13, 1920, 2.

107 Patricia Schechter demonstrates, for example, that Wells-Barnett's "belief was inseparable from faith in God but not reducible to formal religion." Schechter, *Ida B. Wells-Barnett*, 13, 27, 34, 59, 65–66.

108 Obituary, [n.d.], box 8, folder 1, IMGP.

109 "Minutes, Chicago Illinois August 9, 1924, 9.20 A.M.," box 309, NHBP; Collier-Thomas, *Daughters of Thunder*, 12, 22–25, 105, 106. As historian Bettye Collier-Thomas

explains, holiness doctrine was especially significant for preaching women like Randolph, who "believed that the Holy Spirit empowered them to act, think, speak, and simply be" despite men's opposition. Collier-Thomas, *Daughters of Thunder*, 12.

110 "The Glorious Task of 'Lifting as We Climb,' " *Competitor* 3, no. 1 (January–February 1921): 39–40.

111 "Minutes of the Temporary Organization of the National League of Republican Colored Women, Chicago Ill., Aug. 7th, 1924," box 309, NHBP; "Minutes, Chicago Illinois August 9, 1923, 9.20 A.M.," box 309, NHBP.

112 Estelle R. Davis, "Speaking in Kansas and Michigan," *National Notes* 27, no. 4 (January 1925): 13.

113 Mrs. R. T. Tanner to Nannie Helen Burroughs, October 18, 1924, box 29, NHBP.

114 Louise M. Fayerweather to Nannie Helen Burroughs, August 26, 1924, box 8, NHBP.

115 Four years earlier, Republican women also described turning to clergy for assistance in reaching voters. For instance, New Jersey canvasser Mary Burrell, during the 1920 campaign in Essex County, reported, "The clergy in particular, helped to make a difficult task easier by their timely offers of the churches as meeting places." M. E. Burrell, "In the Political Arena: Women's Work in Essex County, N.J.," *Competitor* 3, no. 4 (June 1921): 34.

116 Haynes served on the NLRCW's Publicity Committee at the founding meetings in Chicago. "Bethel AME Church, Chicago, Illinois," August 9, 1924, box 309, NHBP.

117 Elizabeth Ross Haynes to Nannie Helen Burroughs, August 29, 1924, box 11, NHBP.

118 Hallie Quinn Brown to Dear Reverend, September 17, 1924, HQBP.

119 Irene Moats, "West Virginia," *National Notes* 27, no. 3 (December 1924): 3.

120 Bertha G. Higgins, "Rhode Island," *National Notes* 27, no. 3 (December 1924): 7; Rebeque Foree, "Minnesota," *National Notes*, 27, no. 3 (December 1924): 8.

121 Reverdy C. Ransom, "The General Conference of 1920," *AME Church Review* 27, no. 1 (1920): 37.

122 "Women as Delegates to the General Conference," *AME Church Review* 43, no. 169 (July 1926): 25. In 1924 the Presbyterian Church, USA, also granted women the right to be elected to executive committees. "Presbyterian Assembly Gives Women Voice in Chu[rch]," *Negro World*, June 7, 1924, 10.

123 "Women as Delegates to the General Conference," *AME Church Review* 43, no. 169 (July 1926): 25–26; Best, *Passionately Human, No Less Divine*, 131–33.

124 Francis J. Grimké, "Present Day Preaching," *AME Zion Quarterly Review* 36, no. 1 (1925): 38–39.

125 "AME Conference Praises Coolidge," *Chicago Defender*, October 4, 1924, 15.

126 "Democratic Meet Draws Large Crowd," *Chicago Defender*, October 20, 1928, 2.

127 "America Must Mean Equal Training and Opportunity for All," *Competitor* 3, no. 3 (May 1921): 26.

128 For an example of clubwomen urging poor women to pay their poll tax during the 1928 election season, see "Notes from Texas," *National Notes* 30, no. 8 (April 1928): 12.

129 Clemmie White, "Tennessee," *National Notes* 27, no. 3 (December 1924): 7.

130 Amelia W. Sullivan to Nannie Helen Burroughs, February 27, 1925, box 27, NHBP.

131 Schechter, *Ida B. Wells-Barnett*, 156–57, 173.

132 *Negro World*, June 9, 1924, as quoted in Bair, "True Women, Real Men," 156.

133 *Negro World*, June 23, 1923, as quoted in Bair, "True Women, Real Men," 156; White, *Too Heavy a Load*, 120, 286, n. 15.

134 White, *Too Heavy a Load*, 120–24.

135 Burkett, *Black Redemption*, 3; Rolinson, *Grassroots Garveyism*, 2–3, 16–17; Spear, *Black Chicago*, 195; Ula Yvette Taylor, *Veiled Garvey*, 40.

136 White, *Too Heavy a Load*, 120–23.

137 "Respect and Protection of Our Women a Vital Question," *Negro World*, August 23, 1924, 16.

138 Ula Yvette Taylor, *Veiled Garvey*, 36.

139 Ibid., 44.

140 Bair, "True Women, Real Men," 155, as quoted in Ula Yvette Taylor, *Veiled Garvey*, 44.

141 Ula Yvette Taylor, *Veiled Garvey*, 41–46, 50–51, 58–59, 63–68.

142 "Mrs. Harding Greets Colored Women of the Nation," *Negro World*, February 26, 1921, 8.

143 "Negro Women to Protest Lynchings," *Negro World*, October 21, 1922, 12.

144 Ula Yvette Taylor, *Veiled Garvey*, 63, 65.

145 "Colored Lady Elected Committeewoman by G.O.P.," *Negro World*, June 21, 1924, 10; "Republican Co. Convention Names Committee Women," *Negro World*, April 5, 1924, 10. These appointments took place at the Christian County Republican Convention.

146 Rolinson, *Grassroots Garveyism*, 17.

147 "Will the Entrance of Women in Politics Affect Home Life?," *Negro World*, June 14, 1924, 12.

148 "Big Political Meeting at Liberty Hall Last Sunday; Tremendous Crowd Listened to Speeches of Candidates," *Negro World*, November 1, 1924, 5; "Enthusiastic Thousands Throng Liberty Hall and Hear Speeches by Candidates for Office," *Negro World*, November 8, 1924, 2; "Davis and Smith Speak at Liberty Hall to Thousands of Negroes Who Root Enthusiastically for Candidates," *Negro World*, November 8, 1924, 5.

149 Spear, *Black Chicago*, 195–97; Drake, *Churches and Voluntary Associations*, 238.

150 Gosnell, *Negro Politicians*, 113, n. 62; "Garveyites Arrested When Parade Permit Is Missing," *Chicago Defender*, April 12, 1924, 4; "Renominate All Congressmen; Returns Slow," *Chicago Tribune*, April 10, 1924, 2.

151 "Will the Entrance of Women in Politics Affect Home Life?," *Negro World*, June 14, 1924, 12.

152 White, *Too Heavy a Load*, 120–24.

153 Myrtle Foster Cook "The Western Division," *National Notes* 27, no. 3 (December 1924): 2.

154 M. C. Lawton, "The Eastern Division," *National Notes* 23, no. 3 (December 1924): 2. Bureau of the Census, *United States Manuscript Census*, Kings County, New York, 1920.

[277]

Notes to Pages 142–46

155 Lynn Ross Carter, "Arizona," *National Notes* 23, no. 2 (December 1924): 5.

156 Clemme White, "Tennessee," *National Notes* 27, no. 3 (December 1924): 7.

157 Edna Anderson to Nannie Helen Burroughs, December 8, 1924, box 1, NHBP.

158 Myrtle Foster Cook, "Political Comment," *National Notes* 27, no. 3 (December 1924): 4; Lillian I. Browder, "Ward and Precinct Work in Chicago," *National Notes* 27, no. 4 (January 1925): 14.

159 Myrtle Foster Cook, "Political Comment," *National Notes* 27, no. 3 (December 1924): 4.

160 Susan E. Morse, "Upper New York State," *National Notes* 27, no. 3 (December 1924): 3.

161 Irene Moats, "West Virginia," *National Notes* 27, no. 3 (December 1924): 3.

162 "Questionnaire," [n.d.], box 308, NHBP; Grace Evans to Nannie Helen Burroughs, December 13, 1924, box 8, NHBP.

163 Sherman, *Republican Party and Black America*, 214–15.

164 "One Joy, Two Sorrows," *National Notes* 28, no. 9 (June 1926): 1.

165 "Meeting of the Executive Committee of the National League of Republican Colored Women, Oakland, California, August 6, 1926," box 309, NHBP.

Chapter 4

1 *The Prohibition Issue as a Smoke Screen*, [n.d.], box 334, folder 1, CABP.

2 Weiss, *Farewell to the Party of Lincoln*, 10.

3 Among the several studies on the history of repeal, some of the most significant include Kyvig's *Repealing National Prohibition*, Pegram's *Battling Demon Rum*, Cashman's *Prohibition*, and Clark's *Deliver Us from Evil*. Kyvig offers a paragraph on the relationship between repeal and voter trends in the 1920s and 1930s but does not specifically address black voting patterns. Kyvig, *Repealing National Prohibition*, 201. The two classic treatments of the black voting realignment remain Weiss's *Farewell to the Party of Lincoln*, and Sitkoff's *A New Deal for Blacks*.

4 White, *Too Heavy a Load*, 129–30.

5 For a fuller treatment of racial uplift ideology, see Kevin K. Gaines's *Uplifting the Race*.

6 Frances Willard, "The Race Problem: Miss Willard on the Political Puzzle of the South," *The Voice*, October 23, 1890, 8; Ida B. Wells, "Mr. Moody and Miss Willard," *Fraternity*, May 1894, scrapbook 69, *Temperance and Prohibition Papers*; Lady Henry Sumerset, "White and Black in America: An Interview with Miss Willard," *Westminster Gazette*, May 21, 1894, 3; Ida B. Wells, letter to the editor, *Westminster Gazette*, May 22, 1894, 2. Wells discusses her heated exchanges with Willard in chapters 15 and 25 of her autobiography. Wells-Barnett, *Crusade for Justice*, 209. For a more detailed analysis of the controversy, see chapter 3 of Schechter's *Ida B. Wells-Barnett*.

7 Ida B. Wells, "Symposium—Temperance," *AME Church Review* 7, no. 4 (April 1891): 380.

8 Ivy, *No Saloon in the Valley*, 45, 91.

9 Cashman, *Prohibition*, 246–47.

10 Harper, "Work among Colored People," 218–19; Alison Parker, "Frances Watkins

Harper's Federal Legislative Reform Agenda," 7–8, 13–14; Foster, "Harper, Frances Ellen Watkins (1825–1911)," 535–36.

11 Bordin, *Woman and Temperance*, 82–84, 117–18; Gilmore, " 'A Melting Time,' " 157–58, 162–63. In those areas where women had acquired partial suffrage, black women reformers claimed that women had voted against liquor. Adella Hunt Logan, "Woman Suffrage," *Colored American Magazine* 9, no. 3 (September 1905): 488.

12 "Ida Wells-Barnett Speaks," *Chicago Defender*, April 11, 1914, 2.

13 "The Following Is the Very Excellent Paper Which Was Read by Miss Anna Duncan, President of the State Federation of Alabama," *National Notes* 3, no. 12 (December 1900): 3.

14 Hamm, *Shaping the Eighteenth Amendment*, 182, 188.

15 Pegram, *Battling Demon Rum*, 107, 112, 139–40; Hamm, *Shaping the Eighteenth Amendment*, 227–35.

16 Kyvig, *Repealing National Prohibition*, 10–13; Kerr, *Organized for Prohibition*, 192–93, 198–99; Party Platforms of 1912, 1916, 1920, 1924, 1928, in Schlesinger, *History of American Presidential Elections*, 3:2167–2203, 2271–93, 2387–2427, 2500, 2507, 2621, 2637.

17 After women's federal enfranchisement, NACW activists urged members to elect representatives committed to national prohibition. At the 1922 convention, for instance, a Mrs. Hill from Texas "made a plea for prohibition and urged that the women uphold prohibition with their vote." "Minutes of the Thirteenth Biennial Convention of the National Association of Colored Women, August 6–12, 1922, Held at Richmond, Virginia," 41, *NACWP*.

18 "N.A. Colored Women's Convention," *National Notes* 17, no. 2 (November–December 1913): 3.

19 Editorials, *National Notes* 17, no. 4 (March–April 1915): 10.

20 Kyvig, *Repealing National Prohibition*, 10; Pegram, *Battling Demon Rum*, 146–48.

21 Davis, *Story of the Illinois Federation*, 127.

22 "Minutes from the Biennial Convention of the National Association of Colored Women," [1914], 40, *NACWP*; "Minutes of the Eleventh Biennial Convention of the National Association of Colored Women, July 8 to 13, 1918, at Shorter Chapel A.M.E Church, Denver, Colo.," 54, *NACWP*.

23 Prohibition actually went into effect in July 1919 under the Wartime Prohibition Act. Isaac, *Prohibition and Politics*, 259.

24 "Minutes of the Twelfth Biennial Convention of the National Association of Colored Women, July 12th to 16th, 1920, Held at Tuskegee Institute, Alabama," *NACWP*.

25 Eric Foner, *A Short History of Reconstruction*, 195, 234.

26 Eva Wright, "Our Women Take Part in Suffrage Memorial Ceremonies," *Competitor* 3, no. 2 (April 1921): 31.

27 Asbury, *Great Illusion*, 314–17, 321; Merz, *Dry Decade*, 213; Rose, *American Women and Repeal*, 72, 83.

28 Hadley, "Law Making and Law Enforcement," 645–46; "An Editorial," *Chicago Tribune*, June 14, 1932, 1; Dobyns, *Amazing Story of Repeal*, 343. For other contemporary

pieces that couched their opposition to the Eighteenth Amendment and plans for circumventing it in the racially exclusive rhetoric of states' rights and white supremacy, see Fabian Franklin, *What Prohibition Has Done to America*, and Towne, *The Rise and Fall of Prohibition*.

29   "Here and There," *Colored American Magazine* 4, no. 1 (November 1901): 54. This article originally appeared in the Massachusetts-based *Springfield Republican*.

30   Woodward, *Origins of the New South*, 480; Williamson, *Crucible of Race*, 246–47.

31   Kyvig, *Repealing National Prohibition*, 59–60.

32   M. E. Burrell, "Citizenship Department: Sane, Sensible, Practical, Aggressive Work in New Jersey," *National Notes* 26, no. 1 (July 1924): 7.

33   "Platform of the Colored Women of America," *Competitor* 2, no. 1 (July 1920): 140.

34   Kyvig, *Repealing National Prohibition*, 61–62, 69–70.

35   "Minutes of the National Association of Colored Women, Held at Oakland, California, August 1–5, 1926," 45, *NACWP*.

36   "Rhode Island 23rd Annual Convention," *National Notes* 29, no. 9 (May 1927): 7.

37   "Editorials: Amendments to the Constitution," *National Notes* 28, no. 8 (May 1926): 4.

38   Rose, *American Women and Repeal*, 116; O'Connor, *First Hurrah*, 196.

39   Hicks, *Republican Ascendancy*, 50, 66, 69–73, 232; Sherman, *Republican Party and Black America*, 83–85, 153–60, 230, 237–40.

40   "Organization of the Colored Women's Department under the Republican National Committee 1924," *National Notes* 27, no. 3 (December 1924): 2.

41   "Republican Colored Women Hold Three Day Session behind Closed Doors," [1928], box 309, NHBP.

42   Republican National Committee, *Republican Campaign Text-Book, 1924*, no page number; Freeman, *A Room at a Time*, 188.

43   Willie Walker Caldwell, who was married to Virginia lawyer Manley Morrison Caldwell, is typically listed in Republican literature only by her married name, Mrs. M. M. Caldwell. Seymour, *Lineage Book*, 11:107.

44   "Republican Colored Women Hold Three Day Session behind Closed Doors," [1928], box 309, NHBP.

45   Republican National Committee, *Republican Campaign Text-Book, 1924*, 449; Republican National Committee, *Republican Campaign Text-Book, 1928*, 425.

46   In the 1930s, Caldwell went on to publish an equally sentimental biography about her father, James A. Walker, a former Confederate general and two-term Republican congressman. Rosenburg, review of *Stonewall Jim*, 731–32; Blight, *Race and Reunion*, 4–5, chaps. 6 and 7.

47   Sherman, *Republican Party and Black America*, 151–57, 230.

48   "Republican Colored Women Hold Three Day Session behind Closed Doors," [1928], box 309, NHBP.

49   "G.O.P. Women Meet 3 Days at Capital," *Baltimore Afro-American*, [May 1928], box 324, NHBP.

50 "Republican Colored Women Hold Three Day Session behind Closed Doors," [1928], box 309, NHBP.

51 Sherman, *Republican Party and Black America*, 230.

52 Ibid.

53 National League of Republican Colored Women to Mrs. Mabel Willebrandt, August 4, 1928, box 21, NHBP.

54 "Says G.O.P. Made Her Sit in 'Buzzard Roost,'" *Chicago Defender*, October 27, 1928, 5.

55 "Women's Bureau," [1928], box 12-1, folder 8, Jeannette Carter Papers, Moorland-Spingarn Research Center, Howard University, Washington, D.C.

56 Ibid.; "Political Organization among Colored Women," [n.d.], box 12-1, folder 7, Carter Papers.

57 "Summary of Report by (Miss) Nannie H. Burroughs, Washington, DC," box 309, NHBP.

58 Julian D. Rainey to Mr. S. D. Brooks, October 3, 1928, box 24, NHBP.

59 Kevin K. Gaines, *Uplifting the Race*, 210–11; "Two Dyer Bill Opponents Not Re-elected," *Chicago Whip*, November 18, 1922; Dunbar-Nelson, "Politics in Delaware," *Opportunity: A Journal of Negro Life* 2, no. 23 (November 1924): 339; Hull, *Works of Alice Dunbar Nelson*, 1:lix.

60 Hutson, "Bearden, Bessye (c. 1891–1943)," 97–98.

61 Weiss, *Farewell to the Party of Lincoln*, 9; Tatum, "Changed Political Thoughts," 538.

62 "Mrs. B. J. Bearden Thrills Hearers," *Chicago Defender*, October 27, 1928, 2; Weiss, *Farewell to the Party of Lincoln*, 8.

63 "Why I Am a Democrat in 1924," series III.4, box 22, folder 418, Alice Dunbar-Nelson Papers, Special Collections, University of Delaware Library, Newark; Alice Dunbar-Nelson, "The Negro Woman and the Ballot," *Messenger* 9, no. 4 (April 1927): 111.

64 Dunbar-Nelson, "The Negro Woman and the Ballot," *Messenger* 9, no. 4 (April 1927): 111.

65 Williams, "Women in Politics," *Woman's Era* 1, no. 8 (November 1894): 13.

66 Dunbar-Nelson, "The Negro Woman and the Ballot," *Messenger* 9, no. 4 (April 1927): 111.

67 Ibid.

68 "The Negro Vote," *Negro World*, April 28, 1928, 1; "Who Will Be Next President of the U.S.?" *Negro World*, May 12, 1928, 5.

69 "All Negroes Should Vote for Al Smith and the Democratic Party in November; 'Smith Better Than Hoover,' the Slogan," *Negro World*, July 28, 1928, 1.

70 "Al Smith for President," *Negro World*, August 4, 1928, 4; "Garvey Linking Hoover and Firestone in Sinister Liberian Rubber Project," *Negro World*, September 1, 1928, 1; "Smith, Safe and Sound," *Negro World*, September 1, 1928, 4; "Marcus Garvey States Why He Is for Smith and against Hoover," *Negro World*, September 29, 1928, 5;

"Every Negro with a Ballot Must Vote for Alfred Smith," *Negro World*, October 20, 1928, 1; "Misleading the People," *Negro World*, October 20, 1928, 4; "To the Polls for Smith!," *Negro World*, November 3, 1928, 4.

71 "Democratic Meet Draws Large Crowd," *Chicago Defender*, October 20, 1928, 2.

72 Ibid.

73 Wills, "Reverdy Ransom," 189, 195–96, 202; Spear, *Black Chicago*, 95.

74 "Philadelphia Pays Fine Tribute to Mrs. Garvey, Back from Europe," *Negro World*, November 10, 1928; Ula Yvette Taylor, *Veiled Garvey*, 94–98, 101–5.

75 "Baptist Women Hear Plea for Hoover," [1928], newspaper clipping, box 338, folder 4, CABP; Higginbotham, *Righteous Discontent*, 2, 8.

76 "Baptist Women Hear Plea for Hoover," [1928], newspaper clipping, box 338, folder 4, CABP.

77 "Summary of Report by (Miss) Nannie H. Burroughs, Washington, DC," box 309, NHBP; Daisy Lampkin to Nannie H. Burroughs, October 16, 1928, box 17, NHBP.

78 "Says Baptists Must Stick," [1928], newspaper clipping, source unidentified, box 338, folder 3, CABP.

79 Ione E. Gibbs, "Woman's Part in the Uplift of the Negro Race," *Colored American Magazine* 12, no. 4 (April 1907): 267.

80 Kelly Miller, "Kelly Miller Says: Wet or Dry?" *Light and Heebie Jeebies* 4 (December 1927): 12–13.

81 Ibid., 12.

82 Cashman, *Prohibition*, 23; Goldstein, *Effects of Adoption of Woman Suffrage*, 168–69. These percentages are rounded. Gosnell, "How Negroes Vote in Chicago," 242.

83 Herd, "Paradox of Temperance," 78; Herd, "Prohibition, Racism and Class Politics," 85–88; Cartwright, *Triumph of Jim Crow*, 202–8, 210–12; Cashman, *Prohibition*, 246–47; Woodward, *Origins of the New South*, 171; *Journal of the Proceedings of the Constitutional Convention of the State of Mississippi Begun at the City of Jackson on August 12, 1890, and Concluded November 1, 1890*, 88–95, 253–54; Wharton, *Negro in Mississippi*, 207–8.

84 Herd, "Paradox of Temperance," 367–68; Herd, "Prohibition, Racism and Class Politics," 78.

85 *Columbus Enquirer-Sun*, December 29–30, 1906, as quoted in O'Neal, "1907 Georgia Prohibition Act," 47–48, n. 9; O'Neal, "1907 Georgia Prohibition Act," 42, 57–59, 68, 87, 95; Crowe, "Racial Violence and Social Reform—Origins," 251.

86 *Dawson News*, January, 23–30, 1907, as quoted in O'Neal, "1907 Georgia Prohibition Act," 59, n. 24.

87 *Milledgeville Union Recorder*, January 1, 1907, as quoted in O'Neal, "1907 Prohibition Act," 55, n. 19.

88 Crowe, "Racial Violence and Social Reform—Origins," 237–38.

89 Herd, "Paradox of Temperance," 368–71.

90 Baldwin, *Chicago's New Negroes*, 22, 25, 44–49, 92; Kenney, *Chicago Jazz*, 9, 15, 18.

91 Duis, *Saloon*, 157–59; Mumford, *Interzones*, 20, 22–27, 35.

92   Duis, *Saloon*, 157–59.

93   Mumford, *Interzones*, 20–27.

94   Wolcott, *Remaking Respectability*, 95.

95   "N.A. Colored Women's Convention," *National Notes* 17, no. 2 (November–December 1913): 5.

96   Mumford, *Interzones*, 20–27, 35; Baldwin, *Chicago's New Negroes*, 46.

97   Reckless, *Vice in Chicago*, 31; Chicago Commission on Race Relations, *Negro in Chicago*, 331–32; Wolcott, *Remaking Respectability*, 110–11, 113.

98   As quoted in Drake and Cayton, *Black Metropolis*, 597. This quotation comes from the 1930s. The Chicago Commission on Race Relations' 1922 study, *Negro in Chicago*, suggests that such statements would have been applicable during the 1920s as well. See especially pp. 331–32.

99   As quoted in Drake and Cayton, *Black Metropolis*, 598.

100 His information came from the Committee of Fifteen reports. Founded in 1908, this committee was charged with investigating and prosecuting prostitution. The Committee of Fifteen investigated a total of 459 vice establishments in 1929. The committee found that 44.2 percent of these establishments were entirely black, whereas 1.3 percent of the establishments had both black and white women working in them. Reckless, *Vice in Chicago*, 25, 254.

101 Ibid., 21–22, 25.

102 Ibid., 79–80, 87, 93; Bukowski, *Big Bill Thompson*, 222–23; Haller, "Policy Gambling," 727.

103 Haller, "Policy Gambling," 728.

104 Drake and Cayton, *Black Metropolis*, 248.

105 Reckless, *Vice in Chicago*, 96–97.

106 Haller, "Policy Gambling," 725–28.

107 "Prohibition Looms Up as Home-Wrecker," *Negro World*, May 31, 1924, 10.

108 "Prohibition," *Negro World*, July 7, 1928, 4.

109 "Democratic Meet Draws Large Crowd," *Chicago Defender*, October 20, 1928, 2.

110 The police force in Chicago, for instance, was notorious for its heavy-handedness in the city's predominantly black South Side. The 1922 study that was commissioned after the 1919 race riot describes this mistreatment of black citizens at the hands of city police and judges. Chicago Commission on Race Relations, *Negro in Chicago*, 332, 335–36, 345, 351, 353–54; Gosnell, *Negro Politicians*, 245–46.

111 "Likes Negro World Stand on Prohibition and Smith," *Negro World*, July 21, 1928, 8.

112 *The Prohibition Issue as a Smoke Screen*, [n.d.], box 334, folder 1, CABP.

113 White, *Too Heavy a Load*, 37, 120.

114 Williams, "Opportunities and Responsibilities of Colored Women," 149, 154.

115 "Prohibition Looms Up as Home-Wrecker," *Negro World*, May 31, 1924, 10; "Prohibition," *Negro World*, July 7, 1928, 4.

116 White, *Too Heavy a Load*, 124.

[283]

117 "To the Polls for Smith," *Negro World*, November 3, 1928, 4. See chapter 4 of Wolcott's study *Remaking Respectability* for a discussion of the ways that this rhetoric of masculine self-defense of the home played out in Detroit during the 1920s.

118 White, *Too Heavy a Load*, 124–28; Wolcott, *Remaking Respectability*, 93–103, 110, 113, 130; "Prohibition," *Negro World*, July 7, 1928, 4.

119 White, *Too Heavy a Load*, 128–30.

120 Ida B. Wells-Barnett to Claude Barnett, October 21, 1928, box 333, folder 5, CABP.

121 Ibid.

122 Myrtle Foster Cook to Dear Friend, [1928], box 334, folder 1, CABP.

123 Terborg-Penn, *African American Women in the Struggle for the Vote*, 59, 68.

124 See also chapter 5 and the conclusion for such evidence.

125 Weiss, *Farewell to the Party of Lincoln*, 9–10; Julian D. Rainey to S. D. Brooks, October 3, 1928, box 24, NHBP.

126 "Summary of Report by (Miss) Nannie H. Burroughs, Washington, DC," box 309, NHBP.

127 Ibid.

Chapter 5

1 "Women Open War on Mrs. Ruth McCormick," *Chicago Defender*, October 19, 1929, box 102–9, folder 210, MCTP.

2 See chapter 4 for a discussion of this celebration and the formation of the NLRCW.

3 Significantly, Susie Myers directed canvassing work among black women for the McKinley campaign. *Light and Heebie Jeebies*, November 19, 1927; "Minutes of the National Association of Colored Women, Held at Oakland, California, August 1–5, 1926," *NACWP*, 77; Sherman, *Republican Party and Black America*, 214.

4 Gosnell, "Chicago 'Black Belt' as a Political Battleground," 330.

5 Philpott, *Slum and the Ghetto*, 116, 127, 132–33, 168–69, 181, 189–92. According to Philpott, among African American residents of Chicago in 1930, two out of three lived in neighborhoods that were 90 percent or more black. Philpott, *Slum and the Ghetto*, 127.

6 LeRoy Hardin to Ruth Hanna McCormick, November 6, 1929, box 68, HMFP. These included the following wards: Fifth (12,000); Fourteenth (6,000); Twenty-eighth (5,000); Twentieth (4,000); First (3,000); Sixth (2,000); Eighth (1,500); Sixteenth (2,000); Seventeenth (2,500); Nineteenth (2,500); Twenty-sixth (3,000); Thirty-second (1,500); and Forty-second (3,000). Hardin does not indicate the source of this information.

7 Ibid. The largest concentrations could be found in St. Clair (East St. Louis) and Madison Counties (Alton), numbering up to 7,000 and 5,000 respectively. According to Hardin, as many as 3,000 African American voters lived in the midstate counties of Sangamon (Springfield) and Vermillion (Danville), and between 1,000 and 2,500 had settled in at least thirteen other counties. These included Rock Island County; Cook's

neighboring counties of Lake (Waukegan), Kane (Aurora), and Will (Joliet); the mid-state counties of Champaign (Champaign and Urbana), Macon (Decatur), Adams (Quincy), Peoria (Peoria), and McLean (Bloomington); and, finally, the downstate counties of Massac (Metropolis), Jackson (Carbondale and Murphysboro), Pulaski (Mound City), and Marion (Centralia and Colp). At least eight other counties each claimed between 400 and 800 African American voters.

8 "An Appeal to Colored Women to Vote and Do Their Duty in Politics," *National Notes* 28, no. 2 (November 1925): 1, 5.

9 Gosnell, "How Negroes Vote in Chicago," 238.

10 "Biographical Sketch of Irene McCoy Gaines," *Negro History Bulletin*, [n.d.], scrapbooks, IMGP; Obituary, box 1, folder 8, IMGP.

11 Johnson-Odium, "Gaines, Irene McCoy," 294; Davis, *Story of Illinois Federation*, 52; "Life Story of Mrs. Irene McCoy Gaines," *Fisk News*, newspaper clipping, scrapbooks, IMGP.

12 "Our Brilliant Ladies Recognized," December 23, 1911, newspaper clipping, IMGP.

13 Miller, *Ruth Hanna McCormick*, 53–54.

14 McGerr, *Decline of Popular Politics*, 14, 140–45, 154, 163, 182, 207; Gustafson, *Women and the Republican Party*, 179. McGerr points out that neither Hanna nor McKinley was solely responsible for ushering in this new era. For fuller discussion of the multiple factors contributing to the rise of what historian McGerr characterizes as "advertised politics," see his study *The Decline of Popular Politics*, especially chap. 6.

15 Miller, *Ruth Hanna McCormick*, 2, 20–21, 28–39, 56–57, 97, 104, 110–12, 133, 136, 140–41, 151.

16 Ibid., 92–93.

17 Hendricks, *Gender, Race, and Politics*, 90–93; Schechter, *Ida B. Wells-Barnett*, 200.

18 Miller, *Ruth Hanna McCormick*, 74–75. Alice Paul still headed the NAWSA's congressional committee when this 1913 suffrage parade took place.

19 "Chicagoan Makes Record as Solon," March 4, 1933, newspaper clipping, scrapbooks, IMGP.

20 Flyer, box 1, folder 6, IMGP.

21 Gilmer, a well-known precinct worker in the Thirtieth Ward, would go on to become one of the founding members of the NLRCW two years later. L. W. Collins to Ruth Hanna McCormick, August 28, 1922, box 14, HMFP; William Huff to Ruth Hanna McCormick, August 24, 1922, box 14, HMFP; Irene M. Gaines to Ruth McCormick, July 25, 1922, box 13, HMFP; Ada McKinley to Ruth Hanna McCormick, July 12, 1922, box 13, HMFP; Elizabeth Lindsay Davis to Ruth Hanna McCormick, July 18, 1922, box 13, HMFP; Davis, *Story of Illinois Federation*, 52.

22 "Life Story of Mrs. Irene McCoy Gaines," *Fisk News*, [n.d.], newspaper clipping, scrapbooks, IMGP.

23 Obituary, box 1, folder 8, IMGP; Bates, *Pullman Porters*, 79; "Chicago Women to Help Hughes Win," *New York Age*, November 12, 1916, 1; "To the Board of Directors of the Illinois League of Women Voters," [1923], folder 93, League of Women Voters of

Chicago Papers, Special Collections Department, University of Illinois at Chicago; "Illinois Women Organize, G.O.P. Given Endorsement," *Chicago Defender*, October 25, 1924, 10; "Illinois Women's Clubs Elects New Officers," *Chicago Defender*, September 13, 1924, 5; "Organization of the Colored Women's Department under the Republican National Committee, 1924," *National Notes* 27, no. 3 (December 1924): 2; Davis, *Story of Illinois Federation*, 7.

24 "Life Story of Mrs. Irene McCoy Gaines," *Fisk News*, [n.d.], newspaper clipping, scrapbooks, IMGP.

25 "Illinois Women Organize, G.O.P. Given Endorsement," *Chicago Defender*, October 25, 1924, 10; Gosnell, *Negro Politicians*, 157.

26 Miller, *Ruth Hanna McCormick*, 3, 85, 98, 120, 125, 128–29, 131, 133, 138, 142–44; Freeman, *A Room at a Time*, 58, 171–72; Gustafson, *Women and the Republican Party*, 170–81; Rymph, *Republican Women*, 15–16, 18, 20–21, 25–27.

27 Miller, *Ruth Hanna McCormick*, 163–64.

28 *Congressional Record*, 67th Cong., 2nd sess., 1922, pt. 2: 1795.

29 "Rathbone, Friend of Race, Cleared of Ku Klux Stigma," *Chicago Defender*, February 26, 1927, 1.

30 "Congressman Rathbone Urges U.S. to Buy Lincoln Relics," *Chicago Defender*, February 2, 1924, 1; "Rathbone, Friend of Race, Cleared of Ku Klux Stigma," *Chicago Defender*, February 26, 1927, 1; "Congressman Rathbone Speaks at Howard U," *Chicago Defender*, January 21, 1928, 4; *Congressional Record*, 68th Cong., 1st sess., 1924, 65, pt. 4: 4102–3; *Congressional Record*, 69th Cong., 1st sess., 1926, 67, pt. 11: 12582–85; *Congressional Record*, 70th Cong., 1st sess., 1928, 69, pt. 5: 5589, 5604.

31 Miller, *Ruth Hanna McCormick*, 52, 114, 186–87; McGerr, *Decline of Popular Politics*, 144.

32 Miller, *Ruth Hanna McCormick*, 186–87.

33 Form letter by Irene Goins, 1928, box 29, HMFP.

34 "Official Report of the Proceedings of the Provisional National Progressive Committee . . . ," August 3–5, 1912, 47, Roosevelt Memorial Association Collection, Widener Library, Harvard University, as quoted by Sherman, *Republican Party and Black America*, 106.

35 Sherman, *Republican Party and Black America*, 165; Renda, *Taking Haiti*, 191; *Inquiry into Occupation and Administration of Haiti and the Dominican Republic, 67th Congress, 2nd Session*, 35, as quoted by Suggs, "Response of African American Press," 36.

36 "Dyer Anti-Lynching Bill," *Crisis* 25, no. 1 (November 1922): 24–26; "How Senators Dodged Lynch Bill Issue," *Chicago Whip*, October 7, 1922, 1–2.

37 Bertha Montgomery also served on this committee. "The Medill McCormick for United States Senator Republican Women's Loyalty Campaign Committee . . . ," *Broad Ax*, August 10, 1918, 1.

38 "Ruth Hanna McCormick Opens Campaign Office," *Chicago Bee*, October 20, 1929, box 102–9, folder 210, MCTP.

39 Miller, *Ruth Hanna McCormick*, 190–91.

40 Ibid., 150.

41 See opening vignette to chapter 3. "Politicians! Politicians! Constructively So!" *Competitor* 3, no. 2 (April 1921): 28.

42 Margaret O. Gainer to Ruth Hanna McCormick, October 2, 1927, box 15, HMFP.

43 "Women's Loyalty Meeting Indorses Hon. Medill McCormick for United States Senator and the Brundage County Ticket," *Broad Ax*, July 20, 1918, 1.

44 Major Singleton to Ruth Hanna McCormick, June 4, 1927, box 15, HMFP; Bureau of the Census, *United States Manuscript Census*, Jefferson County, Illinois, 1920, 1930.

45 Ruth Hanna McCormick to Lester Lowe, November 8, 1927, box 26, HMFP; Etta McPherson to Ruth Hanna McCormick, November 9, 1927, box 16, HMFP. During November and December 1927, McCormick campaign headquarters sent form letters to black and white Republicans throughout the state announcing her candidacy and inquiring about local sentiment toward her bid for the House of Representatives.

46 Bureau of the Census, *United States Manuscript Census*, Sangamon County, Illinois, 1930; Davis, *Story of Illinois Federation*, 21; Letter to Ann Forsyth from Unknown Author, [February 1928], box 29, HMFP; Lelah Morris Brown to Ruth Hanna McCormick Campaign Headquarters, March 28, 1928, box 40, HMFP; Irene Goins to Adena Rich, October 17, 1924, folder 93, League of Women Voters of Chicago Papers.

47 "Proposed Itinerary for Mrs. Margaret Byrd," box 37, HMFP; Margaret Byrd to Anne Forsyth, April 7, 1928, box 37, HMFP.

48 Margaret Byrd to Anne Forsyth, March 2, 1928, box 36, HMFP; Williamson, "Five Ways to Compute," <MeasuringWorth.com, 2006>.

49 Margaret Byrd to Anne Forsyth, March 31, 1928, box 37, HMFP; Form letter by Irene Goins, 1928, box 29, HMFP; Lillian H. Wheeler to Ruth Hanna McCormick, May 4, 1928, box 40, HMFP.

50 Jessie Slaughter to Ruth Hanna McCormick, March 10, 1928, box 35, HMFP; Margaret Byrd to Anne Forsyth, March 31, 1928, box 37, HMFP. The documents do not reveal if the Colored Women's Republican Club of Decatur held a formal membership in the CWRCI.

51 Martha L. Connole to Anne Forsyth, March 14, 1928, box 33, HMFP; Martha L. Connole to Anne Forsyth, 1928, box 32, HMFP. The McCormick campaign also paid Yancy and Reeves forty dollars each for extra expenses. No author indicated [possibly LeRoy Hardin] to Anne Forsyth, 1928, box 29, HMFP.

52 Williamson, "Five Ways to Compute," <MeasuringWorth.com, 2006>; Miller, *Ruth Hanna McCormick*, 154.

53 Form letter by Irene Goins, 1928, box 29, HMFP; Bureau of the Census, *United States Manuscript Census*, St. Clair County, Illinois, 1930.

54 Pinkie B. Reeves to Ruth Hanna McCormick, April 30, 1928, box 39, HMFP.

55 Ibid.; Form letter by Irene Goins, 1928, box 29, HMFP.

56 "Ruth McCormick, Rathbone Win; Yates Defeated," *Chicago Tribune*, April 11, 1928, 2.

57 Pinkie B. Reeves to Ruth Hanna McCormick, April 30, 1928, box 39, HMFP.

58   Marry Rucker to Ruth Hanna McCormick, April 4, 1924, box 39, HMFP.
59   Jennie Coleman McClain to Ruth Hanna McCormick, April 16, 1928, box 40, HMFP.
60   Ruth Hanna McCormick to Cyril Reed, August 11, 1928, box 42, HMFP.
61   "An Appeal to Colored Women to Vote and Do Their Duty in Politics," *National Notes* 28, no. 2 (November 1925): 1, 5.
62   Gosnell, *Negro Politicians*, 80. This percentage is based on data from the 1930 census.
63   "Women Perfect Campaign Drive," *Chicago Daily News*, September 19, 1927, box 1, folder 8, IMGP; "Life Story of Mrs. Irene McCoy Gaines," *Fisk News*, 20, newspaper clipping, scrapbooks, IMGP.
64   "Illinois Women Gather to Honor National Leaders," *Chicago Defender*, September 22, 1928, 5.
65   Miller, *Ruth Hanna McCormick*, 186–87.
66   "Up to Date," *Chicago Defender*, October 6, 1928, 2.
67   "Amendment Quiz Causes Solons Panics," *Chicago Defender*, October 27, 1928, 4.
68   "Amendment Enforcement Lacks Congressional Support," *Chicago Defender*, November 10, 1928, 4.
69   "Ruth Hanna McCormick Opens Campaign Office," *Chicago Bee*, October 20, 1929, box 1, folder 8, IMGP.
70   Miller, *Ruth Hanna McCormick*, 193; "Congressman H. R. Rathbone Dies Suddenly," *Chicago Defender* July 21, 1928, 2.
71   Brown and Joplin each received just over and just under 600,000 votes respectively. "City and Cook County Vote," *Chicago Tribune*, November 8, 1928, 4.
72   Miller, *Ruth Hanna McCormick*, 196; "Mrs. McCormick Has Large Lead Over Democrats," *Chicago Tribune*, November 7, 1928, 6.
73   Gosnell, *Negro Politicians*, 180–83.
74   "Five Elected to Illinois Legislature," *Chicago Defender*, November 17, 1928, 10; Branham, "Transformation of Black Political Leadership," 42.
75   "Weekly Report of Irene M. Gaines, Chairman State Work among Colored Women, Week Ending January 18th, 1930," box 72, HMFP.
76   James White to James Snyder, January 8, 1929, box 47, HMFP; James Snyder to James White, January 9, 1929, box 47, HMFP; E. P. Easterday to Ruth Hanna McCormick, November 4, 1929, box 65, HMFP; James Snyder to E. P. Easterday, November 5, 1929, box 65, HMFP; James Snyder to James White, November 15, 1929, box 65, HMFP; Bureau of the Census, *United States Manuscript Census*, Pulaski County, Illinois, 1930.
77   Rosa Davy to Ruth Hanna McCormick, October 31, 1929, box 65, HMFP; Ruth Hanna McCormick to Rosa Davy, November 2, 1929, box 65, HMFP; James Snyder to Mary Silvis, November 12, 1929, box 65, HMFP; Ruth Hanna McCormick to Rosa Davy, November 12, 1929, box 65, HMFP; Mary Silvis to James Snyder, November 10, 1929, box 65, HMFP; Bureau of the Census, *United States Manuscript*, Massac County, Illinois, 1930.

78   Eleanor Bainum to Ruth Hanna McCormick, October 20, 1929, box 67, HMFP.

79   "Democrats Still Going Strong as G.O.P. Eases Up," *Chicago Tribune*, November 5, 1928, 9.

80   "Ruth Hanna McCormick Opens Campaign Office," *Chicago Bee*, October 20, 1929, box 1, folder 8, IMGP.

81   Elizabeth Lindsay Davis to Ruth Hanna McCormick, November 12, 1928, box 44, HMFP.

82   Miller, *Ruth Hanna McCormick*, 203.

83   In January 1932 Democrat Hattie Caraway of Arkansas became the first woman to be elected to the Senate. "This Week in America; Democrats Hopeful," *New York Times*, January 17, 1932, E5.

84   "Politicians! Politicians! Constructively So!" *Competitor* 3, no. 2 (April 1921): 29.

85   Irene McCoy Gaines, "Colored Women's Republican Clubs," *The Republican Woman*, October 1929, IMGP; Effie Humphris Hale to Cornelius J. Doyle, August 29, 1930, box 96, HMFP; Obituary, box 1, folder 8, IMGP.

86   Gosnell, *Negro Politicians*, 180–84.

87   "Congressman Tells Plans for Future," *Chicago Defender*, November 24, 1928, 2.

88   Sherman, *Republican Party and Black America*, 171.

89   *Congressional Record*, 71st Cong., 1st sess., 1929, pt. 3: 2348; Macmahon, "First Session," 57.

90   *Congressional Record*, 71st Cong., 1st sess., 1929, pt. 3: 2455, 2458, 2616. The exception entailed the Bankhead amendment vote, which McCormick voted against and on which Tinkham did not vote. *Congressional Record*, 71st Cong., 1st sess., 1929, pt. 3: 2456–57.

91   "Ruth Hanna McCormick Opens Campaign Office," *Chicago Bee*, October 20, 1929, box 1, folder 8, IMGP.

92   Black representative Edward Green, who had been sent to the General Assembly by Chicago's black voters with a mandate to represent the race, was responsible for introducing and shepherding the act through the state assembly. McDermott, "An Outrageous Proceeding," 61–65, 67, 74; Wells-Barnett, *Crusade for Justice*, 309–20; Schechter, *Ida B. Wells-Barnett*, 138–41.

93   Asa J. Wilbourn to Ruth Hanna McCormick, January 10, 1930, box 69, HMFP; Bureau of the Census, *United States Manuscript Census*, Alexander County, Illinois, 1930.

94   Schechter, *Ida B. Wells-Barnett*, 9, 256, n. 7; Duster, Introduction, xxx; Wells-Barnett, *Crusade for Justice*, 317, 319–20.

95   "Chicagoan Makes Record as Solon," March 4, 1933, newspaper clipping, scrapbooks, IMGP; Branham, "Transformation of Black Political Leadership," 279–80.

96   As the story goes, Edward H. Wright, who at the time was only the third black man from Chicago to be elected county commissioner and who was beginning his own political climb, stalled appropriations for the state's attorney's office until Deneen fulfilled his promise to make the Barnett appointment. For the next two decades,

Barnett and Wells-Barnett were, as historian Charles Branham puts it, Deneen's "staunchest and best known black supporters." Gosnell, *Negro Politicians*, 154–55; Branham, "Transformation of Black Political Leadership," 54–55, 60, 78.

97 Wells-Barnett's unsuccessful primary run for state senator further complicated her relationship with Deneen in that the Deneen machine was already supporting a candidate for the Third District state senate seat. Schechter, *Ida B. Wells-Barnett*, 241, 242, 320, n. 146; Duster, Introduction, xxix.

98 Branham, "Transformation of Black Political Leadership," 268.

99 Gosnell, *Negro Politicians*, 180–81.

100 Branham, "Transformation of Black Political Leadership," 280.

101 Terrell, *A Colored Woman in a White World*, 355.

102 Irene M. Gaines to Hallie Quinn Brown, December 14, 1929, HQBP.

103 "This Week in America; Democrats Hopeful," *New York Times*, January 17, 1932, E5.

104 Irene M. Gaines to Hallie Quinn Brown, December 14, 1929, HQBP.

105 Eleanor Bainum to Ruth Hanna McCormick, October 20, 1929, box 67, HMFP.

106 "Ruth Hanna McCormick Opens Campaign Office," *Chicago Bee*, October 20, 1929, box 102-9, folder 210, MCTP.

107 *Light and Heebie Jeebies*, November 19, 1927; "Minutes of the National Association of Colored Women, Held at Oakland, California, August 1–5, 1926," 77, *NACWP*; Sherman, *Republican Party and Black America*, 214.

108 "Women Voters Oust Defender Reporter," [n.d.], box 102-9, folder 210, MCTP.

109 Ibid.

110 "Women Voters Oust Defender Reporter," [n.d.], box 102-9, folder 210, MCTP; "Women Open War on Mrs. Ruth McCormick," unidentified newspaper clipping, October 19, 1929, box 102-9, folder 210, MCTP.

111 Irene M. Gaines to Hallie Quinn Brown, December 14, 1929, HQBP.

112 "Women Voters Oust Defender Reporter," [n.d.], box 102-9, folder 210, MCTP.

113 "Under the Lash of the Whip," *Chicago Whip*, October 19, 1929, box 1, folder 8, IMGP; Gosnell, *Negro Politicians*, 210. Bundesen was a Democrat.

114 "Women Voters Oust Defender Reporter," [n.d.], newspaper clipping, box 102-9, folder 210, MCTP.

115 Ibid.

116 Irene M. Gaines to Hallie Quinn Brown, December 14, 1929, HQBP. The "Mrs. Joan Snowden" to whom Gaines refers is Joanna Snowden Porter. By the late 1920s, Snowden Porter seems to have stopped using "Porter." Elsewhere in the chapter, however, I continue to refer to her as Joanna Snowden Porter.

117 Miller, *Ruth Hanna McCormick*, 225.

118 Drake, *Churches and Voluntary Associations*, 241–52; Robb, *The Negro in Chicago*, 2:233.

119 Irene M. Gaines to Hallie Quinn Brown, December 14, 1929, HQBP; James Snyder to Eleanor Bainum, November 6, 1929, box 67, HMFP.

120 Irene McCoy Gaines, "Colored Women's Republican Clubs," *The Republican Woman*, October 1929, IMGP; Effie Humphris Hale to Cornelius J. Doyle, August 29, 1930,

box 96, HMFP; "Ruth Hanna McCormick Opens Campaign Office," October 20, 1929, *Chicago Bee*, box 1, folder 8, IMGP.

121 "Mrs. Irene M. Gaines Again Heads Republican Women," *Chicago Defender*, April 26, 1930, 19.

122 The women's division consisted of Gaines, Lawrence, and Sutton until early December 1929, when the number of permanent staff employed in the office rose to four with the hiring of Joanna Snowden Porter. LeRoy Hardin, "Weekly Report Col. Men's Div. for Week Beginning Dec. 2nd and Ending Dec. 8th," box 70, HMFP.

123 LeRoy Hardin to Ruth Hanna McCormick, November 6, 1929, box 68, HMFP.

124 "Report of Jennie Lawrence, Chairman Cook County Work among Colored Women from December 30th, 1929, to January 5th, 1930," box 72, HMFP.

125 "Report of Jennie E. Lawrence, Chairman Cook County Work among Colored Women, Feb. 3rd to Feb. 10th, 1930," box 74, HMFP.

126 "Budget for Women's Department, Period beginning December 1929, Ending April 1st, 1930," box 68, HMFP.

127 James Snyder to Eleanor Bainum, November 6, 1929, box 67, HMFP; LeRoy Hardin, "Total Expenses for Period Beginning Oct. 14th and Ending April 7th," box 86, HMFP; "Colored Department, Salary and Expenses," box 114, HMFP.

128 "Report of Jennie E. Lawrence, Chairman Cook County Work among Colored Women, from Week Beginning Dec. 23rd to Dec. 29, 1929," box 70, HMFP.

129 "Weekly Report of Irene M. Gaines, Chairman State Work among Colored Women, Week Ending November 9, 1929," box 68, HMFP; "Weekly Report of Irene M. Gaines, Chairman State Work among Colored Women, Week Ending November 16, 1929," box 68, HMFP.

130 "Budget of Colored Headquarters, for Period Beginning December 1, 1929 and Ending April 1, 1930," box 68, HMFP.

131 James Snyder to Eleanor Bainum, November 6, 1929, box 67, HMFP; LeRoy Hardin, "Total Expenses for Period Beginning Oct. 14th and Ending April 7th," box 86, HMFP; "Colored Department, Salary and Expenses," box 114, HMFP.

132 Davis, *Story of Illinois Federation*, 55; "DePriest Will Be Speaker of Evening," *Chicago Whip*, September 30, 1922, 5; "Property Owners Association in Sunday Afternoon Meeting," *Chicago Defender*, July 22, 1922, 2; *Polk's Chicago Directory, 1923* (Chicago: R. L. Polk, 1923), 1834.

133 Bureau of the Census, *United States Manuscript Census*, Cook County, Illinois, 1920.

134 Gilmore, " 'A Melting Time,' " 162, 165–66.

135 Mumford, *Interzones*, 25.

136 Bureau of the Census, *United States Manuscript Census*, Cook County, Illinois, 1930.

137 The Second Ward, by contrast, was the most densely populated black ward. The Second Ward was nearly 87 percent black with a total black population of 40,735. Gosnell, "How Negroes Vote in Chicago," 242.

138 Irene M. Gaines to Hallie Quinn Brown, December 14, 1929, HQBP.

139 Weekly Reports of Jennie E. Lawrence, Chairman Cook County Work among Col-

ored Women: November 4–11, 1929; Week Ending December 1, 1929; Week Ending December 7, 1929; January 6–12, 1930; January 20–26, 1930; February 17–24, 1930; February 24–March 2, 1930; March 2–9, 1930; March 10–16, 1930; March 17–24, 1930, boxes 68, 70, 72, 74, 80, HMFP.

140 "Weekly Report of Irene M. Gaines, Chairman State Work among Colored Women, Week Ending January 18th, 1930," box 72, HMFP; "Weekly Report of Irene M. Gaines, Chairman State Work among Colored Women, for Week Ending January 25, 1930," box 72, HMFP; "Report of Irene M. Gaines, Chairman of State Work among Colored Women, Week Ending February 22, 1930," box 74, HMFP.

141 "Report of Irene M. Gaines, Chairman State Work among Colored Women, Week Ending March 29th, 1930," box 80, HMFP.

142 "Officers of the Douglass League of Women Voters," June 25, 1927, file 93, League of Women Voters of Chicago Papers; "Illinois League of Women Voters: Report of Appointments," November 6, 1927, folder 93, League of Women Voters of Chicago Papers.

143 "Irene Goins to the President, Delegates and Members Assembled," November 20, 1923, file 93, League of Women Voters of Chicago Papers; Membership Count, January 1, 1929, February 1, 1930, and January 1, 1931, box 5, folder 35, Illinois League of Women Voters Papers, Chicago Historical Society; "Weekly Report of Irene M. Gaines, Chairman State Work among Colored Women, for Week Ending March 1st, 1930," box 80, HMFP; "Weekly Report of Irene M. Gaines, Chairman State Work among Colored Women, for Week Ending March 8th, 1930," box 80, HMFP; "Weekly Report of Irene M. Gaines, Chairman State Work among Colored Women, for Week Ending March 15, 1930," box 80, HMFP; "Report of Irene M. Gaines, Chairman State Work among Colored Women, Week Ending March 22nd, 1930," box 80, HMFP.

144 For example, five of the eleven Chicago-based CWRCI officers in 1929 were listed as members of the Douglass League of Women Voters in 1928. "Members of the Douglass League—January 9, 1928," file 93, League of Women Voters of Chicago Papers; Irene McCoy Gaines to Hallie Quinn Brown, December 14, 1929, HQBP.

145 Bates, *Pullman Porters*, 64–66, 72–83.

146 "Open Labor Conference," *Chicago Defender*, January 25, 1930, 1, 3.

147 Bates, *Pullman Porters*, 86, 102, 110.

148 Ibid., 108.

149 "Weekly Report of Jennie E. Lawrence, Chairman Cook County Work among Colored Women, from January 26th to February 3rd, 1930," box 74, HMFP.

150 Untitled Speech ("I am here today to speak to you . . ."), [1929], box 1, folder 8, IMGP.

151 "Labor Issues Challenge," *Chicago Defender*, February 1, 1930, 1.

152 "775,000 Negro Women Are Now of Voting Age," *Negro World*, January 12, 1924, 4.

153 Groups mentioned by name in Lawrence's and Gaines's weekly campaign reports include the Elks and the Northern Lights Chapter of the Order of the Eastern Star, "Report of Jennie E. Lawrence, Chairman Cook County Work among Colored

Women, for Week of March 17th to March 24, 1930," box 80, HMFP; "Weekly Report of Irene M. Gaines, Chairman State Work among Colored Women, Week Ending January 18th, 1930," box 72, HMFP; "Report of Irene M. Gaines, Chairman State Work among Colored Women, Week Ending March 22nd 1930," box 80, HMFP.

154 Skocpol, Liazos, and Ganz, *What a Mighty Power We Can Be*, 5, 13, 38–39, 216. Significantly, while Ella Berry remained a committed Republican in 1928, her male counterpart in the Elks, J. Finley Wilson, came out for the Democratic presidential candidate in 1928. "J. Finley Wilson, Leader of Elks, for Al Smith," *Chicago Defender*, October 17, 1928, 5.

155 "Elks 'March On' Chicago," *Chicago Defender*, September 1, 1928, 1.

156 "Temple Boosts Mrs. Berry," *Chicago Defender*, February 25, 1928, 2; "Daughter Elks Join Brothers in Convention," *Chicago Defender*, September 1, 1928, 3.

157 Skocpol, Liazos, and Ganz, *What a Mighty Power We Can Be*, 59, 69–77.

158 "Leaders at Breakfast Conference," *Chicago Defender*, November 9, 1929, 10. Berry is among the women standing in a picture captioned, "Ruth Hanna McCormick Republican Candidate for United States Senate, and Her Executive Committee Meet in the Chin Chow Café, 47th St. and South Parkway," *Chicago Bee*, November 10, 1929, 1.

159 "Mrs. Berry to Head Women Elks Again," *Chicago Defender*, September 8, 1928, 1; "Loses Brother," *Chicago Defender*, March 22, 1939, 1.

160 "In Our Churches," *Chicago Defender*, October 13, 1928, 2.

161 "Report of Jennie E. Lawrence, Chairman Cook County Work among Colored Women, from Jan. 6th to Jan. 12th, 1930," box 72, HMFP; "Report of Jennie E. Lawrence, Chairman Cook County Work among Colored Women, from Feb. 10th to Feb. 17th, 1930," box 74, HMFP.

162 Mary Church Terrell to Ruth Hanna McCormick, November 24, 1929, box 67, HMFP.

163 Mary Church Terrell to Ruth Hanna McCormick, December 6, 1929, box 67, HMFP.

164 Best, *Passionately Human, No Less Divine*, 7, 40.

165 Drake, *Churches and Voluntary Associations*, 184.

166 The four Baptist churches mentioned by name in campaign reports were Ebenezer, Salem, Friendship, Church, and Greater St. John. The six AME, CME, or AME Zion churches mentioned by name in campaign reports were Bethel AME, Friendship AME, Quinn Chapel AME, Allen Temple AME, St. Paul's CME, and Walters AME Zion. The other community church they canvassed was Progressive. They also addressed Lincoln Memorial Congregational Church, which was part of the independent church movement. "Report of Jennie E. Lawrence, Chairman Cook County Work among Colored Women, for Week of March 17th to March 24, 1930," box 80, HMFP; "Report of the Work of Jennie E. Lawrence, Organizer of the Colored Women in Chicago and Cook County, from November 11th to November 17th, 1929," box 68, HMFP; "Report of Jennie E. Lawrence, Chairman Cook County

Work among Colored Women, from Week Beginning Dec. 23rd to Dec. 29, 1929," box 70, HMFP; "Weekly Report of Jennie E. Lawrence, Chairman Cook County Work among Colored Women, from January 20th to January 26th, 1930," box 72, HMFP; "Weekly Report of Jennie E. Lawrence, Chairman Cook County Work among Colored Women, Week Ending December 14th, 1929," box 70, HMFP; "Report of Jennie E. Lawrence, Chairman Cook County Work among Colored Women, from Jan. 6th to Jan. 12th, 1930," box 72, HMFP; "Report of Irene M. Gaines, Chairman, State Work among Colored Women, Week Ending April 8th, 1930," box 86, HMFP; "The History of Lincoln Memorial Congregational Church," box 45, folder 19, IWP.

167 "Weekly Report of Irene M. Gaines, Chairman State Work among Colored Women, for Week Ending March 8th, 1930," box 80, HMFP; "Report of Jennie E. Lawrence, Chairman Cook County Work among Colored Women, for Week of March 17th to March 24, 1930," box 80, HMFP; "Report of Jennie E. Lawrence, Chairman Cook County Work among Colored Women, from Jan. 13th through Jan. 19, 1930," box 72, HMFP; "Report of Jennie E. Lawrence, Chairman, Cook County Work among Colored Women, from Feb. 17th to Feb. 24th, 1930," box 74, HMFP. The memberships of each of these churches had expanded by at least 80 percent as a result of the influx of southern migrants during the 1910s and 1920s. Drake, *Churches and Voluntary Associations*, 147.

168 "Report of Jennie E. Lawrence, Chairman Cook County Work among Colored Women, from March 2nd to March 9th, 1930, inclusive," box 80, HMFP; Best, *Passionately Human, No Less Divine*, 44–45.

169 Albert Clay Zumbrunnen, *The Community Church: A Probable Method of Approach to and Bases for Denominational Unity* (Chicago: University of Chicago Press, 1922), 78, as quoted by Best, *Passionately Human, No Less Divine*, 45, 136.

170 Best, *Passionately Human, No Less Divine*, 40.

171 Ibid., 137.

172 Drake, *Churches and Voluntary Associations*, 204.

173 Spear, *Black Chicago*, 177.

174 Ibid., 178.

175 Drake, *Churches and Voluntary Associations*, 204.

176 Pilgrim, Progressive, Provident, Liberty, and Monumental Baptist Churches all started out as informal prayer meetings during this period. Spear, *Black Chicago*, 176.

177 Best, *Passionately Human, No Less Divine*, 33, 52, 55, 63–66, 69; Drake, *Churches and Voluntary Associations*, 149.

178 Spear, *Black Chicago*, 174–77; Drake, *Churches and Voluntary Associations*, 148. The Holiness and Spiritualist Churches emphasized healing, perfectionism, and the "giving of messages," or tongues. Drake, *Churches and Voluntary Associations*, 191, 195.

179 Mitchell, *Righteous Propagation*, 9–10.

180 Best, *Passionately Human, No Less Divine*, 55.

181 Rosa Gordon Newton to Jennie E. Lawrence, March 11, 1930, box 80, HMFP.

182   Ibid.

183   Branham, "Transformation of Black Political Leadership," 254.

184   Untitled Speech ("I am here today to speak to you . . ."), [1929], box 1, folder 8, IMGP; Gosnell, *Negro Politicians*, 59.

185   Untitled Speech ("I am here today to speak to you . . ."), [1929], box 1, folder 8, IMGP.

186   "Candidate," *Chicago Defender*, April 5, 1930, 4; "Tells How Deneen Leader Slighted Woman Candidate," *Chicago Defender*, April 5, 1930, 8.

187   Untitled speech 2 ("Mrs. McCormick has been . . ."), box 102-3, folder 109, MCTP.

188   Ibid.

189   Untitled speech 1 ("Send her to the . . ."), box 102–3, folder 108, MCTP.

190   The returns were as follows: 4,758 for McCormick and 1,399 for Deneen in the Second Ward; 8,484 for McCormick and 2,675 for Deneen in the Third Ward; and 8,083 for McCormick and 2,078 for Deneen in the Fourth Ward. "US Senate Vote First to Sixth Wards," *Chicago Defender*, April 12, 1930, 2.

191   "DePriest Wins; George Beaten?," *Chicago Defender*, April 12, 1930, 1; "Double Winner," *Chicago Defender*, April 12, 1930, 24; "Defeated," *Chicago Defender*, April 12, 1930, 24.

192   Branham, "Transformation of Black Political Leadership," 268–72.

193   Irene M. Gaines to Katherine Hamill, April 20, 1930, box 86, HMFP.

194   Graham T. Perry to James Snyder, October 18, 1930, box 101, HMFP.

195   Irene McCoy Gaines to Mrs. George R. Dean, September 20, 1930, box 101, HMFP.

196   "An Appeal to Colored Women to Vote and Do Their Duty in Politics," *National Notes* 28, no. 2 (November 1925): 1, 5.

197   Cornelius Doyle to Party Leader, October 25, 1930, box 101, HMFP; "Harry Knighten, Veteran Railroad Employee, Dead," *Chicago Defender*, August 16, 1930, 7.

198   Irene McCoy Gaines to Mrs. George R. Dean, September 20, 1930, box 101, HMFP.

199   *The Plain Truth* 1, no. 1 (October 1930): 3, 5, box 102, folder 3, Charles E. Merriam Papers, University of Chicago Library, Special Collections Research Center.

200   " 'This Is A White Man's Country,' Says Jam Ham Lewis," *The Plain Truth* 1, no. 1 (October 1930): 1–4, box 102, folder 3, Merriam Papers.

201   "Igoe Flays Negroes in Harsh Terms" and "Kick Out Cermak, an Enemy of the Race," *The Plain Truth* 1, no. 1 (October 1930): 1, 5–6, 9, 10, box 102, folder 3, Merriam Papers.

202   "Democrats Show Gain in 3d Ward," *Chicago Defender*, April 12, 1930, 6.

203   *The Plain Truth* reprinted a speech that Michael Igoe delivered on behalf of William Dever during the 1927 mayoral contest: "There is just one issue in this campaign. That is a south side issue; if you folks want to keep the south side white you go out and vote election day." Three years prior Igoe told the white crowd gathered at Pershing Palace, "If you folks that live on the south side of Chicago, if you want to educate your children here, if you want to own your property here, and if you want to maintain that property, then you have got to go out on the day of April 5th and vote for the only white candidate of the campaign, William E. Dever." Of course, Dever's opponent for

the mayor's office, Thompson, was white, and so the reprinted speech was all the more incendiary in that it implied that white politicians who represented black residents had betrayed their race. "Igoe Flays Negroes in Harsh Terms," *The Plain Truth* 1, no. 1 (October 1930): 1, 5, box 102, folder 3, Merriam Papers.

204 "Democratic Party Grows Fast in Chicago," in Robb, *The Negro in Chicago*, 2:156–57.

205 "Third Ward Democrats Aid Poor," *Chicago Defender*, January 4, 1930, 18; "Mrs. Brewin Hostess," *Chicago Defender*, October 25, 1930, 7; Irene McCoy Gaines, "Negro Woman in Politics," 2:206.

206 Miller, *Ruth Hanna McCormick*, 221, 229–31, 233; "Decision on Wet and Dry Vote Up to J. Ham Lewis," *Chicago Tribune*, May 20, 1930, 4.

207 "Ten Years of Prohibition," *Chicago Defender*, January 11, 1930, 3.

208 "Vote by Ward on Prohibition Questions," *Chicago Tribune*, November 6, 1930, 5.

209 This is assuming the voting pattern of the most heavily black-populated wards—the Second, Third, and Fourth—were representative of black voters throughout the city. Independent candidate Lottie O'Neil opposed the referendum and, in fact, split from the Republican Party, along with the Anti-Saloon League, precisely because she viewed McCormick as too lenient on prohibition enforcement. Miller, *Ruth Hanna McCormick*, 221, 224, 229.

210 Bukowski, *Big Bill Thompson, Chicago*, 230.

211 Branham, "Transformation of Black Political Leadership," 271.

212 Gosnell, *Negro Politicians*, 33.

Conclusion

1 "Wire-Tappings," *Chicago Defender*, October 29, 1932, 19.

2 *The Plain Truth* 1, no. 1 (October 1930): 9, box 10, folder 3, Charles E. Merriam Papers, University of Chicago, Special Research Collections Research Center.

3 "Women's G.O.P. Club to Hold Mass Meeting," *Chicago Defender*, September 24, 1932, 2.

4 "Race Voters Determined to Re-Elect Oscar DePriest," *Chicago Defender*, October 1, 1932, 3.

5 Elizabeth Lindsay Davis to Nannie Helen Burroughs, November 1, 1932, box 6, NHBP; Francis Wells to Nannie Helen Burroughs, August 22, 1932, box 30, NHBP.

6 Drake, *Churches and Voluntary Associations*, 203–6.

7 Grace Presbyterian Church Records, vol. 2, Chicago Historical Society. In its minutes from April 1932, the Grace Presbyterian Church Council listed Lawrence as among those members who had "neglected the ordinances of the church for one year." The following year, Lawrence successfully requested that the church restore her to the roll of active members. She was taken off the roll of suspended congregants in April 1933. Grace Presbyterian Church Records, vol. 2.

8 Glenda Gilmore suggests that some southern black women who migrated to the

North in the 1920s after the enactment of the Nineteenth Amendment did so with a deep resentment toward the Republican Party in the South. Mary Reynolds did indeed attribute her support for the Democratic Party to southern roots, but she pushed the timeline for the origins of this support much earlier to the 1890s. As she explained to white Democratic leader Molly Dewson in 1936, "My father 'Dr. Key' of Nashville Tenn was a Democrat when I was a child 8 years old & I was 50 yrs old the 15th of Sept. this year." Although a small group, the presence of some black Democrats in the 1890s inspired Reynolds to work on each of the Democratic presidential campaigns that had transpired since the Nineteenth Amendment's enactment. Gilmore, "False Friends and Avowed Enemies," 224–25, 231; Mary Ann Reynolds to Mary Dewson, October 4, 1936, box 5, WDNCP; William Thompkins to Frank Reed, October 6, 1932, box 1, folder 7, Arthur W. Mitchell Papers, Chicago Historical Society, Chicago, Illinois; Mary Ann Reynolds to James A. Farley, February 19, 1934, box 5, WDNCP; Mary Ann Reynolds to Miss Fickel, July 9, 1934, box 5, WDNCP; "In East," *Chicago Defender*, July 9, 1938, 14.

9   Smith earned about 27 percent of the vote in Chicago's black precincts in 1928. Weiss, *Farewell to the Party of Lincoln*, 10, 29–33.

10   Branham, "Transformation of Black Political Leadership," 279; "Wets Capture 24 of Illinois' Congress Seats," *Chicago Tribune*, November 10, 1932, 5.

11   "DePriest Is Re-elected to Congress Seat," *Chicago Defender*, November 12, 1932, 1.

12   Nannie Helen Burroughs to Mrs. M. J. Pius, November 16, 1932, box 41, NHBP.

13   Nannie Helen Burroughs to Bessie C. Jones, December 22, 1933, box 38, NHBP; Davis, *Lifting as They Climb*, 147.

14   See especially Gosnell, *Negro Politicians*, 90–91; and Weiss, *Farewell to the Party of Lincoln*, 84–89.

15   "Democratic Race Women Form New Organization," *Chicago Defender*, October 13, 1934, 20; "Mrs. Rachel Bright Gets Appointment," *Chicago Defender*, September 1, 1935, 13; Bureau of the Census, *United States Manuscript Census*, Cook County, Illinois, 1930.

16   "200 Attend Banquet Given in Honor of Mayor Kelly," *Chicago Defender*, March 30, 1935, 5.

17   Some of the pieces that appeared in the *Chicago Defender* denouncing prohibition in the months prior to the election included "What the People Say," *Chicago Defender*, April 16, 1932, 14; "What Do You Say about It?," *Chicago Defender*, April 30, 1932, 15; "Wants Pure Liquor," *Chicago Defender*, May 7, 1932, A2; "What Do You Say about It?," *Chicago Defender*, June 18, 1932, 15; "What Do You Say about It?," *Chicago Defender*, August 27, 1932, 15.

18   "What Do You Say about It?," *Chicago Defender*, June 25, 1932, 15; "What Do You Say about It?," *Chicago Defender*, July 2, 1932, 15; Freidel, "Election of 1932," 2727; "Party Platforms of 1932," in Schlesinger, *History of American Presidential Elections, 1789–1968*, 3:2743.

19   Kyvig, *Repealing National Prohibition*, 182.

20   Hanson, *Mary McLeod Bethune*, 124; "Minutes, Chicago, Illinois, August 9, 1924, 9:20 A.M.," box 309, NHBP.

21   Hanson, *Mary McLeod Bethune*, 134–37. For a fuller discussion of Bethune's work on behalf of black youth in the NYA, see chapter 4 of Hanson's *Mary McLeod Bethune*.

22   Hanson, *Mary McLeod Bethune*, 126–31. See also chapter 2, "An Old Deal, A Raw Deal," in Sitkoff's *A New Deal for Blacks*; as well as chapter 2, "New Deal or New Bluff?" of Weiss's *Farewell to the Party of Lincoln*. Hanson documents Bethune's criticisms of racial inequity within New Deal Programs. Hanson, *Mary McLeod Bethune*, 125, 139.

23   Form letter from Crystal Bird Fauset, October 7, 1936, box 315, WDNCP.

24   "Minutes of the Temporary Organization of the National League of Republican Colored Women, Chicago, Ill., Aug. 7th, 1924," box 309, NHBP; Daisy E. Lampkin to Crystal Bird Fauset, October 1, 1936, box 315, WDNCP.

25   Belle Collins to Crystal Bird Fauset, October 4, 1936, box 315, WDNCP.

26   Mrs. John Hope Sr. to Crystal Bird Fauset, October 5, 1936, box 315, WDNCP.

27   Addie W. Hunton to Crystal Bird Fauset, October 22, 1936, box 315, WDNCP.

28   Mary Louise Cornell to Crystal Bird Fauset, October 17, 1936, box 315, WDNCP.

29   M. Mossell Griffin to Crystal Bird Fauset, October 7, 1936, box 315, WDNCP.

30   "Mrs. Nannie Reed Is Selected as Head for New Year," *Chicago Defender*, August 1, 1936, 7; "Deaths," *Chicago Defender*, December 4, 1963, 21.

31   "National Association of Colored Women, Fifteenth Biennial Session, Oakland, California, August 1–5, 1926," 77, *NACWP*.

32   Irene McCoy Gaines, "Negro Woman in Politics," 88; "Says One 'White Supremacy' Democrat Equals One 'Lily White' Republican," *Light and Heebie Jeebies*, September 22, 1928, 11; Telegram of congratulations from Second Ward Ruth Hanna McCormick Volunteer Club to Ruth Hanna McCormick, April 11, 1928, box 37, HMFP.

33   Nannie Reed to Crystal Bird Fauset, October 19, 1936, box 315, WDNCP.

34   Jennie E. Lawrence, Certificate of Death, Cook County Bureau of Vital Statistics, Chicago, Illinois.

35   "Mrs. Mary Terrell, 90 Dies; Anti-Segregation Crusader," *Sunday Star*, July 25, 1954, box 102-2, folder 46, MCTP.

36   "9 Women Seek Primary Votes for Assembly," *Chicago Tribune*, March 24, 1940, box 2, folder 1, IMGP; "Primary Winners," *Chicago Daily News*, April 12, 1950, 1, box 3, folder 1, IMGP; Press release, October 23, 1950, box 3, folder 1, IMGP; "Biographical Sketch of Irene McCoy Gaines," *Negro History Bulletin* [n.d.], scrapbook, IMGP.

37   "Citizens Pay Final Tribute," *New Crusader*, April 18, 1964, scrapbook, IMGP; "Mrs. Gaines Would Have Backed L. B. J.," *Chicago Defender*, October 10, 1964, 9.

Bibliography

Manuscripts

Chicago, Illinois
    Chicago Historical Society
        Claude A. Barnett Papers
        Archibald James Carey Papers
        Flower and Coues Family Scrapbooks
        Grace Presbyterian Church Records
        Illinois League of Women Voters Papers
        Irene McCoy Gaines Papers
        Arthur W. Mitchell Papers
    Cook County Bureau of Vital Statistics
        Death Certificates
    University of Chicago Library, Special Collections Research Center
        Charles E. Merriam Papers
        Ida B. Wells Papers
    University of Illinois at Chicago, Special Collections
        League of Women Voters of Chicago Papers
    Carter G. Woodson Regional Public Library, Vivian G. Harsh Research Collection of
        Afro-American History and Literature
        Illinois Writers Project: "Negro in Illinois" Papers
Evanston, Illinois
    Frances E. Willard Memorial Library and Archives
        Frances E. Willard/WCTU Scrapbook Collection
Frankfort, Kentucky
    Kentucky Historical Society
        Vertical Surname Files
Hyde Park, New York
    Franklin D. Roosevelt Library
        Women's Division of the Democratic National Committee Papers, 1933–1944
Newark, Delaware
    University of Delaware Library, Special Collections
        Alice Dunbar-Nelson Papers

New York, New York
    Schomburg Center for Research in Black Culture, New York Public Library
        Bessye B. Bearden Papers
        Herbert L. Bruce Papers
Salisbury, North Carolina
    Noble-Kelsey Funeral Home
Urbana-Champaign, Illinois
    University of Illinois at Urbana-Champaign
        University Archives
Washington, D.C.
    Manuscript Division, Library of Congress
        Nannie Helen Burroughs Papers
        Hanna-McCormick Family Papers
        Charles Evans Hughes Papers
        Mary Church Terrell Papers
    Moorland-Spingarn Research Center, Howard University
        Jeannette Carter Papers
        Mary Church Terrell Papers
West Branch, Iowa
    Herbert Hoover Presidential Library
        Misrepresentations: Chronological File Series
        Pre-Presidential Papers
        Presidential Papers
Wilberforce, Ohio
    Hallie Q. Brown Memorial Library, Central State University
        Hallie Q. Brown Papers

Collections on Microfilm

Jefferson County, Kentucky, Circuit Court Records, 1902.
Jefferson County, Kentucky, Marriage Bonds (African American), 1894–97.
Jefferson County, Kentucky, Index to Deaths, 1900–1911.
Jefferson County, Kentucky, Register of Deaths, Book 11, 1900–1902.
Jefferson County, Kentucky, Marriage Bond Book (African American), 1898–99.
Lincoln County, Kentucky, Deed Book 11, 1878.
Lincoln County, Kentucky, Deed Book 14, 1881.
Lincoln County, Kentucky, Tax Lists, 1867–69.
Lincoln County, Kentucky, Tax Lists, 1870–75.
Records of the National Association of Colored Women's Clubs, 1895–1992, Part 1: Minutes of National Conventions, Publications, and President's Office Correspondence. Edited by Lillian Serece Williams and Randolph Boehm. Bethesda, Md.: University Publications of America. Microfilm.

Rowan County, North Carolina, Record of Deeds, 1878.

Temperance and Prohibition Papers: A Joint Microfilm Publication of the Ohio Historical Society, Michigan Historical Collections, and the Woman's Christian Temperance Union. Edited by Francis X. Blouin Jr. Columbus: Ohio Historical Society, 1977.

Newspapers and Periodicals

Afro-American Ledger (Baltimore)
AME Church Review (Philadelphia)
AME Zion Quarterly Review (Charlotte)
Broad Ax (Chicago)
Central South Sider (Chicago)
Champion Magazine (Chicago)
Charities and the Commons
Charlotte Democrat
Charlotte Observer
Chicago Bee
Chicago Defender
Chicago Enterprise
Chicago Times
Chicago Tribune
Chicago Whip
Chicago World
Christian Recorder (Philadelphia)
Colored American Magazine (Boston)
Competitor (Pittsburgh)
Conservator (Chicago)
Crisis (New York)
Enterprise (Omaha)
Fraternity
Harper's Weekly (New York)
Indianapolis Freeman
Inter Ocean (Chicago)
Lexington Morning Democrat
Lexington Morning Herald
Lexington Press-Transcript
Light and Heebie Jeebies (Chicago)
Messenger (New York)
National Notes
Negro World (New York)
New York Age
New York Times

New York Tribune
Norfolk Journal and Guide
Opportunity: A Journal of Negro Life (New York)
Southern Workman (Virginia)
The Voice (New York)
Washington Bee
Westminster Gazette
Woman's Era (Boston)

Government Documents

Congressional Record, 1922–30.
Guinn v. United States, 238 U.S. 347 (1915).
Bureau of the Census, *Slave Schedule*.
  Lincoln County, Kentucky, 1850, 1860.
Bureau of the Census, *United States Manuscript Census*.
  Alexander County, Illinois, 1930.
  Clarke County, Georgia, 1910.
  Cook County, Illinois, 1900, 1910, 1920, 1930.
  District of Columbia, 1920.
  Greenville County, South Carolina, 1900.
  Jefferson County, Illinois, 1920, 1930.
  Jefferson County, Kentucky, 1900.
  Kings County, New York, 1920.
  Lincoln County, Kentucky, 1850, 1860, 1870, 1880.
  Massac County, Illinois, 1930.
  Borough Manhattan, New York City, New York, 1920.
  Perry County, Illinois, 1930.
  Pulaski County, Illinois, 1930.
  Rowan County, North Carolina, 1880, 1900.
  Sangamon County, Illinois, 1930.
  St. Clair County, Illinois, 1930.
  Surry County, North Carolina, 1880.

City Directories

Caron's Directory of the City of Louisville. Louisville, Ky.: name of publisher varies, 1882–1915.
Chicago, Illinois, City Directories, title and publisher varies, 1902–30.

Published Records of the Presbyterian Church, USA

*Annual Report of the Presbyterian Board of Missions for Freedmen of the Presbyterian Church, in the
United States of America*, Pittsburgh: name of publisher varies, 1884–1912.

Minutes of the General Assembly of the Presbyterian Church in the United States of America. Name and place of publisher varies, 1876–92.

On-line Resources

Center for Population Economics, University of Chicago. <http://www.cpe.uchicago .edu/publichealth/gis_analysis.html>.

Historical Census Browser, University of Virginia, Geospatial and Statistical Data Center, 2004. <http://fisher.lib.virginia.edu/collections/stats/histcensus/index.html>.

<http://www.jimcrowhistory.org/>.

Sautter, R. Craig. "Political Conventions." In *Encyclopedia of Chicago.* Edited by James Grossman et al. Chicago Historical Society, Newberry Library, and Northwestern University, 2005. <http://www.encyclopedia.chicagohistory.org/>.

Williamson, Samuel H. "Five Ways to Compute the Relative Value of a U.S. Dollar Amount, 1790–2005." <MeasuringWorth.com, 2006>.

Books, Articles, Theses, and Papers

Andersen, Kristi. *After Suffrage: Women in Partisan and Electoral Politics before the New Deal.* Chicago: University of Chicago Press, 1996.

Anderson, James D. *The Education of Blacks in the South, 1860–1935.* Chapel Hill: University of North Carolina Press, 1988.

Anthony, Susan B., and Ida Husted Harper, eds. *History of Woman Suffrage.* Vol. 4, *1883– 1900.* 1902. Reprint, Salem, N.H.: Ayer Company, 1985.

Armfield, Felix. "Bullock, Carrie E. (d. 1961)." In *Black Women in America: An Historical Encyclopedia,* edited by Darlene Clark Hine, Elsa Barkley Brown, and Rosalyn Terborg-Penn, 189. Bloomington: Indiana University Press, 1993.

Asbury, Herbert. *The Great Illusion: An Informal History of Prohibition.* New York: Doubleday, 1950.

Ashbaugh, Carolyn. *Lucy Parsons: American Revolutionary.* Chicago: Charles H. Kerr, 1976.

Avary, Myrta Lockett. *Dixie after the War: An Exposition of Social Conditions Existing in the South, during the Twelve Years Succeeding the Fall of Richmond.* New York: Doubleday, Page, 1906.

Bader, Robert Smith. *Prohibition in Kansas: A History.* Lawrence: University Press of Kansas, 1986.

Bair, Barbara. "True Women, Real Men: Gender, Ideology, and Social Roles in the Garvey Movement." In *Gendered Domains: Rethinking Public and Private in Woman's History,* edited by Dorothy O. Helly and Susan M. Reverby, 154–66. Ithaca: Cornell University Press, 1992.

Baker, Paula. "The Domestication of Politics: Women and American Political Society, 1780–1920." *American Historical Review* 89 (June 1984): 66–91.

———. *The Moral Frameworks of Public Life: Gender, Politics, and the State in Rural New York, 1870– 1930.* New York: Oxford University Press, 1991.

Baldwin, Davarian L. *Chicago's New Negroes: Modernity, the Great Migration, and Black Urban Life*. Chapel Hill: University of North Carolina Press, 2007.

Barr, Alwyn. *Reconstruction to Reform: Texas Politics, 1876–1906*. Austin: University of Texas Press, 1971.

Barrows, Susanna, and Robin Room, eds. *Drinking: Behavior and Belief in Modern History*. Berkeley: University of California Press, 1991.

Bates, Beth Tompkins, *Pullman Porters and the Rise of Protest Politics in Black America, 1925–1945*. Chapel Hill: University of North Carolina Press, 2001.

Bederman, Gail. *Manliness and Civilization: A Cultural History of Gender and Race in the United States, 1880–1917*. Chicago: University of Chicago Press, 1995.

Beeton, Beverly. "How the West Was Won for Woman Suffrage." In *One Woman, One Vote: Rediscovering the Woman Suffrage Movement*, edited by Marjorie Spruill Wheeler, 99–116. Troutdale, Ore.: NewSage Press, 1995.

——. *Women Vote in the West: The Woman Suffrage Movement, 1869–1896*. New York: Garland Publishing, 1986.

Bernhard, Virginia, Betty Brandon, Elizabeth Fox-Genovese, Theda Perdue, and Elizabeth Hayes Turner, eds., *Hidden Histories of Women in the New South*. Columbia: University of Missouri Press, 1994.

Best, Wallace D. *Passionately Human, No Less Divine: Religion and Culture in Black Chicago, 1915–1952*. Princeton: Princeton University Press, 2005.

Blight, David W. *Race and Reunion: The Civil War in American Memory*. Cambridge, Mass.: Harvard University Press, 2001.

Bohlmann, Rachel Elizabeth. "Drunken Husbands, Drunken State: The Woman's Christian Temperance Union's Challenge to American Families and Public Communities in Chicago, 1874–1920." Ph.D. diss., University of Iowa, 2001.

Bordin, Ruth. *Woman and Temperance: The Quest for Power and Liberty, 1873–1900*. Philadelphia: Temple University Press, 1981.

Branham, Charles R. "The Transformation of Black Political Leadership in Chicago, 1864–1942." Ph.D. diss., University of Chicago, 1981.

Brown, Elsa Barkley. "To Catch the Vision of Freedom: Reconstructing Southern Black Women's Political History, 1865–1880." In *African American Women and the Vote, 1837–1965*, edited by Ann D. Gordon et al., 66–99. Amherst: University of Massachusetts Press, 1997.

——. "Womanist Consciousness: Maggie Lena Walker and the Independent Order of Saint Luke." In *The Womanist Reader*, edited by Layli Phillips, 173–92. New York: Routledge, 2006.

Brown, Tulia Kay. "The National Association of Colored Women, 1896–1920." Ph.D. diss., Emory University, 1978.

Brown, William E. "State Coöperation in Enforcement." *Annals of the American Academy of Political and Social Science* 163 (September 1932): 30–38.

Bukowski, Douglas. *Big Bill Thompson, Chicago, and the Politics of Image*. Urbana: University of Illinois Press, 1998.

Bullock, Henry Allen. *A History of Negro Education in the South: From 1619 to the Present.* Cambridge, Mass.: Harvard University Press, 1967.

Burkett, Randall K. *Black Redemption: Churchmen Speak for the Garvey Movement.* Philadelphia: Temple University Press, 1978.

Burkett, Randall K., and Richard Newman, eds. *Black Apostles: Afro-American Clergy Confront the Twentieth Century.* Boston: GK Hall, 1978.

Burner, David. "Election of 1924." In *History of American Presidential Elections, 1789–1968,* vol. 3, edited by Arthur M. Schlesinger Jr., 2459–90. New York: Chelsea House Publishers, 1971.

Callcott, Margaret Law. *The Negro in Maryland Politics.* Baltimore: Johns Hopkins University Press, 1969.

Carby, Hazel V. *Reconstructing Womanhood: The Emergence of the Afro-American Woman Novelist.* New York: Oxford University Press, 1987.

Cartwright, Joseph H. *The Triumph of Jim Crow: Tennessee Race Relations in the 1880s.* Knoxville: University of Tennessee Press, 1976.

Cashman, Sean Dennis. *America in the Gilded Age: From the Death of Lincoln to the Rise of Theodore Roosevelt.* 2nd ed. New York: New York University Press, 1998.

——. *Prohibition: The Lie of the Land.* New York: Free Press, 1981.

Cecelski, David S., and Timothy B. Tyson, eds. *Democracy Betrayed: The Wilmington Race Riot of 1898 and Its Legacy.* Chapel Hill: University of North Carolina Press, 1998.

Chicago Commission on Race Relations. *Negro in Chicago: A Study of Race Relations and a Race Riot.* Chicago: University of Chicago Press, 1922.

Clark, Norman H. *Deliver Us from Evil: An Interpretation of American Prohibition.* New York: W. W. Norton, 1976.

Collier-Thomas, Bettye. *Daughters of Thunder: Black Women Preachers and Their Sermons, 1850–1979.* San Francisco: Jossey-Bass, 1998.

Cooper, Anna Julia. *A Voice from the South.* In *The Voice of Anna Julia Cooper, including A Voice from the South and Other Essays, Papers, and Letters,* edited by Charles Lemert and Esme Bhan, 51–196. New York: Rowman and Littlefield, 1998.

Cott, Nancy F. "Across the Great Divide: Women in Politics before and after 1920." In *Women, Politics, and Change,* edited by Louise A. Tilly and Patricia Gurin, 153–76. New York: Russell Sage Foundation, 1990.

——. *The Grounding of Modern Feminism.* New Haven: Yale University Press, 1987.

Crofts, Daniel W. "The Black Response to the Blair Education Bill." *Journal of Southern History* 37, no. 1 (February 1971): 41–65.

Crowe, Charles. "Racial Violence and Social Reform—Origins of the Atlanta Riot of 1906." *Journal of Negro History* 53, no. 3 (July 1968): 234–56.

Dailey, Jane, Glenda Elizabeth Gilmore, and Bryant Simon, eds. *Jumpin' Jim Crow: Southern Politics from Civil War to Civil Rights.* Princeton: Princeton University Press, 2000.

Dance, Martha Short. *Peabody High School: A History of the First Negro Public High School in Virginia.* New York: Carlton Press, 1976.

Daniel, Pete. "Up from Slavery and Down to Peonage: The Alonzo Bailey Case." *Journal of American History* 57, no. 3 (December 1970): 654–70.

Daniel, Philip T. K. "A History of Discrimination against Black Students in Chicago Secondary Schools." *History of Education Quarterly* 20, no. 2 (Summer 1980): 147–62.

——. "A History of the Segregation-Discrimination Dilemma." *Phylon* 41, no. 2 (1980): 126–36.

Davis, Elizabeth Lindsay. *Lifting as They Climb*. 1933. Reprint, New York: G. K. Hall, 1996.

——. *The Story of the Illinois Federation of Colored Women's Clubs*. African American Women Writers, 1910–1940. Edited by Henry Louis Gates Jr. 1922. Reprint, New York: G. K. Hall, 1997.

Decosta-Willis, Miriam, ed. *The Memphis Diary of Ida B. Wells: An Intimate Portrait of the Activist as a Young Woman*. Boston: Beacon Press, 1995.

Department of the Interior, Bureau of Education. *Negro Education: A Study of the Private and Higher Schools for Colored People in the United States*. Vol. 2. Washington, D.C.: Government Printing Office, 1917.

Dinkin, Robert J. *Before Equal Suffrage: Women in Partisan Politics from Colonial Times to 1920*. Westport, Conn.: Greenwood Press, 1995.

Dobyns, Fletcher B. *The Amazing Story of Repeal: An Exposé of the Power of Propaganda*. Chicago: Willet, Clark, 1940.

Dodge, L. Mara. "Emanuel, Fannie Hagen." In *Women Building Chicago 1790–1990: A Biographical Dictionary*, edited by Rima Lunin Schultz and Adele Hast, 248–49. Bloomington: Indiana University Press, 2001.

Dodson, Jualynne E. *Engendering Church: Women, Power, and the AME Church*. Lanham, Md.: Rowman and Littlefield, 2002.

Drake, St. Clair. *Churches and Voluntary Associations in the Chicago Negro Community*. Chicago: Works Progress Administration, 1940.

Drake, St. Clair, and Horace R. Cayton. *Black Metropolis: A Study of Negro Life in a Northern City*. Rev. and enl. Chicago: University of Chicago Press, 1993.

DuBois, Ellen Carol. *Feminism and Suffrage: The Emergence of an Independent Women's Movement in America, 1848–1869*. Ithaca: Cornell University Press, 1978.

——. "Outgrowing the Compact of the Fathers: Equal Rights, Woman Suffrage, and the United States Constitution, 1820–1878." *Journal of American History* 74 (December 1987): 836–62.

——. "Taking the Law into Our Own Hands: Bradwell, Minor, and Suffrage Militance in the 1870s." In *Woman Suffrage and Women's Rights*, 114–38. New York: New York University Press, 1998.

DuBois, Ellen Carol, and Vicki Ruiz, eds. *Unequal Sisters: A Multi-cultural Reader in U.S. Women's History*. New York: Routledge, 1990.

Du Bois, W. E. B. *Black Reconstruction in America, 1860–1880*. 1935. Reprint, New York: Atheneum, 1992.

Duis, Perry R. *The Saloon: Public Drinking in Chicago and Boston, 1880–1920*. Urbana: University of Illinois Press, 1983.

Duster, Alfreda M. Barnett. Introduction to *Crusade for Justice: The Autobiography of Ida B. Wells*, edited by Alfreda M. Barnett Duster, xiii–xxxii. Chicago: University of Chicago Press, 1970.

Edmonds, Helen G. *The Negro and Fusion Politics in North Carolina, 1894–1901*. Chapel Hill: University of North Carolina Press, 1951.

Edwards, Rebecca. *Angels in the Machinery: Gender in American Party Politics from the Civil War to the Progressive Era*. New York: Oxford University Press, 1997.

Fish, Virginia Kemp. "Breckinridge, Sophonisba Preston." In *Women Building Chicago, 1790–1990: A Biographical Dictionary*, edited by Rima Lunin Schultz and Adele Hast, 114–16. Bloomington: Indiana University Press, 2001.

Fisher, Miles Mark. "Negro Churches in Illinois: A Fragmentary History with Emphasis on Chicago." *Journal of the Illinois State Historical Society* 56 (Fall 1963): 552–69.

Fite, Gilbert C. "Election of 1896." In *History of American Presidential Elections, 1789–1968*, vol. 2, edited by Arthur M. Schlesinger Jr., 1787–1825. New York: McGraw-Hill, 1971.

Flanagan, Maureen A. *Seeing with Their Hearts: Chicago Women and the Vision of the Good City, 1871–1933*. Princeton: Princeton University Press, 2002.

Flexner, Eleanor, and Ellen Fitzpatrick. *Century of Struggle: The Woman's Rights Movement in the United States*. Enl. ed. Cambridge, Mass.: Belknap Press, 1996.

Flug, Michael, comp. "Illinois Writers Project: 'Negro in Illinois' Papers, A Finding Aid to the Manuscript Collection." Chicago: Chicago Public Library, 1997.

Foner, Eric. *Reconstruction: America's Unfinished Revolution, 1863–1877*. New York: Harper and Row, 1988.

———. *A Short History of Reconstruction*. New York: Harper and Row, 1990.

Foner, Philip S. *American Socialism and Black Americans: From the Age of Jackson to World War II*. Westport, Conn.: Greenwood Press, 1977.

———, ed. *The Autobiographies of the Haymarket Martyrs*. New York: Humanities Press, 1969.

———. *History of the Labor Movement in the United States*. Vol. 2: *From the Founding of the American Federation of Labor to the Emergence of American Imperialism*. New York: International Publishers, 1955.

Foner, Philip S., and Ronald L. Lewis, eds. *The Black Worker: A Documentary History from Colonial Times to the Present*. Philadelphia: Temple University Press, 1989.

Foster, Frances Smith. "Harper, Frances Ellen Watkins (1825–1911)." In *Black Women in America: An Historical Encyclopedia*, edited by Darlene Clark Hine, Elsa Barkley Brown, and Rosalyn Terborg-Penn, 532–36. Bloomington: Indiana University Press, 1993.

Frankel, Noralee. *Freedom's Women: Black Women and Families in Civil War Era Mississippi*. Bloomington: Indiana University Press, 1999.

Franklin, Fabian. *What Prohibition Has Done to America*. New York: Harcourt, Brace, 1922.

Franklin, John Hope, and Alfred A. Moss Jr. *From Slavery to Freedom: A History of African Americans*. 7th ed. New York: McGraw-Hill, 1994.

Frazier, E. Franklin. *The Negro Church in America*. New York: Schocken Books, 1974.

Freeman, Jo. *A Room at a Time: How Women Entered Party Politics*. Lanham, Md.: Rowman and Littlefield, 2000.

Freidel, Frank. "Election of 1932." In *History of American Presidential Elections, 1789–1968*, vol. 3, edited by Arthur M. Schlesinger Jr., 2707–39. New York: Chelsea House Publishers, 1971.

Gaines, Irene McCoy. "The Negro Woman in Politics." In *The Negro in Chicago, 1779–1929*, vol. 2, edited by Frederic H. Robb, 88, 206. Chicago: Washington Intercollegiate Club of Chicago, 1929.

Gaines, Kevin K. *Uplifting the Race: Black Leadership, Politics, and Culture in the Twentieth Century*. Chapel Hill: University of North Carolina Press, 1996.

Gaither, Gerald H. *Blacks and the Populist Revolt: Ballots and Bigotry in the "New South."* University: University of Alabama Press, 1977.

Gertz, Gwynne. "Edwards, Thyra J." In *Women Building Chicago, 1790–1990: A Biographical Dictionary*, edited by Rima Lunin Schultz and Adele Hast, 244–47. Bloomington: Indiana University Press, 2001.

Gilman, Sander L. "Black Bodies, White Bodies: Toward an Iconography of Female Sexuality in Late Nineteenth-Century Art, Medicine, and Literature." In *"Race," Writing, and Difference*, edited by Henry Louis Gates Jr., 223–61. Chicago: University of Chicago Press, 1986.

Gilmore, Glenda Elizabeth. "False Friends and Avowed Enemies: Southern African Americans and Party Allegiances in the 1920s." In *Jumpin' Jim Crow: Southern Politics from Civil War to Civil Rights*, edited by Jane Dailey, Glenda Elizabeth Gilmore, and Byrant Simon, 219–38. Princeton: Princeton University Press, 2000.

———. *Gender and Jim Crow: Women and the Politics of White Supremacy in North Carolina, 1896–1920*. Chapel Hill: University of North Carolina Press, 1996.

———. "'A Melting Time': Black Women, White Women, and the WCTU in North Carolina, 1880–1900." In *Hidden Histories of Women in the New South*, edited by Virginia Bernhard, Betty Brandon, Elizabeth Fox-Genovese, Theda Perdue, and Elizabeth Hayes Turner, 153–72. Columbia: University of Missouri Press, 1994.

———. "Pettey, Sarah E. C. Dudley (1869–1906)." In *Black Women in America: An Historical Encyclopedia*, edited by Darlene Clark Hine, Elsa Barkley Brown, and Rosalyn Terborg-Penn, 918. Bloomington: Indiana University Press, 1993.

Goldstein, Joel H. *The Effects of the Adoption of Woman Suffrage: Sex Differences in Voting Behavior—Illinois, 1914–1921*. New York: Praeger, 1984.

Goodwin, Joanne L. *Gender and the Politics of Welfare Reform: Mothers' Pensions in Chicago, 1911–1929*. Chicago: University of Chicago Press, 1997.

Gordon, Ann D., ed. *The Selected Papers of Elizabeth Cady Stanton and Susan B. Anthony*. Vol. 2, *Against an Aristocracy of Sex, 1866 to 1873*. New Brunswick, N.J.: Rutgers University Press, 2000.

Gordon, Ann D., et al., eds. *African American Women and the Vote, 1837–1965*. Amherst: University of Massachusetts Press, 1997.

Gordon, Felice. *After Winning: The Legacy of the New Jersey Suffragists, 1930–1947*. New Brunswick, N.J.: Rutgers University Press, 1986.

Gordon, Fon Louise. *Caste and Class: The Black Experience in Arkansas, 1880–1920.* Athens: University of Georgia Press, 1995.

Gordon, Linda. *Pitied but Not Entitled: Single Mothers and the History of Welfare.* New York: Free Press, 1994.

——, ed. *Women, the State, and Welfare.* Madison: University of Wisconsin Press, 1990.

Gosnell, Harold F. "The Chicago 'Black Belt' as a Political Battleground." *American Journal of Sociology* 39, no. 3 (November 1933): 329–41.

——. "How Negroes Vote in Chicago." *National Municipal Review* 22, no. 5 (May 1933): 238–43.

——. *Negro Politicians: The Rise of Negro Politics in Chicago.* 1935. Reprint, Chicago: University of Chicago Press, 1967.

Green, Elna C. *Southern Strategies: Southern Women and the Woman Suffrage Question.* Chapel Hill: University of North Carolina Press, 1997.

Greene, Jerome D. "The Personal Problem." *Atlantic Monthly* 138 (July–December 1926): 525–28.

Greenwood, Janette Thomas. *Bittersweet Legacy: The Black and White "Better Classes" in Charlotte, 1850–1910.* Chapel Hill: University of North Carolina Press, 1994.

Gregory, James N. *The Southern Diaspora: How the Great Migrations of Black and White Southerners Transformed America.* Chapel Hill: University of North Carolina Press, 2005.

Grossman, James R. *Land of Hope: Chicago, Black Southerners, and the Great Migration.* Chicago: University of Chicago Press, 1989.

Gustafson, Melanie Susan. "Partisan Women: Gender, Politics, and the Progressive Party of 1912." Ph.D. diss., New York University, 1993.

——. *Women and the Republican Party, 1854–1924.* Urbana: University of Illinois Press, 2001.

Gustafson, Melanie Susan, Kristie Miller, and Elisabeth Israels Perry, eds. *We Have Come to Stay: American Women and Political Parties, 1880–1960.* Albuquerque: University of New Mexico Press, 1999.

Guy-Sheftall, Beverly. *Daughters of Sorrow: Attitudes toward Black Women, 1880–1920.* Brooklyn: Carlson, 1990.

Hadley, Arthur Twining. "Law Making and Law Enforcement." *Harper's Magazine* 151 (November 1925): 641–48.

Hall, Clyde W. *Black Vocational, Technical, and Industrial Arts Education: Development and History.* Chicago: American Technical Society, 1973.

Haller, Mark H. "Policy Gambling, Entertainment, and the Emergence of Black Politics: Chicago from 1900 to 1940." *Journal of Social History* 24, no. 4 (Summer 1991): 719–39.

Hamm, Richard F. *Shaping the Eighteenth Amendment: Temperance Reform, Legal Culture, and the Polity, 1880–1920.* Chapel Hill: University of North Carolina Press, 1995.

Hanson, Joyce Ann. *Mary McLeod Bethune and Black Women's Political Activism.* Columbia: University of Missouri Press, 2003.

Harbaugh, William. *Lawyer's Lawyer: The Life of John W. Davis.* New York: Oxford University Press, 1973.

Harlan, Louis R., and Raymond W. Smock, eds. *The Booker T. Washington Papers*. Vol. 2, *1911–12*. Urbana: University of Illinois Press, 1981.

Harper, Frances Watkins. "Work among Colored People." *Minutes of the NWCTU at the Seventeenth Annual Meeting, Atlanta, Georgia, November 14–18, 1890*, 213–21.

Harris, Adlean. "Davis, Elizabeth Lindsay." In *Women Building Chicago, 1790–1990: A Biographical Dictionary*, edited by Rima Lunin Schultz and Adele Hast, 212–13. Bloomington: Indiana University Press, 2001.

Helly, Dorothy O., and Susan M. Reverby, eds. *Gendered Domains: Rethinking Public and Private in Women's History*. Ithaca: Cornell University Press, 1992.

Hendricks, Wanda A. "Davis, Elizabeth Lindsay." In *Black Women in America: An Historical Encyclopedia*, edited by Darlene Clark Hine, Elsa Barkley Brown, and Rosalyn Terborg-Penn, 306–7. Bloomington: Indiana University Press, 1993.

——. *Gender, Race, and Politics in the Midwest: Black Club Women in Illinois*. Bloomington: Indiana University Press, 1998.

Herd, Denise A. "The Paradox of Temperance: Blacks and the Alcohol Question in Nineteenth-Century America." In *Drinking: Behavior and Belief in Modern History*, edited by Susanna Barrows and Robin Room, 354–75. Berkeley: University of California Press, 1991.

——. "Prohibition, Racism and Class Politics in the Post-Reconstruction South." *Journal of Drug Issues* 13, no. 1 (Winter 1983): 77–94.

Hewitt, Nancy A., and Suzanne Lebsock, eds. *Visible Women: New Essays on American Activism*. Urbana: University of Illinois Press, 1993.

Hicks, John D. *Republican Ascendancy: 1921–1933*. New York: Harper and Row, 1960.

Higginbotham, Evelyn Brooks. "African-American Women's History and the Metalanguage of Race." *Signs: Journal of Women in Culture and Society* 17 (December 1992): 251–74.

——. "Burroughs, Nannie Helen (1879–1961)." In *Black Women in America: An Historical Encyclopedia*, edited by Darlene Clark Hine, Elsa Barkley Brown, and Rosalyn Terborg-Penn, 202. Bloomington: Indiana University Press, 1993.

——. "In Politics to Stay." In *Women, Politics, and Change*, edited by Louise A. Tilly and Patricia Gurin, 199–220. New York: Russell Sage Foundation, 1990.

——. *Righteous Discontent: The Women's Movement in the Black Baptist Church, 1880–1920*. Cambridge, Mass.: Harvard University Press, 1993.

Hine, Darlene Clark. "Black Migration to the Urban Midwest: The Gender Dimension, 1915–1945." In *The Great Migration in Historical Perspective: New Dimensions of Race, Class, and Gender*, edited by Joe William Trotter Jr., 127–46. Bloomington: Indiana University Press, 1991.

——. *Black Victory: The Rise and Fall of the White Primary in Texas*. Columbia: University of Missouri Press, 2003.

——. "Rape and the Inner Lives of Black Women in the Middle West: Preliminary Thoughts on the Culture of Dissemblance." In *Unequal Sisters: A Multi-cultural Reader in U.S. Women's History*, edited by Ellen Carol DuBois and Vicki Ruiz, 292–97. New York: Routledge, 1990.

Hine, Darlene Clark, Elsa Barkley Brown, and Rosalyn Terborg-Penn, eds. *Black Women in America: An Historical Encyclopedia*. Bloomington: Indiana University Press, 1993.

Holmes, Dwight Oliver Wendell. *The Evolution of the Negro College*. College Park, Md.: McGrath, 1934.

Holt, Thomas. *Black over White: Negro Political Leadership in South Carolina during Reconstruction*. Urbana: University of Illinois Press, 1979.

Honey, Michael. "Class, Race, and Power in the New South: Racial Violence and the Delusions of White Supremacy." In *Democracy Betrayed: The Wilmington Race Riot of 1898 and Its Legacy*, edited by David S. Cecelski and Timothy B. Tyson, 163–84. Chapel Hill: University of North Carolina Press, 1998.

Hull, Gloria T. "Dunbar-Nelson, Alice Ruth Moore (1875–1935)." In *Black Women in America: An Historical Encyclopedia*, edited by Darlene Clark Hine, Elsa Barkley Brown, and Rosalyn Terborg-Penn, 359–62. Bloomington: Indiana University Press, 1993.

——, ed. *The Works of Alice Dunbar Nelson*. Vol. 1. New York: Oxford University Press, 1988.

Hume, Richard L. "Negro Delegates to the State Constitutional Conventions of 1867–69." In *Southern Black Leaders of the Reconstruction Era*, edited by Howard N. Rabinowitz, 129–53. Chicago: University of Illinois Press, 1982.

Hutchinson, Louise Daniel. "Cooper, Anna Julia Haywood (1858–1964)." In *Black Women in America: An Historical Encyclopedia*, edited by Darlene Clark Hine, Elsa Barkley Brown, and Rosalyn Terborg-Penn, 275–81. Bloomington: Indiana University Press, 1993.

Hutson, Jean B. "Bearden, Bessye (c. 1891–1943)." In *Black Women in America: An Historical Encyclopedia*, edited by Darlene Clark Hine, Elsa Barkley Brown, and Rosalyn Terborg-Penn, 97–98. Bloomington: Indiana University Press, 1993.

Isaac, Paul E. *Prohibition and Politics: Turbulent Decades in Tennessee, 1885–1920*. Knoxville: University of Tennessee Press, 1965.

Ivy, James D. *No Saloon in the Valley: The Southern Strategy of the Texas Prohibitionists in the 1880s*. Waco: Baylor University Press, 2003.

Jerrido, Margaret. "Brown, Lucy Hughes (1863–1911)." In *Black Women in America: An Historical Encyclopedia*, edited by Darlene Clark Hine, Elsa Barkley Brown, and Rosalyn Terborg-Penn, 182. Bloomington: Indiana University Press, 1993.

Johnson, Catherine. "Early, Sarah Jane Woodson (1825–1907)." In *Black Women in America: An Historical Encyclopedia*, edited by Darlene Clark Hine, Elsa Barkley Brown, and Rosalyn Terborg-Penn, 377. Bloomington: Indiana University Press, 1993.

Johnson-Odium, Cheryl. "Gaines, Irene McCoy." In *Women Building Chicago, 1790–1990: A Biographical Dictionary*, edited by Rima Lunin Schultz and Adele Hast, 294–96. Bloomington: Indiana University Press, 2001.

Johnston, Henry Alan. *What Rights Are Left*. New York: Macmillan, 1930.

Jones, Martha S. *All Bound Up Together: The Woman Question in African American Public Culture, 1830–1900*. Chapel Hill: University of North Carolina Press, 2007.

——. "The 'Woman Question' in African-American Public Culture, 1830–1900." Ph.D. diss., Columbia University, 2001.

Journal of the Proceedings of the Constitutional Convention of the State of Mississippi Begun at the City of Jackson on August 12, 1890, and Concluded November 1, 1890. Jackson, Miss.: E. L. Martin, 1890.

Kelley, Robin D. G., "Parsons, Lucy (1853–1942)." In *Black Women in America: An Historical Encyclopedia*, edited by Darlene Clark Hine, Elsa Barkley Brown, and Rosalyn Terborg-Penn, 909–10. Bloomington: Indiana University Press, 1993.

Kenney, William Howland. *Chicago Jazz: A Cultural History, 1904–1930.* New York: Oxford, 1993.

Kerr, K. Austin. *Organized for Prohibition: A New History of the Anti-Saloon League.* New Haven: Yale University Press, 1985.

Keyssar, Alexander. *The Right to Vote: The Contested History of Democracy in the United States.* New York: Basic Books, 2000.

Kleber, John E., ed. *The Kentucky Encyclopedia.* Lexington: University Press of Kentucky, 1992.

Knott, Claudia. "The Woman Suffrage Movement in Kentucky, 1879–1920." Ph.D. diss., University of Kentucky, 1989.

Knupfer, Anne Meis. *Toward a Tenderer Humanity and a Nobler Womanhood: African American Women's Clubs in Turn-of-the-Century Chicago.* New York: New York University Press, 1996.

Kousser, J. Morgan. *The Shaping of Southern Politics: Suffrage Restriction and the Establishment of the One-Party South, 1880–1910.* New Haven: Yale University Press, 1974.

Kraditor, Aileen S. *The Ideas of the Woman Suffrage Movement, 1890–1920.* New York: W. W. Norton, 1981.

Kyvig, David E. *Repealing National Prohibition.* Chicago: University of Chicago Press, 1979.

Ladd, Everett Carll. "Participation in American Elections." In *Voting and the Spirit of American Democracy: Essays on the History of Voting and Voting Rights in America*, edited by Donald W. Rogers, in collaboration with Christine Scriabine, 109–16. Urbana: University of Illinois Press, 1992.

Lampkin, Catheryn Elaine. "McKinley, Ada Sophia Dennison." In *Women Building Chicago, 1790–1990: A Biographical Dictionary*, edited by Rima Lunin Schultz and Adele Hast, 571–73. Bloomington: Indiana University Press, 2001.

Leach, Alan R. "Lincoln County." In *The Kentucky Encyclopedia*, edited by John E. Kleber, 557–58. Lexington: University Press of Kentucky, 1992.

Lebsock, Suzanne. "Woman Suffrage and White Supremacy: A Virginia Case Study." In *Visible Women: New Essays on American Activism*, edited by Nancy A. Hewitt and Suzanne Lebsock, 62–100. Urbana: University of Illinois Press, 1993.

Lemert, Charles. "Anna Julia Cooper: The Colored Woman's Office." In *The Voice of Anna Julia Cooper, including A Voice from the South and Other Essays, Papers, and Letters*, edited by Charles Lemert and Esme Bhan, 1–43. New York: Rowman and Littlefield, 1998.

Lerner, Gerda, ed. *Black Women in White America: A Documentary History.* New York: Pantheon Books, 1972.

Lewis, David Levering. *The Fight for Equality and the American Century, 1919–1963.* New York: Henry Holt, 2000.

Lincoln, Eric C., and Lawrence H. Mamiya. *The Black Church in the African American Experience*. Durham: Duke University Press, 1990.

Link, Arthur S., and William M. Leary Jr. "Election of 1916." In *History of American Presidential Elections, 1789–1968*, vol. 3, edited by Arthur M. Schlesinger Jr., 2245–70. New York: Chelsea House Publishers, 1971.

Litwack, Leon F. *Trouble in Mind: Black Southerners in the Age of Jim Crow*. New York: Vintage Books, 1999.

Lofgren, Charles A. *The Plessy Case: A Legal-Historical Interpretation*. New York: Oxford University Press, 1987.

Logan, Frenise A. *The Negro in North Carolina, 1876–1894*. Chapel Hill: University of North Carolina Press, 1964.

Logan, Rayford W. *The Betrayal of the Negro: From Rutherford B. Hayes to Woodrow Wilson*. New York: Macmillan, 1965.

Lucas, Marion B. *A History of Blacks in Kentucky*. Vol. 1, *From Slavery to Segregation, 1760–1891*. Frankfort: Kentucky Historical Society, 1992.

Mack, Kenneth W. "Law, Society, Identity, and the Making of the Jim Crow South: Travel and Segregation on Tennessee Railroads, 1875–1905." *Law and Social Inquiry* 24, no. 2 (Summer 1984): 521–57.

Macmahon, Arthur W. "First Session of the Seventy-First Congress." *American Political Science Review* 24, no. 1 (February 1930): 38–59.

Majors, Monroe A. *Noted Negro Women: Their Triumphs and Activities*. 1893. Reprint, Freeport, N.Y.: Books for Libraries Press, 1971.

Mansbridge, Jane J. *Why We Lost the ERA*. Chicago: University of Chicago Press, 1986.

Margo, Robert A. "Race Differences in Public School Expenditures." In *African Americans and Education in the South, 1865–1900*, edited by Donald G. Nieman, 203–27. New York: Garland, 1994.

Massa, Ann. "Black Women in the 'White City.'" *Journal of American Studies* (8 December 1974): 319–37.

McCormick, Richard L. *The Party Period and Public Policy: American Politics from the Age of Jackson to the Progressive Era*. New York: Oxford University Press, 1986.

McCoy, Donald R. "Election of 1920." In *History of American Presidential Elections, 1789–1968*, vol. 3, edited by Arthur M. Schlesinger Jr., 2349–85. New York: Chelsea House Publishers, 1971.

McDermott, Stacy Pratt. "An Outrageous Proceeding': A Northern Lynching and the Enforcement of Anti-Lynching Legislation in Illinois, 1905–1910." *Journal of Negro History* 84, no. 1 (Winter 1999): 61–78.

McGerr, Michael. *The Decline of Popular Politics: The American North, 1865–1928*. New York: Oxford University Press, 1986.

———. "Political Style and Women's Power, 1830–1930." *Journal of American History* 77 (December 1990): 864–85.

McKinney, Gordon B. *Zeb Vance: North Carolina's Civil War Governor and Gilded Age Political Leader*. Chapel Hill: University of North Carolina Press, 2004.

McMath, Robert C., Jr. *American Populism: A Social History, 1877–1898*. New York: Hill and Wang, 1993.

McMillen, Neal. *Dark Journey: Black Mississippians in the Age of Jim Crow*. Chicago: University of Illinois Press, 1989.

Mead, Rebecca Joyce. *How the Vote Was Won: Woman Suffrage in the Western United States, 1868–1914*. New York: New York University Press, 2004.

Meier, August. "The Negro and the Democratic Party, 1875–1915." *Phylon* 17, no. 2 (1956): 173–91.

Merriam, Charles Edward, and Harold Foote Gosnell. *Non-Voting: Causes and Methods of Control*. Chicago: Chicago University Press, 1924.

Merz, Charles B. *The Dry Decade*. Garden City, N.Y.: Doubleday, Doran, 1931.

Meyerowitz, Joanne J. *Women Adrift: Independent Wage Earners in Chicago, 1880–1930*. Chicago: University of Chicago Press, 1988.

Miller, Kristie. *Ruth Hanna McCormick: A Life in Politics, 1880–1944*. Albuquerque: University of New Mexico Press, 1992.

Minutes of the NWCTU at the Seventeenth Annual Meeting, Atlanta Georgia, November 14–18, 1890. Chicago: Woman's Temperance Publishing Association, 1890.

Mitchell, Michele. *Righteous Propagation: African Americans and the Politics of Racial Destiny after Reconstruction*. Chapel Hill: University of North Carolina Press, 2004.

Moneyhon, Carl H. *Arkansas and the New South, 1874–1929*. Fayetteville: University of Arkansas Press, 1997.

Montgomery, William E. *Under Their Own Vine and Fig Tree: The African American Church in the South, 1865–1900*. Baton Rouge: Louisiana State University Press, 1993.

Morton, Patricia. *Disfigured Images: The Historical Assault of Afro-American Women*. New York: Greenwood Press, 1991.

Mumford, Kevin J. *Interzones: Black / White Sex Districts in Chicago and New York in the Early Twentieth Century*. New York: Columbia University Press, 1997.

Neverdon-Morton, Cynthia. *Afro-American Women of the South and the Advancement of the Race, 1895–1925*. Knoxville: University of Tennessee Press, 1989.

Niswonger, Richard L. *Arkansas Democratic Politics, 1896–1920*. Fayetteville: University of Arkansas Press, 1990.

Nord, Paul David. *Newspapers and New Politics: Midwestern Municipal Reform, 1890–1900*. Studies in American History and Culture, no. 27. Ann Arbor, Mich.: UMI Research Press, 1981.

O'Connor, Richard. *The First Hurrah: A Biography of Alfred E. Smith*. New York: G. P. Putnam's Sons, 1970.

O'Neal, Max. "The 1907 Georgia Prohibition Act." M.A. thesis, Georgia Southern College, 1974.

Osofsky, Gilbert. *Harlem: The Making of a Ghetto; Negro New York, 1890–1930*. New York: Harper and Row, 1963.

Painter, Nell Irvin. *Exodusters: Black Migration to Kansas after Reconstruction*. New York: W. W. Norton, 1986.

——. *Sojourner Truth: A Life, a Symbol.* New York: W. W. Norton, 1996.

Paris, Peter J. *The Social Teaching of the Black Churches.* Philadelphia: Fortress Press, 1985.

Parker, Alison. "Frances Watkins Harper's Federal Legislative Reform Agenda." Paper presented at the Berkshire Conference of Women Historians, Claremont, California, June 5, 2005.

Parker, Inez Moore. *The Rise and Decline of the Program of Education for Black Presbyterians of the United Presbyterian Church U.S.A., 1865–1970.* San Antonio: Trinity University Press, 1977.

Patton, June O. "Williams, Fannie Barrier." In *Women Building Chicago, 1790–1990: A Biographical Dictionary*, edited by Rima Lunin Schultz and Adele Hast, 977–79. Bloomington: Indiana University Press, 2001.

Pegram, Thomas. *Battling Demon Rum: The Struggle for a Dry America, 1800–1933.* Chicago: Ivan R. Dee, 1998.

——. *Partisans and Progressives: Private Interest and Public Policy in Illinois, 1870–1922.* Urbana: University of Illinois Press, 1992.

Perkins, Linda. "Black Women and Racial 'Uplift' Prior to Emancipation." In *Black Women Cross-Culturally*, edited by Filomina Chioma Steady, 317–34. Cambridge: Schenkman Publishing, 1981.

Perman, Michael. *Struggle for Mastery: Disfranchisement in the South, 1888–1908.* Chapel Hill: University of North Carolina Press, 2001.

Phillips, Kimberly L. *AlabamaNorth: African-American Migrants, Community, and Working-Class Activism in Cleveland, 1915–1945.* Urbana: University of Illinois Press, 1999.

Phillips, Layli, ed. *The Womanist Reader.* New York: Routledge, 2006.

——. "Womanism: On Its Own." In *The Womanist Reader*, edited by Layli Phillips, xix–lv. New York: Routledge, 2006.

Philpott, Thomas Lee. *The Slum and the Ghetto: Neighborhood Deterioration and Middle-Class Reform, Chicago, 1880–1930.* New York: Oxford University Press, 1978.

Pierce, James. *Photographic History of the World's Fair and Sketch of the City of Chicago, Also a Guide to the World's Fair and Chicago.* Baltimore: R. H. Woodward, 1893.

Prather, H. Leon, Sr. *We Have Taken a City: Wilmington Racial Massacre and Coup of 1898.* Cranbury, N.J.: Associated University Presses, 1984.

Raboteau, Albert J. *Slave Religion: The 'Invisible Institution' in the Antebellum South.* New York: Oxford University Press, 1978.

Reckless, Walter C. *Vice in Chicago.* 1933. Reprint, Montclair, N.J.: Patterson Smith, 1969.

Renda, Mary A. *Taking Haiti: Military Occupation and the Culture of U.S. Imperialism, 1915–1940.* Chapel Hill: University of North Carolina Press, 2001.

Republican National Committee. *Republican Campaign Text-Book, 1900.* Philadelphia: Dunlap Printing Company, 1900.

——. *Republican Campaign Text-Book, 1920.* New York: Republican National Committee, 1920.

——. *Republican Campaign Text-Book, 1924.* Chicago: Republican National Committee, 1924.

——. *Republican Campaign Text-Book, 1928*. Chicago: Republican National Committee, 1928.

——. *Text-Book of the Republican Party, 1932*. Chicago: Republican National Committee, 1932.

——. *Text-Book of the Republican Party, 1936*. Chicago: Republican National Committee, 1936.

Richardson, Marilyn, ed. *Maria W. Stewart, America's First Black Woman Political Writer: Essays and Speeches*. Bloomington: Indiana University Press, 1987.

Robb, Frederic H., ed. *The Negro in Chicago*. Vol. 1, *1779–1927*. Chicago: Washington Intercollegiate Club of Chicago, 1927.

——, ed. *The Negro in Chicago*. Vol. 2, *1779–1929*. Chicago: Washington Intercollegiate Club of Chicago, 1929.

Rolinson, Mary G. *Grassroots Garveyism: The Universal Negro Improvement Association in the Rural South, 1920–1927*. Chapel Hill: University of North Carolina Press, 2007.

Rose, Kenneth D. *American Women and the Repeal of Prohibition*. New York: New York University Press, 1996.

Rosenburg, R. B. Review of *Stonewall Jim: A Biography of General James A. Walker, C.S.A.*, by Willie Walker Caldwell. *Journal of Southern History* 58, no. 4 (1992): 731–32.

Ryan, Mary P. *Women in Public: Between Banners and Ballots, 1825–1880*. Baltimore: Johns Hopkins University Press, 1990.

Rycraft, Joan R. "Abbott, Edith." In *Women Building Chicago, 1790–1990: A Biographical Dictionary*, edited by Rima Lunin Schultz and Adele Hast, 3–6. Bloomington: Indiana University Press, 2001.

Rydell, Robert W. *All the World's a Fair*. Chicago: University of Chicago Press, 1984.

Rymph, Catherine E. *Republican Women: Feminism and Conservatism from Suffrage through the Rise of the New Right*. Chapel Hill: University of North Carolina Press, 2006.

Salem, Dorothy. "National Association of Colored Women." In *Black Women in America: An Historical Encyclopedia*, edited by Darlene Clark Hine, Elsa Barkley Brown, and Rosalyn Terborg-Penn, 845. Bloomington: Indiana University Press, 1993.

Saville, Julie. *The Work of Reconstruction: From Slave to Wage Laborer in South Carolina, 1860–1870*. New York: Cambridge University Press, 1994.

Sawyer, Albert E. "The Enforcement of National Prohibition." *Annals of the American Academy of Political and Social Science* 163 (September 1932): 10–29.

Schechter, Patricia A. *Ida B. Wells-Barnett and American Reform, 1880–1930*. Chapel Hill: University of North Carolina Press, 2001.

——. "Temperance Work in the Nineteenth Century." In *Black Women in America: An Historical Encyclopedia*, edited by Darlene Clark Hine, Elsa Barkley Brown, and Rosalyn Terborg-Penn, 1154–56. Bloomington: Indiana University Press, 1993.

Schlesinger, Arthur M., Jr., ed. *History of American Presidential Elections, 1789–1968*. Vols. 2 and 3. New York: Chelsea House Publishers, 1971.

Schultz, Rima Lunin, and Adele Hast, eds. *Women Building Chicago, 1790–1990: A Biographical Dictionary*. Bloomington: Indiana University Press, 2001.

Schuyler, Lorraine Gates. *The Weight of Their Votes: Southern Women and Political Leverage in the 1920s*. North Carolina: University of North Carolina Press, 2006.

Scott, Emmett J., comp. "Additional Letters of Negro Migrants of 1916–1918." *Journal of Negro History* 4 (October 1919): 412–65.

Sernett, Milton C. *Bound for the Promised Land: African American Religion and the Great Migration*. Durham: Duke University Press, 1997.

Seymour, Mary Jane. *Lineage Book National Society of the Daughters of the American Revolution*. Vol. 11. Harrisburg, Pa.: Press of Harrisburg Publishing Company, 1900.

Shaw, Barton C. *The Wool-Hat Boys: Georgia's Populist Party*. Baton Rouge: Louisiana State University Press, 1984.

Sherman, Richard B. *The Republican Party and Black America: From McKinley to Hoover, 1896–1933*. Charlottesville: University Press of Virginia, 1973.

Silber, Irwin, ed. *Songs of the Civil War*. New York: Columbia University Press, 1960.

Silbey, Joel H. *The American Political Nation, 1838–1893*. Stanford, Calif.: Stanford University Press, 1991.

Sitkoff, Harvard. *A New Deal for Blacks: The Emergence of Civil Rights as a National Issue: The Depression Decade*. New York: Oxford University Press, 1978.

Skocpol, Theda, Ariane Liazos, and Marshall Ganz. *What a Mighty Power We Can Be: African American Fraternal Groups and the Struggle for Racial Equality*. Princeton: Princeton University Press, 2006.

Smith, Elaine M. "Bethune, Mary McLeod (1875–1966)." In *Black Women in America: An Historical Encyclopedia*, edited by Darlene Clark Hine, Elsa Barkley Brown, and Rosalyn Terborg-Penn, 113–27. Bloomington: Indiana University Press, 1993.

———. "Scotia Seminary." In *Black Women in America: An Historical Encyclopedia*, edited by Darlene Clark Hine, Elsa Barkley Brown, and Rosalyn Terborg-Penn, 1016–18. Bloomington: Indiana University Press, 1993.

Smith, J. Clay, Jr. *Emancipation: The Making of the Black Lawyer, 1844–1944*. Philadelphia: University of Pennsylvania Press, 1999.

Sneider, Allison Lee. "Reconstruction, Expansion, and Empire: The U.S. Woman Suffrage Movement and the Re-making of National Political Community, 1870–1900." Ph.D. diss., University of California at Los Angeles, 1999.

———. *Suffragists in an Imperial Age: US Expansion and the Woman Question, 1870–1929*. New York: Oxford University Press, 2008.

Spear, Allan H. *Black Chicago: The Making of a Negro Ghetto, 1890–1920*. Chicago: University of Chicago Press, 1967.

Stampp, Kenneth M. *The Era of Reconstruction, 1865–1877*. New York: Alfred A. Knopf, 1965.

Stanton, Elizabeth Cady, Susan B. Anthony, and Matilda Joslyn Gage, eds. *History of Woman Suffrage*. Vol. 1, *1848–1861*. 1881. Reprint, New York: Arno and the New York Times, 1969.

———. *History of Woman Suffrage*. Vol. 2, *1861–1876*. 1882. Reprint, New York: Arno and the New York Times, 1969.

Sterling, Dorothy, ed. *The Trouble They Seen: Black People Tell the Story of Reconstruction.* Garden City, N.Y.: Doubleday, 1976.

———, ed. *We Are Your Sisters: Black Women in the Nineteenth Century.* New York: W. W. Norton, 1984.

Stewart, Maria. "Lecture Delivered at the Franklin Hall, Boston, September 21, 1892." In *Maria W. Stewart, America's First Black Woman Political Writer: Essays and Speeches,* edited and introduced by Marilyn Richardson, 45–49. Bloomington: Indiana University Press, 1987.

———. "Religion and the Pure Principles of Morality, the Sure Foundation on Which We Must Build." In *Maria W. Stewart, America's First Black Woman Political Writer: Essays and Speeches,* edited and introduced by Marilyn Richardson, 28–42. Bloomington: Indiana University Press, 1987.

Strickland, Arvarh E. *History of the Chicago Urban League.* Urbana: University of Illinois Press, 1966.

Suggs, Henry Lewis. "The Response of the African American Press to the United States Occupation of Haiti, 1915–1934." *Journal of Negro History* 73, no. 1 (1988): 70–82.

Tatum, Elbert Lee. "The Changed Political Thoughts of Negroes of the United States, 1915–1940." *Journal of Negro Education* 16, no. 4 (Autumn 1947): 538.

Taylor, A. Elizabeth. "Tennessee: The Thirty-Sixth State." In *Votes for Women! The Woman Suffrage Movement in Tennessee, the South, and the Nation,* edited by Marjorie Spruill Wheeler, 53–70. Knoxville: University of Tennessee Press, 1995.

Taylor, Ula Yvette. *The Veiled Garvey: The Life and Times of Amy Jacques Garvey.* Chapel Hill: University of North Carolina Press, 2002.

Tello, Jean C. "Flower, Lucy Louisa Coues." In *Women Building Chicago, 1790–1990: A Biographical Dictionary,* edited by Rima Lunin Schultz and Adele Hast, 273–76. Bloomington: Indiana University Press, 2001.

Terborg-Penn, Rosalyn. *African American Women in the Struggle for the Vote, 1850–1920.* Bloomington: Indiana University Press, 1998.

———. "African-American Women's Networks in the Anti-Lynching Crusade." In *Gender, Class, Race, and Reform in the Progressive Era,* edited by Noralee Frankel and Nancy S. Dye, 148–61. Lexington: University Press of Kentucky, 1991.

Terrell, Mary Church. *A Colored Woman in a White World.* African American Women Writers, 1910–1940. Edited by Henry Louis Gates Jr. and Jennifer Burton. 1940. Reprint, New York: G. K. Hall, 1996.

Thornbrough, Emma Lou. *T. Thomas Fortune: Militant Journalist.* Chicago: University of Chicago Press, 1972.

Tolnay, Stewart E., and E. M. Beck. *A Festival of Violence: An Analysis of Southern Lynchings, 1882–1930.* Urbana: University of Illinois Press, 1995.

Towne, Charles Hanson. *The Rise and Fall of Prohibition: The Human Side of What the Eighteenth Amendment and the Volstead Act Have Done to the United States.* New York: Macmillan, 1923.

Trotter, Joe William, Jr., ed. *The Great Migration in Historical Perspective: New Dimensions of Race, Class, and Gender*. Bloomington: Indiana University Press, 1991.

Turner, Frederick Jackson. *Rereading Frederick Jackson Turner: "The Significance of the Frontier in American History" and Other Essays*. Commentary by John Mack Faragher. New York: Henry Holt, 1994.

Unger, Nancy C. *Fighting Bob La Follette: The Righteous Reformer*. Chapel Hill: University of North Carolina Press, 2000.

Varon, Elizabeth R. *We Mean to Be Counted: White Women and Politics in Antebellum Virginia*. Chapel Hill: University of North Carolina Press, 1998.

Walker, Clarence E. *A Rock in a Weary Land: The African Methodist Episcopal Church during the Civil War and Reconstruction*. Baton Rouge: Louisiana State University Press, 1982.

Walls, William J. *The African Methodist Episcopal Zion Church: Reality of the Black Church*. Charlotte: AME Zion Publishing House, 1974.

Washington, Booker T. *Up From Slavery*. 1901. Reprint in *Three Negro Classics*. With an introduction by John Hope Franklin. New York: Avon Books, 1965.

Washington, James Melvin, ed. *Conversations with God: Two Centuries of Prayers by African Americans*. New York: Harper Collins, 1994.

Weddle, Carriette. "Bullock, Carrie E." In *Women Building Chicago, 1790–1990: A Biographical Dictionary*, edited by Rima Lunin Schultz and Adele Hast, 128–29. Bloomington: Indiana University Press, 2001.

Weiss, Nancy J. *Farewell to the Party of Lincoln: Black Politics in the Age of FDR*. Princeton: Princeton University Press, 1983.

Wells-Barnett, Ida B. *Crusade for Justice: The Autobiography of Ida B. Wells*. Edited by Alfreda M. Barnett Duster. Chicago: University of Chicago Press, 1970.

Wenger, Tisa. " 'The Women Had Full Sway': Women's Missionary Societies and Racial Uplift in the AME Church, 1860–1910." Unpublished article in author's possession.

Wharton, Vernon Lane. *The Negro in Mississippi, 1865–1890*. New York: Harper and Row, 1965.

Wheeler, Marjorie Spruill. *New Women of the New South: The Leaders of the Woman Suffrage Movement in the Southern States*. New York: Oxford University Press, 1993.

——, ed. *One Woman, One Vote: Rediscovering the Woman Suffrage Movement*. Troutdale, Ore.: NewSage Press, 1995.

——. "A Short History of the Woman Suffrage Movement in America." In *One Woman, One Vote: Rediscovering the Woman Suffrage Movement*, edited by Marjorie Spruill Wheeler, 9–19. Troutdale, Ore.: NewSage Press, 1995.

——, ed. *Votes for Women! The Woman Suffrage Movement in Tennessee, the South, and the Nation*. Knoxville: University of Tennessee Press, 1995.

White, Deborah Gray. *Ar'n't I a Woman?: Female Slaves in the Plantation South*. New York: W. W. Norton, 1985.

——. *Too Heavy a Load: Black Women in Defense of Themselves, 1894–1994*. New York: W. W. Norton, 1999.

Williams, Fannie Barrier. "The Intellectual Progress of the Colored Women of the United States since the Emancipation Proclamation." In *The World's Congress of Representative Women*, edited by May Wright Sewall, 696–711. Chicago: Rand, McNally, 1894.

——. "Opportunities and Responsibilities of Colored Women." In *Afro-American Encyclopedia; or, The Thoughts, Doings, and Sayings of a Race*, edited by James T. Haley, 146–61. Nashville: Haley and Florida, 1895.

Williamson, Joel. *The Crucible of Race: Black-White Relations in the American South since Emancipation*. New York: Oxford University Press, 1984.

Wills, David. "Reverdy Ransom: The Making of an AME Bishop." In *Black Apostles: Afro-American Clergy Confront the Twentieth Century*, edited by Randall K. Burkett and Richard Newman, 181–212. Boston: GK Hall, 1978.

Winson, Robert W. *It's a Far Cry*. New York: Henry Holt, 1937.

Wolcott, Victoria W. *Remaking Respectability: African American Women in Interwar Detroit*. Chapel Hill: University of North Carolina Press, 2001.

Wolgemuth, Kathleen L. "Woodrow Wilson and Federal Segregation." *Journal of Negro History* 44, no. 2 (April 1959): 158–73.

Wolloch, Nancy. *Women and the American Experience*. 3rd ed. New York: McGraw Hill, 2000.

Woodward, C. Vann. *Origins of the New South, 1877–1913*. Baton Rouge: Louisiana State University Press, 1951.

——. *The Strange Career of Jim Crow*. 3rd ed. New York: Oxford University Press, 1974.

——. *Tom Watson: Agrarian Rebel*. New York: Rinehart, 1938.

Wright, George C. *A History of Blacks in Kentucky: In Pursuit of Equality, 1890–1980*. Vol. 2. Frankfort: Kentucky Historical Society, 1992.

——. *Life behind a Veil: Blacks in Louisville, Kentucky, 1865–1930*. Baton Rouge: Louisiana State University Press, 1985.

——. *Racial Violence in Kentucky, 1865–1940: Lynchings, Mob Rule, and "Legal Lynching."* Baton Rouge: Louisiana State University Press, 1990.

Yee, Shirley J. *Black Women Abolitionists: A Study in Activism, 1828–1860*. Knoxville: University of Tennessee Press, 1992.

Zangrando, Robert L. *The NAACP Crusade against Lynching, 1909–1950*. Philadelphia: Temple University Press, 1980.

Index

Louisville, Kentucky, 68–70, 72–74, 101, 260 (n. 51); marriage of, 70; and Medill McCormick's congressional campaign, 195; and middle-class networks in Chicago, 63, 83–84; photographs of, 83, 211; political organizing by, generally, 60, 62, 80, 260 (n. 66); and presidential campaign of 1916, 99, 104–5; and presidential campaign of 1928, 293 (n. 154); public image of, changed from divorcée to widow, 63, 70, 83–84, 258 (n. 37), 263 (n. 119); relocation of, to Chicago, 60, 70, 255 (n. 2); and Ruth H. McCormick's congressional campaign, 215–16; and Second Ward alderman elections of 1910s, 85, 87, 96–97, 106; siblings of, 67–68, 73–74

Berry, William, 70, 263 (n. 119)

Best, Wallace, 36, 216–18

Bethune, Mary McLeod, 67, 160, 235–36, 270 (n. 38), 298 (n. 22)

Black-and-tan convention delegations, 161, 162

Black churches. *See* Churches

Black disfranchisement. *See* Disfranchisement

Black Laws, 22

Black men: alcohol consumption by, 152–54, 172–74; college education of, 25; critique of, by black women, 12, 95, 102–3, 131, 140, 152–53, 166, 179, 182; and Democratic Party, 13–14, 16–19; as elected officials, 10, 85, 96, 97–98, 189, 201, 203, 232, 233, 266 (n. 167), 289 (n. 92, 96); and election fraud during Reconstruction, 5–6; employment of, 1–2, 78–79, 174, 210, 241 (n. 3); and labor movement, 24, 214–15; as political candidates in Chicago, 86–88, 95–98; and Republican Party, 2, 4, 13–14, 17–19, 23, 40, 41–42, 46–47, 58, 233; and Second Ward alderman elections in Chicago of

1910s, 85–88; as teachers, 76, 261 (n. 82); Universal Negro Improvement Association and manhood of, 142–43; and white men at all-male Republican gatherings, 23. *See also* Disfranchisement—of black men; Lynching; Voting—by black men; *and specific men*

Blackwell, Henry, 246 (n. 29)

Black women: college education of, 25; critique of black men by, 12, 95, 102–3, 131, 140, 152–53, 166, 179, 182; and "culture of dissemblance," 83–84; education of, 25, 64–67; education supported by, 31–32; employment of, 1, 18, 24, 28, 65, 70, 78–79, 134, 175–76, 210, 211–12, 213, 241 (n. 3); and fraternal organizations, 69–70, 84, 99, 215–16, 259 (n. 49), 292 (n. 153); and interracial political mobilization for Illinois elections of 1894, 27–28, 31–33; and labor movement, 24, 191–92; moral superiority of, 12–14; and national politics during 1894, 39–59; as New Deal administrators, 236; and political implications of motherhood, 31, 126–27, 144, 167; as prostitutes, 175–76, 213, 283 (n. 100); protective labor legislation for, 126; and Reconstruction electoral politics, 3–8, 166; as reformers generally, 12–13, 145–46; and Republican loyalty of black men, 46–47, 58, 233; and self-help organizations generally, 13, 28, 81; social class and party affiliation of, 135–36; stereotypes of, 45–46, 49, 53, 79, 143; support for white women candidates by generally, 25–26, 186–87, 194–206, 210–27; as teachers, 24–25, 64, 75–77, 101, 261 (n. 82); Universal Negro Improvement Association and respect for, 143–44; and University of Illinois trustee campaign of 1894, 20–21, 25–26, 39, 42, 44, 55; voting rights for black men supported by, 6–7; and white women's racism, 15, 26, 32, 37, 50, 53, 253 (n. 128); and World's Columbian Exposition of 1893 in Chicago, 32, 47, 50. *See also* Antilynching movement; Churches; Democratic Party; Disfranchisement—of black women; Illinois elections of 1894; Prohibition / temperance; Republican Party; Southern migrants; Voting—by women; "Woman's era" philosophy; *and specific women*

Black women's club movement, 28, 38–39, 56–58, 80–82, 84, 87, 92, 146, 214

Blair Education Bill, 40

Blight, David, 162

Booze, Mary Montgomery, 123, 144, 193

Bordin, Ruth, 252 (n. 120)

Boston Guardian, 165

Bradley, William O'Connell, 72–73, 77

Branham, Charles, 225

Bright, Rachel, 232–33

Broad Ax, 92

Brotherhood of Sleeping Car Porters (BSCP), 214–15, 245 (n. 21)

Browder, Lillian, 126

Brown, Charles, 198, 201

Brown, Elsa Barkley, 6

Brown, Fannie, 31, 39, 42, 44, 46, 47, 245 (n. 7)

Brown, Ida, 120

Brown, John M. (bishop), 37

Brown, Lucy Hughes, 258 (n. 36)

Brown, Philip H., 110–11

Brown v. Board of Education, 132

Bryan, Charles, 125

Bryan, William Jennings, 56, 125

BSCP. *See* Brotherhood of Sleeping Car Porters

Bullard, Samuel, 55

Bullock, Carrie, 258 (n. 36), 262 (n. 114)

Bundesen, Herman, 209

Burrell, Mary E., 114, 159, 276 (n. 115)

Burroughs, Nannie Helen: and black

churches, 92, 139; critique of black male voters by, 102–4; on Democratic Party, 223, 232; and National League of Republican Colored Women, 124, 125, 138, 146; and political activism and religious beliefs, 137; and poll tax, 141; and presidential campaign of 1928, 164, 169–70, 182–83; and presidential campaign of 1932, 230, 232; and Progressive Party, 128; and prohibition, 169, 194; and Republican Party loyalty, 133, 232; and Ruth H. McCormick's congressional campaign, 222; and U.S. withdrawal from Haiti and Santo Domingo, 195

Byrd, Margaret, 197–98, 212

Byrd, Robert A., 197

Caldwell, H. C. (elder), 231

Caldwell, Manley Morrison, 280 (n. 43)

Caldwell, Willie Walker (Mrs. M. M.), 162, 280 (nn. 43, 46)

California, 266 (n. 170)

Callcott, Margaret Law, 256 (n. 7)

Callis, Henry J., 91

Carey, Archibald, 90–91, 137

Carlyle, Thomas, 45

Carpenter, Marvelyne, 232–33

Carter, Elizabeth, 148

Carter, Jeannette, 132, 164, 273 (n. 65)

Cashman, Sean Dennis, 278 (n. 3)

Cermack, Anton, 176

Champion Magazine, 105, 106

Charlotte Observer, 17, 18

Chicago: black community in, during nineteenth century, 22–25; black elected officials in, 10, 85, 96, 97–98, 189, 266 (n. 167), 289 (nn. 92, 96); black population of, 9–10, 22, 85, 187, 213, 284 (nn. 5–6), 291 (n. 137); black women's clubs in, 38–39, 56–58, 80–82, 84–85, 87, 92, 214; black women's Republican clubs in, 38, 46, 47, 81–82, 92–93, 95,

96, 99, 108, 275 (n. 106); city council of, 85–86, 96, 189, 263 (n. 128); commercial leisure district ("the Stroll") in, 172–74, 180, 183; Democratic Party in, 53–55, 168, 176, 221–23, 225, 230–33; education of blacks in, 25, 31–32; employment of blacks in, 24, 210; establishment of, as permanent settlement, 22; Frederick Douglass Center in, 28, 101; labor movement in, 24, 214–15; machine politics in, 23–24, 54–55, 86, 90–95, 203, 205–6, 216, 221, 225; mayors of, 53, 175–76, 233, 295–96 (n. 203); NAACP in, 269 (n. 10); opposition to prohibition in, by blacks, 171, 224–25, 234; Phyllis Wheatley Home in, 82–83, 97, 211, 212, 213; police in, 175, 283 (n. 110); postal jobs in, 31, 247–48 (n. 52); prostitution in, 174–75, 283 (n. 100); protests against job discrimination in, 210; and Pullman strike, 39; race riot of 1919 in, 283 (n. 110); radicalism in, 24; Republican National Committee's headquarters in, 10; Republican National Conventions in, 10; saloons in, 173–74; Second Ward aldermen elections of 1910s in, 85–98; settlement houses in, 28, 82–83; southern migrants in, 9–10, 21–22, 63, 82–83; Universal Negro Improvement Association in, 145; Urban League in, 89, 92, 98, 263 (n. 118); vice district in, 174–76, 213; women's political organizing and voting in, during 1894, 19–59; World's Columbian Exposition of 1893 in, 32, 47, 50. *See also* Illinois; Southern migrants

Chicago Bee, 204, 211

Chicago Daily News, 200

Chicago Defender: Abbott as editor of, 98; on Berry, 104, 259 (n. 49); on black clergy, 216; on congressional reapportionment, 200–201; on Democratic Party, 132, 223, 230, 232, 273 (n. 65); on Deneen, 220; on DePriest, 203, 230, 232; on fraternal movement, 259 (n. 49); on Gaines, 239; on Lawrence, 228; and presidential campaign of 1928, 165; on prohibition, 224, 234–35, 297 (n. 17); on Rathbone, 193; on Republican racism, 164; on Second Ward alderman elections of 1910s, 86–88, 91, 95; on Terrell's leadership of Ruth H. McCormick's campaign, 209; on voter registration, 116; on wages for blacks, 78

Chicago School of Civics and Philanthropy (CSCP), 82, 262 (n. 114)

Chicago Tribune: on black women voters, 55, 254 (n. 139); on disfranchisement of women voters, 254–55 (n. 141); on Ida B. Wells Club, 28, 254 (n. 139); on Illinois elections of 1894, 254 (n. 139); and Medill McCormick, 190; and questionnaire on Reconstruction Amendments, 220–21; on Republican Party loyalty, 46; on Volstead Act, 158; on Wells-Barnett, 250 (n. 95)

Chicago Whip, 115, 129, 208–9, 210

Chicago Woman's Club, 50, 56

Child labor, 125, 126–27, 134

Chiles, Mrs. C., 120

Christian Recorder, 37, 140

Church, Robert R., Jr., 117

Churches: attendance decline in, during 1930s, 231; black, during nineteenth century, 22; and black women's clubs, 57, 84–85, 92–94; and black women's political activities, 15–16, 22–23, 33–39, 91–94, 136–41, 216, 230; and Community Church Movement, 217; and education of blacks, 64–67, 76; and Eighteenth Amendment, 169, 170, 182, 224; finances of, 92, 94, 218, 231; male clergy's leadership of, 36–38, 57, 91–94, 139, 140–41, 216, 230; and middle-class blacks, 36; multiple rural black churches run by one minister, 64; political affiliations of, 90–91, 98, 140–41; political rallies and meetings in, 34–39, 41–42, 55, 276 (n. 115); and poor blacks, 217–19, 230–31; and presidential campaign of 1916, 103; and presidential campaign of 1924, 141; and presidential campaign of 1928, 168, 169, 293 (n. 166); and racial uplift, 94; and Ruth H. McCormick's congressional campaign, 214, 216–19; and Second Ward alderman elections of 1910s, 89–94; and social class, 216–19; and southern migrants, 89–91, 216–19, 294 (n. 167); statistics on, 216–17; storefront churches, 93, 217–19; and temperance, 52, 53, 252 (n. 120), 253 (n. 126); and women ministers, 36–37, 248–49 (n. 70), 249 (n. 72); women's role in, 36–37, 94, 137, 139–40, 276 (n. 122)

Civil rights: and New Deal, 237; protection of black citizenship rights by Republican Party, 8–9, 11–12, 21–22, 39, 40, 45, 125; and repeal movement for Eighteenth Amendment, 157–60, 169–70; and temperance and racial uplift before prohibition repeal movement, 152–57. *See also* Reconstruction Amendments; *and specific constitutional amendments*

Civil Rights Act (1875), 8, 29, 69, 156

Civil Rights Act (1964), 239

Clark, Mary G., 221

Clark, Norman H., 278 (n. 3)

Class. *See* Social class

Cleveland, Grover, 39, 40

Cobb, James, 128

Cohen, Walter H., 208

College education. *See specific colleges and universities*

Collier-Thomas, Bettye, 275–76 (n. 109)

Collins, Belle, 236

Colorado, 27, 246 (n. 32)

Colored American Magazine, 73, 158

A Colored Woman in a White World (Terrell), 206

Colored Women for the Democratic Party, 129–30

Colored Women's Department of the Republican National Committee (CWDRNC): and Anti-Lynching Crusaders, 271 (n. 45); and Colored Women's Republican Clubs of Illinois, 207; directorship of, 117; and Goins, 192; leadership of, 99, 110–11, 146–47, 269 (n. 20), 273 (n. 60); planning by, in 1921, 117; and poll tax, 141; and presidential campaign of 1916, 99, 110; and presidential campaign of 1920, 108, 110–11, 114–15; and presidential campaign of 1924, 141, 146, 161; and presidential campaign of 1928, 149, 164, 169–70; and prohibition, 149, 178, 194; and Terrell's leadership in Ruth H. McCormick's campaign, 185, 207

Colored Women's Republican Clubs of Illinois (CWRCI): and DePriest, 203, 206, 221; and elections of 1934, 233; founding of, 136, 189; and Garveyites, 145; leadership of, 186, 189, 203; as permanent organization, 147; and Ruth H. McCormick's congressional campaigns, 186–89, 195, 197, 200, 202–3, 205–7, 210, 212, 221–22, 225–27

Committee of Fifteen, 283 (n. 100)

Communist Party, 235, 245 (n. 18)

Community Church Movement, 217

Competitor, 137

Congress, U.S.: and Bankhead amendment, 289 (n. 90); black members of, 10, 201, 203, 232, 233; and congressional reapportionment, 200–201, 203–4, 230; and Eighteenth Amendment, 156; and equal rights amendment, 126; and Lodge Federal Elections Bill (Force Bill), 40–41, 127; and Nineteenth Amend-

Index

ment, 116; and prohibition, 149, 159–60; and Reconstruction Amendments, 4; Republican control of, after 1894 elections, 55; Republican control of, after 1920 elections, 109, 117; Ruth H. McCormick's congressional campaigns, 185–89, 193–225, 229–30; and Tinkham amendment, 203–4, 226; women in, 12, 207. *See also* Dyer Antilynching Bill

Congress of Representative Women (1893), 32, 47, 50

Constitutional amendments. *See specific amendments*

Cook, W. D., 91

Coolidge, Calvin: and antilynching legislation, 129, 130; and civil rights for blacks, 148; as president following Harding's death, 125; in presidential campaign of 1924, 125, 134, 139, 141, 161; as vice-presidential candidate in 1920, 109, 114, 115. *See also* Presidential campaign—of 1924

Cooper, Anna Julia, 46–47

Cornell, Mary Louise, 237

Cornell Charity Club, 93, 99

Cottrill, Charles A., 117

Cowan, William, 86–88, 91, 95

Crisis: on antilynching movement, 120, 122, 195, 271 (n. 45); on black churches, 92; on black women's voting, 102, 103, 105; on Medill McCormick, 195; on National Association of Colored Women, 80–81; photograph from, of antilynching delegation to Harding, 120

CSCP. *See* Chicago School of Civics and Philanthropy

"Culture of dissemblance," 83–84

Cummings, Ida, 155, 270 (n. 38)

CWDRNC. *See* Colored Women's Department of the Republican National Committee

CWRCI. *See* Colored Women's Republican Clubs of Illinois

Davis, Elizabeth Lindsay: on Berry, 260 (n. 66); and Colored Women's Department of the Republican National Committee, 269 (n. 20); on Democratic Party, 230; and DePriest, 97; and presidential campaign of 1920, 114; and presidential campaign of 1932, 230; relocation of, to Chicago, 267–68 (n. 183); and Republican Woman's Cook County Campaign Committee, 191; and Ruth H. McCormick, 202; and Second Ward alderman elections in Chicago of 1910s, 97, 264 (n. 140); as teacher in South, 25; and Urban League, 263 (n. 118); on women voters, 102

Davis, Estelle, 120, 137

Davis, John, 125, 132

Davy, Rosa, 201–2

Dawes, Charles, 125, 139, 161

Debs, Eugene, 245 (n. 18)

Defender. See *Chicago Defender*

Delaware, 129, 271 (n. 45)

Democratic National Committee, Women's Division, 236

Democratic Party: black disfranchisement by, 1, 2, 11, 40–41, 54–56, 58–59, 61, 72, 77–80, 100; and blacks generally, 2, 6–7, 9, 11, 13–14, 16–19, 127, 150, 151, 182–84, 223; and black women, 53, 114, 122, 124, 128–33, 135–36, 141, 164–69, 182, 223, 227, 231–32, 233–38, 297 (n. 8); Burroughs on, 223, 232; and Dunbar-Nelson, 129–33, 135, 148, 165, 167, 182, 271 (n. 45); economic pressure on blacks for their support of, 18; and elections of 1892, 40, 41; electoral fraud by, 5–6, 161–62; fears of, about black women voters, 115–16; and Illinois congressional campaign of 1928, 198, 201; and Illinois congressional campaign of 1930, 204–6, 208, 214, 219–23, 225–27; and Illinois congressional campaign of 1932, 230, 232; and Illinois congressional campaign of 1934, 232–33; and Illinois elections of 1894, 53–54; Lawrence on, 222–23, 230; and machine politics, 23–24, 54–55; and New Deal, 9, 16, 233, 235–39, 298 (n. 22); and poor blacks, 135–36, 151, 164, 227; and prohibition, 149, 155, 160, 169–71, 235; and protective labor legislation, 127; regional differences in, 132, 171; and Second Ward alderman elections in Chicago of 1910s, 95, 96; and segregation of Washington, D.C., 104; and southern white supremacy, 12, 40, 61, 72, 73, 75, 79–80, 132, 133, 222–23, 236; and violence during Reconstruction elections, 6–7; and vote-buying schemes, 47, 50; and woman suffrage, 73, 115–16. *See also* Presidential campaign; *specific states; and specific party candidates and leaders*

Dempsey, Dillard, 28, 39

Dempsey, Ida: biographical information on, 28; and Illinois Women's Republican Education Committee, 28, 247 (n. 40); photograph of, 48; political organizing by, during Illinois elections of 1894, 31–33, 42, 44–46; and Second Ward alderman elections of 1910s, 88, 264 (n. 139); voter registration by, 55

Deneen, Charles: and black churches, 90; civil rights record of, 204–5; as governor of Illinois, 190, 204–5; and Harris Gaines, 191, 205; Harris Gaines on, 219–20; and Reconstruction Amendments, 220–21; Terrell on, 220–21; and U.S. Senate race of 1924, 190, 208; and U.S. Senate race of 1930, 204–6, 208, 214, 225; and Wells-Barnett, 205, 289–90 (nn. 96–97)

Dennison, Franklin A., 266 (n. 167)

DePriest, Oscar: and break with Thompson machine, 221, 225, 227; as Chicago alderman, 10, 97–98, 189; as Chicago Third Ward Committeeman, 206, 221; church membership of, 98, 266 (n. 166); and Colored Women's Republican Clubs of Illinois, 203, 206, 221; and congressional campaign of 1929–30, 221; and congressional campaign of 1932, 230, 232; corruption charges against, 97, 219; defeat of, in Illinois congressional election of 1934, 232; election of, to U.S. House of Representatives, 10, 201, 203, 213, 215; and labor movement, 215; and Lawrence, 96–98, 210, 212, 213; and Metropolitan Community Church, 217; and Ruth H. McCormick's congressional campaign, 206, 221, 222–23; Ruth H. McCormick's support for seating of, in U.S. Congress, 203; and Second Ward alderman elections of 1910s, 95–98; and Terrell, 207

De Saible, Jean Baptiste Point, 22

Desegregation. *See* Segregation

Dever, William, 295–96 (n. 203)

Dewson, Molly, 297 (n. 8)

Disfranchisement
— of black men: by Democratic Party, 1, 2, 11, 40–41, 54–56, 58–59, 61, 72, 77–80, 100; and Fourteenth Amendment's second section, 201, 203–4; and grandfather clause, 61, 105, 132; Illinois Women's Republican Education Committee on, 249 (n. 84); Jennie Lawrence's awareness of, 61–62, 74–77; and local option prohibition campaigns, 171–72; and National Association of Colored Women, 141; and poll taxes, 30, 56, 61, 141–42, 246 (n. 30); property and educational requirements used for, 26, 56, 61, 76–77, 141, 142, 246 (n. 30); understand-

ing tests used for, 41, 61, 76, 142; violence used for, 8, 54–55, 75. *See also* Racism and white supremacy; *and specific states*
—of black women, 55, 116–17, 141–42, 156–57
—of white women, 254–55 (nn. 140–41)
District of Columbia. *See* Washington, D.C.
Dodson, Louise M., 272 (n. 58)
Douglass, Frederick, 32, 52, 56
Douglass, Louise, 224
Druis, Perry, 174
Du Bois, W. E. B.: on black leadership class, 25, 63, 65; on presidential campaign of 1912, 101; on presidential campaign of 1916, 102, 104, 267 (n. 180); on Progressive Party, 127; on Reconstruction, 8
Dunbar, Paul Laurence, 129
Dunbar-Nelson, Alice: and antilynching legislation, 129, 130, 234, 271 (n. 45); biographical information on, 128–29; on black women voters, 165–67; and Democratic Party, 129–33, 135, 148, 165, 167, 182, 271 (n. 45); and presidential campaign of 1920, 108, 129, 135; and presidential campaign of 1924, 129–33; and presidential campaign of 1928, 164–67; on Republican Party, 130–31, 166; Terrell's criticism of, 132–33; on women's institution building, 135
Duncan, Anna, 154
Dyer, Leonidas, 112, 129, 148
Dyer Antilynching Bill: and Anti-Lynching Crusaders, 121–22, 136–37; and Coolidge, 129, 130, 148; and Dunbar-Nelson, 129–31, 167; filibuster against and defeat of, in U.S. Senate, 122, 129, 130, 193, 195, 234; and Harding, 119, 120, 122, 130; introduction of, into U.S. House of Representatives, 112; introduction of, into U.S. Senate, 119; and Medill McCor-

mick, 195; and NAACP, 112, 122, 129; and National Association of Colored Women, 113–14, 119, 120, 234; passage of, in U.S. House of Representatives in 1922, 119, 129, 193, 270 (n. 41); provisions of, 112; publicity and fundraising campaign supporting, 121–22, 136–37; reintroduction of, in 1923, 129; reintroduction of, in 1926, 185; and Republican Party 1920 and 1924 platforms, 112–14, 129, 234; Wells-Barnett on, 118; Whyte on, 147; and Yates, 193. *See also* Antilynching movement; Lynching

Education: and black colleges, 100, 193; and black men as teachers, 76, 261 (n. 82); of blacks, 24–25, 31–32, 40, 64–67, 101, 193; of black women, 25, 64–67; and black women as teachers, 24–25, 64, 75–77, 101, 229, 261 (n. 82); coeducation at Livingstone College, 258 (nn. 31–32); segregated schools, 69, 71, 101
Edwards, Thyra, 262 (n. 114)
Eighteenth Amendment: black opposition to, 171–80, 182, 223–25, 234–35, 297 (n. 17); black women's support for, 155–57, 169–71, 180–81; enforcement of, compared with that of Nineteenth Amendment, 156–57; enforcement of, compared with that of Reconstruction Amendments, 150–51, 152, 156, 158–60, 169–70, 181, 183, 194, 229; and congressional campaigns of 1929–30, 223–25; date of beginning of national prohibition, 171; economic reasons for opposition to, 173–77; passage and ratification of, 154, 155, 156; and presidential campaign of 1928, 169–79; repeal movement for, 149–51, 157–60, 169–79, 234–35, 278 (n. 3); repeal of, with Twenty-first Amendment, 183, 235; and Ruth H. McCormick, 186, 194, 200;

and vice economy, 174–78; Volstead Act for enforcement of, 149, 156, 157, 159–60, 224, 225. *See also* Prohibition/ temperance

Eisenhower, Dwight D., 239

Elections. *See* Illinois congressional campaigns; Illinois elections of 1894; Presidential campaign; Second Ward alderman elections in Chicago of 1910s; Voting

Elks ("black Elks"), 84, 215–16, 292 (n. 153), 293 (n. 154)

Ellis, Georgia Jones, 220, 221

Elm, Ella, 1–2, 6, 77–78, 80, 241–42 (n. 4), 242 (n. 6)

Elm, Texas, 1–2, 242 (nn. 4, 6)

Emancipation Proclamation, 68, 259 (n. 44)

Emanuel, Fannie Hagen, 262 (n. 114)

Employment: of black men, 1–2, 28, 78–79, 172, 241 (n. 3); of black women, 1, 18, 24, 28, 65, 70, 78–79, 134, 175–76, 210, 211–12, 213, 241 (n. 3); in Chicago, 24; discrimination in, 210; paid Republican campaign work, 197–98, 203, 209–12, 219, 226–27, 230; and patronage appointments for Ruth H. McCormick's supporters, 198–202, 206, 211–12, 226, 227; protective labor legislation, 125, 126, 134; as reason for migration of blacks, 78–79; unemployment in 1893–1894, 39; unemployment in late 1920s–1930s, 209–11, 213, 235–36; wages for blacks, 78, 198, 210, 212. *See also* Labor movement

Enforcement Acts (1870, 1871), 156

Equal rights amendment, 126

Ettelson, Samuel, 95

Fauset, Crystal Bird, 236–38

Fayerweather, Louise, 138

Felts, Alice, 37

Fifteenth Amendment: Burroughs on, and possible repeal of Eighteenth Amendment, 169; *Chicago Tribune* questionnaire on, 220–21; compared with Eighteenth Amendment, 156, 169, 181; Foster Cook on, 160; and grandfather clause, 105; provisions of, 4, 23; repeal movement for, 158; Ruth H. McCormick on enforcement of, 201, 202, 204; and U.S. Congress, 41; U.S. Supreme Court decisions on, 8; Wells-Barnett on, 45, 250 (n. 95); and Williams on black men's misuse of voting rights, 50, 51; and woman's suffrage, 44. *See also* Reconstruction Amendments

Fisher, E. J., 90

Fleming, Lethia, 114, 120

Florida, 78, 101, 114, 118, 271 (n. 45)

Flower, Lucy, 21, 25–27, 33, 44, 50, 51, 55

Force Bill. *See* Lodge Federal Elections Bill

Fortune, T. Thomas, 253 (n. 126)

Foster, J. P. (reverend), 76

Foster Cook, Myrtle, 120, 146–48, 160, 182, 192, 272–73 (n. 60)

Fourteenth Amendment: and antilynching legislation, 112; black women's political activism for enforcement of, generally, 229; Burroughs on, and possible repeal of Eighteenth Amendment, 169; *Chicago Tribune* questionnaire on, 220–21; compared with Eighteenth Amendment, 156, 169, 181; and congressional reapportionment, 201, 203–4; enforcement of, 147, 201–4, 229; Foster Cook on, 160; and New Deal, 237; provisions of, 4, 112, 118, 201, 237; Ruth H. McCormick on enforcement of, 201–4; U.S. Supreme Court decisions on, 8; Wells-Barnett on, 45, 118, 215 (n. 95); Whyte on enforcement of, 147; and woman's suffrage, 44. *See also* Reconstruction Amendments

Fox, Harriet, 33

Fraternal organizations, 69–70, 84, 99, 214–16, 259 (n. 49), 292 (n. 153)
Frederick Douglass Center, 28, 101
Freedmen's Bureau, 24, 259 (n. 44)
Free Speech, 30, 112
Fugitive Slave Law, 157

Gainer, Margaret O., 108, 196, 269 (n. 20)
Gaines, Harris B., 191, 201, 205, 206, 221
Gaines, Harry, 239
Gaines, Irene M.: biographical informa-
    tion on, 189; and Colored Women's
    Department of the Republican National
    Committee, 192, 291 (n. 122), 292 (n. 153);
    and Colored Women's Republican Clubs
    of Illinois, 203, 206, 207; death of, 239; on
    Deneen, 219–20; and Goins, 191, 192;
    and labor movement, 214–15; marriage
    of, 191; photograph of, 211; as political
    candidate, 239; and Republican Party
    loyalty, 239; and Ruth H. McCormick in
    1910s and 1920s, 190–91; and Ruth H.
    McCormick's congressional campaigns,
    199–200, 203–6, 210–11, 214–22; and
    Terrell's leadership of Ruth H. McCor-
    mick's campaign, 207, 209, 212
Gambling, 174, 176
Ganz, Marshall, 69–70
Gardiner, Mary, 134–35
Garvey, Marcus, 142–45, 167–68, 179
George, Albert B., 266 (n. 167)
Georgia: antilynching movement in, 271
    (n. 45); Atlanta Race Riot of 1906 in,
    172; black migrants from, 78; Demo-
    cratic electoral fraud in, 5–6; dis-
    franchisement of women in, 116–17;
    political activities by black women in, 4–
    6; poll tax in, 141–42; presidential cam-
    paign of 1920 in, 116–17; prohibition in,
    172; violence during Reconstruction
    elections in, 7; voter registration in,
    141–42

Georgia State Federation of Colored
    Women's Clubs, 116–17
Gibbs, Ione, 170
Gilmer, Blanche, 191, 285 (n. 21)
Gilmore, Glenda, 10–11, 77, 252 (n. 120),
    257 (n. 28), 258 (n. 31), 261 (n. 82), 296–
    97 (n. 8)
Goins, Irene: biographical information on,
    191–92, 268 (n. 183); and Colored
    Women's Republican Clubs of Illinois,
    136, 186, 197; death of, 203; and Gaines,
    191, 192; and labor movement, 191–92,
    214–15; and Negro Women's Republican
    League, 270 (n. 38); and presidential cam-
    paign of 1916, 192; religious beliefs and
    church membership of, 136; relocation of,
    to Chicago, 191; and Ruth H. McCor-
    mick's congressional campaigns, 194, 196,
    197; and Urban League, 263 (n. 118)
Goldwater, Barry, 239
Gosnell, Harold, 79, 247–48 (n. 52)
Graham, D. A. (reverend), 253 (n. 126)
Granady, Octavius, 219–20
Grandfather clause, 61, 105, 132
Grant, Ulysses S., 4
Gray, Monen L., 117–18, 123–24, 144, 272
    (n. 58)
Green, Edward, 289 (n. 92)
Griffin, Charles, 95, 96
Griffin, Mazie Mossell, 159, 237–38, 273
    (n. 60)
Grimké, Francis, 140
Guinn v. United States, 105, 132

Hadley, Arthur Twining, 157–58
Haiti, 195
Haley, Victoria Clay, 114
Hall, Charles, 111
Hall, George Cleveland, 98, 266 (n. 167)
Hall, S. R., 178
Halley, Victoria Clay, 270 (n. 38)
Hanna, Mark, 189–90, 285 (n. 14)

Hanson, Joyce Ann, 298 (nn. 21–22)
Hardin, LeRoy, 210, 284–85 (nn. 6–7)
Hardin, Lil, 173
Harding, George, 86, 90, 95–96
Harding, Mrs. Warren G., 144
Harding, Warren G., 108–17, 119, 122, 125, 130, 196
Hardwick, Thomas, 158
Harlem Renaissance, 130
Harper, Frances Ellen Watkins, 12, 52–53, 153–54, 253 (n. 128)
Harper's Magazine, 157
Harris, George W., 105
Harrison, Benjamin, 40
Harrison, Carter, 53
Hawkins-Brown, Charlotte, 270 (n. 38)
Haymarket Riot, 24
Haynes, Elizabeth Ross, 125, 138–39
Henderson, Levi, 213
Hendricks, Wanda, 81, 88
Hert, Sallie, 161, 162
Higginbotham, Evelyn Brooks, 46, 92, 272 (n. 54)
Higgins, Bertha, 139
Higher education. *See specific colleges and universities*
Hinds, James, 6
Hine, Darlene Clark, 83–84
Hobson, Richmond, 155
Hobson-Sheppard Amendment, 155
Holiness doctrine, 137, 275–76 (n. 109)
Hoover, Herbert: black women's support for, 178–79, 234; and Eighteenth Amendment, 160, 169, 194, 234; and presidential campaign of 1928, 149–50, 162, 164, 178–79, 183, 194; and presidential campaign of 1932, 230. *See also* Presidential campaign—of 1928
Hopkins, John (mayor), 54
Horne, Cora, 120
House of Representatives, U.S. *See* Congress, U.S.

Howard University, 193
Hughes, Charles Evans, 98–106, 110, 137, 155, 192, 267 (n. 180)
Hughes, Sarah, 37
Hull House, 82
Humphrey, Hubert, 239
Hunter, Alberta, 173
Hunton, Addie, 237

Ida B. Wells Club (Chicago), 28, 38, 56, 58, 254 (n. 139)
IFCWC. *See* Illinois Federation of Colored Women's Clubs
Igoe, Michael, 223, 295–96 (n. 203)
Illinois: antilynching law in, 204–5; Black Laws in, 22; black population of, 9–10, 22, 187, 284–85 (n. 7); education of blacks in, 25, 31–32; legislature of, 201, 205, 221, 239; local option campaigns for prohibition in, 154; machine politics in, 23–24, 54–55, 86, 90–95, 195, 203, 205–6, 216, 221, 225; southern migrants in, 9–10, 21–22, 63, 78; Springfield Riot of 1908 in, 220; woman suffrage in, 9, 15, 20, 59, 60, 80, 81, 244 (n. 2). *See also* Chicago; Illinois congressional campaigns; Illinois elections of 1894; Southern migrants
Illinois Association of Colored Women, 238
Illinois Commission on Race Relations, 266 (n. 164)
Illinois congressional campaigns: of 1928, 193–202, 225–27, 287 (nn. 45, 51); of 1930, 202–27, 229–30; of 1932, 230, 232; of 1934, 232–33
Illinois Democratic Women's Club, 232–33
Illinois elections of 1894: black manhood and Republican Party loyalty for, 41–42; and black women on Republican loyalty of black men, 46–47; black women's organizing separately and through

churches for, 33–39; and black women's Republican Party loyalty, 42, 44–47, 50–51, 55; and Democratic Party, 53–54, 253–54 (n. 132); and disfranchisement of black men by Democratic Party, 54–55; disfranchisement of black women for, 55; disfranchisement of white women for, 254–55 (nn. 140–41); and Ida B. Wells Club (Chicago), 28, 38; interracial political mobilization by women for, 27–28, 31–33; and national politics, 39–59; opposition to split-ticket voting by black women for, 42, 44–47, 50–51, 62; and People's Party, 51–52, 251 (n. 114); political rallies in churches for, 34–39, 41–42, 55; Prohibition Party in, 52–53; University of Illinois trustee campaign, 20–21, 25–26, 27, 39, 42, 44, 52, 55; and vote-buying schemes of Democratic Party, 47, 50; women's ballot for, 20, 43; women's voter registration for, 55, 254 (nn. 139–40); women's voting in, 20–59

Illinois Equal Suffrage Association, 190

Illinois Federation of Colored Women's Clubs (IFCWC), 81, 99, 121, 192

Illinois Prohibition Act, 224, 225

Illinois Women's Republican Education Committee (IWREC), 27–28, 53, 55, 249 (n. 84), 250 (n. 93), 254 (n. 139)

Immigration Act (1924), 215

Independent Order of Saint Luke, 119

Indiana, 60, 232

Industrial Workers of the World, 245 (n. 18)

International Glove Workers Union, 192

Inter Ocean, 23, 34, 43, 54, 55, 254 (nn. 139–40)

Iowa, 271 (n. 45)

IWREC. *See* Illinois Women's Republican Education Committee

Jackson, Mary B., 120

Jackson, Moses (reverend), 98

Jackson, Robert R., 96, 97

Jacques Garvey, Amy, 143–44, 167–69, 182

Johnson, Henry Lincoln, 117

Johnson, James Weldon, 129

Johnson, Lillian, 128, 133

Johnson, Lorraine, 210

Johnson, Lyndon B., 239

Jones, Bessie, 232

Jones, John, 85

Joplin, C. D., 198, 201

Kansas, 137, 266 (n. 170)

Kellogg-Briand Pact, 194, 200

Kelly, Edward, 176, 233

Kentucky: antilynching law in, 72; Ella Berry's ties to Louisville, 68–70, 72–74, 101, 260 (n. 51); black male voting in, 62, 72–73, 256 (n. 7); black migrants from generally, 62, 63; black Republican women's clubs in, 74; Democratic electoral fraud in, 161; Democratic Party in, 73–74, 256 (n. 7); Freedmen's Bureau in, 259 (n. 44); freedom for slaves in, 259 (n. 44); lynchings in, 71–72, 260 (n. 64); racial violence in, 68–69, 71, 259 (n. 44); Republican Party in, 72–73, 77, 87, 144, 256 (n. 7); segregation in, 70–71, 260 (n. 57); woman suffrage in, 27, 73, 247 (n. 33)

Knighten, Grace, 222

Knights of Labor, 24, 245 (n. 21)

Knupfer, Anne Meis, 81

Kraditor, Aileen S., 246 (n. 29)

Krout, Mary, 55, 249 (n. 84), 254 (n. 140)

Ku Klux Klan, 7, 30, 128, 129, 131, 132, 182–83

Kyvig, David E., 278 (n. 3)

Labor legislation, 125, 126

Labor movement, 24, 39, 191–92, 214–15, 245 (n. 21). *See also* Employment

La Follette, Robert, 125, 127–28, 134

190–91; Gaines's roles in congressional campaigns of, 199–200, 203–6, 210–11, 214–22; Goins on, 194; immigration policy of, 215; and labor movement, 215; marriage of, 189, 190; and National American Woman Suffrage Association, 190–91; paid campaign work for, 197–98, 203, 209–12, 219, 226–27, 230; patronage and employment for black supporters of, 198–202, 206, 211–12, 226, 227; photograph of, 211; and policy issues, 194, 200; and Progressive Party, 189, 190; and Reconstruction Amendments, enforcement of, 201–6, 226; Republican Party leadership by, 191–93; Senate race (1929–30) of, 202–25, 229–30; Terrell's roles in political campaign of, 185–86, 187, 199, 204, 206–10, 212; in U.S. Congress, 12, 201–2

McCoy, Irene. *See* Gaines, Irene M.

McCurdy, Mary, 252 (n. 125)

McGerr, Michael, 285 (n. 14)

McIntosh, Ida. *See* Dempsey, Ida

McKinley, Ada Dennison, 99–100, 191, 201

McKinley, William, 56, 58, 189, 285 (n. 14)

McKinley, William Brown, 119, 148, 185–86

McLean, Alexander, 55

McPherson, Etta, 196–97

Meier, August, 51

Memphis Evening Star, 29

Memphis Free Speech and Headlight, 29, 30

Merriam, Charles, 79

Messenger, 165–67

Michigan, 60, 133, 137, 253 (n. 126), 256 (n. 4)

Middle-class blacks: in Chicago, 28; and churches, 36; and college education, 25; Du Bois on, 25, 63, 65; migration by, from South, 63; and Republican Party, 135–36. *See also* Black women's club

movement; Racial uplift/racial destiny ideology

Migrants. *See* Southern migrants

Milledgeville Union Recorder, 172

Miller, Kelly, 170–71

Mississippi: black disfranchisement in, 41, 59, 74; black migrants from, 78; constitutional convention of 1890 in, 123; presidential election of 1868, 4; prohibition in, 171–72; unjust prosecution of black Republican leaders and appointees from, 163

Missouri, 182

Mitchell, Arthur, 10, 232

Mitchell, Marie, 88, 264 (n. 140)

Mitchell, Michele, 12–13

Moats, Irene, 133, 139, 147

Montgomery, Bertha, 115, 195, 207–9

Montgomery, Isaiah, 123

Moody Bible Institute, 100–101

Moore, Alice Ruth. *See* Dunbar-Nelson, Alice

Moore, Mrs. D. P., 33, 53

Moore, Marie, 224

Morton, Ferdinand Q., 165

Motherhood, political implications of, 31, 126–27, 144, 167

Mother's clubs, 28

Myers, Elmer, 195

Myers, Susie, 195, 207–8, 230, 233, 284 (n. 3)

NAACP: and antilynching legislation, 112, 122, 129; in Chicago, 269 (n. 10); and erosion of clergy's political power, 92; in Harlem, 165; and presidential campaign of 1920, 110; and southern influence in U.S. Congress, 128

NACW. *See* National Association of Colored Women

National American Woman Suffrage Association (NAWSA), 26, 190–91

National Association for the Advancement of Colored People. *See* NAACP

National Association of Colored Women (NACW): and antilynching movement, 112, 113, 114, 119–20, 122, 124, 234; Citizenship Department of, 141; and clerical animosity toward women's organizations, 93–94; founding of, 58, 255 (n. 152); membership statistics of, 80–81; motto of, 57; partisan/nonpartisan policy of, 113, 124–25, 262 (n. 111), 272–73 (nn. 58–60), 274 (n. 69); and presidential campaign of 1916, 103, 104, 110; and presidential campaign of 1920, 108–9, 110–11, 113, 114; and prohibition, 154–56, 158–60, 179, 279 (n. 17); and racial uplift, 57, 94, 180–81; religious convictions of membership of, 136–37, 237; strategies against disfranchisement, 141; and Terrell, 185, 188, 216; on vice districts, 174

National Colored Democratic Association, 232

National Federation of Afro-American Women, 57–58

National League of Colored Women, 255 (n. 152)

National League of Republican Colored Women (NLRCW): and Colored Women's Republican Clubs of Illinois, 207; and Coolidge administration, 148; and creation of national network of black Republican women, 186; and disappointment with Republican Party, 162–63, 227; founding of, 123–25, 185, 235, 236, 285 (n. 21); and Garveyites, 145; and National Association of Colored Women, 124–25, 272–73 (nn. 59–60); and presidential campaign of 1924, 125–26, 134–39, 146, 161; and presidential campaign of 1928, 161–63; and prohibition, 150; questionnaire by, 147

National Notes: on antilynching legislation, 148; on church work by women, 94; on Colored Women's Republican Clubs of Illinois, 147; and equal rights amendment, 126; and nonpartisanship policy of NACW, 124, 272–73 (n. 60), 274 (n. 69); on political strategies, 188; on presidential campaign of 1924, 133, 146; on Progressive Party, 127–28; on prohibition/temperance, 154, 155, 159, 160; on Republican presidential campaign of 1924, 272–73 (n. 60)

National Prohibition Act. *See* Volstead Act

National Woman Suffrage Association (NWSA), 44

National Women's Political Study Club, 164, 273 (n. 65)

National Youth Administration (NYA), 236–37

NAWSA. *See* National American Woman Suffrage Association

Nebraska, 249–50 (n. 85)

Negro Women's Republican League (NWRL), 117–18, 123–24

Negro World, 144, 168, 169, 177–80, 215

New Deal, 9, 233, 235–39, 298 (n. 22)

New Jersey, 114, 116, 159, 164

New Negro movement, 111, 130, 131, 132, 138, 179

Newton, Rosa Gordon, 219, 227

New York: black population of, 187; Democratic Party in, 145, 164–65, 223; Republican Party in, 100, 145, 147; vice economy in Harlem, 177; Waytes in, 101; women's voting in, 60, 256 (n. 4)

New York Age, 105–6, 116

New York Freeman, 253 (n. 126)

New York News, 105

New York Times, 5, 122

New York World, 46

Nineteenth Amendment: compared with

—of 1896, 56, 58
—of 1912, 101–2
—of 1916, 59, 80, 98–106, 110, 192, 266 (n. 170), 267 (n. 180)
—of 1920, 108–17, 276 (n. 115)
—of 1924: and Democratic Party, 122, 125, 127, 128–34, 155; and Republican Party, 122–48, 155, 161
—of 1928: and Democratic Party, 145, 149–51, 160, 164, 168–69, 182, 293 (n. 154); and Republican Party, 149, 151, 160–84
—of 1932, 230, 232
—of 1936, 183, 232, 235–36, 238
—of 1952, 238–39
—of 1964, 239
Progressive Party, 101–2, 125, 127–28, 134, 189, 195, 266 (n. 167)
Prohibition Party, 52–53, 155, 252 (nn. 117–118), 253 (n. 126)
Prohibition / temperance: and alcohol consumption by black men, 152–54, 172–74; black men's support of, 170; black opposition to, 171–80, 182, 223–25, 234–35, 297 (n. 17); black women's support for, 15, 52–53, 152–57, 169–71, 179–81, 252 (nn. 120, 125), 279 (nn. 11, 17); Chicago city council votes on, 97; civil rights, temperance, and racial uplift before Prohibition repeal movement, 152–57; and Colored Women's Department of the Republican National Committee, 149, 178; and congressional campaigns (1929–30), 223–25; and Democratic Party, 149, 155, 160, 169–71, 235; and disfranchisement of black men in South, 171–72; enforcement of, compared with that of Reconstruction Amendments, 150–52, 156, 158–60, 169–70, 181, 183, 194, 229; and Illinois elections of 1894, 52–53; local option campaigns for, 153–54, 171–72; and National Association of Colored

Women, 154–56, 179, 279 (n. 17); passage and ratification of Eighteenth Amendment, 154, 155, 156; and presidential campaign of 1928, 169–79; and racial uplift ideology, 151, 170, 181–82; repeal movement for Eighteenth Amendment, 149–51, 154, 157–60, 223–25, 234–35, 278 (n. 3); repeal of Eighteenth Amendment, 183, 235; and Republican Party, 15, 148–51, 155, 160, 169–71, 235; and Ruth H. McCormick, 186, 194, 200, 225, 230; and Universal Negro Improvement Association, 176–77, 179, 180; and urban leisure culture, 172–74, 180; and vice economy, 174–78, 180, 181, 213; and violence against black communities, 177–78. *See also* Anti-Saloon League; Prohibition Party; Woman's Christian Temperance Union
Prostitution, 174–76, 213, 283 (n. 100). *See also* Vice economy

Quinn Brown, Hallie: and antilynching movement, 119; and black clergy, 139; and Negro Women's Republican League, 270 (n. 38); photograph of, 120; and presidential campaign of 1920, 110–11, 114; and presidential campaign of 1924, 139; at RNC convention of 1928, 164; and Terrell's leadership of Ruth H. McCormick's campaign, 207, 209; on woman's suffrage, 156–57

Race riots, 126, 172, 220, 283 (n. 110). *See also* Violence against blacks
Racial uplift / racial destiny ideology: and churches, 94; and civil rights and temperance before prohibition repeal movement, 152–57; decline of, 16, 151–52, 179–80, 182–83, 234; for discrediting black Democrats, 151–52; and education of blacks, 77; meaning of, 151; and

middle-class status for blacks, 12–13; and National Association of Colored Women, 57, 94, 180–81; and political implications of motherhood, 126–27; and presidential campaign of 1924, 126; and presidential campaign of 1928, 151–52, 181–82; and prohibition, 151, 155, 170, 181–82; and self-help institutions, 13; and social class, 152, 218–19; and temperance, 52, 152–57; and "woman's era" philosophy, 12–13, 151, 234

Racism and white supremacy: and Democratic Party, 12, 40, 61, 72, 73, 75, 79–80, 132, 133, 222–23, 236; by Republican Party against black women, 14–15, 161–64, 229, 233; and southern lily-white Republicans, 109, 161–63; and southern strategy of woman's suffrage movement, 26, 32, 37. *See also* Disfranchisement; Segregation

Randolph, A. Philip, 245 (n. 21), 274 (n. 73)

Randolph, Florence (reverend), 137, 276 (n. 109)

Randolph, Lucille, 274 (n. 73)

Ransom, Reverdy, 139–41, 168, 177, 182

Rathbone, Henry, 193, 198, 201

Reckless, Walter, 175–76

Reconstruction, 3–8, 19, 21, 39, 45, 166

Reconstruction Act (1867), 4

Reconstruction Amendments: *Chicago Tribune* questionnaire on, 220–21; compared with Eighteenth Amendment, 150–51, 152, 156, 158–60, 169–70, 181, 183, 194, 229; defiance of, 157–58; and Deneen, 220–21; enforcement legislation for, 4; enforcement of, as campaign issue, 163, 166, 201–6, 226, 240; McCormick and enforcement of, 201–6, 226; and New Deal, 237; provisions of, 4; repeal movement for, 150–51, 158; and Republican Party loyalty by blacks, 9, 11, 21, 39; U.S. Supreme Court decisions

on, 8, 44; Wells-Barnett on, 44–45, 250 (n. 95); and woman's suffrage movement, 44–45. *See also* Fifteenth Amendment; Fourteenth Amendment; Thirteenth Amendment

Reed, Nannie, 238

Reeves, Pinkie B., 198–99, 287 (n. 51)

Repeal movement for Eighteenth Amendment, 149–51, 154, 157–60, 169–79, 194, 200, 223–25, 234–35, 278 (n. 3). *See also* Eighteenth Amendment; Prohibition/temperance

Republican National Committee (RNC): Colored Voters' Division of, 110–11; headquarters of, in Chicago, 10; and presidential campaign of 1916, 99; and presidential campaign of 1920, 108, 110–11, 119; and women delegates to 1924 convention, 193; Women's Division of, 161, 192–93. *See also* Colored Women's Department of the Republican National Committee

Republican Party: abandonment of, by black women in 1920s, 109–10, 113–14, 128–33, 135, 151, 164–69, 233–34; and abolitionism, 21, 39, 45; and antilynching movement, 58, 81, 109, 112–14, 118–22, 125, 128–31, 134, 148, 234; and black-and-tan convention delegations, 161, 162; black manhood and loyalty to, 41–42, 233; and blacks generally, 2–19, 21–23, 40; black women's local Republican clubs, 38, 46, 47, 81–82, 92–93, 95, 96, 99, 108–9, 136, 275 (n. 106); black women's loyalty to, 2–16, 42, 44–47, 50–51, 55, 58, 87–88, 96–97, 106–7, 109, 113–14, 133–48, 150, 161–63, 166, 178–84, 227, 233, 238–40; black women's strategies within, 229–30; black women's support for white versus black Republican candidates, 85–98; Dunbar-Nelson on, 130–31, 166; and Ku Klux

Klan, 128, 131; and Lodge Federal Elections Bill (Force Bill), 40–41; and machine politics, 23–24, 90–95, 195, 203, 205–6, 216, 221, 225; national conventions of, in Chicago, 10; New Right in, 239; and patronage, 31, 198–202, 206, 211–12, 215, 226, 227, 247–48 (n. 52); People's Movement in, 96–98; and prohibition, 15, 148–51, 155, 160, 169–71, 235; and protection of black citizenship rights, 8–9, 11–12, 21–22, 39, 40, 45, 125; and protective labor legislation, 125, 134; racism against black women by, 14–15, 161–64, 229, 233; and Reconstruction, 21, 39, 45; regional differences in, 171; and Ruth H. McCormick's congressional campaigns, 185–89, 193–227; and Second Ward alderman elections in Chicago of 1910s, 85–98; and southern lily-white Republicans, 109, 161–63, 171, 178; and tariff, 39–40; Vance on, 17; and white women, 192–93. *See also* Illinois congressional campaigns; Illinois elections of 1894; *specific Republican organizations; specific states, party leaders, and candidates*

Republican-Populist "fusion" party, 52, 74

Reynolds, Mary, 231–32, 297 (n. 8)

Rhode Island, 139, 160

RNC. *See* Republican National Committee

Roberts, Aldelbert H., 170

Roberts, Anna, 125–26

Roosevelt, Franklin D., 9, 16, 67, 232, 233, 235–38

Roosevelt, Theodore, 101–2, 190, 195

Rose, Mrs. E. G., 120

Rucker, Marry, 199

Ruffin, Josephine St. Pierre, 246 (n. 30)

Russell, Al, 96

Sanford, Amelia, 52

Santo Domingo, 195

Saville, Julie, 242 (n. 18)

Schechter, Patricia, 98, 112, 275 (n. 107)

Schenck, John, 17–18

Scotia Seminary, 65–67, 75, 257 (nn. 22, 27), 258 (nn. 31, 36)

Scott, Minnie, 120

Second Ward alderman elections in Chicago of 1910s, 85–98

Segregation: at Democratic National Convention of 1928, 165; and desegregation of Chicago Woman's Club, 50, 56; of New Deal programs, 236; of public transportation, 29, 70, 105, 260 (n. 57); and "separate but equal" doctrine, 8, 56, 132; in South, 61, 70–71, 260 (n. 57); of Washington, D.C., 104

Senate, U.S. *See* Congress, U.S.

"Separate but equal" doctrine, 8, 56, 132

Sernett, Milton, 93

Settlement house movement, 28, 82–83

Shaw, Blanche, 264 (n. 139)

Shaw University, 100

Sheppard, Morris, 155

Shortridge, Samuel, 119

Simmons, Roscoe Conklin, 127, 274 (n. 76)

Singleton, Lucy B. C., 196

Singleton, Major, 196

Skocpol, Theda, 69–70

Slaughter, Jessie, 198

Slemp, C. Bascom, 162

Smith, Alfred E., 145, 149–50, 160, 164–69, 177–83, 232, 238. *See also* Presidential campaign—of 1928

Smith, Ellison D., 116

Smith, Julia Holmes, 50, 252 (n. 117), 253 (n. 132)

Smith, Lucy, 218

Snowden Porter, Joanna: and Colored Women's Department of the Republican National Committee, 269 (n. 20); and Lawrence, 83; name of, 290 (n. 116); and presidential campaign of 1920, 115;

on Progressive Party, 127–28; and Ruth
H. McCormick's political campaign,
210, 212, 291 (n. 122); and Terrell's lead-
ership of Ruth H. McCormick's cam-
paign, 209; and Urban League in Chicago, 263 (n. 118)
Social class: and churches, 216–17; and
Garvey movement, 142–45, 167–69; and
party affiliation, 135–36; and racial
uplift / racial destiny ideology, 152, 218–
19; and "woman's era" philosophy, 138.
See also Middle-class blacks; Poor blacks
Social Gospel, 101
Socialist Party, 267 (n. 180), 274 (n. 73)
Social Security, 236
The Souls of Black Folk (Du Bois), 25
South Carolina: black disfranchisement in,
41, 56, 100; black migrants from, 78;
education of blacks in, 76, 100, 229;
woman's suffrage in, 242 (n. 18)
Southern Illinois Penitentiary, 201–2
Southern migrants: alcohol consumption
by, 172–73; arrival of, in Chicago, 9–10,
21–22, 82–83; and churches, 89–91,
140, 216–19, 294 (n. 167); from Deep
South, 78–79; and elections for Chicago
Second Ward aldermen of 1910s, 85–98;
and employment opportunities in Midwest, 78–79; and Great Migration during World War I, 11, 61, 78, 175; and
integrating into midwestern politics,
80–85; in middle class, 63; origins of,
and political lessons from South, 1, 2,
58–59, 61, 63–80, 106, 239; Phyllis
Wheatley Home for migrant women,
82–83, 97, 211, 212, 213; politics of, during 1910s, 60–107; and presidential campaign of 1916, 98–107; and presidential
campaign of 1924, 133–34; statistics on,
9–10, 22, 78, 99; from Upper South, 63;
as voting bloc, 60–61
Star of Zion, 66, 258 (n. 36)

Starr, Ellen Gates, 82
Stereotypes of blacks, 12–13, 45–46, 49, 53,
79, 143, 152, 172
Stevenson, Adlai, 239
Stokes, Ora Brown, 161–62, 270 (n. 38)
Strikes, 24, 39. *See also* Labor movement
Suffrage. *See* Voting
Sullivan, Amelia, 141–42
Sumner, Charles, 29
Supreme Court, U.S.: on Alabama's
peonage laws, 105; and Civil Rights Act
of 1875, 8, 29; on grandfather clause,
105, 132; Hughes as justice of, 98, 105;
and Reconstruction Amendments, 8, 44;
on "separate but equal" doctrine, 8, 56,
132. *See also specific cases*
Sutton, Alice, 210, 212, 291 (n. 122)
Swift, George W., 34

Taft, William, 102
Talbert, Mary, 93–94, 113, 121, 123, 202
Tariff, 39–40
Taylor, Julius F., 92
Taylor, Nathan S., 145
Taylor, Rebecca Stiles, 117
Taylor, Ula, 143–44
Temperance. *See* Prohibition / temperance;
Woman's Christian Temperance Union
Tennessee: antilynching movement in, 271
(n. 45); black disfranchisement in, 30;
black migrants from, 63; Democratic
Party in, 30, 165; lynching in, 30; newspapers in, 29; and Nineteenth Amendment, 113, 116; poll tax in, 141; and presidential campaign of 1928, 165; Republican Party in, 146
Terrell, Mary Church: autobiography of,
206; on black churches, 94, 216; and
congressional reapportionment, 200–
201; death of, 239; on Deneen, 220–21;
on Dunbar-Nelson in Democratic Party,
132–33; on independent voting versus

Republican loyalty of black women, 238; and McKinley senatorial campaign of 1926, 185–86, 207; and National Association of Colored Women, 185, 188, 216; photograph of, 211; on political strategies, 188; and presidential campaign of 1920, 108, 114, 185; and presidential campaign of 1924, 132–33; and Republican party loyalty, 238–39; and Ruth H. McCormick's congressional campaign, 185–87, 199, 204, 206–10, 212, 214–22; and U.S. withdrawal from Haiti and Santo Domingo, 195; in women's political organizations, 185, 188, 270 (n. 35)

Texas, 78, 100, 153

Third Ward Republican Organization (TWRO), 206, 213–14

Thirteenth Amendment: and Alabama's peonage laws, 105; Burroughs on, and possible repeal of Eighteenth Amendment, 169; compared with Prohibition Amendment, 156, 169; Foster Cook on, 160; provisions of, 4, 105, 259 (n. 44). *See also* Reconstruction Amendments

Thomas, John Francis, 90–93, 95

Thompson, Emma, 132, 273 (n. 65)

Thompson, William Hale "Big Bill," 90, 175–76, 195, 206, 216, 221, 223, 296 (n. 203)

The Tie That Binds (Caldwell), 162

Tillman, Ben, 41, 56, 158

Tinkham, George, 203–4, 289 (n. 90)

Tinkham amendment, 203–4, 226

Townsend, J. M. (reverend), 40, 41–42

Truth, Sojourner, 252 (n. 125)

Tucker, Dave, 67

Tucker, Ella. *See* Berry, Ella G.

Tucker, Maggie, 260 (n. 51)

Turner, Henry McNeal, 37

Twenty-first Amendment, 183, 235

Twenty-third Amendment, 268 (n. 184)

TWRO. *See* Third Ward Republican Organization

UBF. *See* United Brothers of Friendship and Sisters of the Mysterious Ten

Understanding tests, 41, 61, 76, 142

Unemployment. *See* Employment

UNIA. *See* Universal Negro Improvement Association

Unions. *See* Labor movement

United Brothers of Friendship and Sisters of the Mysterious Ten (UBF), 69–70, 84

Universal Negro Improvement Association (UNIA), 142–46, 167–69, 176–77, 179, 180

University of Illinois: black enrollment at, 25; election of woman trustee for, 20–21, 55; trustee campaign of 1894 for, 20–21, 25–27, 39, 42, 44, 52, 55; women's enrollment at, 25

Urban League, 89, 92, 98, 165, 263 (n. 118)

Vance, James Madison, 58, 59

Vance, Zebulon, 17–19, 64

Vardaman, James, 158

Vice economy, 174–78, 180, 181, 213. *See also* Prostitution

Vice in Chicago (Reckless), 175–76

Violence against blacks: for disfranchisement and segregation, 6–8, 54–55, 75; race riots, 126, 172, 220, 283 (n. 110); racial violence in Kentucky, 68–69, 71, 259 (n. 44); during Reconstruction elections, 6–7; Wells-Barnett on, 53. *See also* Ku Klux Klan; Lynching

Virginia: black migrants from, 63; Democratic electoral fraud in, 161; election day in, 6; fears about woman suffrage in, 115–16; political activities by black women in, during Reconstruction, 4–5; Republican Party in, 119, 161–62; voting rights for black males in, 6

A Voice from the South (Cooper), 46–47

Volstead Act, 149, 156, 157, 159–60, 224, 225

Voting

—by black men: black manhood and Republican Party loyalty, 41–42, 233; black women's support for, 5–7; critique of, by black women, 12, 51, 95, 102–3, 131, 140, 166, 179, 182; economic pressure on, by Democratic Party, 18; in Illinois generally, 22–23; in Kentucky, 62, 72–73, 256 (n. 7); and Lodge Federal Elections Bill (Force Bill), 40–41, 127; in Maryland, 256 (n. 7); Williams on, 51. *See also* Disfranchisement—of black men; Fifteenth Amendment

—by women: Democrats' fears about black women voters, 115–16; disfranchisement of black women, 55, 116–17, 141–42, 151, 156–57; disfranchisement of white women, 254–55 (nn. 140–41); Dunbar-Nelson on black women voters, 165–67; effectiveness of black women's voting for progress, 102–3, 106; in Illinois elections of 1892, 244 (n. 2); in Illinois elections of 1894, 20–59; Illinois laws on, 9, 15, 20, 59, 60, 80, 81, 98, 244 (n. 2); in Indiana, 60; in Kentucky, 27, 73, 247 (n. 33); in Massachusetts, 27, 246 (n. 30); in Michigan, 60, 256 (n. 4); in New York, 60, 256 (n. 4); in Ohio, 60, 256 (n. 4); and presidential campaign of 1916, 59, 80, 98–107, 110, 266 (n. 170); and presidential campaign of 1920, 108–17; and presidential campaign of 1924, 122–46; registration of black women voters in Illinois elections of 1894, 55; and religious beliefs, 137–38; in Second Ward alderman elections of 1910s, 85–87, 91, 95–97; in South, 116–17; southern strategy of woman's suffrage movement, 26, 32, 37; split-ticket voting by black women,

42, 44–47, 50–51, 62, 238; statistics on black women voters, 99, 101, 106, 110; in West, 27, 266 (n. 170); Williams on importance of black women's vote, 51; women's ballot in Illinois, 20, 43. *See also* Illinois elections of 1894; Nineteenth Amendment; Woman's suffrage movement

Voting Rights Act (1965), 239

Walker, James A., 280 (n. 46)

Walker, Maggie Lena, 119

Wallace, William, 168

Waring, Mary, 270 (n. 38)

Washington, Booker T., 56, 174

Washington, Margaret, 174

Washington, D.C., 63, 104, 140, 268 (n. 184)

Washington State, 266 (n. 170)

Waytes, Alice Thompson, 100–102, 267 (n. 176)

WCTU. *See* Woman's Christian Temperance Union

Wells, Hattie J., 202, 207

Wells, Jim, 30

Wells-Barnett, Ida B.: on alcohol consumption by black men, 153; and Alpha Suffrage Club, 87; antilynching work by, 30–31, 34, 112, 118–20, 153; and black women's Republican clubs, 81, 95; church membership and religious belief of, 98, 275 (n. 107); as civil rights and women's rights advocate, 29, 44–45; death of, 29; and Deneen, 205, 290 (nn. 96–97); early life of, in South, 28–30, 70, 112, 244 (n. 7); *Free Speech* article by, 30, 112; and Illinois elections of 1894, 33–34, 39, 42, 44, 62; and Illinois Women's Republican Education Committee, 28; as journalist, 29; and labor movement, 214–15; on loyalty of black women to Republican Party, 62; marriage of, 32, 86; photographs of, 49, 120; as political candidate, 205, 208, 221, 290 (n. 97); on political implications of motherhood, 31; and presidential campaign of 1912, 102; and presidential campaign of 1916, 99; and presidential campaign of 1928, 181; and prohibition, 153, 154, 181, 194; and racism of white suffragists, 190–91; on Reconstruction Amendments, 44–45, 250 (n. 95); relocation of, to Chicago, 28, 31, 112; and Second Ward alderman elections of 1910s, 87, 95; and segregated public transportation, 29, 70; and Terrell's leadership of Ruth H. McCormick's campaign, 208; and Universal Negro Improvement Association, 142–46; on violence against southern blacks, 53; and World's Columbian Exposition of 1893, 32

West, Cordelia, 264 (n. 139)

West Virginia, 63, 133, 139, 147

Wheeler, Burton, 125

Whip. See Chicago Whip

White, Clemmie, 141

White, Deborah Gray, 12, 56–57, 142, 180–81, 269 (n. 9)

White, Eartha, 114

White supremacy. *See* Disfranchisement—of black men; Disfranchisement—of black women; Racism and white supremacy; Segregation

White women: black women's support of, as political candidates, 25–26, 186–87, 194–206, 210–27; and Chicago Woman's Club, 50, 56; college education of, 25; and Democratic Party, 253–54 (n. 132); disfranchisement of, in Illinois elections of 1894, 254–55 (nn. 140–41); and equal rights amendment, 126; and interracial political mobilization for Illinois elections of 1894, 27–28, 31–33; and Prohibition

Party, 252 (n. 119); as prostitutes, 283 (n. 100); racism of, and relationship with black women, 15, 26, 32, 37, 50, 53, 253 (n. 128); and Republican Party, 161–62, 192–93; and southern strategy of woman's suffrage movement, 26, 32, 37; and temperance movement, 52, 53; as University of Illinois trustee candidates, 20–21, 25–26, 42, 44, 55. *See also specific women*

Whyte, Georgiana, 147

Willard, Frances, 52, 53, 153, 155, 252 (n. 118)

Willebrandt, Mabel, 163

Williams, Fannie Barrier: and Chicago Woman's Club, 50, 56; and Congress of Representative Women, 32, 47; and fraternal movement, 84; on independent voting versus Republican loyalty of black women, 50–51, 62, 166; on Phyllis Wheatley Home, 82; and presidential campaign of 1916, 102; relocation of, to Chicago, 267 (n. 183); as teacher, 25; on temperance, 179; on voting as effective weapon against prejudice and discrimination, 102; and "woman's era" philosophy, 51, 102, 179

Williams, Lacy Kirk, 90

Williams, Mary Miller, 116–17, 123, 270 (n. 38)

Williams, Susie, 201

Wilson, J. Finley, 293 (n. 154)

Wilson, Woodrow, 98–106, 155, 156

Winters, Mrs. Peal, 120

Wisconsin, 271 (n. 45)

Wolcott, Victoria W., 180, 284 (n. 117)

Woman's Journal, 26

Woman's Christian Temperance Union (WCTU), 52, 53, 153, 155, 213, 252 (nn. 117–18), 252 (n. 120), 253 (n. 128)

Woman's Era, 27, 50, 51, 166, 246 (n. 30)

"Woman's era" philosophy: and Dunbar-